MARTIN TAYLOR'S COMPLETE

JAZZ**GUITAR**
METHODCOMPILATION

Master Jazz Guitar Chord-Melody, Walking Basslines & Single-Note Soloing

MARTIN**TAYLOR**

FUNDAMENTAL**CHANGES**

Martin Taylor Complete Jazz Guitar Method Compilation

Master Jazz Guitar Chord-Melody, Walking Basslines & Single-Note Soloing

ISBN: 978-1-78933-148-6

Published by www.fundamental-changes.com

Copyright © 2019 Martin Taylor & Joseph Alexander

Edited by Tim Pettingale

The moral right of this author has been asserted.

All rights reserved. No part of this publication may be reproduced, stored in a retrieval system, or transmitted in any form or by any means, without the prior permission in writing from the publisher.

The publisher is not responsible for websites (or their content) that are not owned by the publisher.

www.fundamental-changes.com

Twitter: @guitar_joseph

Over 10,000 fans on Facebook: **FundamentalChangesInGuitar**

Instagram: **FundamentalChanges**

For over 350 Free Guitar Lessons with Videos Check Out

www.fundamental-changes.com

Cover Image Copyright:

Foreword

Welcome to the *Martin Taylor Complete Jazz Guitar Method Compilation*. This book comprises Martin's three bestselling books:

- *Beyond Chord Melody*
- *Walking Basslines for Jazz Guitar*
- *Single-Note Soloing for Jazz Guitar*

Together these books teach the most important aspects of jazz guitar playing.

Beyond Chord Melody

First, learn Martin's proven 7-step method to creating solo chord-melody arrangements that will unlock your creativity. This book goes beyond simply "arranging" chords and melodies – it teaches guitarists how to achieve a polyphonic approach to playing, where chords, basslines and melodic lines all move as independent voices. It's the antidote to formulaic methods and opens the door to real creativity.

Walking Basslines for Jazz Guitar

Next, dig into the art of jazz guitar comping. Here Martin teaches the skill of playing walking basslines on guitar and combining them with chord stabs. Learn how to harmonise chords on chromatic notes to create rich musical textures, and discover the secrets of syncopation that will make you an interesting and versatile accompanist.

Single-Note Soloing for Jazz Guitar

Finally, take your single-note soloing skills to the next level with Martin's creative, melodic guide. Here Martin distils more than 40 years of wisdom into a comprehensive resource that helps you to play authentic jazz guitar solos. Learn how a virtuoso jazz guitarist thinks and constructs melodic ideas to create rich, engaging jazz solos. As well as teaching you how to develop the skill of melodic variation, Martin dedicates time to teaching the one skill that sets the great jazz guitarists apart from everyone else: being able to play exactly what you hear in your head. Find out how in the pages ahead.

I trust you'll enjoy this goldmine of jazz guitar knowledge from one of the best in the world!

Joseph

Contents

Book 1: Martin Taylor Beyond Chord Melody — 1

Introduction — 2
Get the Audio — 3
Get the Video! — 4
Chapter One: One-String Scales and Intervals — 5
Chapter Two: Movement with 3rds and 7ths — 19
Chapter Three: Combining 10ths, 7ths and Bass Movement — 28
Chapter Four: Adding Melodies to 7ths and 10ths — 36
Chapter Five: Minor Scales — 42
Chapter Six: The CAGED System — 46

Part Two: Seven Steps to Arranging Heaven — 51
Chapter Seven: Step One - Harmony — 54
Chapter Eight: Step Two - Melody — 57
Chapter Nine: Step Three - Chord Melody — 61
Chapter Ten: Step Four - Melody and Bass — 69
Chapter Eleven: Step Five - Inner Lines — 75
Chapter Twelve: Step Six - Melody, Bass and Inner Lines — 79
Chapter Thirteen: Step Seven - Melodic Variation — 87

Book 2: Martin Taylor Walking Basslines For Jazz Guitar — 92

Introduction — 93
Get the Audio — 94
Get the Video — 94
Chapter One – Essential Chord Voicings — 95
Chapter Two – Simple Walking Bass — 103
Chapter Three – Chords and Harmonised Basslines — 109
Chapter Four – Syncopation and Separation — 116

Chapter Five – Imitating Drums with the Pick	124
Chapter Six – Walking Bass Variations	129
Chapter Seven – Jazz Skips	136
Chapter Eight – Thumb Flicks	143
Chapter Nine – Decorated Basslines	148
Chapter Ten – Walking into the Bar	155
Chapter Eleven – Jazz Blues	160
Chapter Twelve – Autumn Leavers	162
Chapter Thirteen – All The Things You Aren't	167
Conclusion and Further Listening	172

Book 3: Martin Taylor Single Note Soloing For Jazz Guitar	**173**
Introduction	174
Get the Audio	177
Get the Video	177
Chapter One – Melody and Variation	178
Chapter Two – Other Target Notes and Colour Tones	192
Chapter Three – Baa Baa Black Sheep	206
Chapter Four – Developing Vocabulary and Phrasing	216
Chapter Five – Swing, Rhythm and Timing	229
Chapter Six – Playing Out of the Box	237
Chapter Seven – Creating Interest and Structure in your Solos	246
Chapter Eight – Piecing it all Together	255
Conclusion and Further Reading	267
Other Jazz Guitar Books From Fundamental Changes	268

About the Authors

Dr Martin Taylor MBE is a virtuoso guitarist, composer, educator and musical innovator.

Acoustic Guitar magazine has called him, "THE acoustic guitarist of his generation." Chet Atkins said that Martin is, "One of the greatest and most impressive guitarists in the world," and Pat Metheny commented that, "Martin Taylor is one of the most awesome solo guitar players in the history of the instrument."

Widely considered to be the world's foremost exponent of solo jazz and fingerstyle guitar playing, Martin possesses an inimitable style that has earned him global acclaim from fellow musicians, fans and critics alike. He dazzles audiences with a signature style which artfully combines his virtuosity, emotion and humour with a strong, engaging stage presence.

Martin has enjoyed a remarkable musical career spanning five decades, with more than 100 recordings to his credit. Completely self-taught, beginning at the early age of 4, he has pioneered a unique way of approaching solo jazz guitar that he now breaks down into seven distinct stages in order to teach others.

Joseph Alexander is one of the most prolific writers of modern guitar tuition methods.

He has sold over 500,000 books that have educated and inspired a generation of upcoming musicians. His uncomplicated tuition style is based around breaking down the barriers between theory and performance, and making music accessible to all.

Educated at London's Guitar Institute and Leeds College of Music, where he earned a degree in Jazz Studies, Joseph has taught thousands of students and written over 40 books on playing the guitar.

He is the managing director of *Fundamental Changes Ltd.*, a publishing company whose sole purpose is to create the highest quality music tuition books and pay excellent royalties to writers and musicians.

Fundamental Changes has published over 120 music tuition books and is currently accepting submissions from prospective authors and teachers of all instruments. Get in touch via **webcontact@fundamental-changes.com** if you'd like to work with us on a project.

MARTIN TAYLOR
BEYOND CHORD MELODY

Master Jazz Guitar Chord Melody with Virtuoso Martin Taylor MBE

WITH
JOSEPH ALEXANDER

FUNDAMENTAL CHANGES

Introduction

In this book you'll learn a unique approach to solo guitar playing that will set a foundation for going beyond traditional chord melody playing.

Most chord melody teaching is based on traditional chord "grips", with students being encouraged to locate melody notes inside set shapes. But this immediately limits the player to the geometry of the guitar and, in my opinion, stifles true expression. The 7-step approach in this book is different. Melody notes, bass lines and chords are viewed as separate, independent voices. "Chords" are stripped down to their essential components to open up a freedom of movement that offers many more musical options.

I describe the way I play as a *polyphonic* improvised approach to the guitar. By polyphonic I mean that the three elements of melody, chords and bass all operate independently. My aim is to help you develop a similar freedom and independence on the guitar that will allow you to develop your own voice and break out of the "boxes" in which us guitar players tend to play.

This is a *ground-up* method, beginning with simple one-string scales, moving through simple chord inversions, finding the most important intervals, to advice on voicings, melodies, basslines, moving internal voices and much, much more.

We'll start very simple and each step will build on the previous one to enhance your arrangements. Throughout this book, the emphasis is on exploration and experimentation, rather than set rules and theory. The first examples are simple, but they evolve as the book progresses.

In time, you will find that you approach the guitar differently, as you begin to move away from familiar boxes and grids, and develop your own, truly polyphonic, jazz arrangements.

Each example/exercise is accompanied by audio examples which you should download. Sometimes music looks very complex on paper, but the audio will make it come alive.

Get the audio from **www.fundamental-changes.com/download-audio**

You can also watch a number of video demonstrations along the way that will give you an insight into my phrasing and note choices. I hope you find these helpful. These videos are available from:

https://fundamental-changes.teachable.com/p/martin-taylor-beyond-chord-melody

Most of all, remember to have fun and enjoy the music!

Martin.

Get the Audio

The audio files for this book are available to download for free from **www.fundamental-changes.com** and the link is in the top right corner. Simply select this book title from the drop-down menu and follow the instructions to get the audio.

We recommend that you download the files directly to your computer, not to your tablet, and extract them there before adding them to your media library. You can then put them on your tablet, iPod or burn them to CD. On the download page there is a help PDF and we also provide technical support via the contact form.

Get the Video!

As a special bonus to buyers of this book, Martin Taylor has created some videos, explaining key elements of technique, that are not available anywhere else.

You can get it here:

http://geni.us/martintaylor

Please note, there is no www in this address!

Or the full link is here:

https://fundamental-changes.teachable.com/p/martin-taylor-beyond-chord-melody

If you type above link into a browser, please note that there is no "www." You can also scan the QR code below to view the videos on your smartphone:

Chapter One: One-String Scales and Intervals

Most guitarists begin learning scales as blocks that go across the fretboard. In other books I have put great emphasis on the CAGED System and learning scales vertically around chord shapes. For example, here is the scale of G Major built around a G Major barre chord:

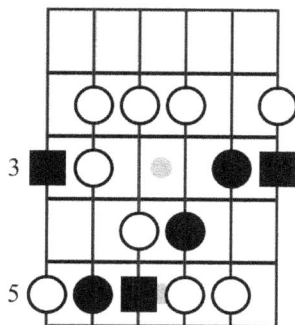

However, when it comes to building chord melody-style improvisations it is essential to learn scales *horizontally* along the guitar neck. Learning scales along one string allows access to basslines, melodies and internal chord voicings without getting trapped in "traditional" chord grips.

When playing chord melody, we see the guitar almost as if it was three instruments:

• Basslines are played on the lower two strings.

• Chord voicings and *counter melodies* are played on the middle strings.

• Main melodies are played on the top two strings.

Of course, the above points are only guidelines and some crossover will occur. However, by mentally dividing the guitar into three melodic sections we can stop thinking about the guitar as one single voice.

Everything begins with one-string scales on the bass strings and you will see how important this approach is when we build polyphonic (many voices) improvisations later.

We will begin by learning the G Major scale along the sixth (E) string of the guitar.

Example 1a:

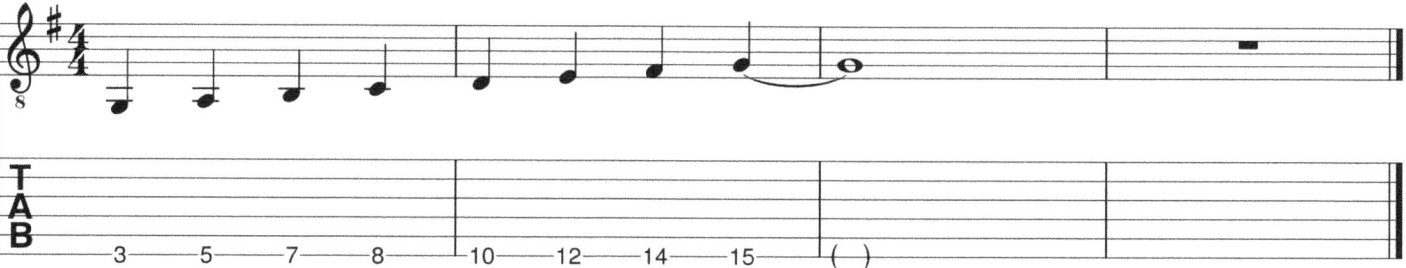

Play up and down this scale to memorize both its pattern and sound using just one finger to play every note. Learn the scale with just your first finger and then learn it with your second and third fingers too.

This scale on the sixth string will form the bass part of all your future improvisations. Often you will need to fret notes with your second, third, or even fourth fingers in order to reach melody and chord tones with your first finger.

The following pattern teaches you to make melodic jumps in the bass and helps you to memorize the scale more fully. Repeat the exercise using a different finger each time.

Example 1b:

Now learn the G Major scale on the fifth string. Remember that both the lowest strings are used for bass lines, so we must know them inside out.

Example 1c:

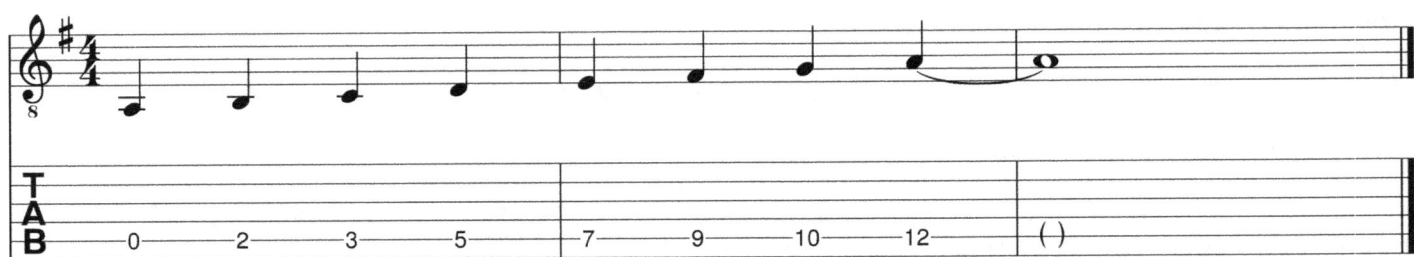

Repeat example 1b using the notes from G Major on the fifth string.

Transition Points

It is important to explore different ways to ascend and descend the major scale and change strings at different points. The point at which we change string is called a transition.

For example, we could ascend the G Major scale in the following ways:

Example 1d:

Example 1e:

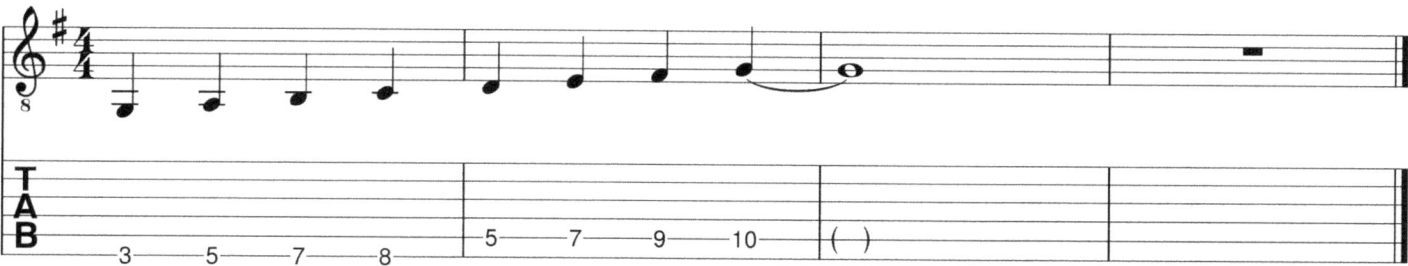

We could descend the G Major scale in the following ways:

Example 1f:

Example 1g:

Spend time exploring the G Major scale and find as many transition points as you can.

Adding Guide Tones

In any chord, the intervals of a 3rd and a 7th are the most important notes. The 3rd defines whether the chord is major or minor and the 7th defines whether the chord is major 7th, minor 7th or dominant 7th (7).

A major 3rd is two tones (whole steps) above the root note. For example, in the scale of G,

G A B C D E F# G

The major 3rd is the note B.

On the guitar, a major 3rd looks like this:

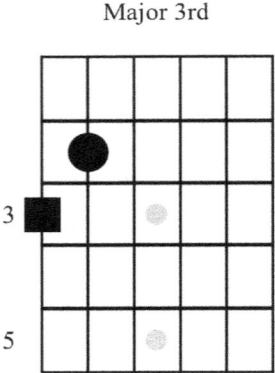

Major 3rd

A *minor* 3rd is smaller; only one-and-a-half tones above the root.

You can create a minor 3rd by flattening a major 3rd by a semitone (half step). So, while a major 3rd above G is B, a *minor 3rd* above G is the note *Bb*.

A minor 3rd looks like this on the guitar:

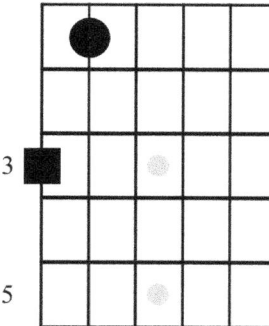

Minor 3rd

If a chord contains a major 3rd, it is a major chord. If a chord contains a minor 3rd, it is a minor chord.

3rds define the chord type, but they're not much good to us on the bass strings. In fact, playing 3rds on the bass strings of the guitar can sound very "muddy". It is much better to shift these 3rds up by an octave and place them on the middle strings of the guitar.

When a 3rd is moved up an octave it could be called a *10th* as it is now ten notes above the root:

G A B C D E F# G A B

Although musicians normally still call it a 3rd for simplicity, we will use the names "3rd" and "10th" interchangeably throughout this book.

A major 3rd between the sixth (E) string and third (G) strings looks like this:

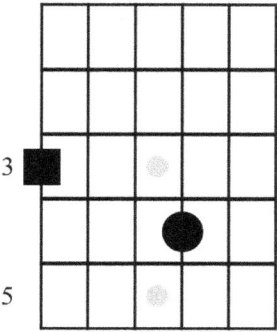

Major 3rd

Unsurprisingly, a minor 3rd between the sixth (E) string and third (G) strings looks like this:

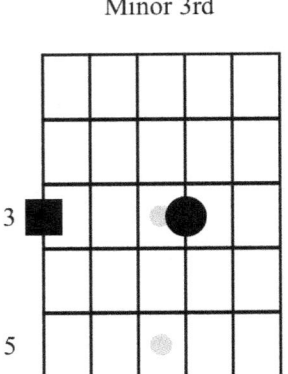

Minor 3rd

Let's play through the G Major scale and add 10ths on the third string. Notice that some are major and some are minor.

Example 1h:

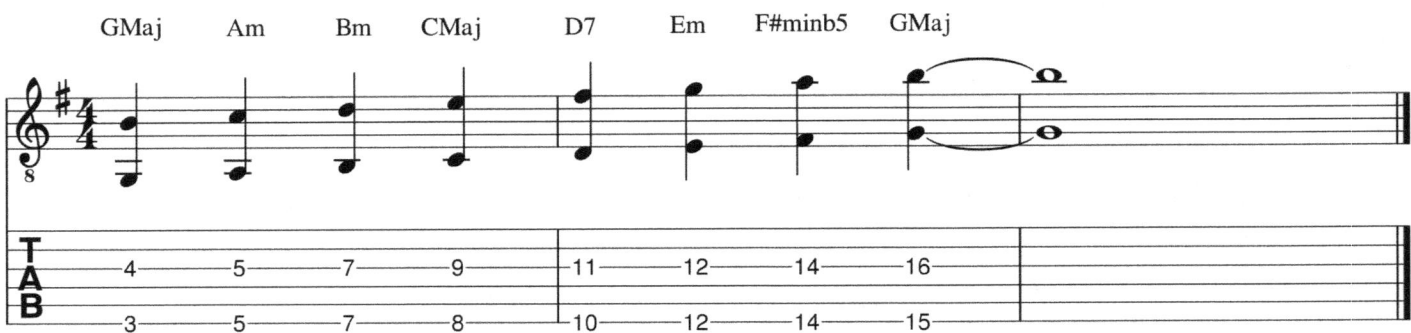

Practise ascending and descending this chord scale until you know it inside out, just like you did with the single-string scales in the previous section. Try the following exercises to help you get inside the chord scale.

Example 1i:

10

Example 1j:

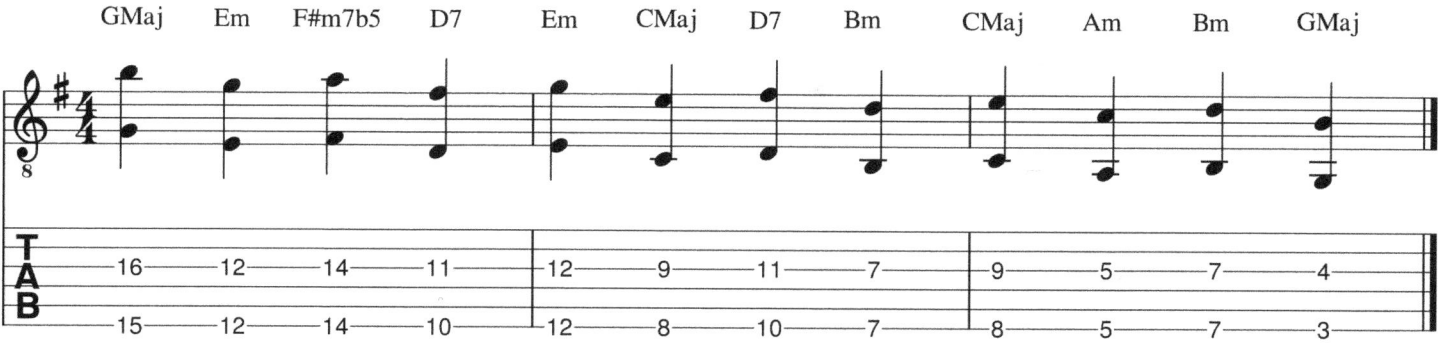

Having embedded this sound in your head, the next step is to begin experimenting, making up short melodies and getting creative by adding your own melodic leaps.

When you played through Examples 1h – 1j, you probably placed your first finger on the sixth string and used your third finger to play the notes on the third string. After all, that is the most intuitive way to finger these intervals.

The following exercises are some of the most important in this book. These are the ones that will *free you* from traditional chord grips and open up the fretboard to infinite melodic possibilities. They may feel unnatural at first, especially if you have played a lot of jazz rhythm and are used to fretting chords in a specific way.

Play through exercise 1h again, but this time use *only* your second finger to play the bass notes on the sixth string. You must use either your third or your fourth finger to play the intervals on the third string.

Ascend and descend the chord-scale many times using only your second finger on the sixth string. First use your third finger exclusively to fret the notes on the third string, then use your fourth finger exclusively. This will feel alien and awkward at first, but you will gradually get used to it.

Play through examples 1i and 1j in this manner and then start to add your own leaps.

Next, repeat the above steps again, but now with your third finger on the sixth string. You must play all the 10ths on the third string with your little (fourth) finger.

These exercises will feel a little strange, but the idea is to free up the fingers of your fretting hand, so that you can add melodies later. We will look at this idea in detail in chapter 4, but for now, check out the following idea to understand how we can unlock the guitar by using different fingerings.

The next example shows a short melodic pattern built around the 10th. Throughout, I fret the root note with my 2nd finger and use only my third and first fingers on the G string.

Example 1k:

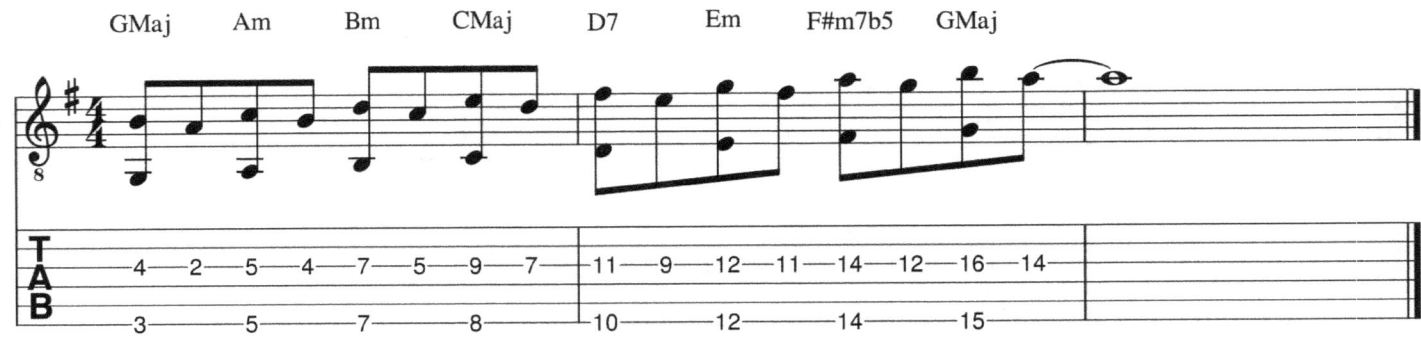

Next, we will transfer these approaches to the G Major scale played on the fifth string.

Due to the difference in tuning between the G and B strings, major and minor 3rds look different when played between the fifth and second strings.

The following diagrams will help you to visualise these intervals.

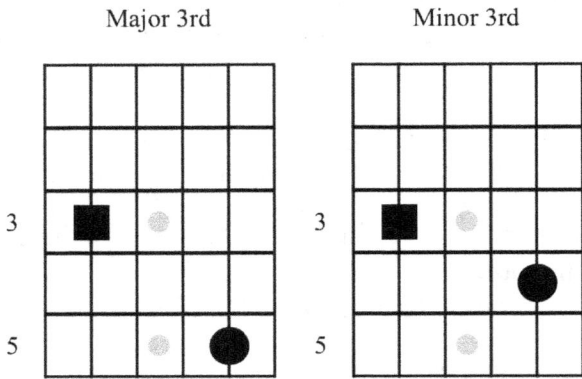

Next, play through the chord-scale of G Major, beginning from the lowest available fretted note on the fifth string.

Example 1l:

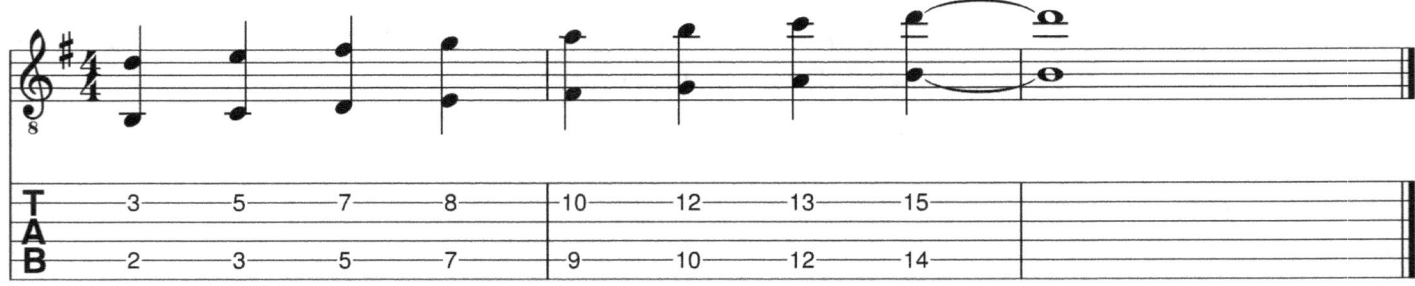

Again, practise these intervals in 3rds to help you memorize and hear the scale shape.

Example 1m:

Example 1n:

It is essential to break away from using just your first finger on the bass notes. Play through examples 1l, 1m and 1n using your second finger on the bass note exclusively.

It is very difficult to use your third finger on the bass note and still fret the 10th effectively, so I would avoid this for now. However, with your second finger on the bass note you can experiment with which finger you use to play the 10th. Both your third and fourth fingers should be available.

As mentioned, we will look at adding melodies in chapter 4 but for now, see how many ways you can find to fret the following example that incorporates a simple movement on the B string. Use your second finger to fret the bass notes.

Example 1o:

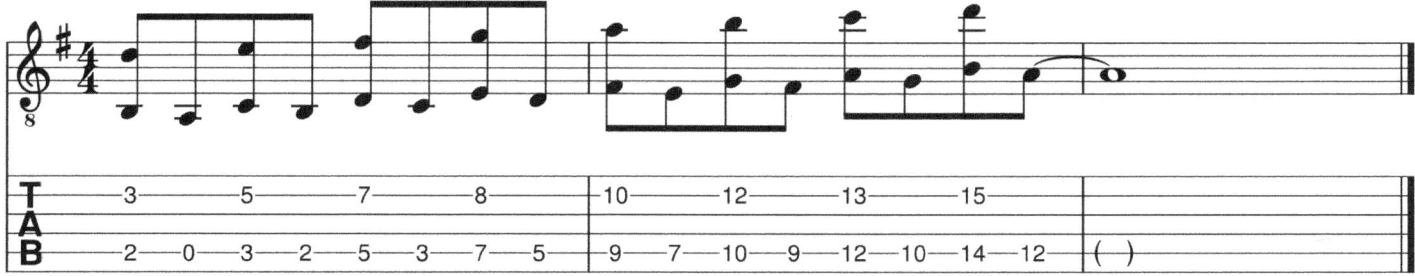

Practise the previous idea descending and try to create your own melodies.

Transition Points with 10ths

Just as we learnt to transition between strings with one-string scales, we must practise transitioning across strings using roots and 3rds. If you practised thoroughly earlier, the following exercises shouldn't be too challenging. The key to progressing is to explore the guitar by finding as many transition points as possible, and experiment with which finger plays the bass note.

Example 1p:

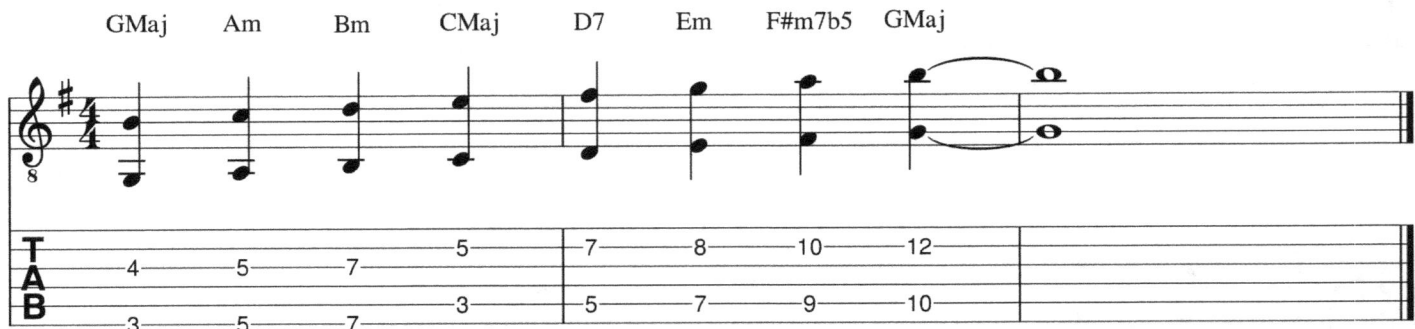

Example 1q:

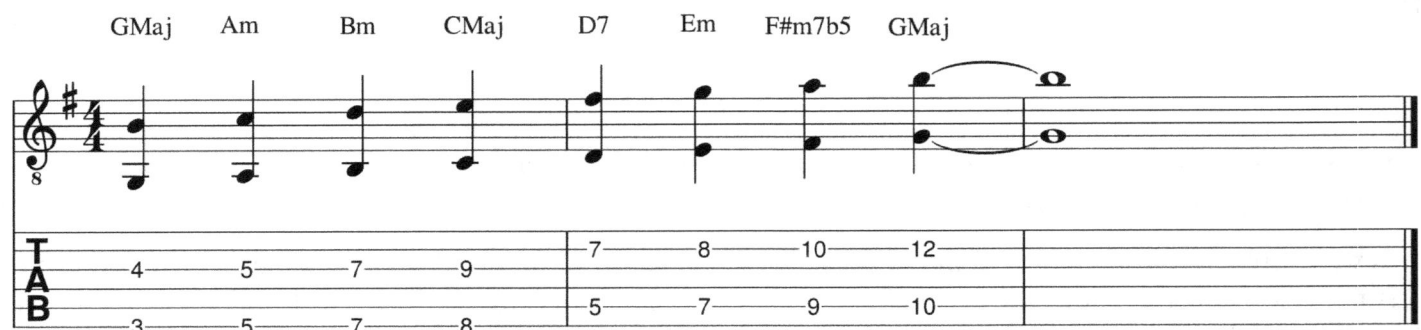

Try both the previous examples ascending and descending. Play them initially with the first finger in the bass, then the second finger and finally use the third finger where you can on the sixth string.

Extend these examples by finding your own transition points or by adding a simple decoration to the 10th as shown in example 1o. Moving these decorations across strings may initially require some careful planning of your fingering, but this will become more intuitive over time.

Spend time working to achieve the smooth, melodic transitions across strings that is an intrinsic part of polyphonic guitar playing.

Adding 7ths

We've discussed that the next most important note in any chord is the 7th. It tells us whether a chord is a major 7th, minor 7th or dominant 7th. The theory can get a little complex, but the following table shows you how 3rds and 7ths combine to form different types of 7th chord.

Chord Type	Root	Third	Fifth	Seventh
Major 7	1	3	5	7
7	1	3	5	b7
Minor 7	1	b3	5	b7
Minor 7b5	1	b3	b5	b7

• Major 7th chords contain major 7ths.

• Minor 7 and Dominant 7 chords contain minor 7ths

Just as we have intervals of major and minor 3rds, we have intervals of major and minor 7ths. A major 7th is seven steps above (or a semitone below) the root. The major 7th of G major is the note F#:

G A B C D E F# (G)

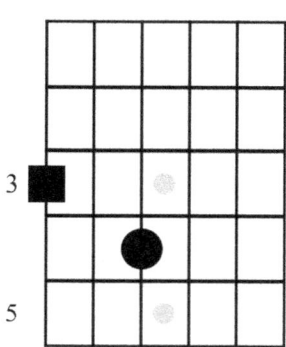

Major 7th

A minor 7th is simply a major 7th that has been flattened by a semitone (just as a minor 3rd is a major 3rd that has been flattened). A minor 7th is always one tone below the root:

G A B C D E F (G)

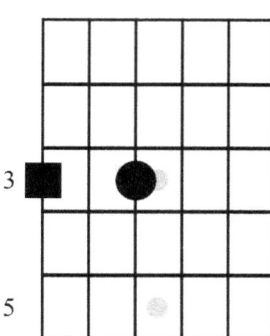

Minor (or 'b') 7

Compare the two diagrams above and ensure you understand the difference between major and minor 7ths.

(N.B. Jazz musicians don't normally say "minor 7th", we say b7. We will normally call the major 7th the "natural" 7th, or just the "7th")

Playing through the chord scale with just roots and 7ths sounds a little unusual. They're not as rich as 3rds, but they are an essential part of the middle-string voicings and really come into their own later when combined with 10ths and melodic movements. For now, I'll ask you to trust me and learn the chord-scale of G Major 7ths.

Example 1r:

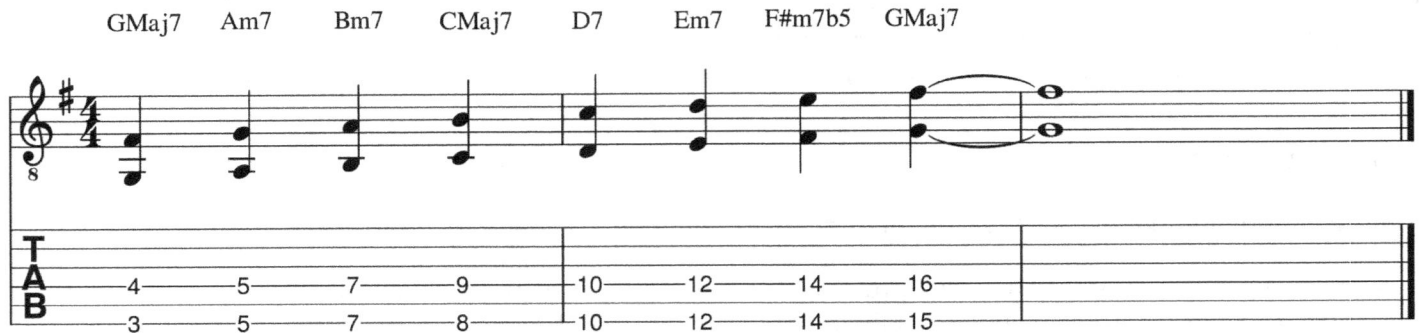

Practise this chord-scale ascending and descending until you know it inside out, just like you did with roots and 10ths earlier. Try the following exercises to help you get inside the chord scale.

Example 1s:

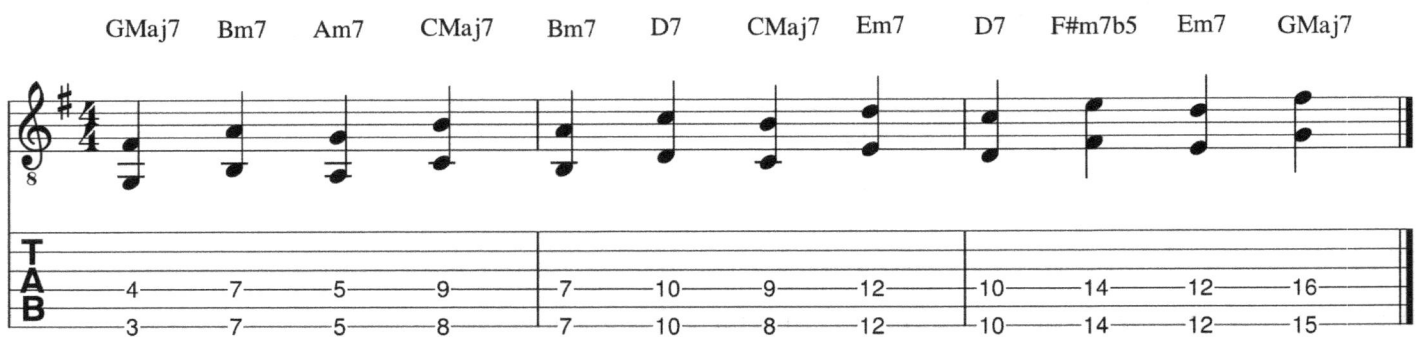

Example 1t:

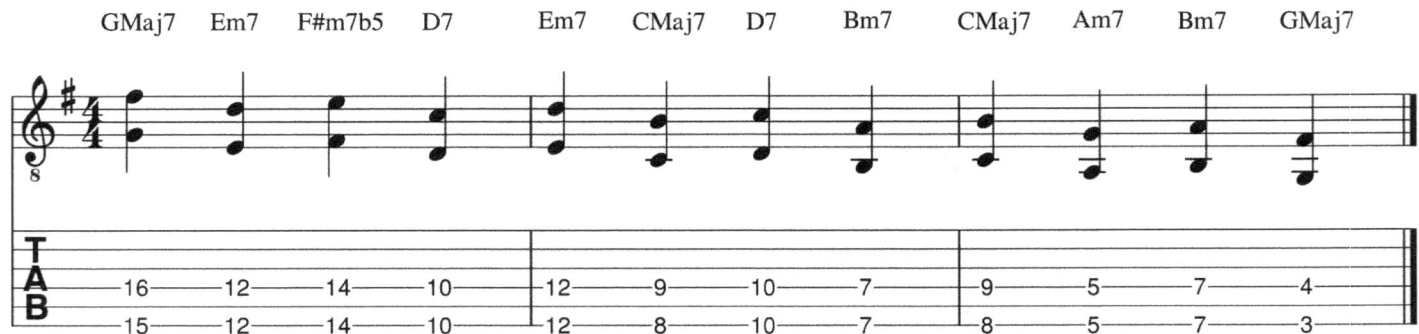

Practise the previous three exercises using a different finger to fret the bass note on the sixth string.

Next, play the G Major scale in 7ths between the fifth and third strings. Notice that the interval shapes remain the same as on the sixth string.

Example 1u:

Again, practise playing interval skips of a 3rd to help you memorize and hear this scale shape.

Example 1v:

Example 1w:

Again, I can't stress enough the importance of practising using different fingers to fret the bass notes. Play through these exercises and experiment by using *just* the first finger to play the bass. Then spend a few days using *just* the second finger to play the bass. When you're playing 7ths, you can use the third finger to play the bass notes without too much trouble.

You can spend a few days experimenting with different fingerings to see just how much you can free up the spare fingers of the fretting hand.

17

Now that you know the chord-scale of G Major in 7ths on both the sixth and fifth strings, find as many transition points as you can – both ascending and descending the scale. The more time you can explore this idea the better. You will start to find that the guitar neck really opens up and you gain a new-found freedom.

Gradually start to add simple melodies to decorate the 7th while you play through the chord scale. Here's just one possible example:

Example 1x:

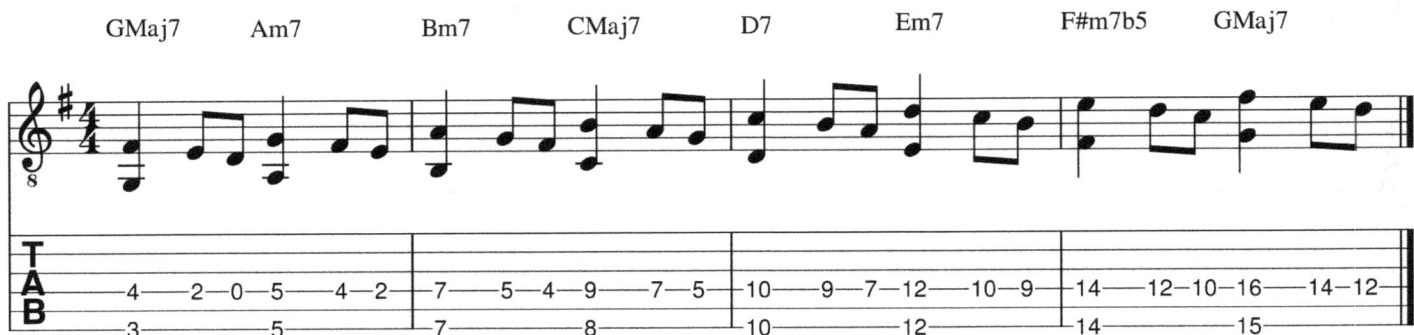

There are also some points where you can move between chords chromatically. This works especially well with root and 10th, but you can try it with root and 7th also. Here are two points in the scale where you can shift between minor chords while moving in semitones.

Example 1y:

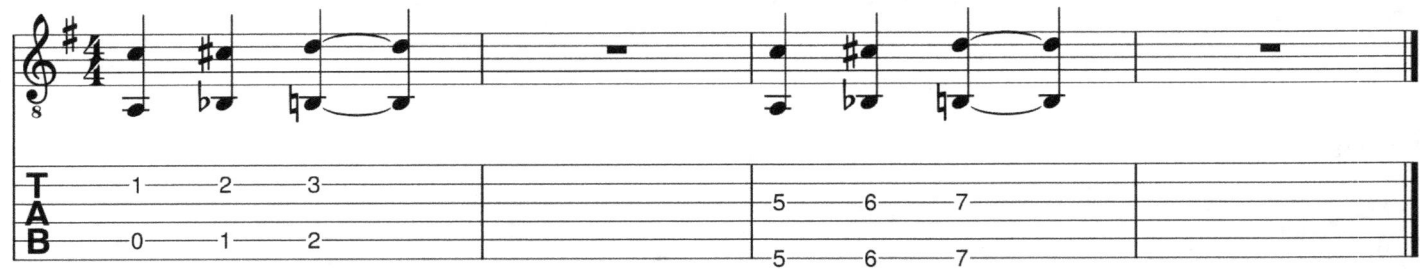

Example 1z:

This has been a long chapter, but it lays the groundwork for developing a truly free and polyphonic style of chord melody playing. Learning to re-finger chords while reducing them to their most important constituents allows us to access some incredible melodies and intricate techniques.

Chapter Two: Movement with 3rds and 7ths

This chapter is where we really start to break away from fixed, traditional chord shapes. It's like going on a little spacewalk: we're still tethered to the craft (the scale) but we get to go outside and explore the universe as we please!

10ths on the Sixth String

We will continue playing the G Major scale in 10ths, but now look in more detail at how we can add movement to the 10th.

Don't worry too much about the fingering of the following examples. Just go with what works. It will, of course, be beneficial to play through the following examples using a different finger to play the bass (root) note. But if you are comfortable, and can control the notes in the upper voice, then that is good enough for now.

Let's dive in and begin by playing up the chord scale of G Major with the root on the sixth (E) string. The 10th is played on the third (G) string. Here's an ascending idea that adds simple decoration to the 10th.

Example 2a:

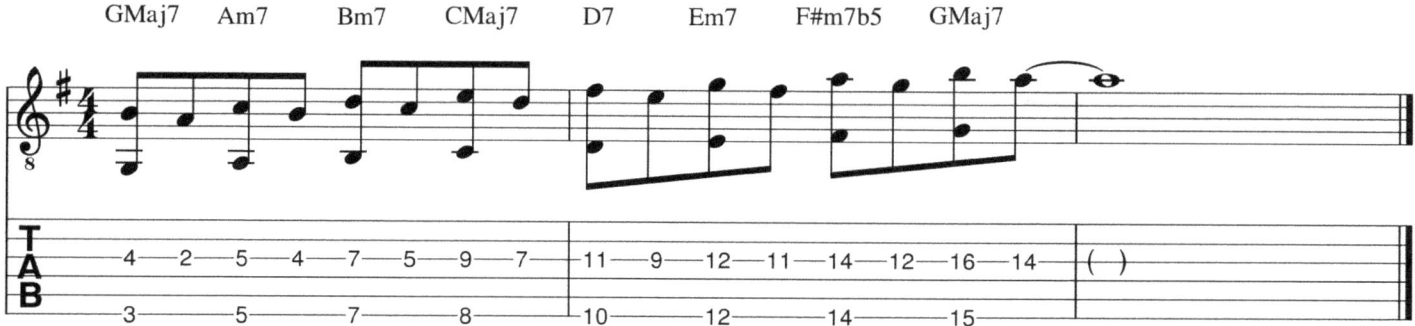

Next, let's play that idea descending.

Example 2b:

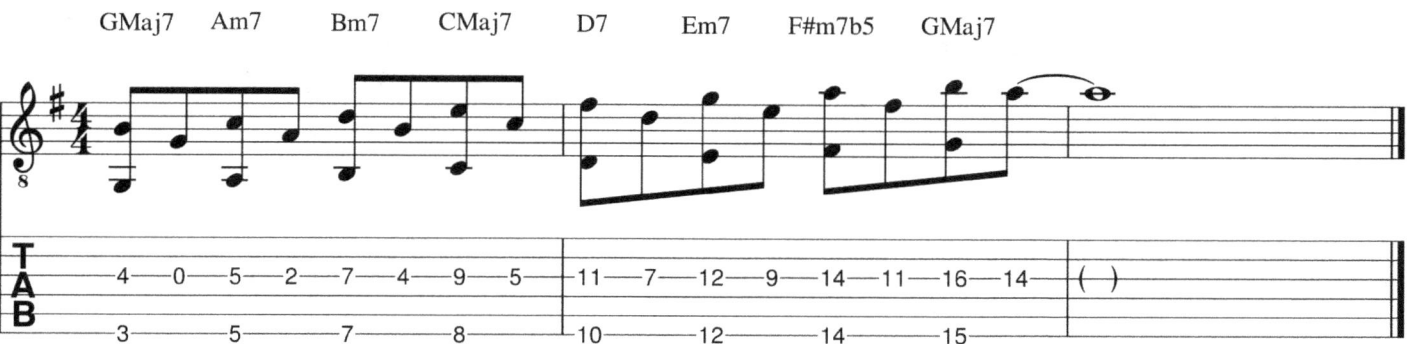

Here's another ascending idea that adds a simple step-wise melody to the 10th:

Example 2c:

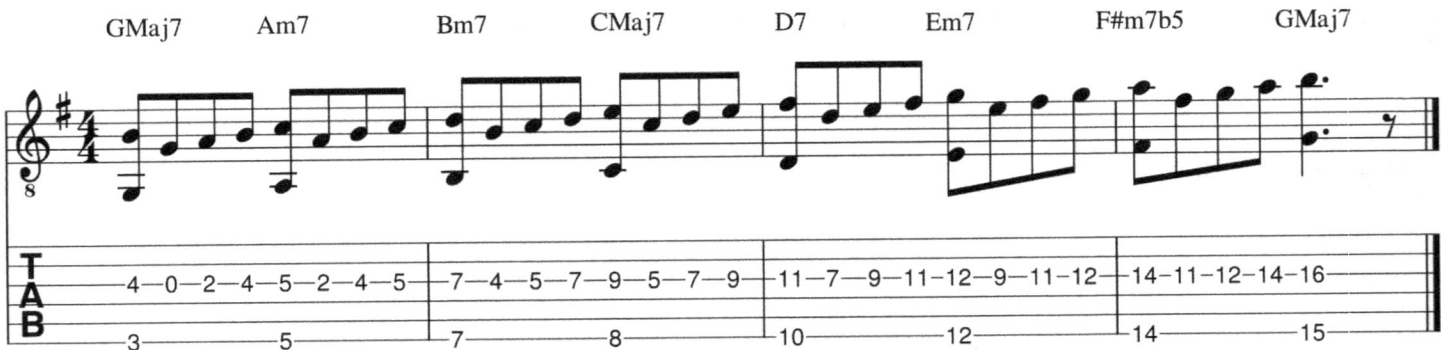

Now play it descending the neck.

Example 2d:

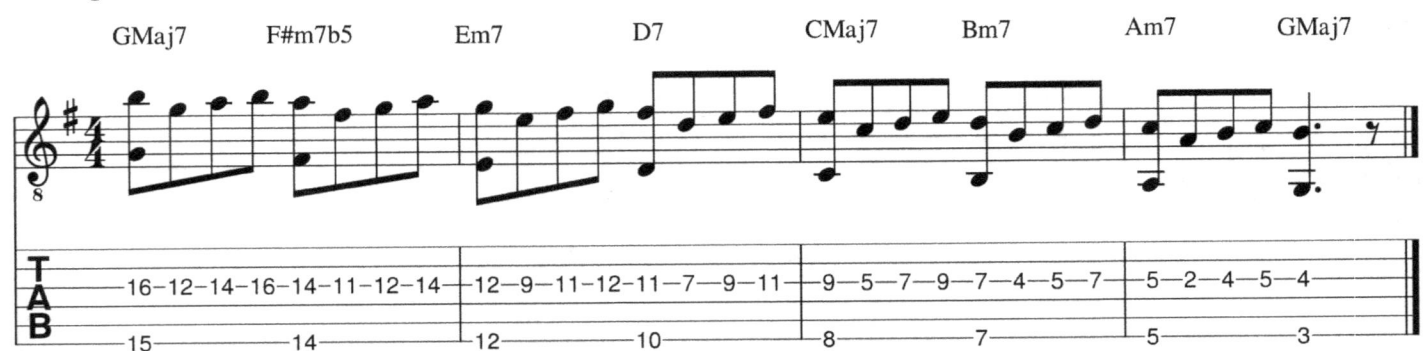

The following idea is more intricate.

Example 2e:

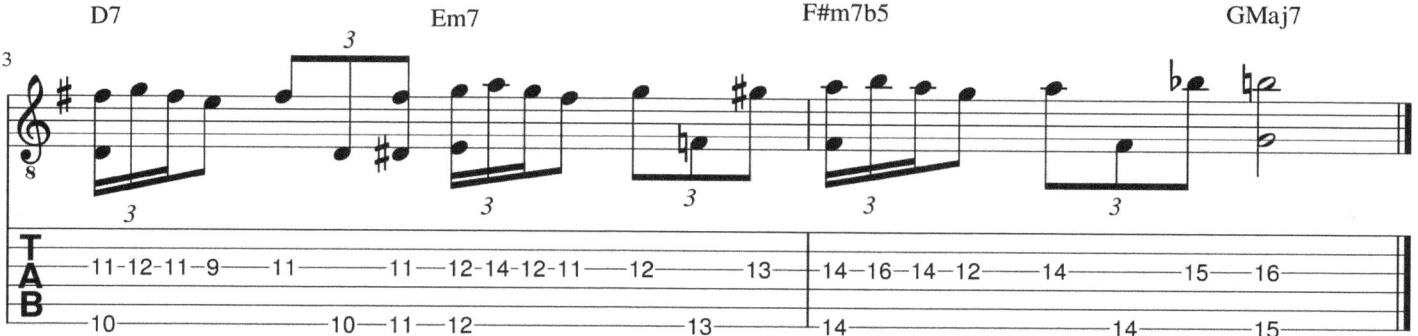

I advise you to explore as many possibilities as you can find with this type of movement on the 10th. If you use a different finger on the sixth string, you can access different melodic ideas. For instance, you can extend the decoration of the 10th onto the B string:

Example 2f:

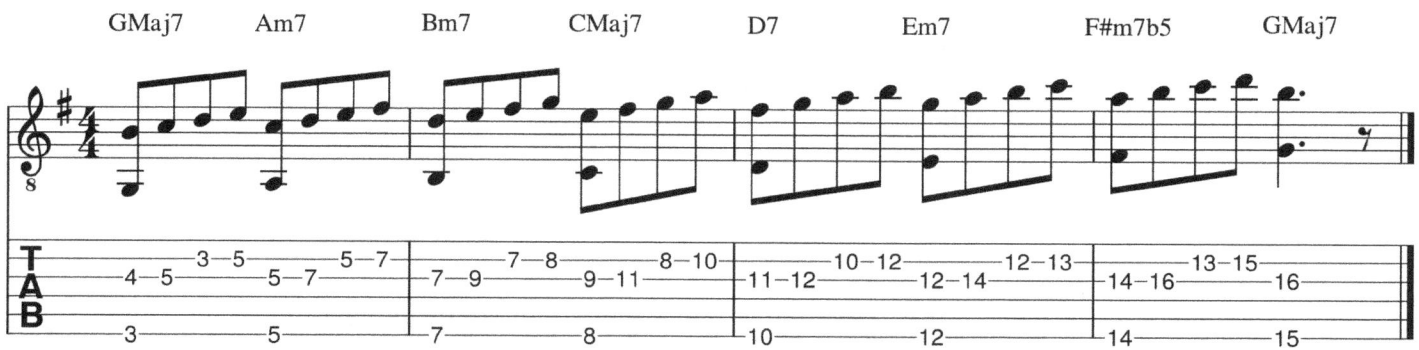

You can take it down on to the D String:

Example 2g:

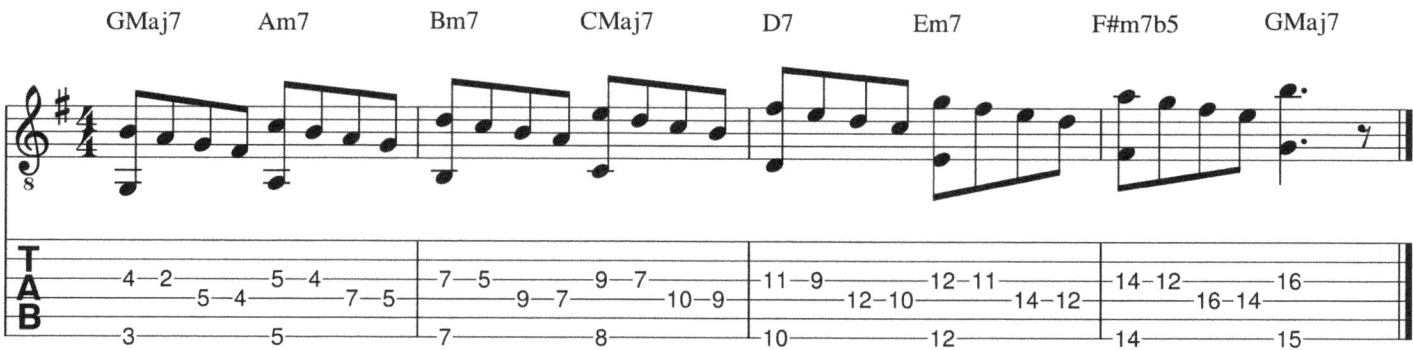

Or you could combine both ideas into longer lines.

Example 2h:

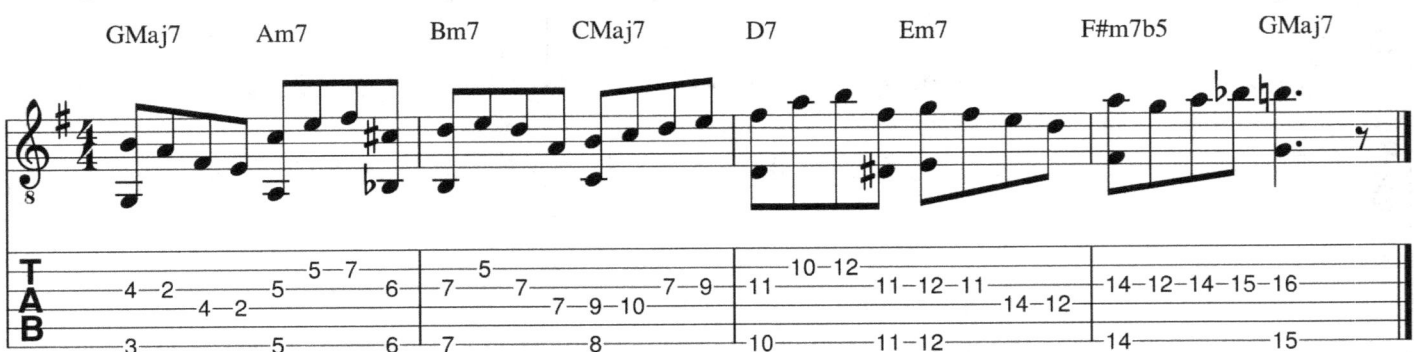

Practise these concepts ascending and descending the guitar neck. You will occasionally find that melodic ideas that cross strings are challenging to fret. It is your job to find a fingering that works.

If you struggle to get creative with your melodies, think about rhythm. Playing a similar phrase, with just one note that sounds for longer can take you to a completely different melodic place. Check out the difference a small rhythmic alteration makes in the following similar ideas:

Example 2i:

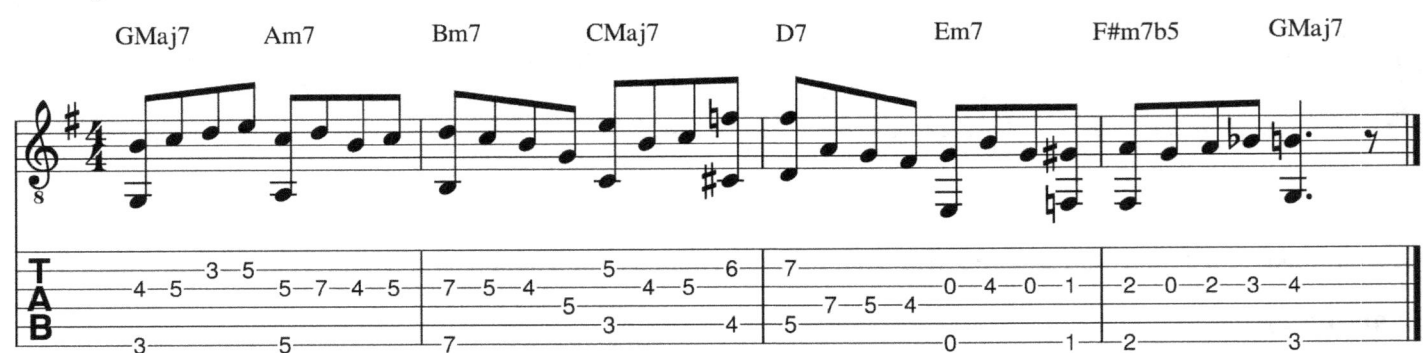

Example 2j:

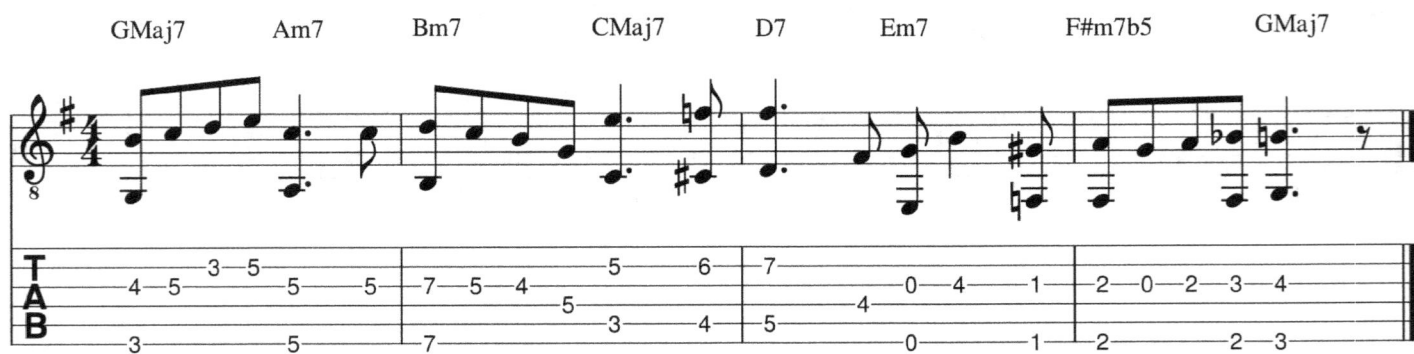

So far, each chord change has moved through the scale in a stepwise manner. You can also move the chord in 3rds or even play through a simple chord progression:

Here is an example that moves in 3rds:

Example 2k:

Have some fun and experiment.

10ths on the Fifth String

Let's transfer all the previous exercises (and your own melodic explorations) on to the fifth (A) string. We learnt the G Major scale on the fifth string in the previous chapter, so it shouldn't be too difficult to use your ears to translate the melodies and concepts across a string.

The following examples show how to play the first few ideas in this chapter with the root played on the fifth string.

Example 2m:

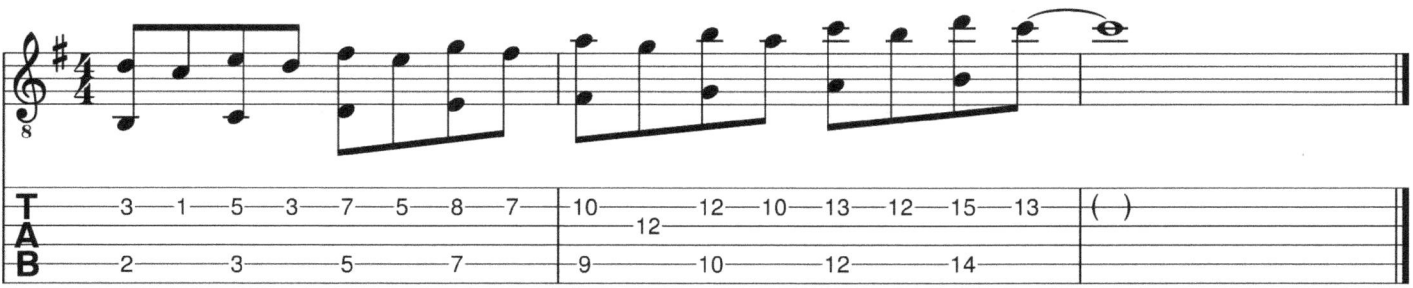

Example 2n:

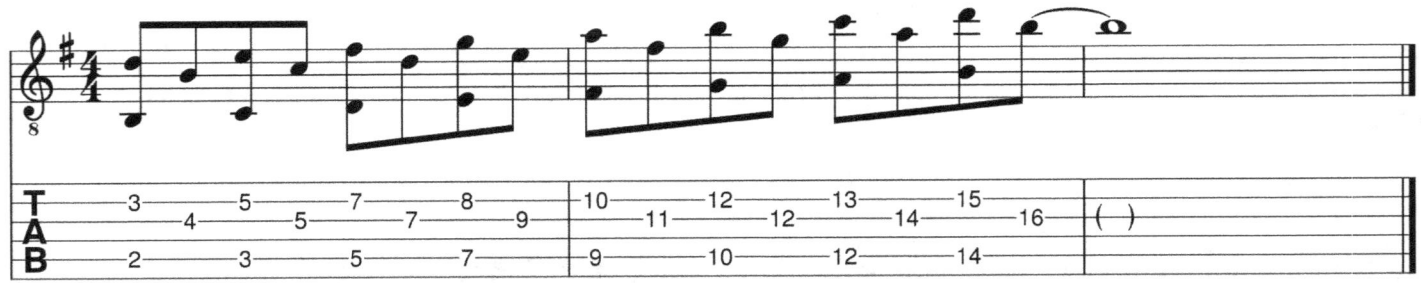

Don't forget you can extend the melodies onto the higher and lower strings:

Example 2o:

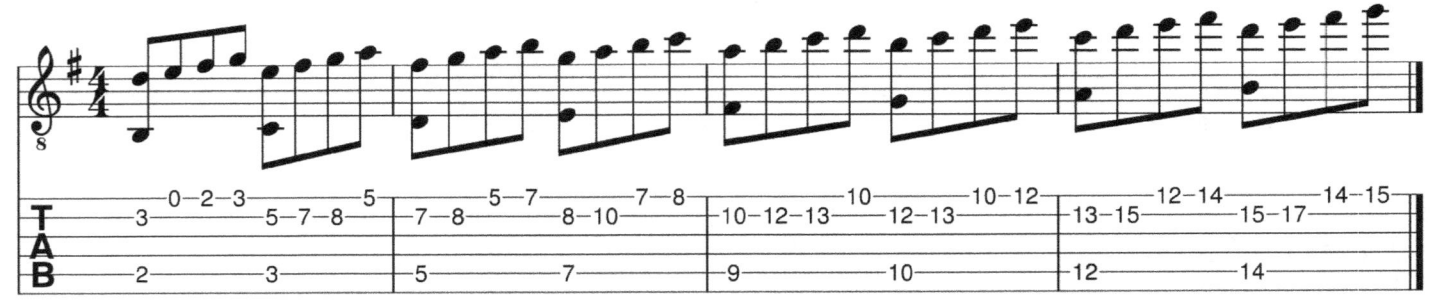

Example 2p:

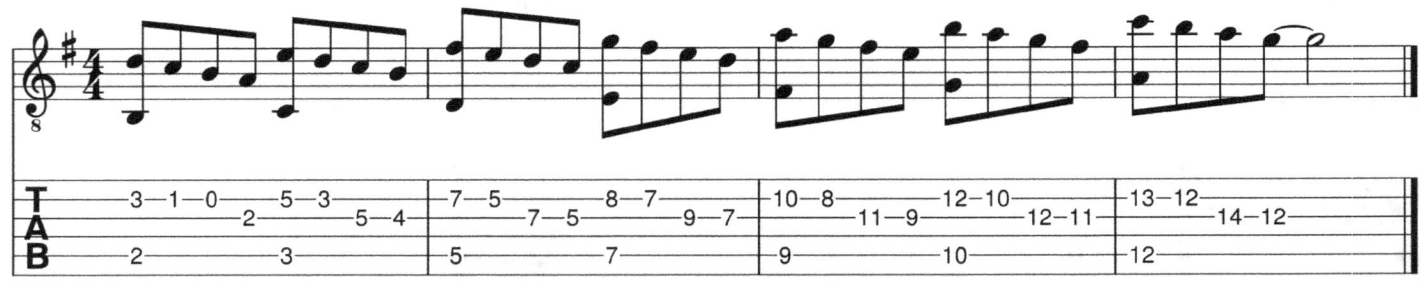

Work through the above examples and spend time experimenting with rhythm and melody. Remember to try your melodic ideas over simple chord sequences or using intervallic jumps in the bass part.

When you have these ideas mastered on the fifth string, we will examine some transition points to help you avoid large physical leaps.

Transitions

Just as with the scales in the previous chapter, it is important to explore transition points between the sixth and fifth strings with 10ths. The goal is to learn to transition across the strings whenever we choose, without losing the rhythm or flow of the melody. This allows us to keep our chord voicings close together (if we should choose to) and gives more control over our playing.

There is a big difference in tone between a melody played on the second string and one played on the third string, especially if you're using a jazz guitar with a wound G (third) string. Learning to transition across strings allows you to control the tone and feeling of the melody to a much greater degree. Listen to the audio tracks. You will notice a distinct tonal shift whenever I change strings.

There are no rights or wrongs when it comes to melody placement; it's all a matter of personal taste. The only caveat I would add is to not forget you are trying to communicate the melody to your listeners, so it should shine through your arrangements. But, by building fluency and control we can gain more control over how our music sounds – and this can only be a good thing!

The following exercises show different ways to transition a simple 10ths melody across the strings. Each transition occurs at a different point. Treat these exercises as a starting point and explore as many transitions as you can find.

Example 2q:

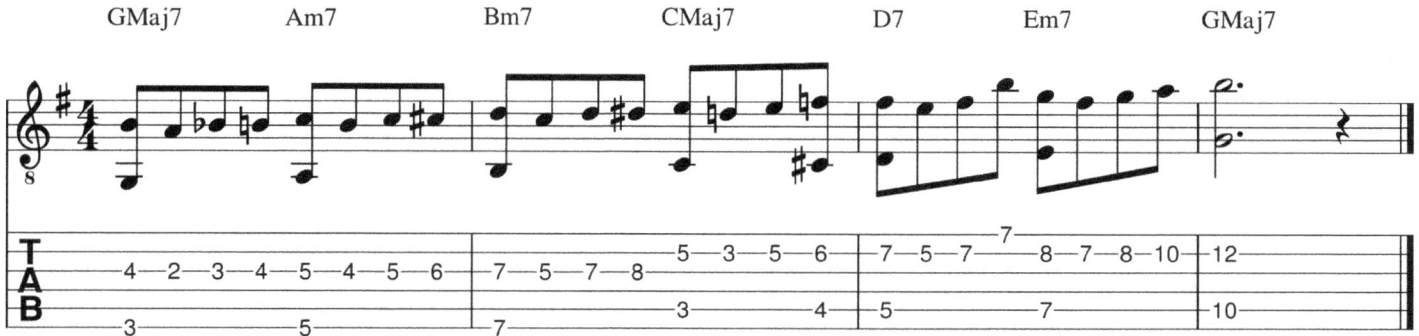

Example 2r:

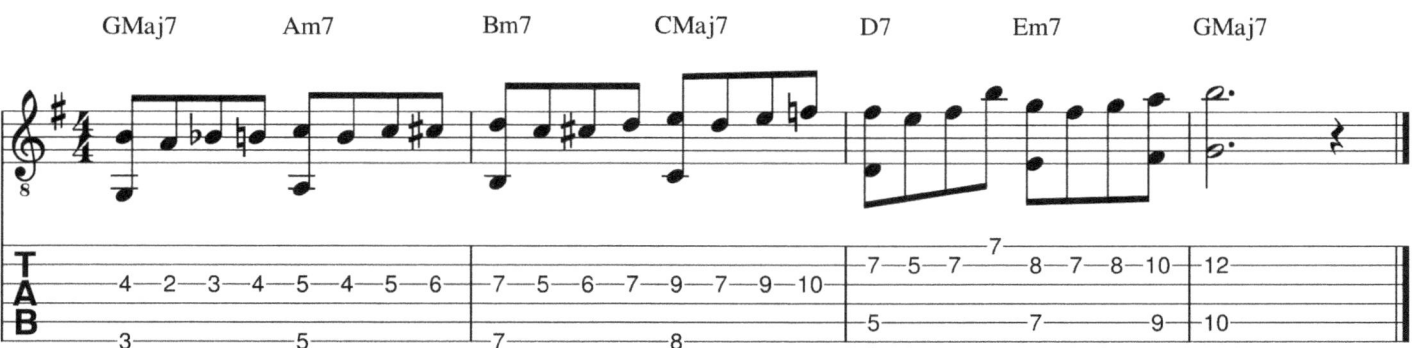

Example 2s:

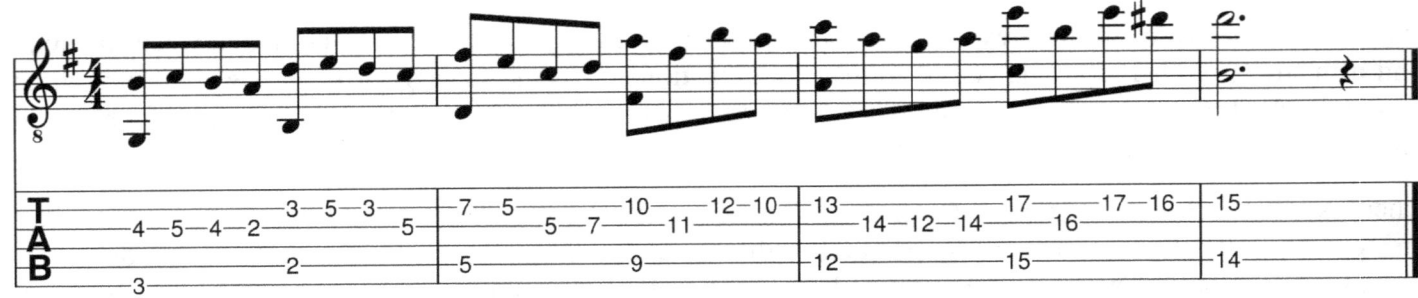

Try using the following root movements to explore transitions while keeping the melodic pattern on the 10th smooth and consistent.

Example 2t:

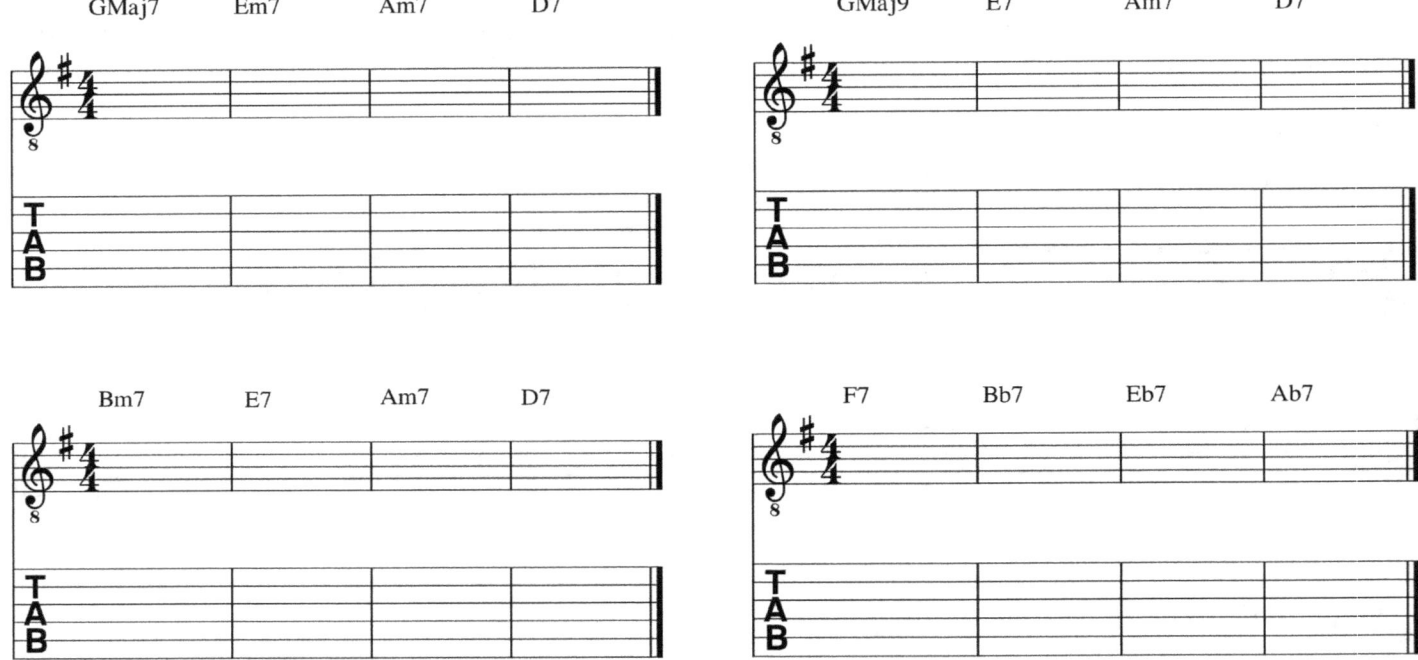

Movement with 7ths

Now it's time to apply everything we've discussed in this chapter to root-and-7th voicings. You may remember that 7ths have quite an "unresolved" sound, but when we add melody they quickly become much more appealing.

Work through exercises 2a to 2t again, but this time apply each melodic pattern to the root and 7th interval instead of the root and 10th.

You would play example 2a in the following way:

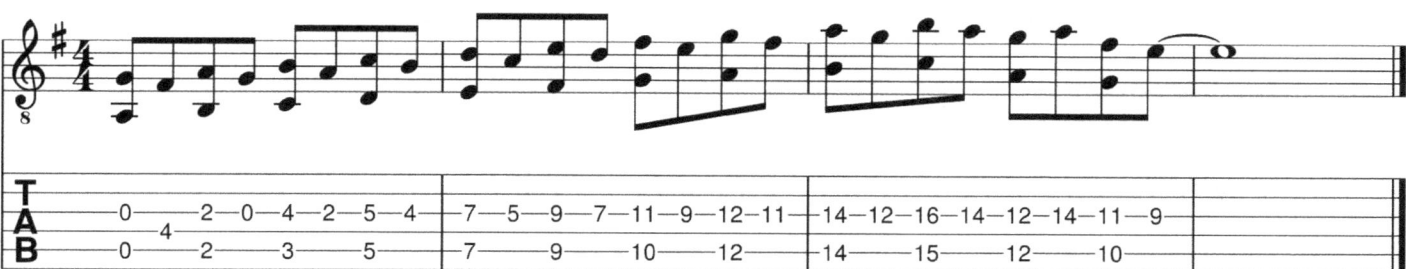

Play through the chord-scale with roots on both the sixth and fifth strings and explore the transition points as fully as you can. The information in this chapter may take a few days or weeks to digest, but the more comfortable and proficient you become, the better.

Finally, work through this and the previous chapter again, but repeat everything in the key of C Major. The scale diagrams for 10ths and 7ths are shown below.

C Major 7ths and 10ths

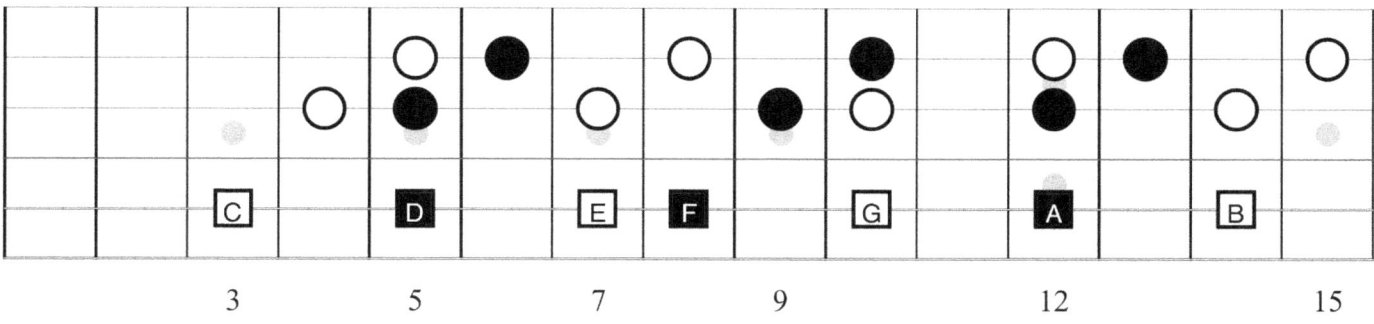

Work in other keys like Bb, D and A whenever you can.

Chapter Three: Combining 10ths, 7ths and Bass Movement

Before we look at combining movements on the 10ths and 7ths, we will examine how to add movement to the *root note* of each interval and begin to mix these movements across both voices.

Let's start with a simple movement added to the root while ascending the G Major scale with 10ths. Think carefully about how you can finger the following examples to reach every note fluently. Some of these bass movements may be a slight stretch to begin with.

Example 3a:

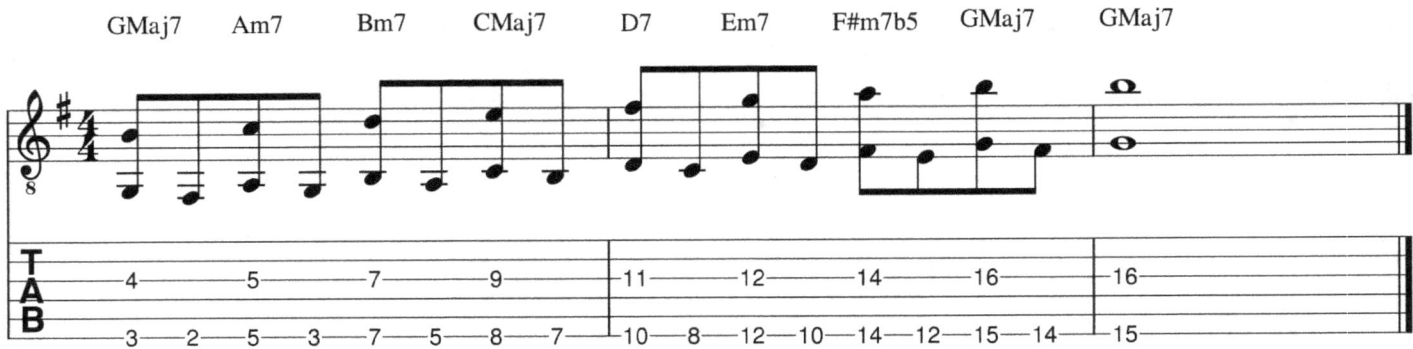

Now play the same idea descending

Example 3b:

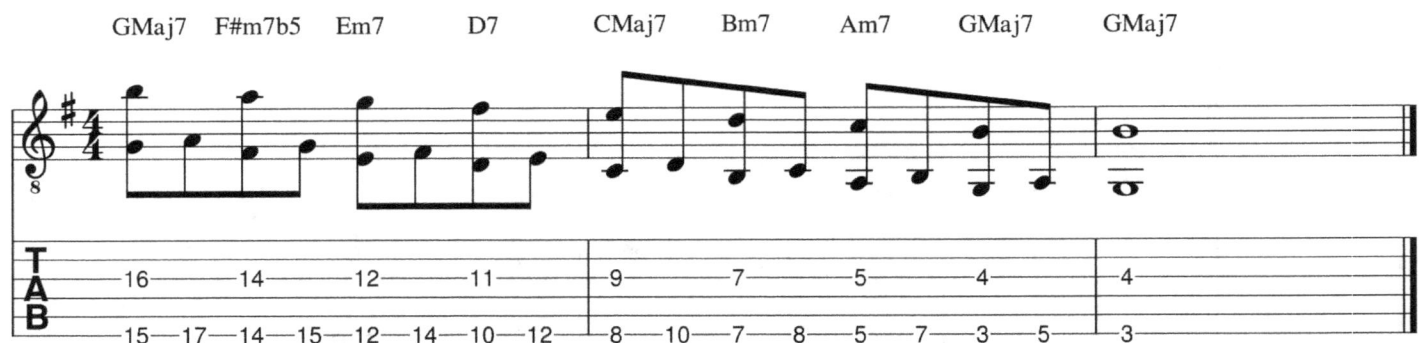

Let's add a bit more movement with the bass. You may be forced to slide to the higher note in each movement and stop holding the 10th. This is fine!

Example 3c:

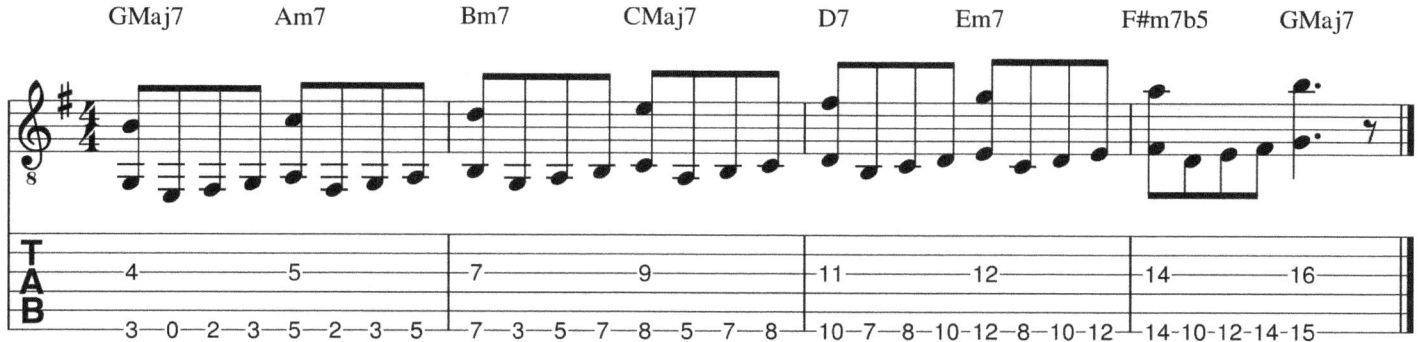

Next play a similar descending figure.

Example 3d:

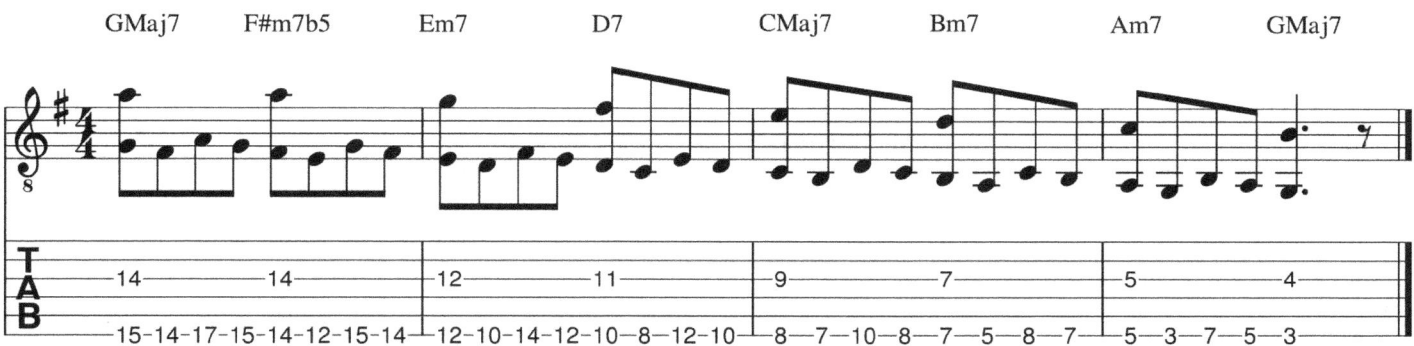

Spend some time exploring bass movements with 10ths.

The previous examples showed you how to use *diatonic* scale steps to create movements around the roots. However, it is also common to use *chromatic* (non-scale) notes to move between scale steps and decorate the bass part.

The following two examples will teach you a couple of ways to use chromatic notes and you should use them as a starting point for your own exploration.

Example 3e:

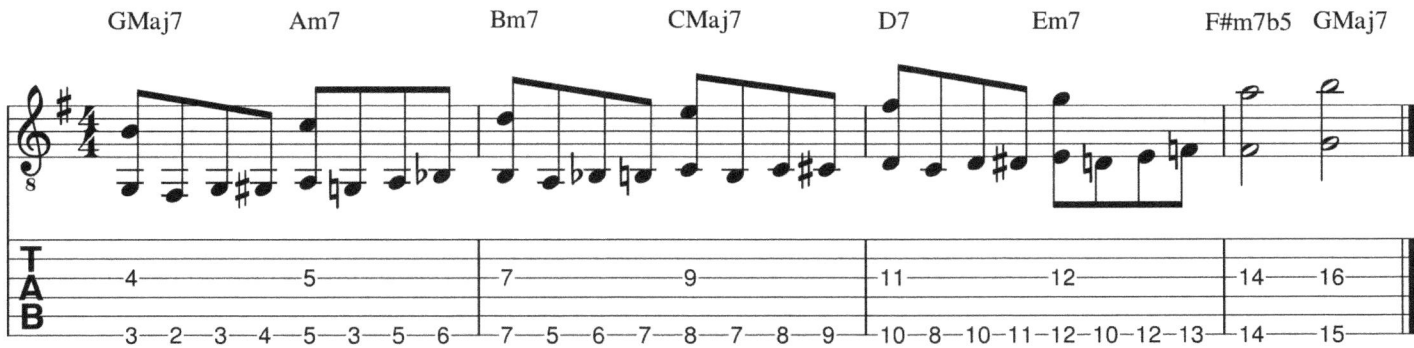

Example 3f:

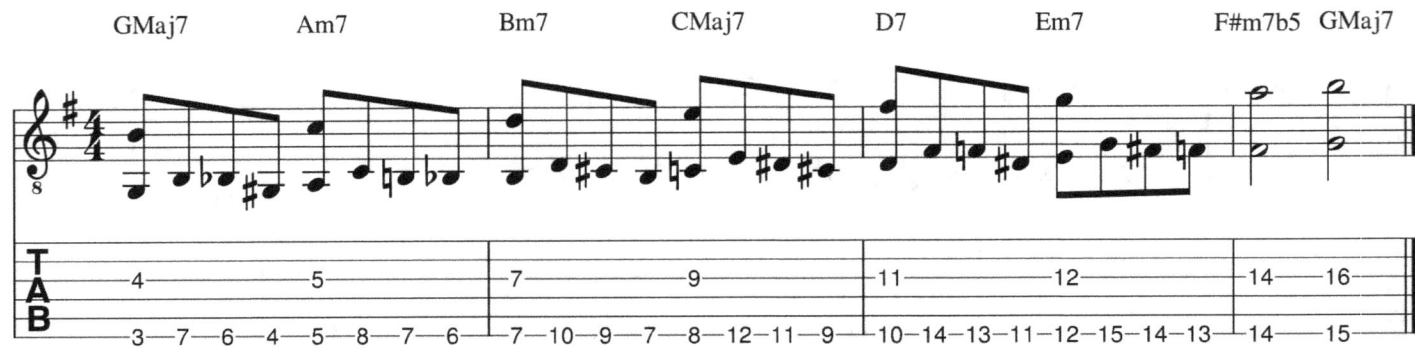

When you are comfortable adding movement to the bass note on the sixth string, try repeating the previous six exercises with roots on the fifth string.

The following exercise will get you started.

Example 3g:

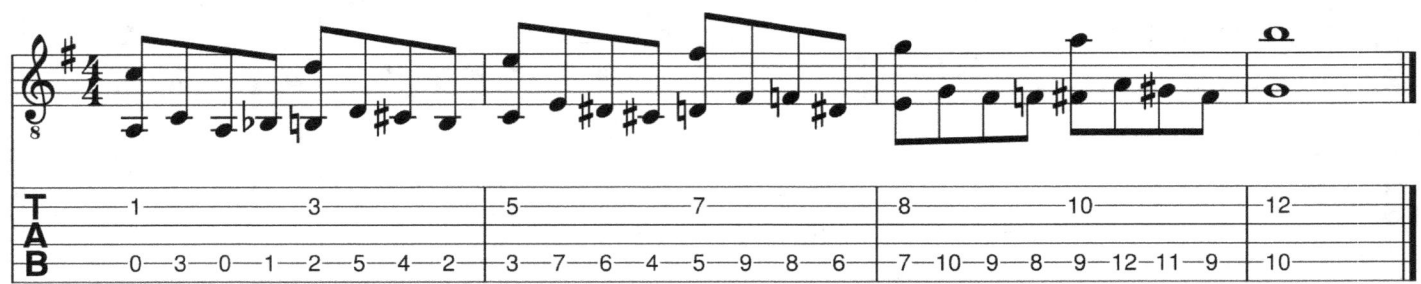

Again, spend time exploring your own variations.

Finally, begin to investigate transition points between the sixth and fifth strings. Use the exercises in chapter 2 to help you get going. A useful exercise is to take a consistent bass movement across the transition. Keep the movement, pattern and rhythm constant as you learn to change string. This will teach you control before you start to create your own melodies. Here's one pattern to get you going:

Example 3h:

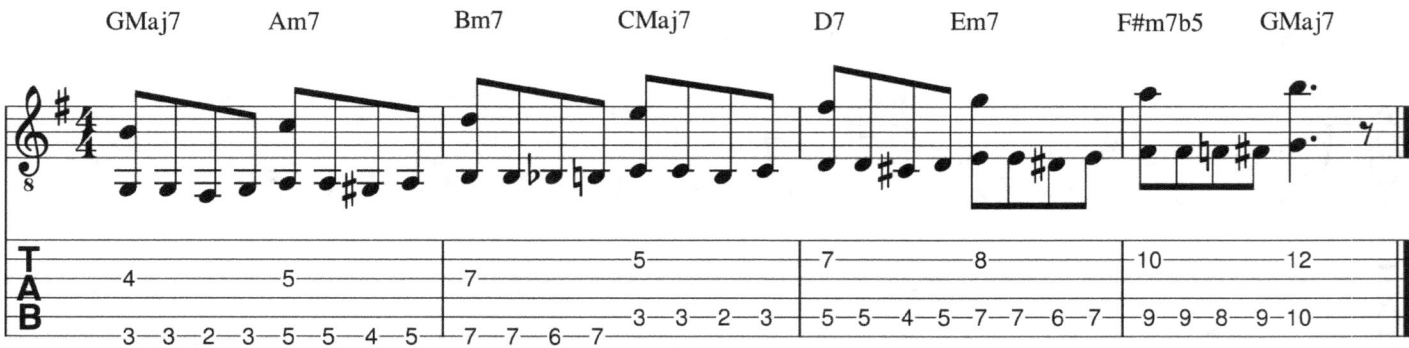

Spend as much time as you can to explore these ideas.

When we started this journey, we broke our approach down into a skeleton which included just the basic constituent parts of chords: the root and 10th and the root and 7th.

When we combine the root, 10th and 7th into one voicing, we arrive back at block chord shapes you may already know and which are used commonly in jazz. Now, however, you have a much greater insight about how each note in the chord can function as an individual voice and are able to add musical movement to each one.

Returning to these block chords is just a momentary stepping-stone on our journey to creative freedom!

Here is the chord-scale of G Major played on the sixth string with both 10ths and 7ths. Try fretting these voicings using the second finger on the sixth string.

Example 3i:

Here is the chord-scale ascending the fifth string.

Example 3j:

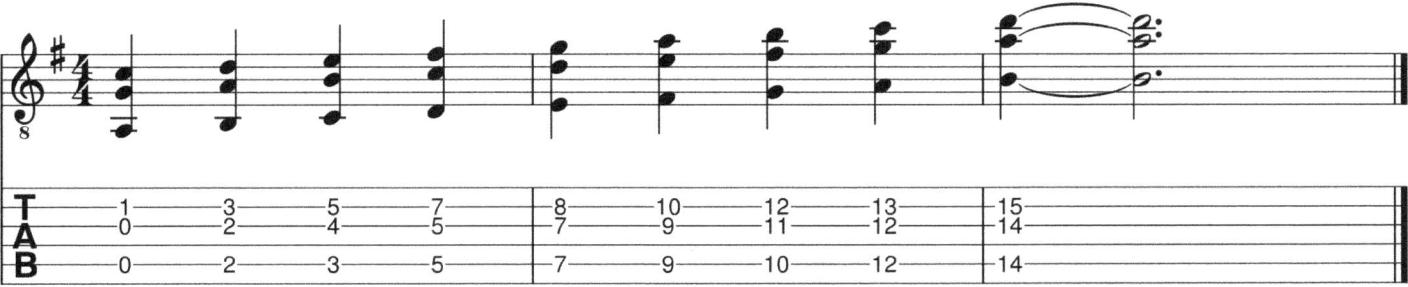

Make sure you are comfortable with these shapes on both strings and once again see how many ways you can find to transition across the strings. If you did your homework in the previous chapter, this should be a fairly easy task.

Let's begin by adding movement to the 10ths in each of these voicings. Again, you may wish to begin with your second finger playing the root notes.

Example 3k:

Example 3l:

Now apply these ideas to the fifth string. Here are some new movements for the 10th.

Example 3m:

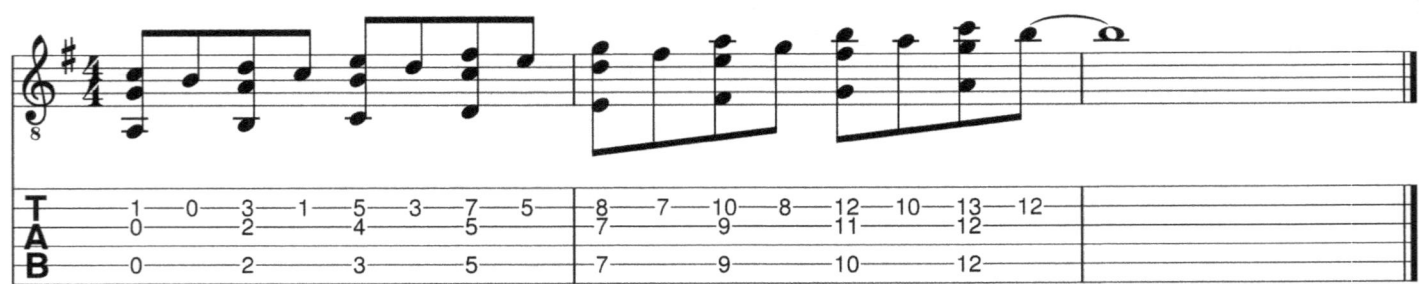

Example 3n:

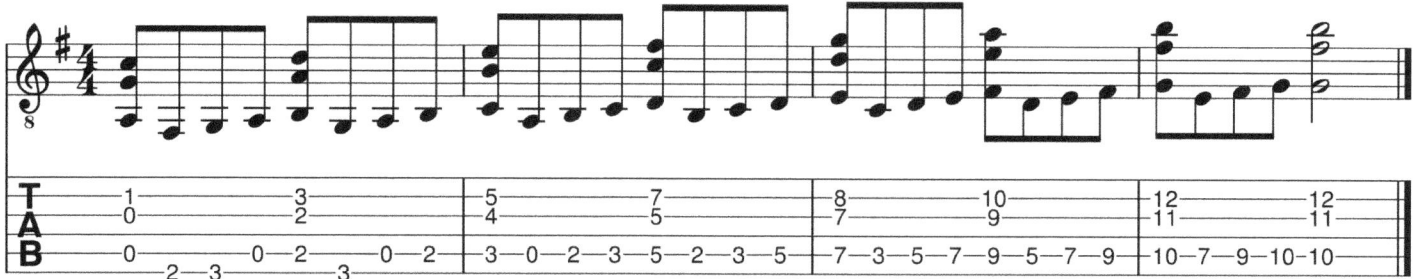

Now find some transition points between strings.

These voicings may feel unusual or uncomfortable to you at first. They may even go against what you thought you knew about fingering chord shapes correctly! However, just as all those jazz chords you already know became second nature, these fingerings will too. In fact, you will quickly find that you have many more options and much greater freedom for chord voicings and improvisation than you had before.

You may remember from the previous chapter that root and 7th voicings sound a little awkward. What you'll find now is that when combined with the 10th, and with some movement added, everything starts to fall into place. The 10th *supports* the 7th and allows the music to "carry" this slightly dissonant interval.

Try adding some movement to the 7th. You may find that you occasionally need to lift your finger from the root or 10th to play what you hear.

Example 3o:

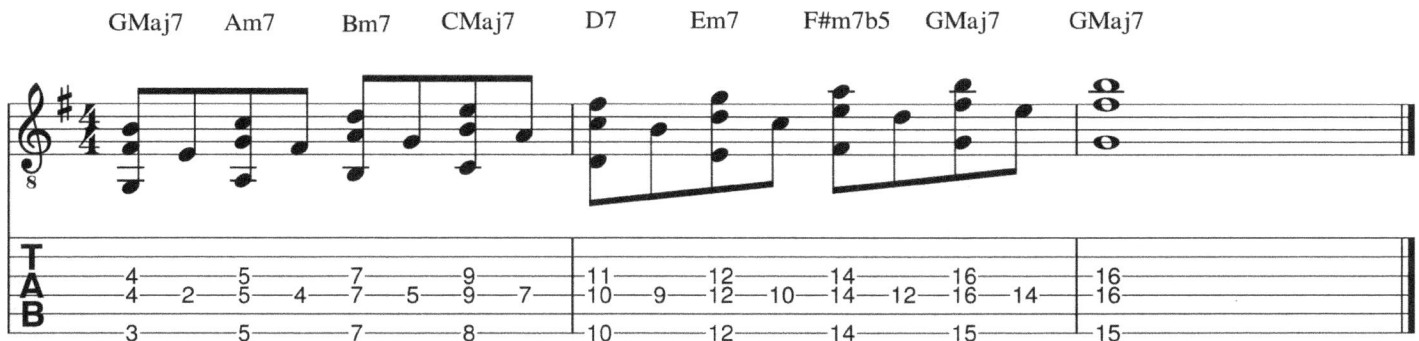

Example 3p:

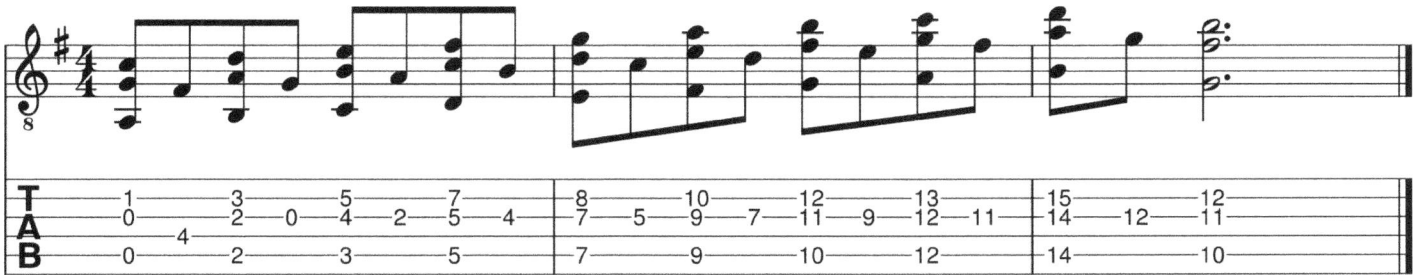

Example 3q:

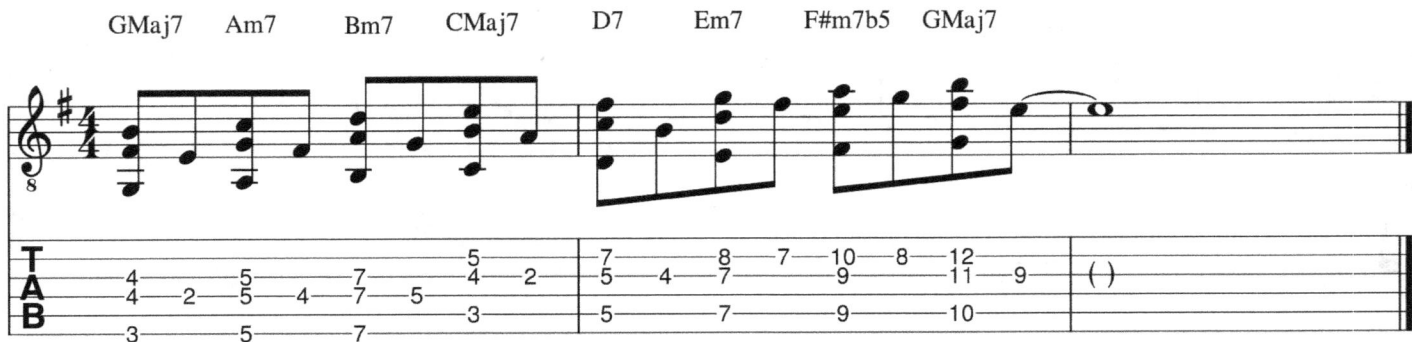

Now it's time to lose the restrictions! The following examples combine movements with 7ths and 10ths. Don't worry about rhythm, just explore the guitar and see what sounds different fingerings offer you.

Example 3r:

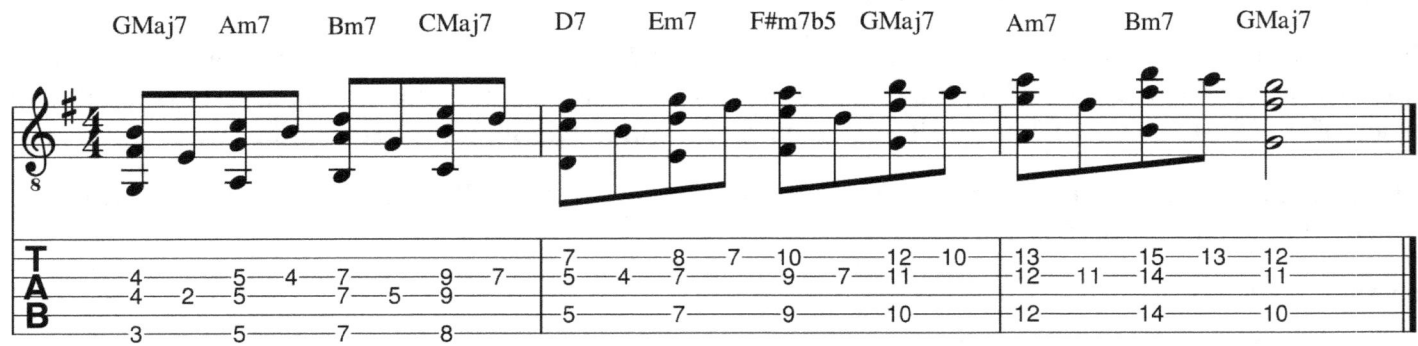

Example 3s:

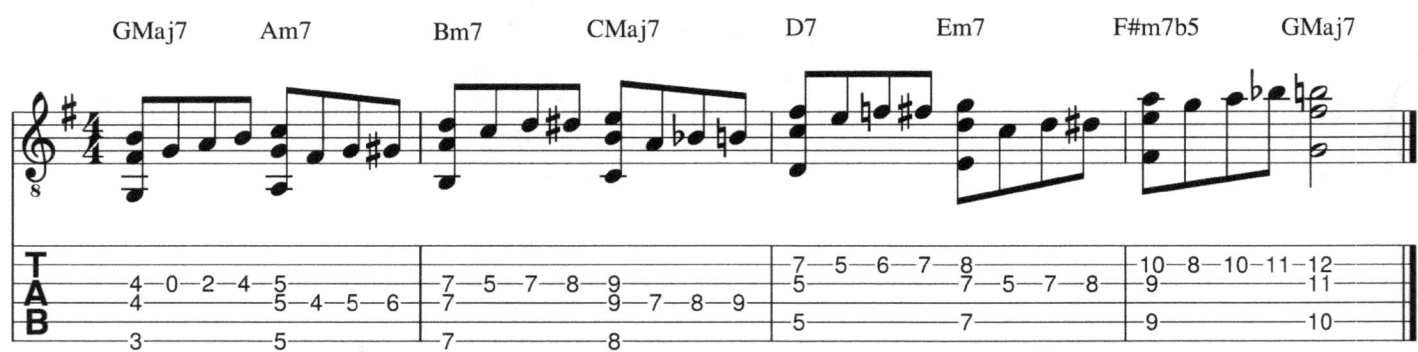

Finally, let's add movements on the root back into the mix, so that now there is the possibility of creating melody on any of the three independent voices.

Example 3t:

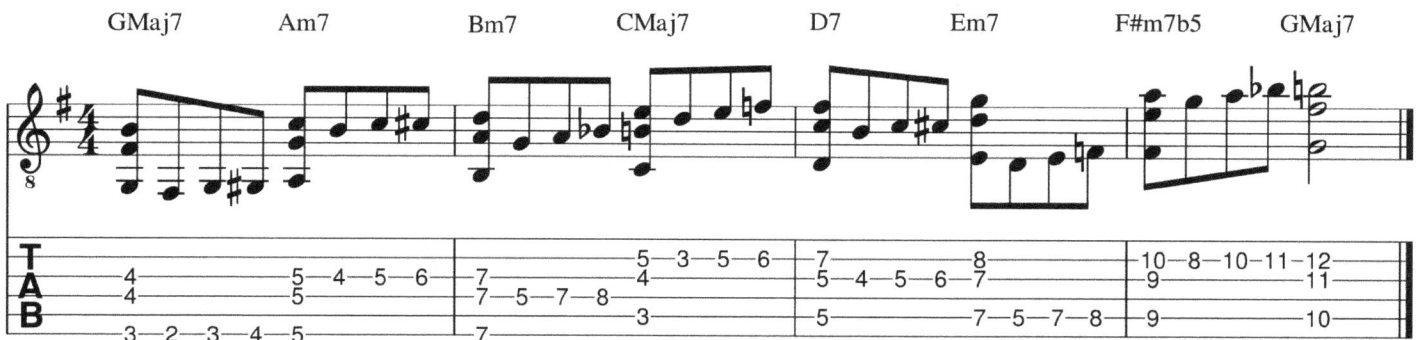

It's up to you how musical you make this process. I've given you some material and ways to experiment, but you can get as creative as you like! Try to break out of set patterns and create movements and melodies that are different on each note.

The exercises in this chapter are based around scale steps, but why not try them with some familiar chord sequences or around the circle of fifths?

Learn to play all the ideas in this book in *every* key. When you're comfortable working in the key of G Major, try C Major and then E Major. Find as many different transition points as you can, and then see if you can find voicings with the root on the fourth (D) string.

Even if you only work through a few new key centres, the guitar neck quickly opens up in ways you never considered possible. It's all to play for, so set aside some time each day and really get to know your guitar!

Chapter Four: Adding Melodies to 7ths and 10ths

Now we're going to get creative and have some fun with melody!

In the previous chapter we learned to decorate 10ths, 7ths and root notes with patterns while moving in scale steps. Now it's time to move away from scale steps and think about adding melody over chord movements.

To begin with, let's work with a common jazz chord sequence.

iii vi ii V I (Diatonic) in G

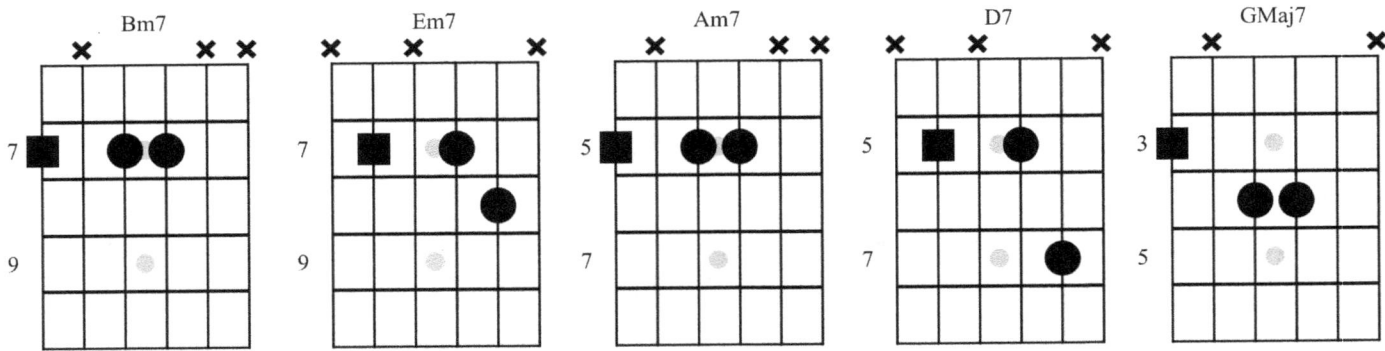

The first step is to add a melody on top of the root, 10th and 7th voicings of the above chords.

It's important you know that the following melodies were *improvised* before being transcribed. As with every example in this book, they are intended to be a starting point for your own exploration on the guitar. Creating improvised melodies can be a challenge to begin with, which is why I'm giving you some initial ideas here. After a short time, however, you will start to find your own melodies by simply exploring the notes that are available around each chord and trying different ideas.

I teach all my students to work at *internalizing* music. In other words, hearing an idea in your head, then transferring it to the guitar. It often helps to sing ideas out loud. This nearly always results in helping you to express more "musical" ideas and is another way in which you can help yourself to break out of those familiar boxes.

It is also important to stress that there is no "correct" fingering to play the examples in this, or any other chapter. Often the choice of fingering is governed by the *target* note of the melody. All melodies have some strong notes (usually a chord tone), and some supporting notes that decorate these targets. Target notes are like an island chain in my sea of melody! If I know I need to use a particular finger to reach an island in a few notes time, then I will subconsciously organise the fingering of other melody notes around this.

When I started playing in this style, learning which fingers to use was a case of very slow practise. I figured out how to play what I heard in my heard, translated it onto the guitar, then organised my fingers accordingly.

Most often, my choice of fingering is dictated by the *next* chord voicing I will play. If I know a specific finger is used on a specific chord tone, I can quickly work my improvised melody around it. Practise makes perfect and you will find that you get much quicker at this process until the point where it becomes unconscious. At the core of it all, you simply need to look ahead to what you'll be playing in a few beats time.

As your skills develop, you will naturally start to feel where the target notes are and know which finger needs to be used. The notes that *support* this target note can be fingered in any way that allows you to access them smoothly.

The first example shows how I can add an improvised melody to the above chord sequence. Notice that I am playing just root and melody, and the melody is played on just the first and second string.

Example 4a:

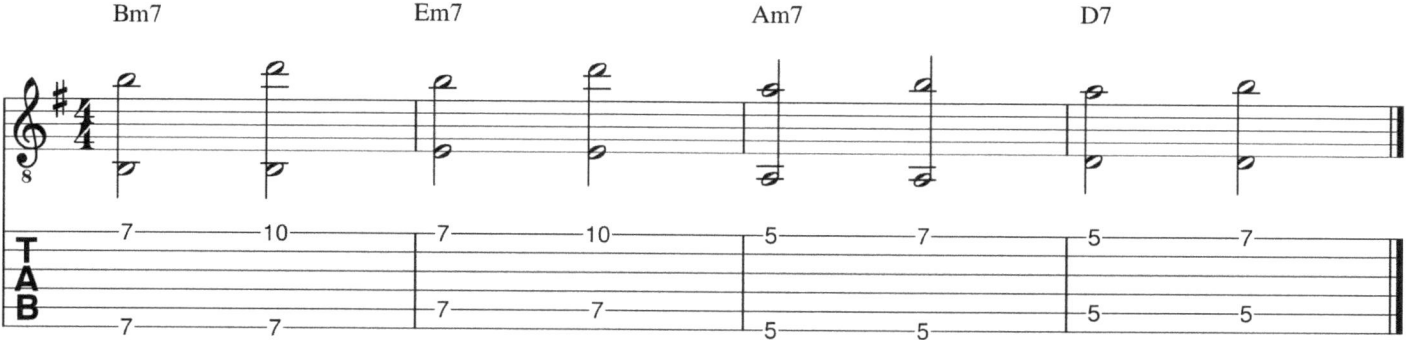

Let's add the third back in while playing the same melody.

Example 4b:

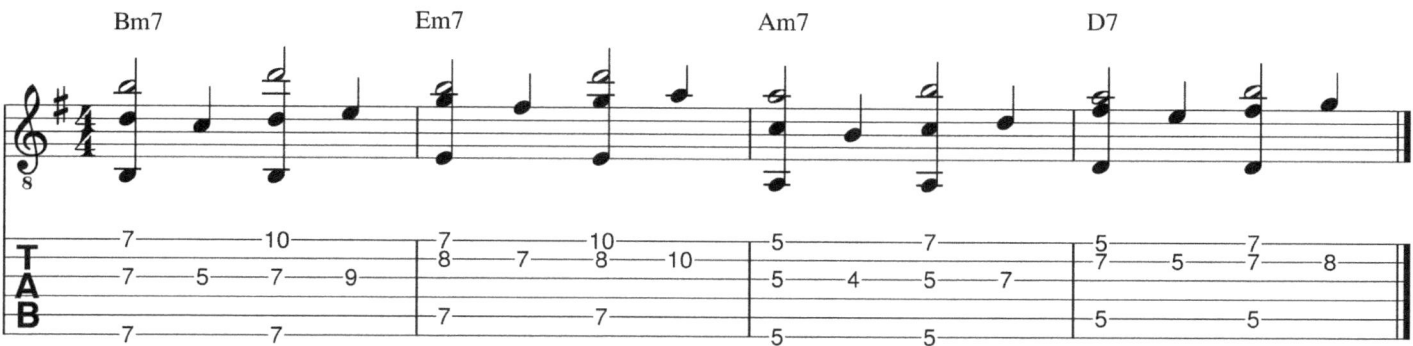

Now, retain the top melody and add some decoration to the third. Notice that the part based around the 3rd dovetails with the melody being played on the top strings. Crucially, the top melody is still heard as the most important part. I've also dropped the bass note to give the melody some "air".

Example 4c:

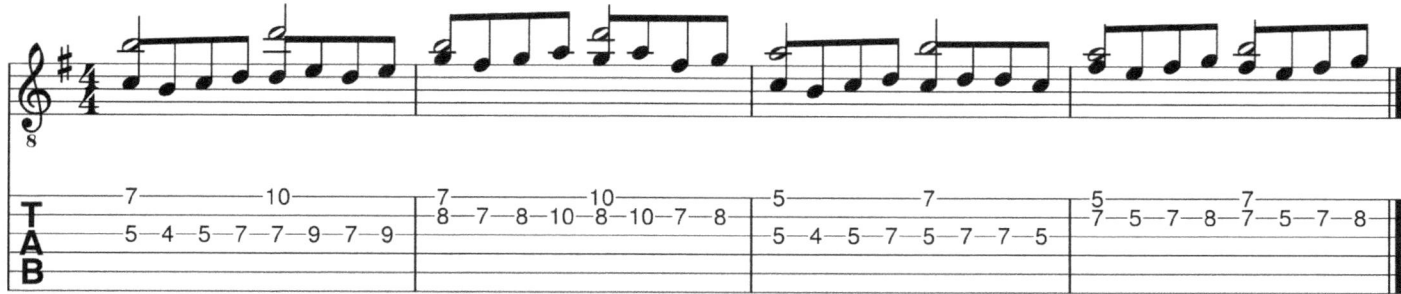

Now reintroduce the bass and add some decoration

Example 4d:

Now let's combine some other movements with the bass movements.

Example 4e:

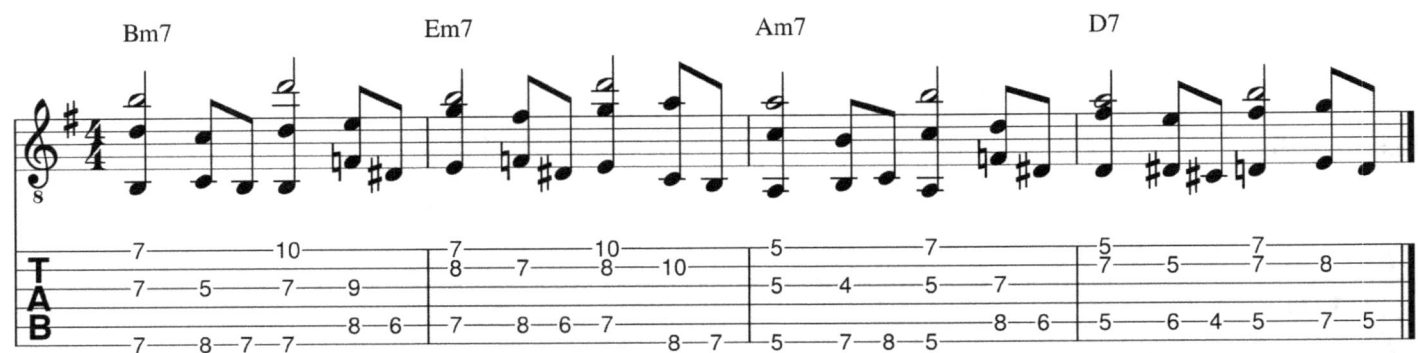

We can reintroduce the 7th and add some movement there.

Example 4f:

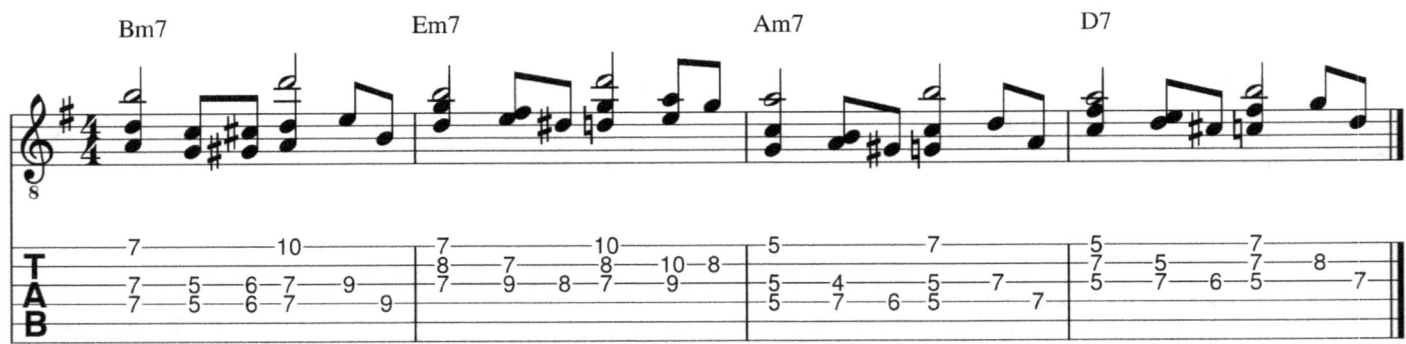

Finally let's combine aspects of all three parts.

Example 4g:

Spend as much time as you can finding new ways to play through this chord sequence using the same melody. You may decide to decorate the 3rd in bar one, the root in bar two and the 7th in bar three. The next time through, you could vary the root in bar one and the 7th in bar two. There are unlimited permutations, so get exploring – just be organised in your approach.

Now I want you to get creative and find new melodies over the previous chord sequence. Begin with just root and melody, then introduce the 3rd, decorations, 7ths, 7th decoration, and finally combine everything into a short piece of music. Remember, you don't have to play everything all at once and it's perfectly fine to drop the bass while you focus on other parts.

Whatever style of music we play, there are certain chord sequences that crop up all the time. It is important to get a feel for these sequences and learn to add melody and movement so that you can train your ears to hear the possibilities.

Here's a common chord sequence to explore.

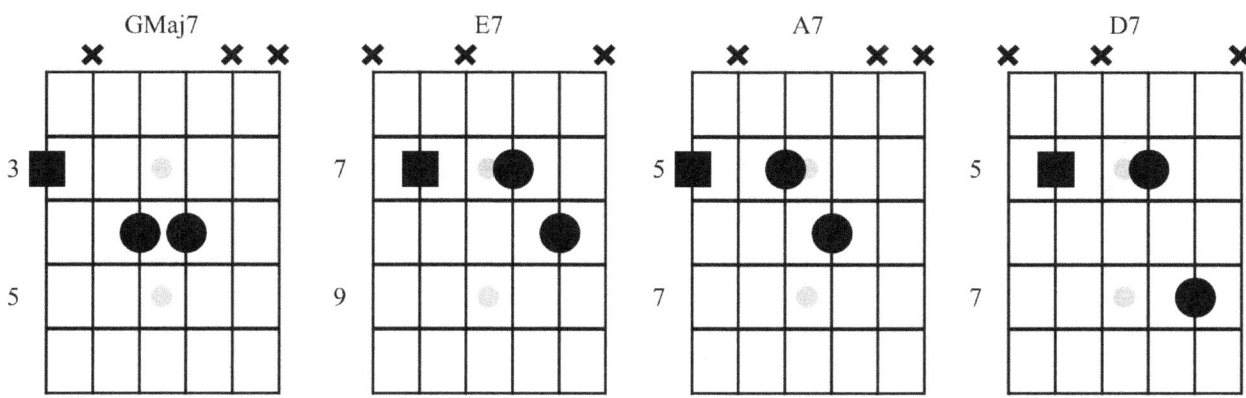

Here's a melody you could use as a starting point.

Example 4h:

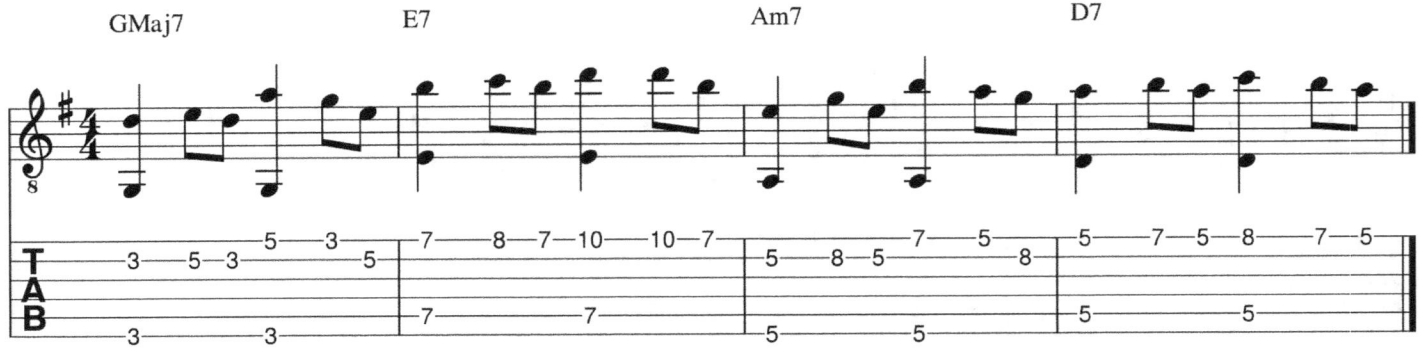

Here is one way to decorate the 10ths

Example 4i:

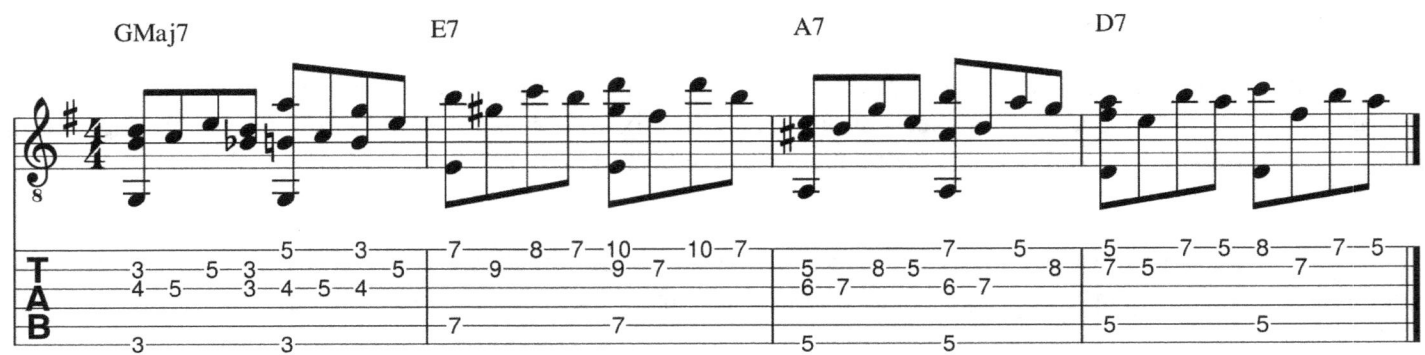

Now try adding movement to the root.

Example 4j:

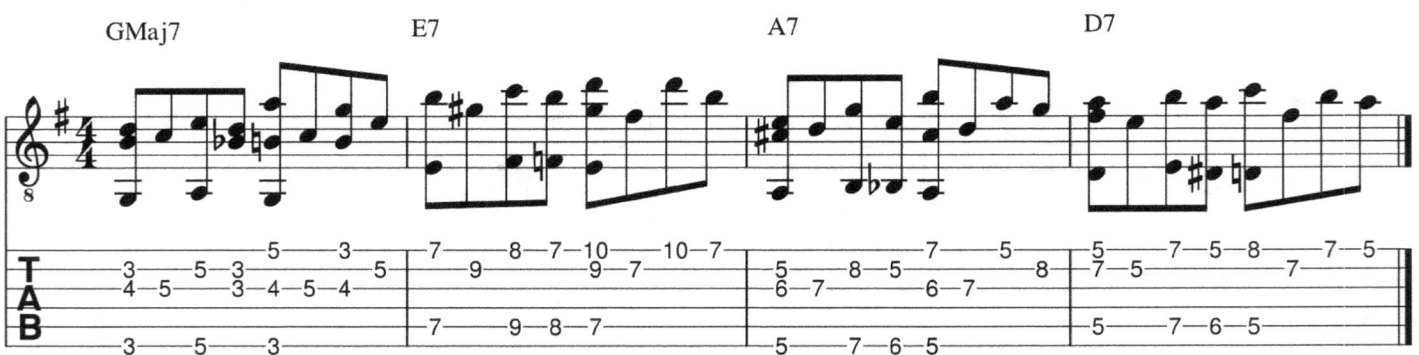

Repeat the steps in examples 4a-4g to add your own variations to the 10th, root and 7th before combining them.

Here are two more examples with improvised melodies. Repeat steps 4a to 4g on each of them.

Example 4k:

Example 4l:

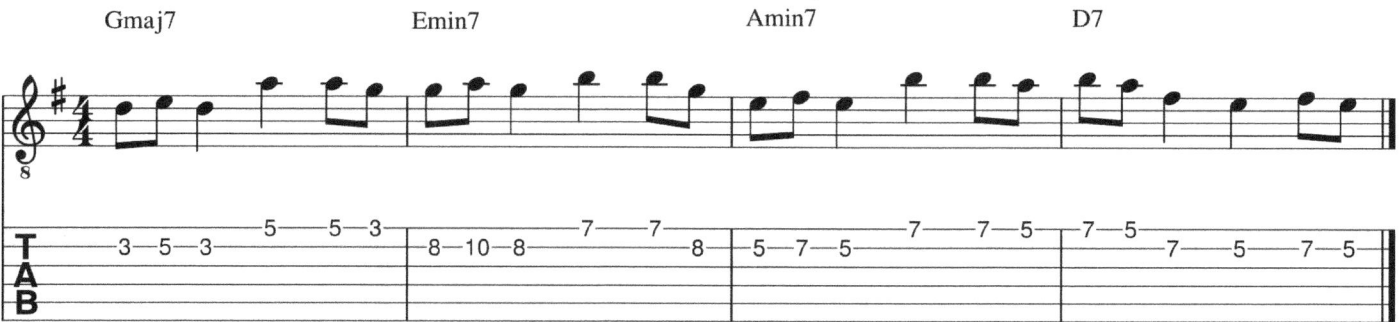

The previous ideas are a starting point for your own exploration. They aren't designed to be "masterpieces", they're just here to get you thinking about the fretboard in a different way. Try playing the chords on different strings and in different keys.

When you're exploring these concepts, try to keep things simple – there is no need for complexity at this stage; you are laying foundations for your future playing.

Chapter Five: Minor Scales

Throughout this book, we have been working exclusively with the Major scale. While the Major scale is an important part of music it's certainly not the whole story and we need to take a brief look at Minor scales before moving on.

There are three types of traditional minor scale (if we ignore certain minor modal scales such as Dorian and Phrygian). These three minor scales have, along with the Major scale, formed the backbone of Western music for over eight hundred years.

Natural Minor Scales

Let's begin with the *Natural Minor*. You may have heard this scale called the Aeolian mode before. It has a slightly Spanish flavour.

If the Major scale has the *formula* 1 2 3 4 5 6 7

The Natural Minor scale has the formula 1 2 b3 4 5 b6 b7

With a root note of G, that formula creates the notes

G A Bb C D Eb F G

These notes can be played like this on the sixth string.

Example 5a:

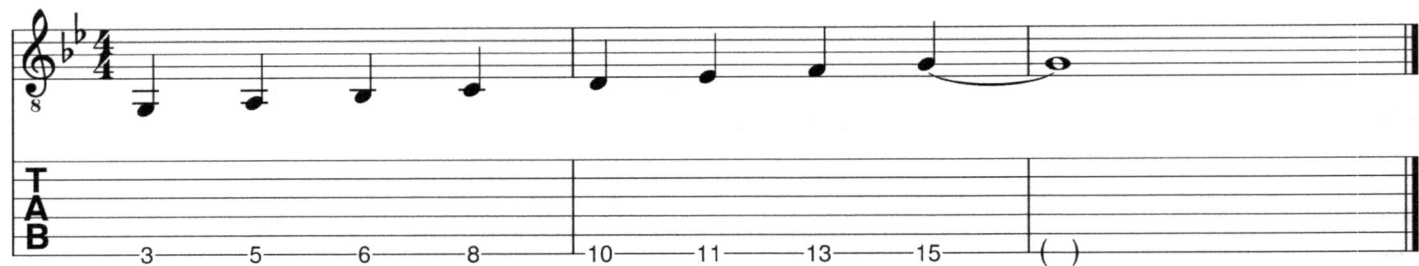

Harmonic Minor Scales

The next scale to look at is the *Harmonic Minor* scale. The formula for a harmonic minor scale is

1 2 b3 4 5 b6 7

With a root note of G, that formula creates the following scale:

G A Bb C D Eb F#

42

These notes can be played like this on the sixth string.

Example 5b:

Melodic/Jazz Minor Scales

Finally, there is the *Melodic Minor* scale. The Melodic Minor scale is a bit awkward because it is often played differently when ascending and descending. When ascending, the melodic minor is just like a major scale with a flattened third. The formula is,

1 2 b3 4 5 6 7

Giving the notes

G A Bb C D E F#

Example 5d:

When descending, the Melodic Minor is played as the Natural Minor scale.

b7 b6 5 4 b3 2 1

Giving the notes

G F Eb D C Bb A.

43

Example 5e:

The full ascending and descending Melodic Minor scale sounds like this:

Example 5f:

However, many jazz musicians tend to ignore the descending form of the Melodic Minor and simply ascend and descend the Melodic Minor scale in the *ascending* form (1 2 b3 4 5 6 7). This is often referred to as the "Jazz Minor Scale".

Example 5g:

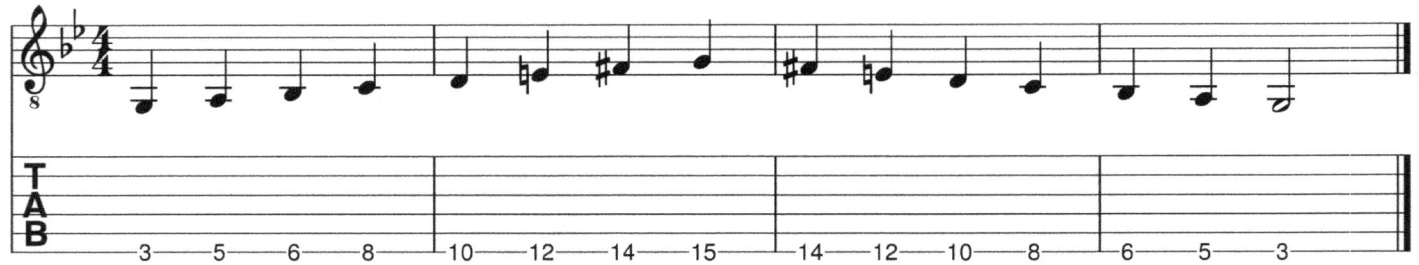

Relative Minor Scales

Every major scale has a *relative minor* scale that shares the same key signature. The relative minor scale always begins six scale notes above the root of the major scale.

For example, in the scale of G Major we have the notes,

G A B C D E F# G

The relative minor scale begins on the sixth note, E.

44

E Minor is the *relative* minor to G Major.

The E *Natural Minor* scale contains *exactly* the same notes as G Major, just starting from the note E:

E F# G A B C D E

However, we can use any of the scales in this chapter as a relative minor scale, so the scales of:

- E Natural Minor
- E Melodic Minor

And,

- E Harmonic Minor

Are all treated as *relative* minor scales of G Major.

Major and relative minor keys share the same *key signature,* even though the melodic and harmonic minor scales introduce notes from outside the key of G Major.

Test yourself:

What is the relative minor of C Major?

Scale of C Major: C D E F G A B C.

The sixth note is A, so A minor is the relative minor of C major.

A Natural Minor contains the same notes as C Major:

A B C D E F G A (Formula 1 2 b3 4 5 b6 b7)

A Melodic Minor ascending has the formula 1 2 b3 4 5 6 7 giving the notes

A B C D E F# G# A

A Harmonic Minor has the formula 1 2 b3 4 5 b6 7 giving the notes

A B C D E F G# A

All the techniques studied in the previous chapters can be applied to each of these minor scales and I strongly suggest exploring every exercise in Part One with minor scales as a productive side project. Begin with the Harmonic minor scale in the key of A and then investigate the Melodic and Natural minor scales.

Chapter Six: The CAGED System

I wish the CAGED system had been as widely taught as it is now, when I first learned to play guitar.

As I never had what you might call a "formal" guitar lesson, it took me a long time to learn my way around the fretboard. Over the years, I've come across the CAGED system and realised that it is an accurate summation of how I view the guitar. While it took me many years to develop my fretboard knowledge, The CAGED system can help you build the same insights much more quickly. It's a great system to help you find your way around the neck and it does provide an accurate roadmap for how I view the guitar – particularly regarding the chord voicings and inversions that I use.

Think for a minute about what playing "chord melody" means: playing chords and melody *at the same time*. Most of the time, the melody note needs to be placed as the top voice (highest-pitched note) in the chord, so that the listeners' ears can pick it out above the rest of the notes being played.

For instance, what happens if you only know this voicing of a GMaj7 chord?

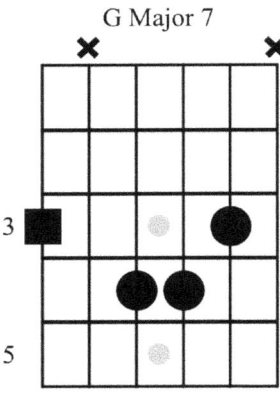

But the melody note is a high D at the 10th fret.

Unless you have hands the size of shovels, playing the melody and chord voicing at the same time is impossible. So, it makes sense to use a voicing of GMaj7 that is geographically close to the melody note.

Here's a chord shape you may already know that places the GMaj7 chord close to the D melody note. In fact, the D is the top (highest-pitched) note in this voicing, so this voicing is a great choice to use in this situation.

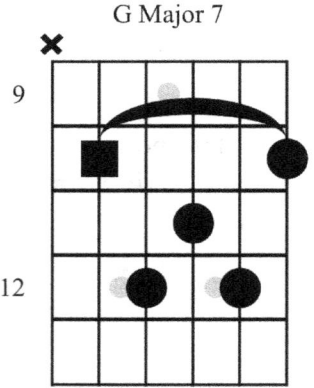

The CAGED system allows us to break the fretboard into *five* different chord shapes that help us to place *any* melody note at the top of *any* voicing of a chord. These five voicings are normally played as some sort of barre chord voicing of the *open position* "campfire" chords of C, A, G, E and D Major that you learnt as a beginner.

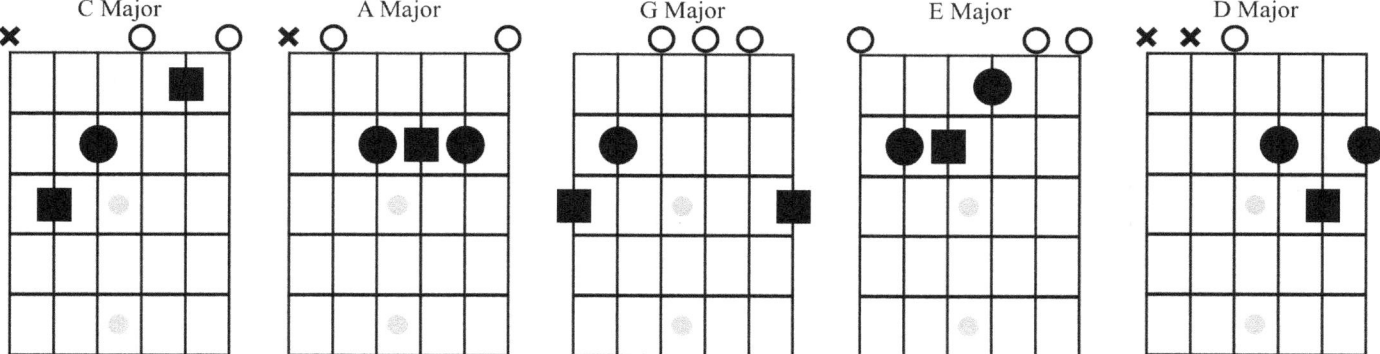

Here's how the above chords are turned into barre chords. Pay attention to the square markers, these are the root notes of each shape.

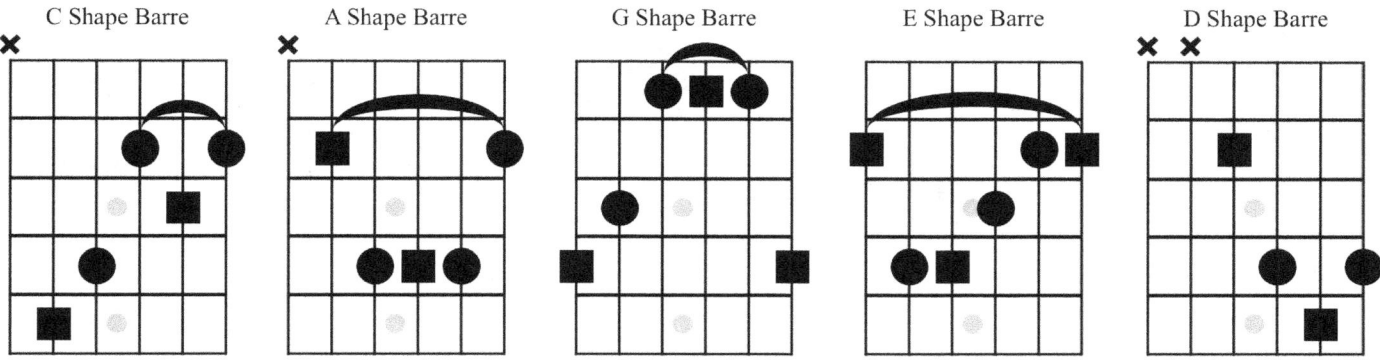

As barre chords are all movable shapes, we can play each of them as a different voicing of a G Major. We will deal with maj7, m7, 7 and m7b5 chords in a minute.

Here are five different *voicings* of a G Major chord:

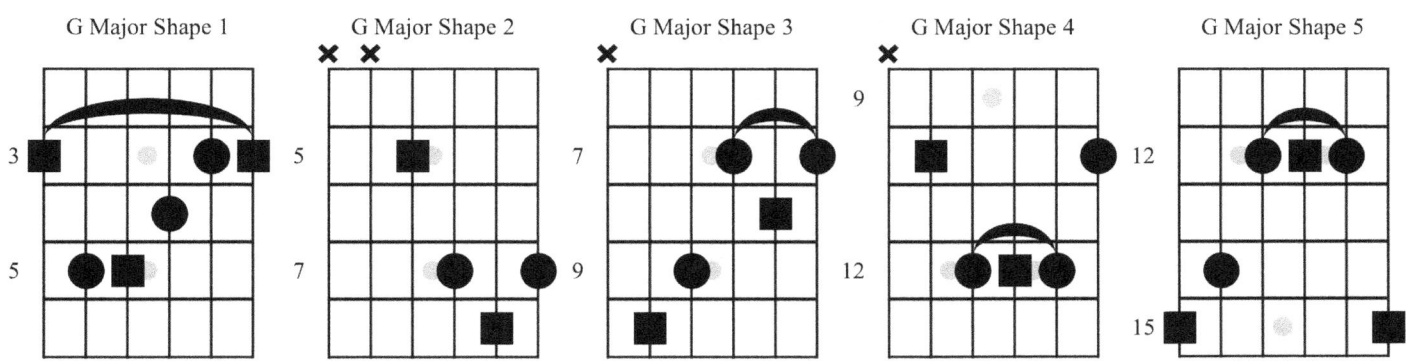

Using these voicings, it is possible to place any note in the chord of G Major (G, B or D) as the highest, which in turn gives us great freedom when creating a chord melody part.

Of course, in jazz we use many types of chords, the main ones being major 7th, minor 7th, dominant 7 and minor 7b5 (minor 7 "flat" 5). It is important to learn the CAGED voicings for these chord types because they crop up all the time in every song we play.

I'm reluctant to give you a list of chords you must learn, but by absorbing the following shapes and incorporating them into your playing as soon as possible, you will quickly develop the ability to play *any* song, anywhere on the guitar.

Here are all the CAGED voicings of the chords listed above. They're shown with a root of G for reference but, just like any barre chord, they can be shifted up and down the neck to easily to reach other chords. For example, a Gm7 voicing can be shifted up the neck two frets to create an Am7 chord. At this point, many of my students realise they need to go and revise the note names on the fourth (D) string!

In the following diagrams, only play the black dots. The hollow dots show where the rest of the CAGED notes lie on the neck in shape 5, but they are not played due to awkward fingering on the guitar.

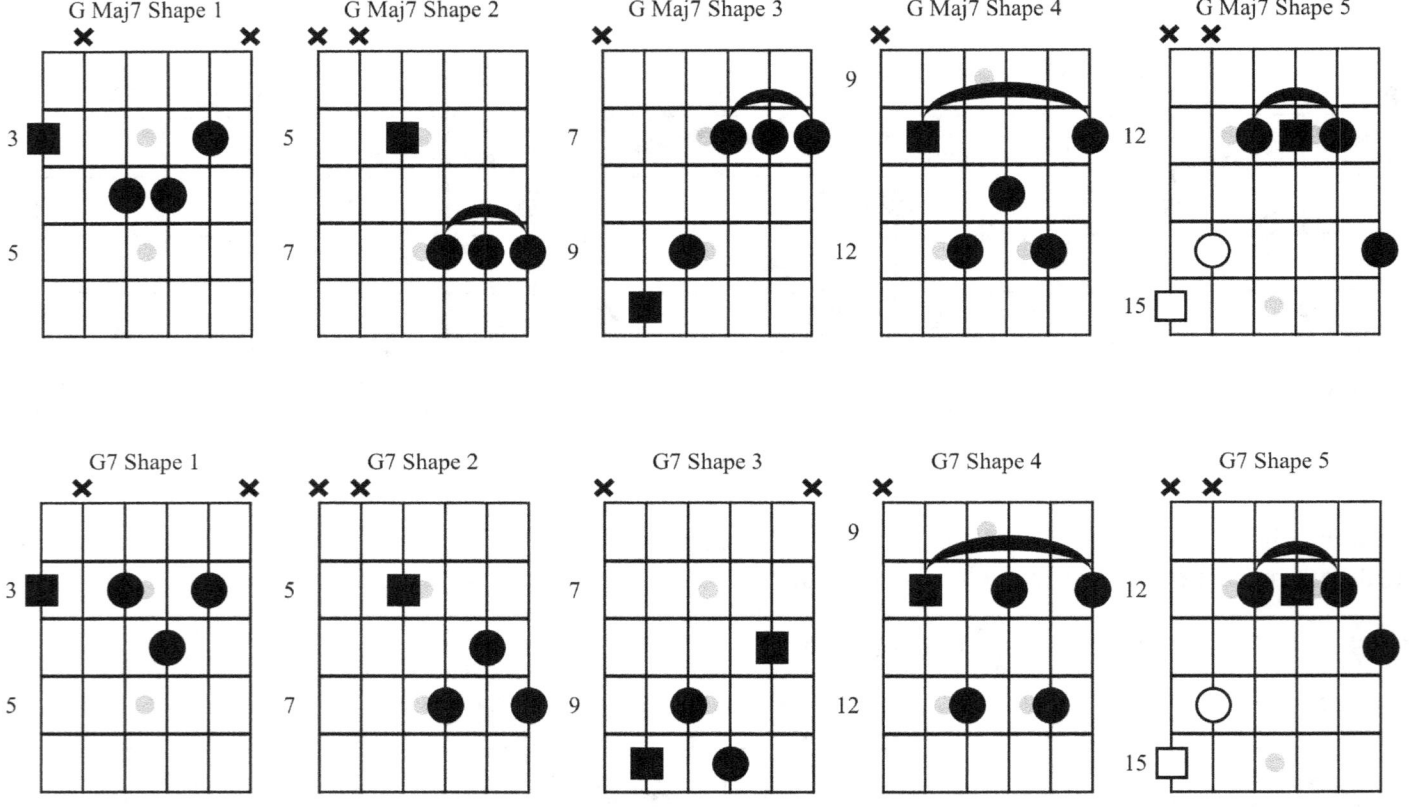

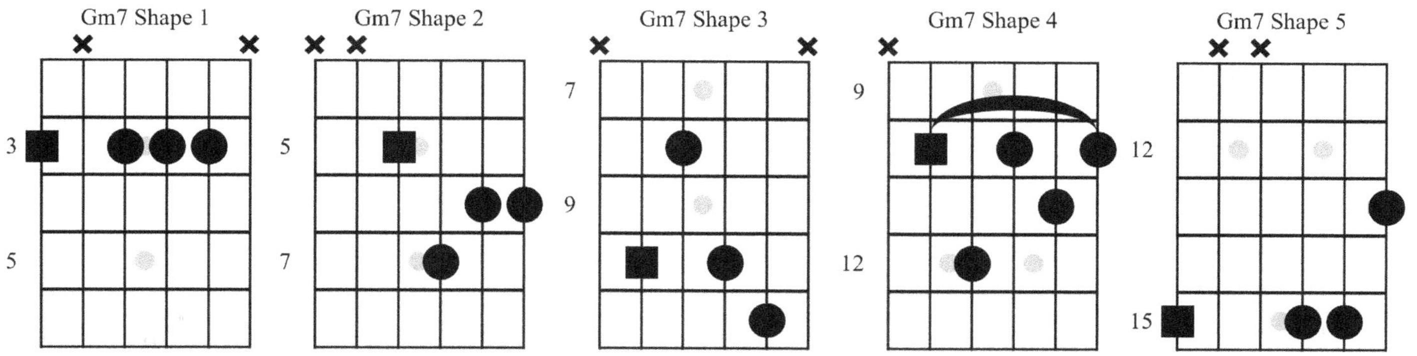

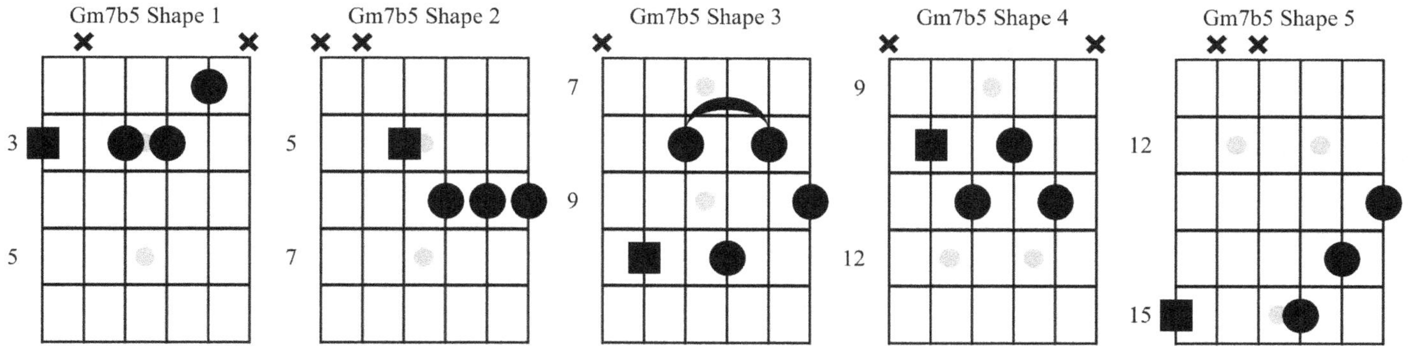

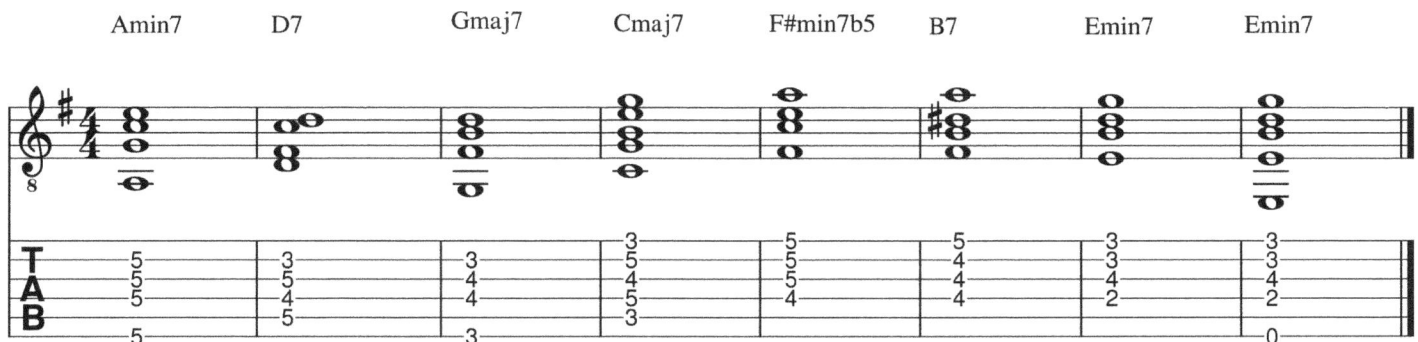

To learn these chords, try playing though any jazz standards you know, and begin from a different chord voicing each time you start a new chorus.

Try to move to the closest possible voicing of the subsequent chord and keep your playing in one small area of the guitar. For example, you could play the following chord sequence with the voicings shown below.

Don't worry about whether a chord is a "C shape" or a "D shape", just learn the voicings and the roots, and then piece the information together to create a smooth, flowing sequence of chords. It will take time, but it is one of the most valuable skills you can learn as a guitarist.

Some good tunes to practise are,

- All the Things You Are
- Autumn Leaves
- Someday my Prince Will Come
- All of Me
- Stella by Starlight
- Blue Bossa

These CAGED shapes will become essential in Part Two when we look at creating actual polyphonic music.

Part One of this book has been a primer to help you understand and get *inside* the biggest conceptual hurdles to polyphonic playing. These ideas really come into their own in Part Two, when we look at how they find their way into my music. Part Two takes an actual piece of music and shows you the exact process I use to create my own arrangements.

Before we move into Part Two we need to quickly address minor scales and the CAGED System. You will find the ideas in the following chapters helpful in everything you play.

Part Two: Seven Steps to Arranging Heaven

Part One of this book laid the foundations for a lifetime of study exploring how to get inside jazz guitar parts using the building blocks of polyphonic solo guitar. We covered the technical process of breaking down a scale into bass notes, 10ths, 7ths, and how to combine them all. Then we looked at how to combine these intervals to create moving parts within scales and chord sequences.

In Part Two we will discover how to put these important skills into practise in the context of real music. I have composed an original tune, just for this book, based on the chord changes of the important jazz standard, *Autumn Leaves*. Autumn Leaves is a great example to use because it brings together so many elements common to all jazz standards, especially the combination of both major and minor ii V I sequences. Unlike some standards, however, there are no unexpected key changes in the music, so you can concentrate on developing your polyphonic chord melody skills with no distractions.

In the recording of this composition I am deliberately playing it "straight" with very little embellishment. This is to make it easy for you to learn the melody and memorize it. If you're a good reader, you may find that, at times, the notation doesn't perfectly match the audio. The guitar is capable of so many subtle nuances that it can prove difficult to convey all of that artistic expression on the page.

The work you've already done in Part One should have prepared your ears for this, and you will begin to recognise sounds and patterns you've discovered yourself, in your own studies and exploration. But even if you don't – please don't panic! You don't need to treat the notated parts in this book as gospel. They are a guide and an example. If your ears suggest going somewhere else musically, and you want to add your own unwritten embellishments – great! This is really the point of this book. Don't just learn the exercises verbatim. Instead, use them as a springboard for your own creativity. What would really make me happy is for you to develop your own, unique voice.

However, do learn the melody of this piece precisely as it is the workhorse of Part Two of the book. Play it straight and commit it to memory. In fact, this advice applies to any jazz standard you choose to tackle. The melody is your lifeline (and your audience's, too!). Keep it playing in your head at all times and you'll never get lost. As you progress through the seven stages in Part Two, you will gradually learn to take more liberties with the melody, but at first, take the time to memorize it (in a few positions on the neck if you can) as accurately as possible. Structure comes first, musicality comes later.

All the skills in this book are transferable, like learning a new language. A great storyteller uses the same words to tell many different stories. Every approach that follows is transferable to any future piece of music you learn. While some of the steps here are challenging, and will take time to explore, realise that you are learning a language that will transfer to every song you play. Be patient and don't move forward too quickly; there's no rush!

This transferable language can be "categorised" for use in various different situations. The work you have put into chord sequences such as the ii V I, for instance, will pay dividends when you approach other tunes containing that very familiar pattern. To get the best out of all you've learnt so far, and to become fluent in this new language, don't forget to apply the knowledge to other keys. Your vocabulary will quickly grow, and you will find yourself with multiple ways to tackle many chord sequences.

When you learn the harmony of any tune, remember that the strongest interval is always created by the root and 10th. By learning the chord sequence as roots and 10ths you will develop a series of distinct "landmarks" that give you a simple map of the entire piece. This is the skeleton outline of the song on which you can build many different chords, embellishments, variations and melodies. 10ths are your best friend when mastering the harmony of any tune, so make time to build at least one unshakeable route around the chord sequence.

You can hear the following example piece played on the audio download.

Autumn Breeze

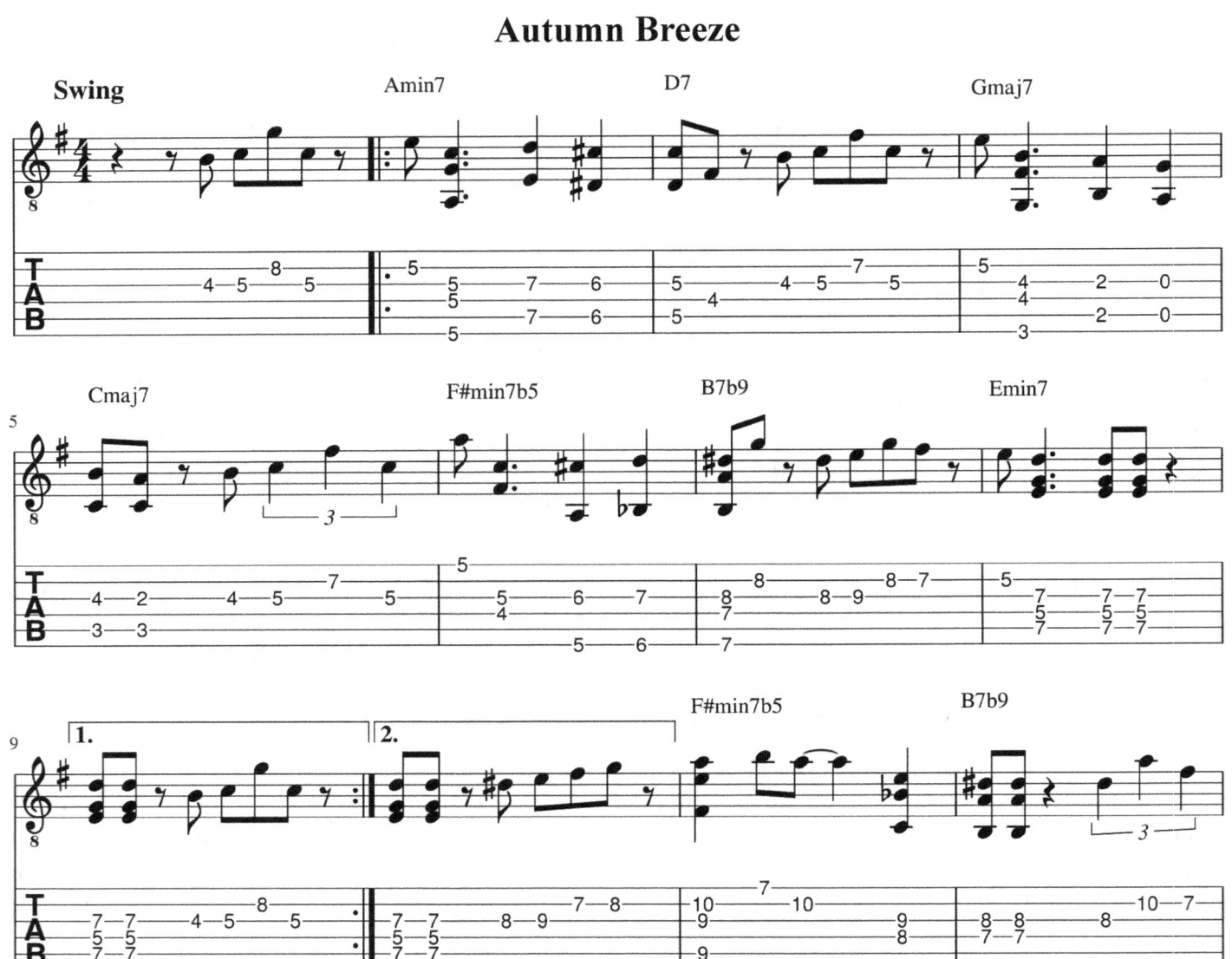

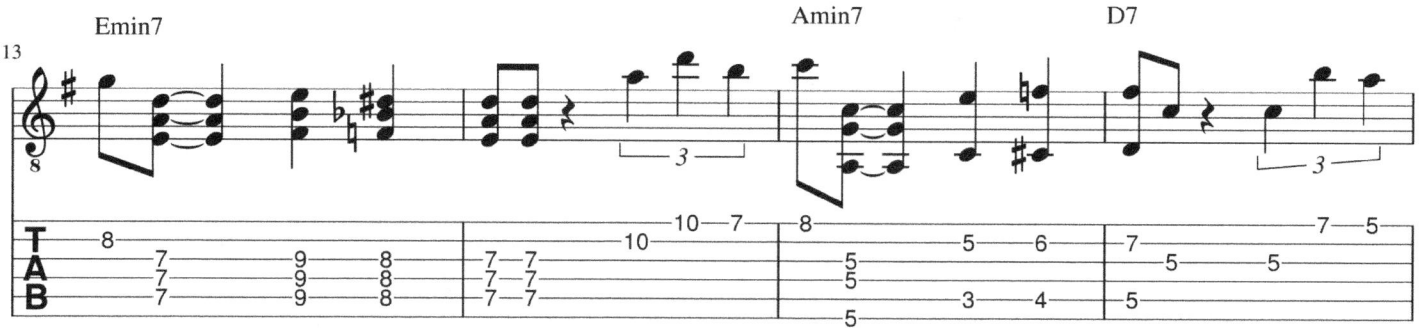

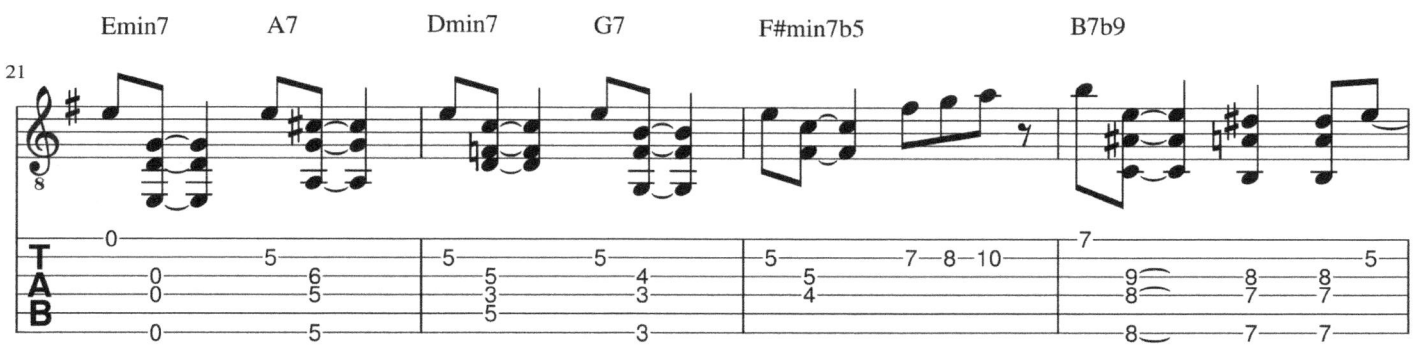

Chapter Seven: Step One - Harmony

Now we come to practical, creative and exciting task of creating a new arrangement from scratch.

The first step in learning a fingerstyle approach for a new tune is to break it down into *just* the chords. For this we will use voicings that contain the root, 3rd and 7th. Below is a chord chart outline for our example tune.

Use *any* chord voicings you know at this stage. All we want to do is to develop a strong feeling for the music's harmony – to get that sound in our head, and to know where it's going. The harmony is the bedrock of the song and knowing it inside-out will be a great help later when our playing becomes more intricate.

Start by playing through the changes slowly and steadily using four strums per bar.

In this chapter, we are focusing only on the first eight bars shown below as an example, but you should work your way through the whole sequence yourself.

Example 7a:

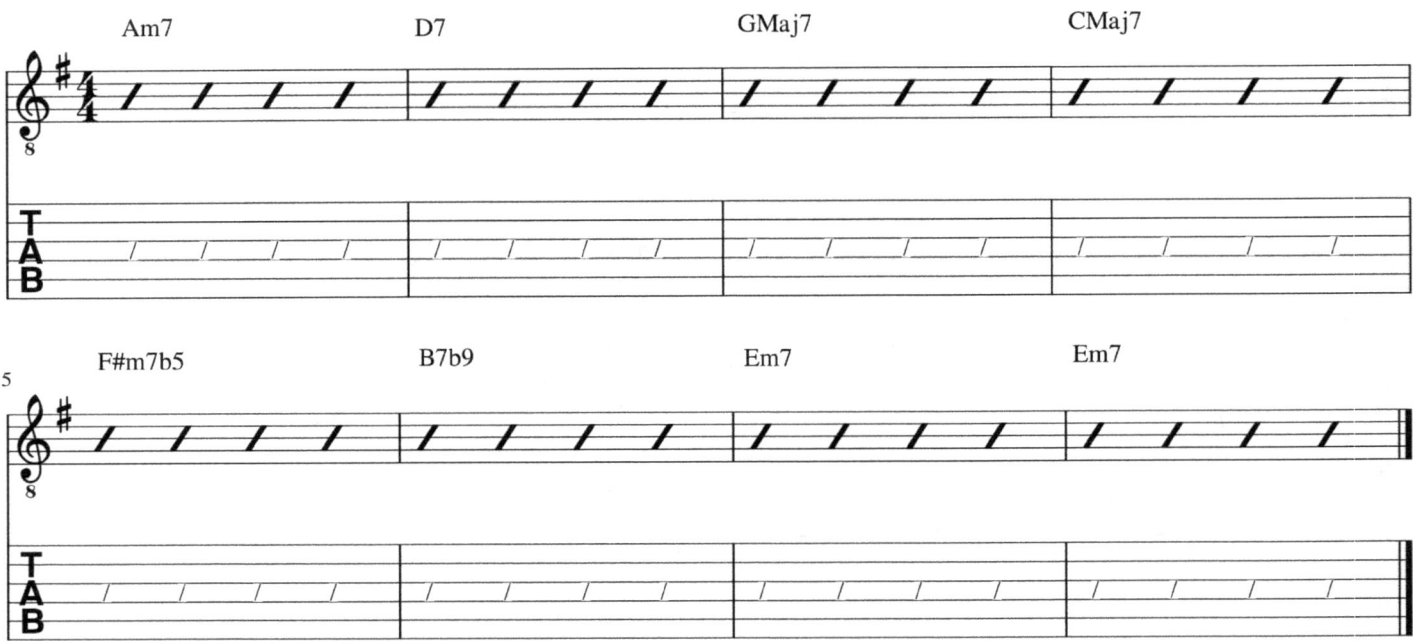

Now, play through the sequence again, but this time start with a voicing of the Am7 chord that begins on the fifth string and find your way through the changes in a new way.

Example 7b:

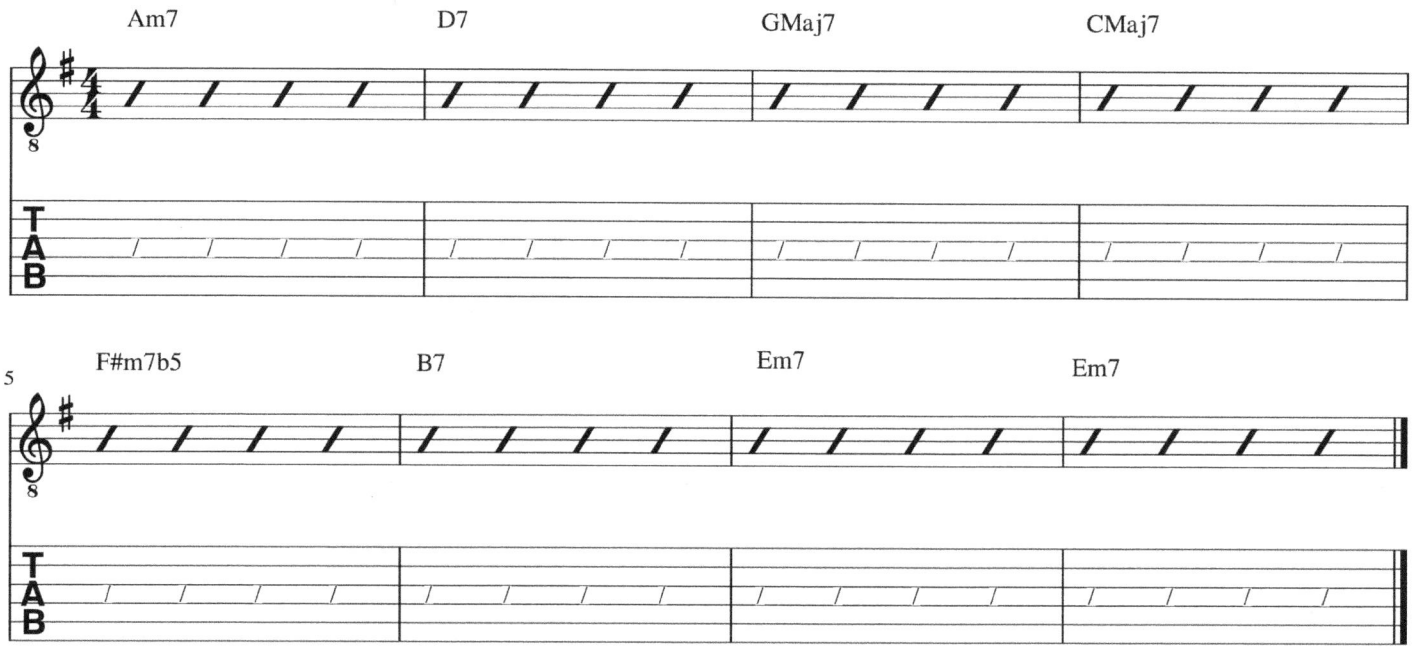

Many guitarists shy away from the next stage, but it is actually one of the most important parts of learning to play.

When you have memorized the chord sequence, play along with the recording of the tune and *sing* or *hum* the melody while you play. Don't worry if you're not a confident singer, no one has to hear you! The point is to internalize the harmony and melody *together*. This helps to cement the foundation of the tune, so that you can hear the music as a whole. This way, you'll never get lost.

I'm serious, if you don't sing the melody you'll really struggle to learn the song. If you do sing it, everything that follows is much, much easier. It will also help you later when you want to create melodic improvisations. Ideas that are sung to begin with are always more musical. Otherwise, us guitar players easily revert to the not-very-musical running up and down scales.

Once you've learnt the full block chords, start to simplify the voicings and reduce each chord to its simplest form of root and 10th. If you like, you can still fret the block voicings shown above, but be careful to only play the root and 10th. The ideal scenario is that your fingers "hover" in a chord shape just above the string, but you only make contact with the selected notes.

Play through the sequence just with roots and 10ths, beginning with the Am voicing on the sixth string. Here are the first eight bars:

Example 7c:

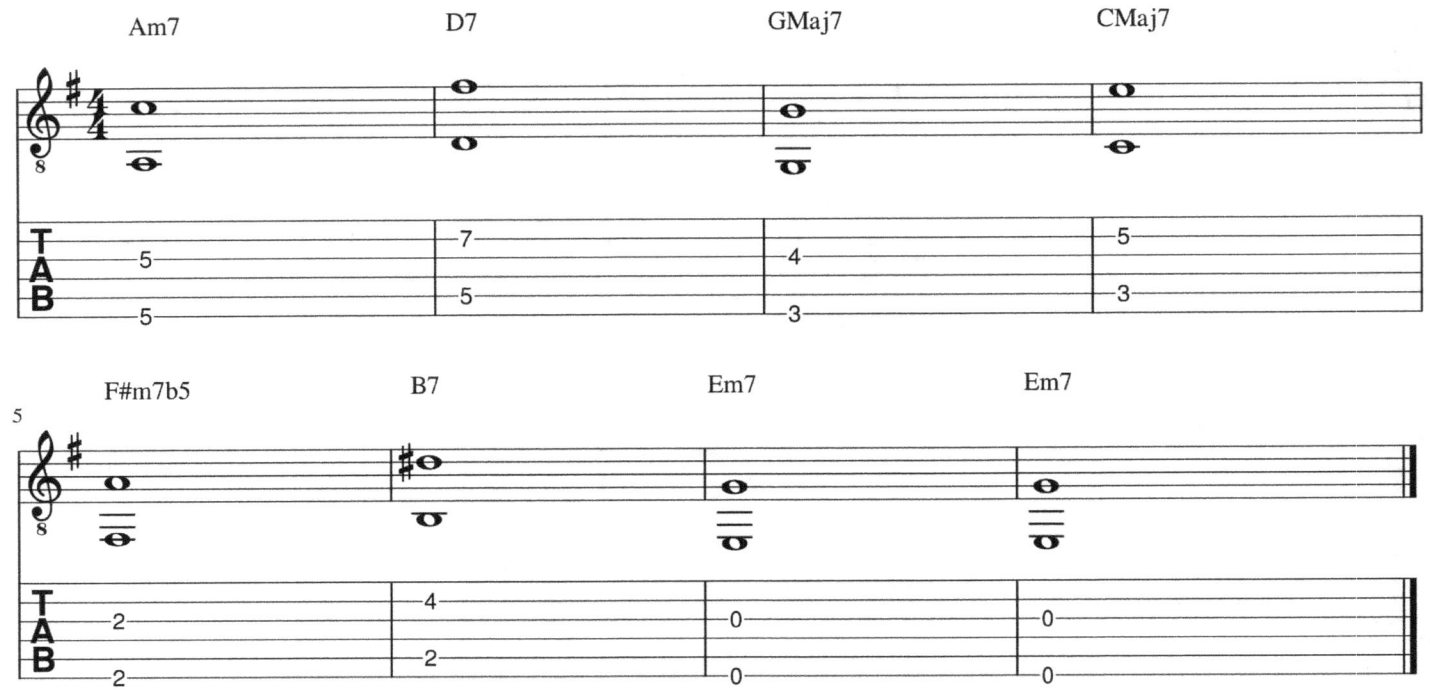

Now repeat this process starting on the fifth string, as with example 7b.

Again, sing or hum the melody over these chords as soon as you are comfortable playing through the changes. I can't stress enough how much this will help you. We've also included an unaccompanied recording of the melody in example 7a, so you can play the root and 10th accompaniment to it.

Step one may appear deceptively simple, but don't rush this stage. You need strong foundations to build a fortress.

If you want to get deeper into the changes and learn the fretboard, try staying in a small, four-to-five-fret area of the neck and using the CAGED shapes from chapter 6. Repeat this process all over the neck. However, while working through the CAGED chords is a useful skill, I advise saving this for later and moving onto Step 2 as soon as you're comfortable playing through the changes in the two different ways outlined above.

Chapter Eight: Step Two - Melody

Once you have a strong foundation of block chords, roots and 10ths, and are happily singing through the tune as you play the chords, it is time to learn the melody. The melody is *the most important part* of any song and you should devote a large percentage of your early practise time to learning, memorising and *revoicing* it in as many ways as you can find.

The goal is to get *inside* the melody and *feel* it in your body like a second heartbeat. It needs to be under your skin. Without melody, there is no song and therefore no music. The melody is the framework of the composition and all the melodic ideas we add later (be they embellishment, inner voices, decoration, bass lines or chord substitutions) fit *around* the melody. The melody is The Boss and demands your respect!

The melody from the lead sheet on pages 55-56 is played without accompaniment in audio example 8a.

Example 8a:

Begin by learning the melody as written above. Use the tablature to copy the location where I play it on the fretboard.

Now sing the melody as you play and "hear" the chords changes in your head. Play along with my recording of the tune from example 8a to mimic my phrasing.

Now I want you to find three other ways to play the melody on the guitar. You could start by playing all the notes on just the top E string, like this:

Example 8b:

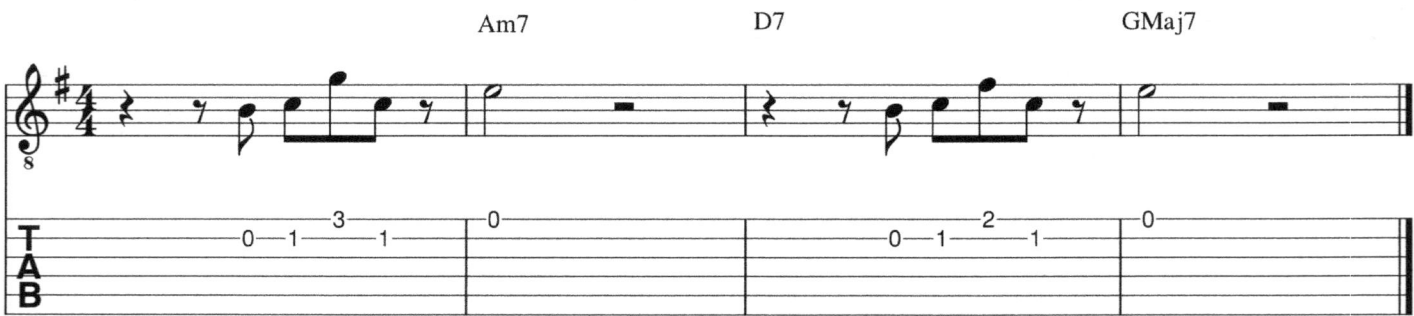

Now play as much of the melody as you can on the second (B) string.

You could move the whole thing to a different position on the fretboard like this:

Example 8c:

There are normally many possible positions and fingerings to voice a melody, so the more you explore the guitar the more fluent you will become.

It's also useful to learn the melody an octave lower than written, although this does make it almost impossible to place chords underneath. In fact, you will often find that you need to shift a written melody an octave higher when arranging it for solo guitar.

By learning the melody on different strings and in different positions you will find that the tone of the melody varies dramatically. Some positions will sound brighter/richer than others and this will affect your rendition of the piece.

It's also worth mentioning that you can vastly affect the feeling of the music by changing the key of the song.

Traditional "guitar" keys like G, C, E and A will sound brighter and more resonant, while saxophone/trumpet keys like Bb, Eb, and Ab will often sound darker and moodier. Neither effect is better, but you may wish to create a particular mood in your playing. These effects are more pronounced on a good-quality acoustic or semi-acoustic guitar.

The important thing when learning any melody is to *keep it simple!* Now is not the time to be adding embellishments and variation. Practise the melody with only a metronome and, if you can, set the metronome to tick on just beats two and four. Don't rely on a backing track to help you find your way through the tune – it needs to be solid in your own mind. Don't forget to sing!

A Note on Learning Other Tunes

It is rare to hear a jazz musician play any melody without adding their own embellishments, phrasing and personality. When other jazz musicians hear these embellishments, they copy them and add their own ideas. Some of these decorations and phrasings have been handed down through the generations and replaced the original written tunes in the consciousness of contemporary students. For example, John Coltrane's version of *My Favourite Things* is very different from the original version written by Rodgers and Hammerstein. Coltrane's 14-minute long extended improvisation rewrote the rules on how this tune could be played and became one of his signature tunes in live performance. If you'd never heard the original song, however, you might not realise that Coltrane was taking great liberties with the phrasing and articulation of the melody and base your version on his, not the original tune.

For this reason, I do recommend that when you learn new songs you go back to the source and learn the music from The Great American Song Book or The Real Book. While the odd mistake has been known to creep into both publications, they give you a good idea of what the composer originally intended.

When you study jazz recordings of your chosen songs, try to listen to "straight ahead" singers and musicians like Tony Bennett, Frank Sinatra or Peggy Lee, who remained faithful to the original music and had very musical phrasing. Make sure you learn the melody in as original a form as possible, then develop your own personal interpretation later.

Chapter Nine: Step Three - Chord Melody

Step Three is where all the work you did on the CAGED system comes into play. The goal of this chapter is to add simple chord voicings to the melody while keeping flowing in the top voice.

This stage is where most chord melody guitarists stop, and if it hadn't been for guitarist Ike Issacs, I might have stopped too!

I remember when I was 19, I sat down and played my chord melody arrangement of a tune for Ike. He listened carefully and said, "Well, it's okay, but it's not very interesting!"

I asked Ike how he would play it and he started to play the song with many different melodic lines weaving through the music. It had direction and momentum, but also harmonic interest. This was my introduction to polyphonic playing and we will look at how to add all these lines in the later chapters. For now, Step Three is where we combine the chord and melody parts from the previous two chapters.

The most important thing to remember is that the melody is still The Boss! Any chords we add underneath the melody must work around the tune. *You should never alter the tune for the sake of a chord*. The melody *always* has priority.

We looked in detail at the CAGED system so that we can always find a chord voicing close to a melody note. If the melody note isn't in a chord, we can always find a chord voicing where the top note can be altered to fit.

Before we get started, a key realisation is that *not every melody note needs to be harmonised*.

Listen to some of the great jazz chord melody guitarists, such as Joe Pass. In Joe's playing there are many times where the melody is played without a chord or just one note is harmonised. Quite often that sparse harmony is just a bass note or the 10th.

Unfortunately, it is impossible for me to sit here and tell you exactly which notes to harmonise with a full chord, which to harmonise with a bass note, which to harmonise with an interval, or which notes not to harmonise at all because it will always be a personal choice. However, I can tell you that the way I learnt to make these choices was listening to pianists like Bill Evans.

Pianists approach their instrument in a different way to guitarists. They are used to having many notes available constantly. As the piano is a rich, powerful instrument, a pianist couldn't continually harmonise every note in a melody with six-part chords, because it would be very loud and fatiguing for the audience. Pianists quickly learn when to support a melody with the fewest possible notes and when to let the melody carry itself in isolation.

Listen to pianists playing unaccompanied jazz standards and you will quickly develop a feel for what to include, but more importantly, what to leave out.

While there are no hard and fast rules, a good tip to begin with is to harmonise the notes that fall on beat one of the bar. Yes, this will be a little "square", but it provides a starting point for your journey.

Let's look at how I could add simple chords under the first four bars of our melody.

Example 9a:

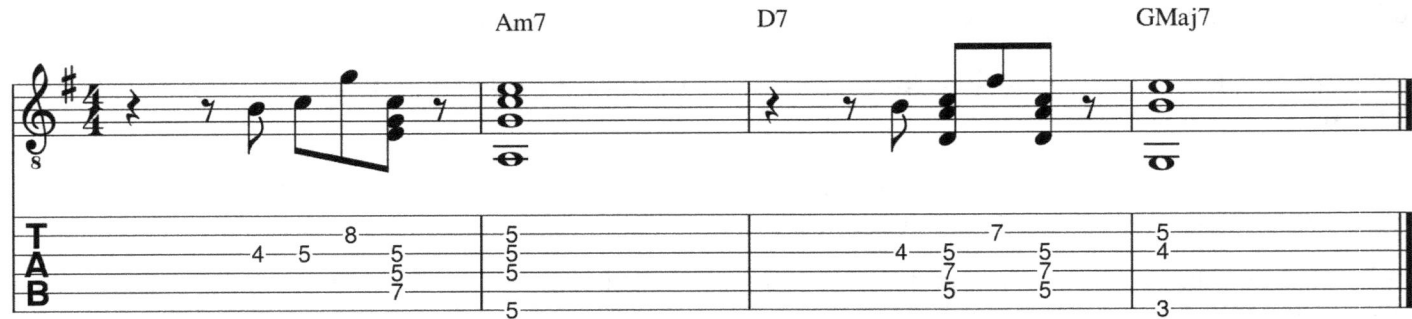

Notice that I often don't play all the notes in the chord, even though I regularly hold the full chord down. Sometimes my hand hovers over the chord shape and I only connect with a couple of notes.

Now look at how I approach the second four bars. Again, everything is very simple and you can see that I'm using basic CAGED shapes to find voicings that fit nicely under the melody.

Example 9b:

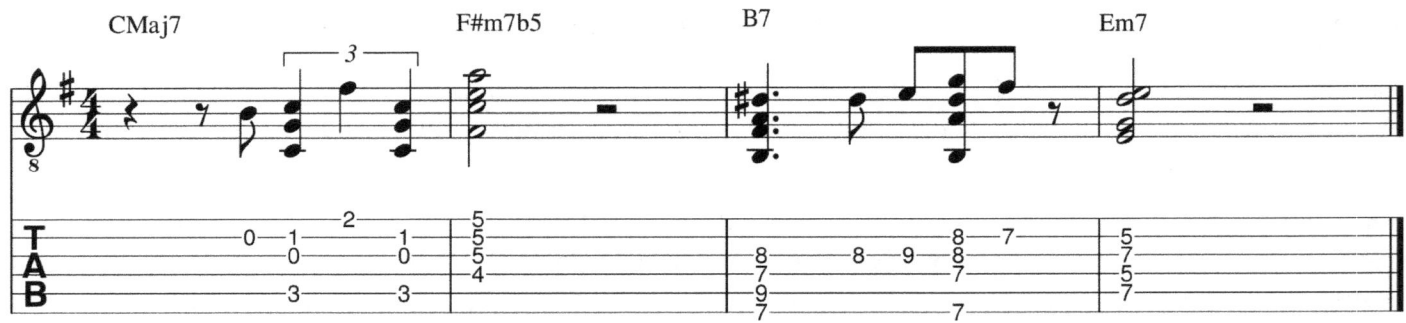

Notice how I make use of open strings, chord fragments, and isolated melody to make harmonisation easier.

To give you a starting point, I'll now play through the whole tune using this approach, broken and then break it down into four-bar sections, so you can understand what I'm thinking.

Example 9c:

Now let's break down each section in turn.

Example 9d:

Bar 1: the bar opens with the melody unaccompanied, to create a strong lead in to the tune before resolving to an Am7 chord (5th fret CAGED chord shape) in bar two.

Bar 3: I use another CAGED shape for the D7 chord at the 5th fret, still under your fingertips, but break the chord down to keep the melody as part of the accompaniment, leading to the resolution in bar 4.

Bar 5: Here we have a mixture of the CAGED shape for the C Major 7 chord, and a similar fragmented idea in bar 3 to keep the melody in line with the accompaniment.

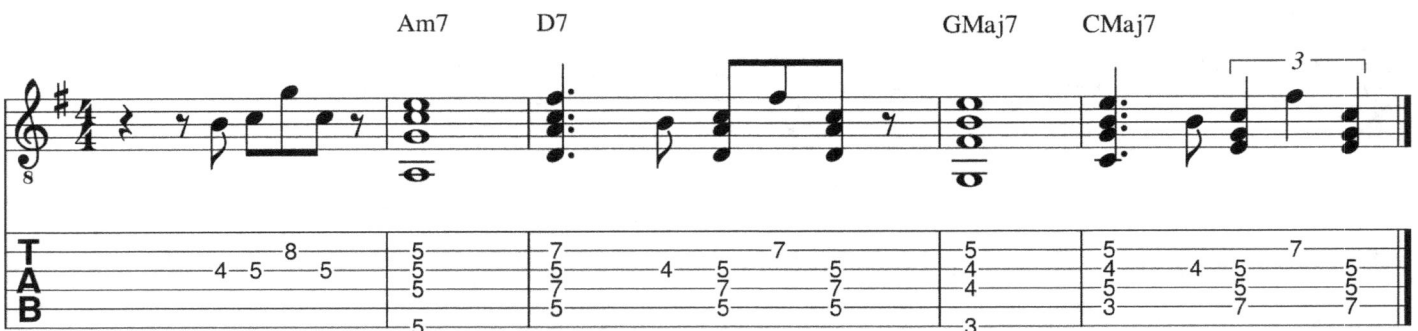

Example 9e:

Bar 6: Here, the melody note lies on the top of this chord and is strict, simple chord melody style.

Bar 7: Is a mixture of using the basic 10th + 7th framework, but allowing the melody to breath and weave its way to resolve through tension into the minor chord of bar 8.

Bar 9: This is an example of a turnaround based on the opening melodic phrase in example 9d, but bringing in some chordal accompaniment to the melody too. All CAGED shapes can be used sparingly and with just enough of the chord to imply the harmony, and you can still keep your melody on the top of the chord. Try and fit what chord shape works best for you!

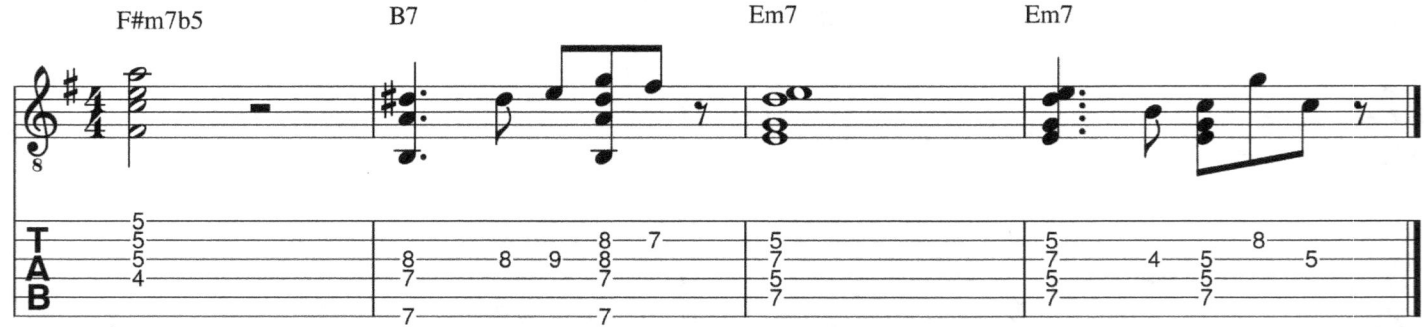

Example 9f:

Bar 10: Shows you that you establish the harmony for the listener with the chord, and then carry on with your melody, leading towards the harmonic tension of bar 11.

Bar 11: Here is your next chord to the pattern, and used simply but very effectively to keep melody and harmony neatly balanced, and not having too much of melody or of the chord.

Bar 12: Here is the basic 10th + 7th chord shape used as a dominant 7th chord, establishing the harmonic content for the melody to then take over and lead us again to the resolution of the minor chord.

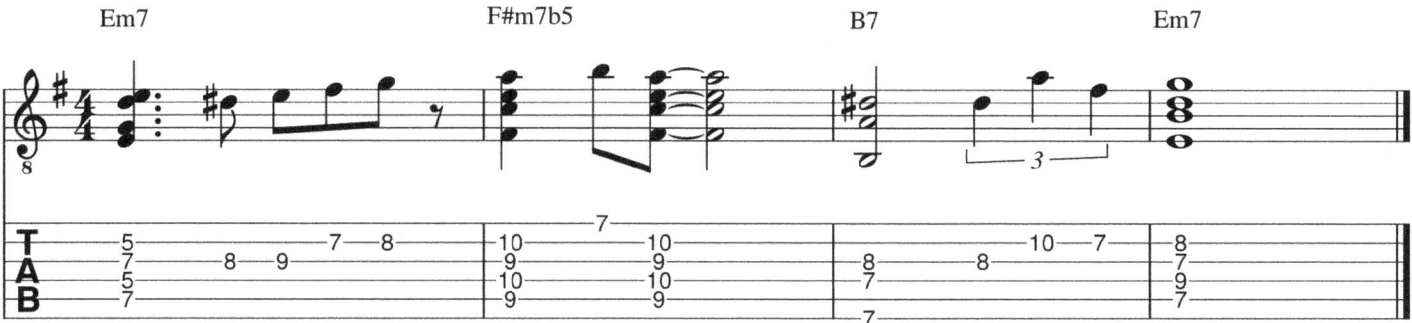

Example 9g:

Bar 14: There's no need for every note to be harmonised when playing polyphonic guitar. Space is good!

Bar 15: Notice that although this chord shape is a barre, we are only playing four notes. Again, you don't have to play every note, just enough to convey harmonic clarity and to bring your melody note in too. It helps to make your arrangement sound more sophisticated.

Bar 16: We start with an outline of the D7 by playing the chord shape itself, but then we have a perfect example of choosing what notes of the chord to use to harmonise the melody. Take little chunks of the chord and use them for your melody. Don't bog yourself down by trying to play everything all the time.

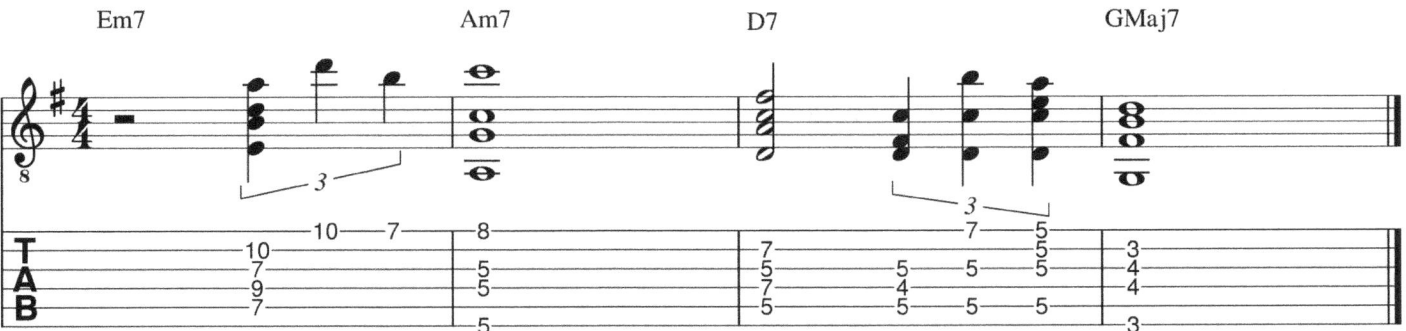

Example 9h:

Bars 18-21: The C Major 7 chord establishes the harmony strongly enough for the melody to then take over leading us into the next chord and changing the harmony. We are still weaving the melody around chordal stabs (notice we are not playing the whole chord!) Less is more when playing chord melody. It is a constant balancing act and is the road to true polyphonic guitar playing. The last bar leads into a cycle of 4ths, eventually bringing us to the final turnaround of the tune, taking us back to the top.

Example 9i:

Bar 22: Here we have simple CAGED system chords outlining the harmony, but combined with the melody also. Notice how you would barre the whole chord for the G7, but not play the full chord. You play only the information you want to convey. This is a very smart and economical way to arrange solo guitar.

Bar 23: Is the perfect example of using a partial chord to kick us into single note melody. Notice how simple this is, and you don't have to have the most complicated of chords and finger movements. Simple goes a long way when playing Jazz.

Bar 24: This section looks more complicated than it is! Notice the use of the low and high string together. Having made this barre with our hand, we can free ourselves to bring in the other notes of the chord and melody. Doing this keeps any guitar arrangement light and manageable, but still strong in harmony and melody.

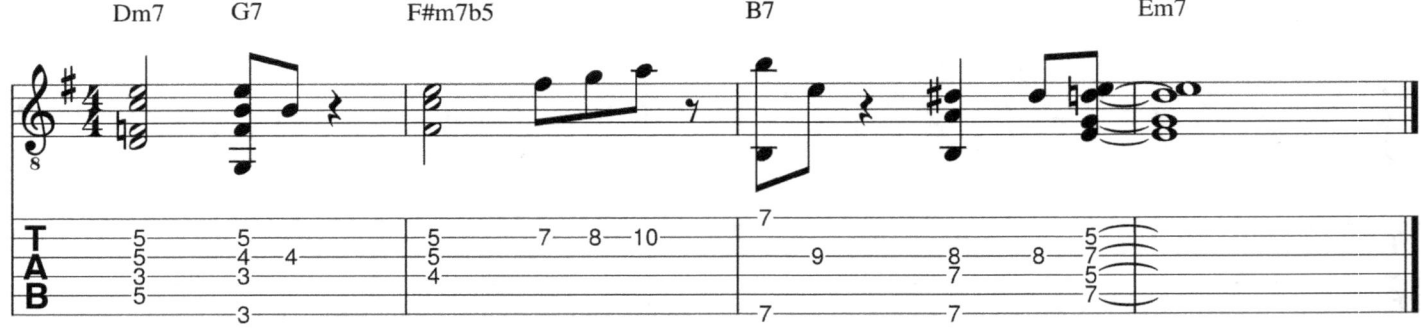

The examples above show you one route through the changes. Once you're comfortable playing my ideas, start to experiment with the note choices within each chord.

Play through the song again, but this time *only* use root and 3rd voicings under the melody.

Play through again and only use bass notes and melody.

Next, try selecting different combinations of intervals from the full chord voicings I used. For example, where I've played a full chord, try playing just the root or root and 10th. You could even play just the 10th and 7th. Learning to hear these different possibilities will help you develop a palette of different colours that you can use to give subtly different inflections to your music.

Consider how many notes you will play from each chord, but also consider whether you want to strum, pick or arpeggiate a voicing if it fits the melody. There are so many creative choices available it can be a bit bewildering for a student, so I suggest you take just one idea at a time and spend a full practice session exploring the possibilities. Different choices will take you down new paths and create widely varying feelings in your playing.

If the examples above are just *one possible route* through the chord changes, how might you revoice the chords and play them in different locations while keeping the melody on top? By learning different ways to play the chord melody part, you access new colours and inflections in your music.

This whole process can be daunting for indecisive players. There can often be a nagging doubt asking you, "But what if this isn't the best voicing? What if *that* one is better?!"

Don't worry, there no "best voicing", just different choices. The key is to listen to pianists and chord melody guitarists and explore as much as possible on your own. You'll quickly start to make informed, creative choices. Throughout, the only important question is, *how do your choices make you feel?* If you like them, keep them, if you don't, change them. Sometimes the only answer may be to throw my method out of the window and make your own choices. I heartily endorse this approach!

As you progress and improve as a musician you will find that Step Three quickly becomes Step One in your arranging process. You will have discovered enough chord voicings to jump straight to this step and immediately be able to create a passable chord melody arrangement of any tune.

Tips for creating a simple chord melody arrangement.

- K.I.S.S. Keep It Simple, Stupid! Even very simple choices sound great in this style. There's no need to add complexity.

- Don't embellish the melody. Begin by playing the melody as it is written. Adding chords underneath is challenging enough, so focus on building a solid chord melody structure that works.

- Use CAGED – these chord shapes allow you place any melody note as the top voice in at least one chord

- You don't have to always harmonise the melody! This point is often ignored by students, but when you listen to great pianists and guitarists you'll be surprised by what they don't harmonise. If you can't find a chord, just play the melody.

- Choose your notes. Even if you're holding down a full chord, you don't have to play every note. Experiment by leaving notes out.

- Find a route. Your first goal should always be to find one solid path through the song using chord melody. This is your foundation and means you can always explore new ideas with a safety net to fall back on.

- Make decisions. There are no bad chord choices. You can always change your mind later. If you're not making decisions, you're not moving forward.

- Deal with non-chord tones. The melody note on beat one isn't always in the chord. Either isolate it or adjust a CAGED shape.

- Remember: melody is The Boss. Chords work either with, or around the melody, and melody should never be sacrificed to harmony.

Sometimes you must just put the method aside and go with your gut feeling. That's the most musical way. The joy of music is in experimentation and investigating possibilities.

Chapter Ten: Step Four - Melody and Bass

Now we have developed a framework for the chords and melody, it's time to simplify our playing. After all the work in Step Three it may seem counterintuitive to cut out most of what we've done, but as you'll quickly see, this is the secret to going beyond chord melody and building truly polyphonic playing.

Occasionally you will of course hear me play straight ahead chord melody, but my playing really goes beyond that. In fact, I'm normally composing with three or more separate voices at the same time. To achieve this, I must begin by cutting everything back to just melody and bass. It is ironic that this apparent move backwards is what allows me to play very complex music easily.

When I strip the music back to just the bass and melody I am still *thinking* chord shapes, in that my hand still hovers over the fretboard in the CAGED voicings I showed you previously. Occasionally, I'll even fret the chord without playing the inner notes. This is why building a strong foundation was so important in Step Three. Creating a solid route around the changes allows me to quickly find the bass note of the chord.

This is how I play the first eight bars of our example piece with just bass and melody. Remember, my hand is hovering over the chord position.

Example 10a:

It shouldn't take you long to apply this approach to the rest of the tune.

When you're confident, you can begin to add some chromatic movement or melodies to the bass note. You may wish to do this by ear, but taking an organised approach can help you find new options you never would have thought of.

Begin by adding a semitone below the target bass note. Notice that I don't force myself to play this on every chord change.

Example 10b:

Try the same thing but place the semitone approach note *above* the target note.

Example 10c:

Another common approach is to run down into the target bass note in semitones from a tone above.

Example 10d:

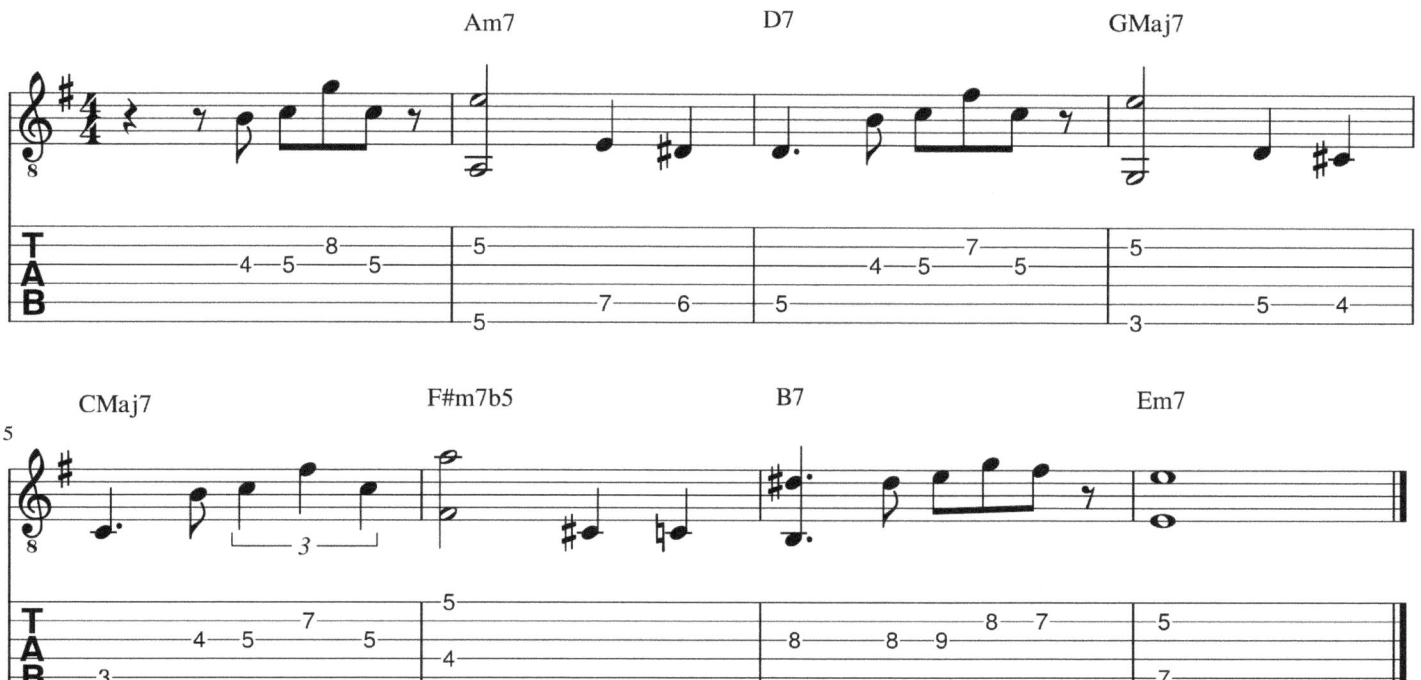

Again, there is no reason to place these movements on every bass note if the melody doesn't allow you to do it easily. Later, you can experiment by adding bass movement *while* you play the melody, but this really requires some creative fingering!

The next idea is to play a semitone below the target and then a tone above.

Example 10e:

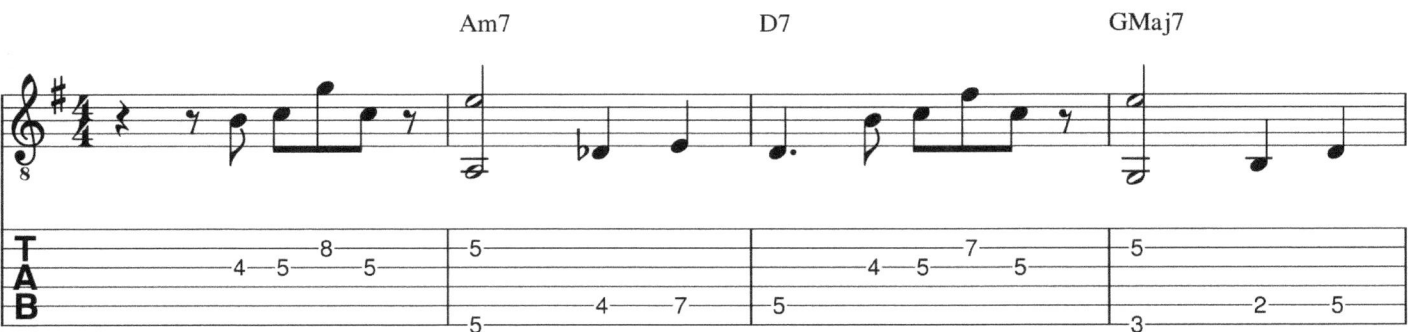

Occasionally, your ears may tell you to play a semitone above the root instead of a tone. That's also fine, so go with your gut!

Finally, reverse the previous pattern so that you play a tone above, then a semitone below the bass.

Example 10f:

Finally, let's combine the stepwise descending movement from example 10d with a semitone below the root:

Example 10g:

The previous steps developed quite a formal, structured approach to learning bass movements, but of course when I play I use many combinations of these ideas. They are so internalised I can easily create melodies in the bass parts, just as I showed you in chapter 3.

Here are the first eight bars of our tune with me playing various ideas in the bass.

Example 10h:

As you can hear, even simple ideas combine easily to create something that sounds very complex. Have some fun and get creative. We will begin to develop inner lines in the next step.

Chapter Eleven: Step Five - Inner Lines

Now we know how to get the bass notes moving, let's add an *inner* voice.

I'll keep this simple to begin with and get more advanced in Step Six. All we will do for now is add a short melody that moves stepwise into the 10th of the following chord. This all happens while playing the melody and bass note.

The trick is to visualise and target a chord tone of the *following* chord. For example, the first chord change is between Am7 and D7, so the inner melody begins on the Am7 chord and resolves (for the moment) to the 10th of the D7 chord on beat one.

I'll show you what I mean by playing just one note that moves to the 10th of the next chord over the first eight bars.

Example 11a:

75

Now try the same thing approaching the 7th.

Example 11b:

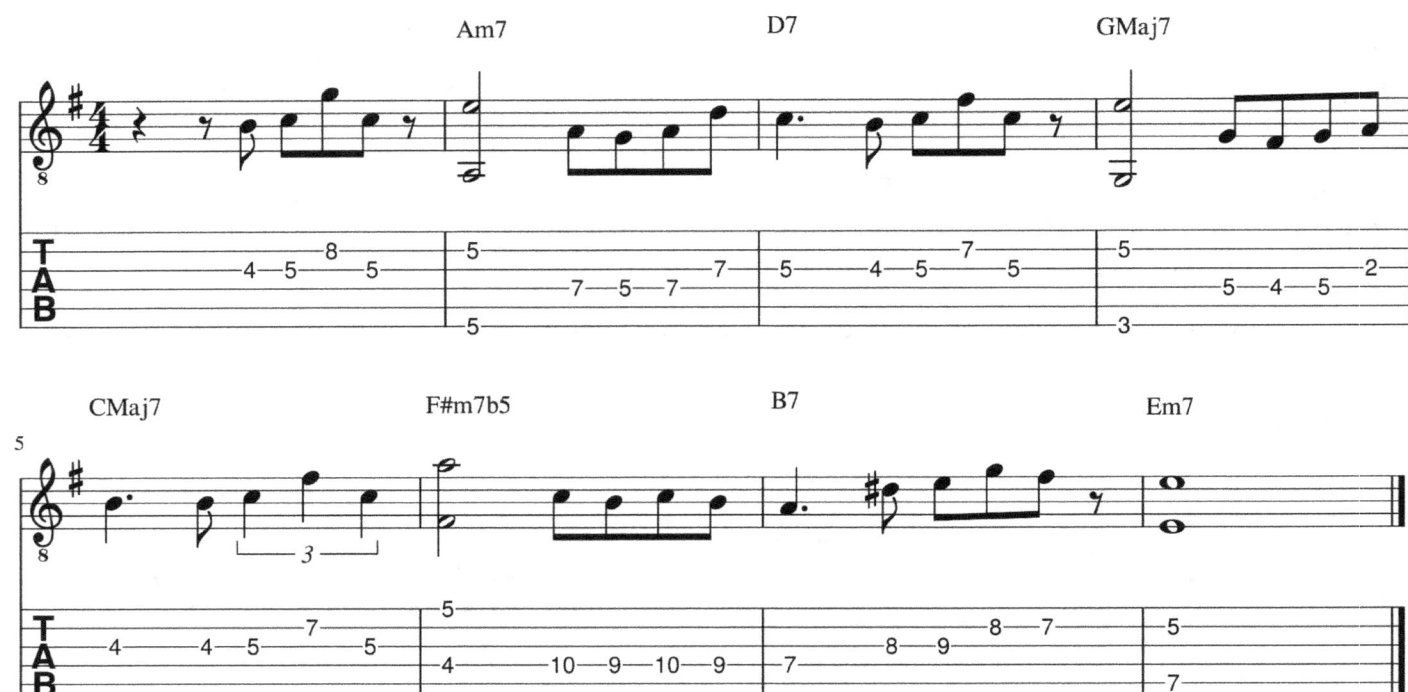

This time I will switch between targeting the 10th and the 7th of the following chord as the mood takes me.

Example 11c:

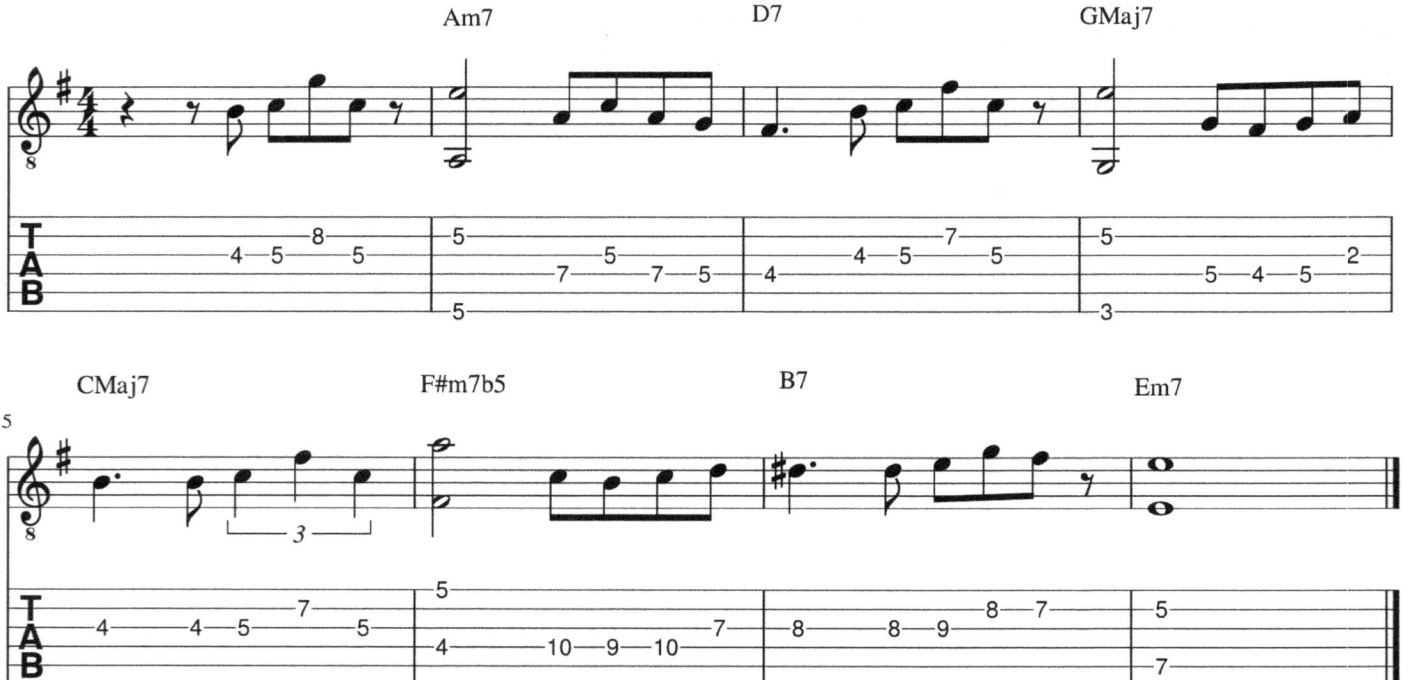

The next stage is to make these lines a little longer. Keep the melody and bass line constant. You don't need to vary them yet. Don't worry about playing in time either – a consistent tempo will come later. For now, just concentrate on making melodies that target the 10ths and 7ths of the next chord.

Example 11d:

Here are a few other ways you could decorate the inner parts.

Example 11e:

77

Example 11f:

Think about which direction you want the melody of the inner lines to move. If the actual tune of the music is ascending, it can work well to descend with the inner parts, and vice versa.

As always, respecting the written melody is paramount! All the melodic lines you add, either in the inner parts or in the bass *must* work around the song's melody.

Chapter Twelve Step Six - Melody, Bass and Inner Lines

In Step Six, we build on the ideas in Step Five to use longer inner lines and create more interest in the many parts. It is here that much of the work you did in chapters 2 and 3 will become relevant.

For the moment, forget about playing the bass note; we will add it back in later.

The first step in building longer lines is to think about using scales to help find the notes that will work. Our example tune is in the key of G Major, so it makes sense to use the G Major scale to build the inner melodic lines.

The goal is to play the melody, add an inner melodic line to target a chord tone of the next chord, and then continue the melody. It is very important when you're learning to play longer inner lines that you initially do *not* play in time! It's not often you'll hear a musician say that, but don't worry too much if you accidentally play too much in the space available for your melodic "fill".

First, let's explore a G Major melodic line that targets the 10th of the D7 chord.

Example 12a:

Now let's play the first part of the melody that lands on the Am7 chord, then add the previous melodic line.

Example 12b:

Don't worry about this inner line being a written part for now. You will start to improvise your own lines soon. Also, remember to visualise the block chord throughout all these examples. This will help you to find both the inner lines and return accurately to the melody of the song.

Now let's repeat the process with the second phrase of the melody. This time, however, the inner line from example 12a is adapted to target the 10th of the CMaj7 chord. Notice that the shape and rhythm of the melody is identical, it is just shifted or "translated" to begin a tone lower.

Example 12c:

Here's the same idea again: the third melody phrase is played and the inner line melody is shifted down to target the 10th of B7. I finish by playing the final part of the melody to end on the Em7 chord. Notice that we need to adjust the scale slightly, because some of the notes of B7 aren't in the G Major scale.

Example 12d:

Here's a different inner line you could play over the first eight bars.

Example 12e:

The previous lines used scale steps taken from G Major and were adjusted when the chord demanded it. Now, let's try another line that targets the 3rd of the chord, but this time we will add a couple of chromatic notes.

Example 12f:

Try playing these lines in different positions on the fretboard.

Here's another chromatic line that targets the 10th. Apply it to the whole chord sequence yourself.

Example 12g:

Now you have built up a few pieces of vocabulary, play through the tune again and use a different fill on each chord change. This will help you internalise the rhythm and placement of inner-voiced lines and build your own ideas based on these fragments.

Do the same thing, but now use your own fills. Use your ears and aim for the 10th of each chord that follows the melody line. You can spend a great deal of time here (years in fact!) finding lines that work. As mentioned in Step Five, listen to piano players and guitarists like Joe Pass and myself to accustom your ears to the possibilities, both in terms of rhythm and melody.

Next, move on to finding longer lines that target the 7th of each chord. Here are two to get you started.

Example 12h:

Example 12i:

Learn to apply each of the above lines individually before combining them and then mixing them with the lines targeting the 10th from above.

The next stage is to add the bass line back in. Play the melody and bass line *straight* and unaltered. Here are two ways to play through the first eight bars with longer inner lines and a bass note. Don't forget to visualise the chord melody shapes you learnt earlier.

Example 12j:

Example 12k:

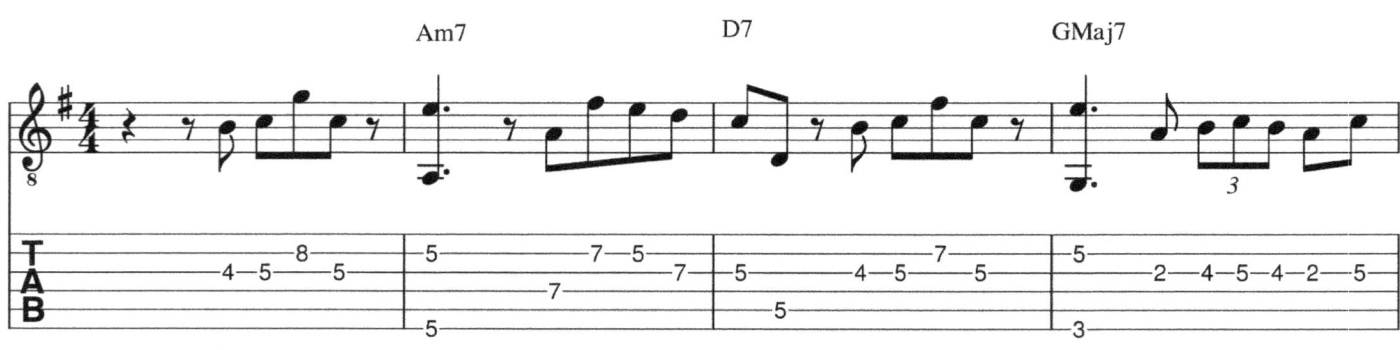

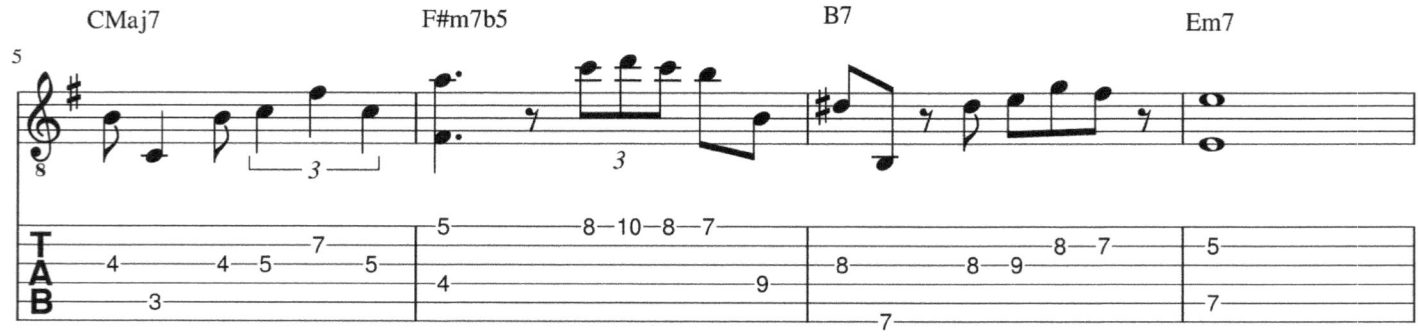

Now, let's add a little bit of movement to the bass part too. Notice that I don't do this on every chord. Sometimes I will play a bass line, sometimes I will play an inner voice fill, and sometimes I will do both!

The following example is a complete recording of our reference tune. I am playing more freely here, but staying well within the confines of the first six steps. I combine inner voices, chromatic approach notes, and bass movement while keeping the written melody fixed and in time. Notice that the melody is still the most important voice and if I can't reach a bass note or inner voice I will miss it out in order to play the tune.

Example 12l:

The next stage is to learn to vary the melody while incorporating everything shown in the first six steps. We're nearly there!

Chapter Thirteen: Step Seven - Melodic Variation

The final step in my method is to learn to vary the main melody of the song. Notice that the melody is the last component to be altered because the melody is The Boss!

When I talk to students about creativity, often I see that they are intimidated by the word *improvisation*. Improvisation can be a daunting prospect, so I prefer to talk about *variation*.

By gradually varying a melody, even if just by a few notes, you can quickly find yourself playing musical ideas that are distinct, yet strongly related to the original melody of the tune. Remember I mentioned learning jazz melodies from singers like Tony Bennett, rather than from players like John Coltrane? Gradually, over time, the embellishments and variations that players like Coltrane added have become *compounded* and taken us away from the original melody of the song.

However, when we intentionally vary a melody, taking a few liberties is exactly what we want to do! Having varied the melody, you can then vary the *new melody* you've created; then continue the process. What you'll have is an evolving improvisation that is strongly related to the original tune. It's like an acorn growing into a massive oak tree. Everything originated from that first acorn, but now all the variations and possibilities expand as the branches and leaves overlap to form a beautiful tree that looks nothing like the original seed.

Improvisation may seem daunting, but varying a melody is easy!

Let's look at the first phrase of our melody again:

Example 13a:

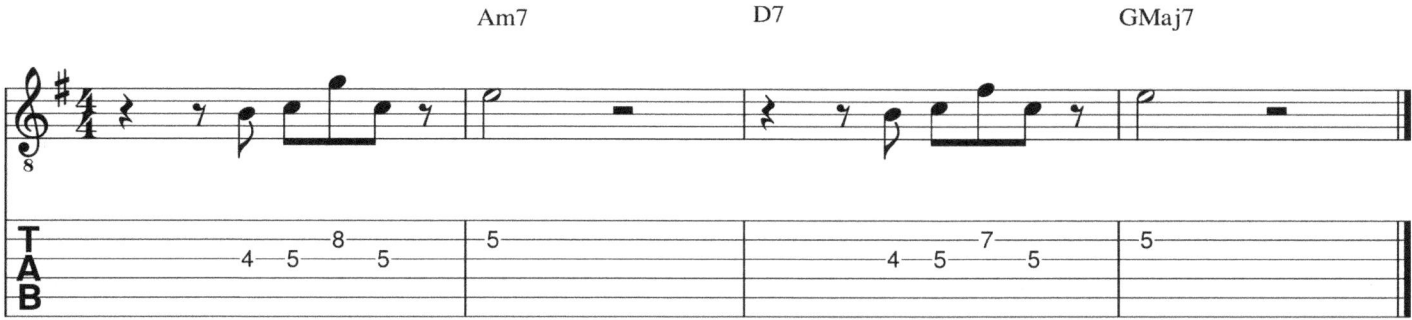

Here are just two ways we could vary the melody to form a different, yet related, musical idea.

Example 13b:

Example 13c:

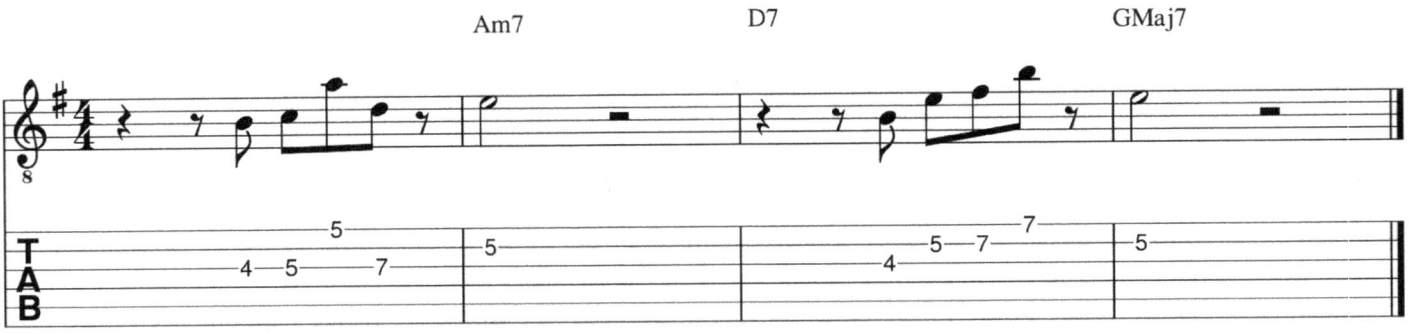

Just to show you how these variations can quickly compound, here is a variation of the previous variation:

Example 13d:

Notice how this idea is completely different from the original melody, yet it works well because we developed it in logical, musical steps.

Just as our verbal responses in a conversation are (hopefully!) related to the words another person just said, the inner voices and basslines we create while improvising will relate to the variations in the melody. As we vary the melody, our *melodic answers* will vary too!

Of course, it takes time to build these skills and I've been playing since the '60s, but the more you listen to great musicians and the more you work on your own variations, the more creative you will get with your music.

Wayne Shorter said that when he composes he improvises slowly, and when he improvises he composes quickly. This is a great way to think about varying the melody; you're just composing quickly.

Let's look again at the original four bars of our piece and then play through some variations on the melody. Notice that as I vary the melody, I often play different inner voice and bass line ideas.

Example 13e:

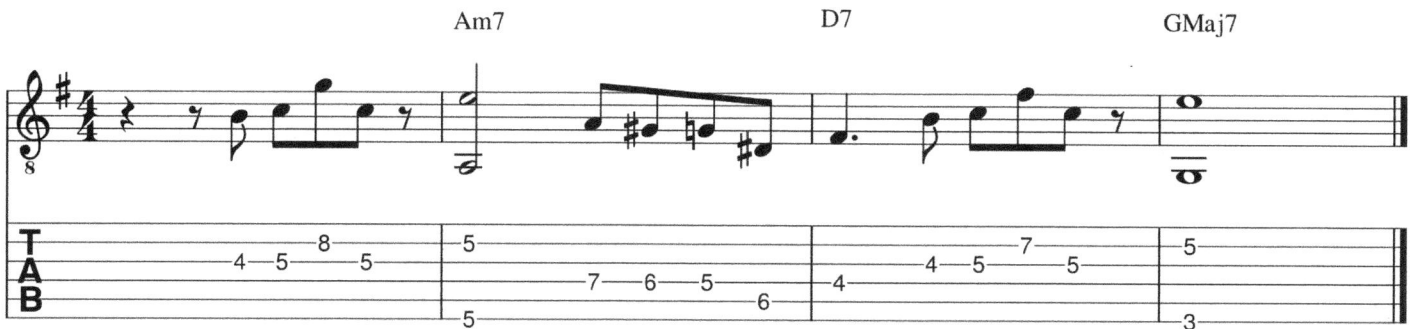

Example 13f:

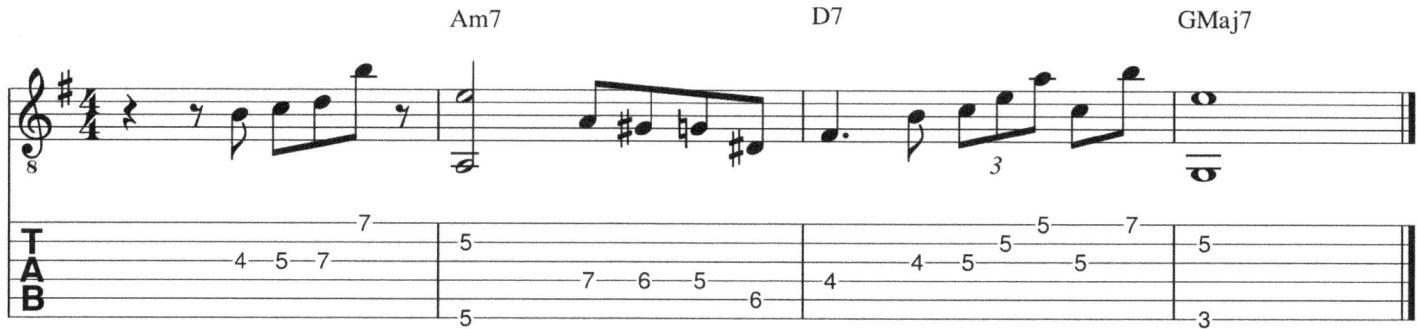

Example 13g:

Sometimes I will play different ideas simply because my melody variation took me to a different area on the fretboard.

Finally, here is a complete chorus of *Autumn Breeze,* where I vary the full melody as I like and use many different approaches on the inner voice melodies and bass parts. I recorded this in one take, as if it was my first solo after playing the written melody. It was transcribed by Joseph and given to you here as an insight into my style.

Good luck and have fun!

Martin Taylor MBE

Example 13h:

90

MARTIN TAYLOR
WALKING BASSLINES FOR JAZZ GUITAR

Learn To Masterfully Combine Jazz Guitar Chords With Walking Basslines

MARTIN TAYLOR

FUNDAMENTAL CHANGES

Introduction

One of the things I'm most often asked is how to play walking basslines on guitar. Between my private students and at every guitar retreat I teach, inevitably someone will ask me how to combine chords with walking basslines while keeping a tight jazz groove and driving the song forward.

It's a great question. Being able to play chords and basslines at the same time is the ultimate accompanist's skill for a jazz guitarist, whether you're jamming in a guitar duo, working with a singer, or even playing in a bigger band with a piano. In fact, my chord and bassline approach sits at the core of my playing, so mastering it will give you a deep insight into my chord melody style.

This book will teach my technique of combining chords and walking basslines from the ground up, starting with the most important chord shapes and fingerings, right through to constructing basslines and mastering the jazz swing feel.

I'll teach you how to introduce syncopation, mimic jazz drummers, add the bass player's iconic "skip" and give you plenty other tricks of the trade. All this will help turn you into a groovy accompanist that other musicians will be dying to work with.

At the heart of all groove is the skill of *listening*. It's very important that you check out a number of great bass players, so you can hear how these lines should actually sound. Everything we do in this style is about imitating the bass player, so if you've not heard the musicians listed below, it will be worth your while to seek them out and spend some time listening before diving into Chapter One.

Some of my favourite bass players include:

- Niels-Henning Ørsted Pedersen
- Ray Brown
- Oscar Pettiford
- Jaco Pastorius

Listen to these incredible musicians and focus on their groove and note placement to capture their feel. If you like, you can try to copy their feel by playing along on a muted bass string.

Before we get going, I want to give you one final piece of advice: *Please* don't play walking basslines when you're playing with an actual bass player. You'll create loads of clashes and just get in their way. Playing walking basslines is the bass player's job, after all, so only use these wonderful techniques when there's no bass player available. Your band will thank you!

Now that's out of the way, let's dive into Chapter One and look at some of the most appropriate chord shapes to use when playing walking bass. Pay attention to the fingerings as they might not be quite what you're used to.

Get the Audio

The audio files for this book are available to download for free from **www.fundamental-changes.com.** The link is in the top right-hand corner. Click on the "Guitar" link then simply select this book title from the drop-down menu and follow the instructions to get the audio.

We recommend that you download the files directly to your computer, not to your tablet, and extract them there before adding them to your media library. You can then put them onto your tablet, iPod or burn them to CD. On the download page there are instructions and we also provide technical support via the contact form.

For over 350 Free Guitar Lessons with Videos Check out:

www.fundamental-changes.com

Twitter: **@guitar_joseph**

Over 10,000 fans on Facebook: **FundamentalChangesInGuitar**

Instagram: **FundamentalChanges**

Get the Video

As a special bonus to buyers of this book, Martin Taylor has two videos that explain every key element of his walking bass and chords technique, that are not available anywhere else. Follow this link to view/download the content:

https://fundamental-changes.teachable.com/p/martin-taylor-walking-bass-for-jazz-guitar

Or use the short link:

http://geni.us/walkingbassvideo

If you type above link into a browser, please note that there is no "www."

You can also scan the QR code below to view the videos on your smartphone:

Chapter One – Essential Chord Voicings

While most jazz guitarists know some big and impressive guitar chords with terrifying names, it's most common (and more effective) to use very small fragments of chords when learning to play chords in tandem with a walking bassline.

These fragments are called "root and guide tone" voicings, as they contain just the root of the chord, normally played on the 6th or 5th string, and the *guide tones* of the chord (the 3rd and 7th) which are played on two of the middle strings of the guitar. The 3rd and 7th are the notes that best define the sound of a chord and indicate whether it is a major 7th (Maj7), minor 7th (m7), or dominant 7th (7).

Throughout this book you won't see a single note played on the high E string. We're only concerned with the bass notes and middle chord voices, and you'll be amazed how intricate and grooving we can make just these small fragments sound when they're combined with a jazz walking bass.

As you probably know, there are some important chord changes in jazz that crop up time and time again, and we are going to use one of these as the framework to hang all our walking bass ideas on. The progression is a I VI II V (pronounced One Six Two Five) sequence in the key of G Major. You may know this sequence as a *rhythm changes* progression, as it forms the backbone of the song *I Got Rhythm*, and many other standard jazz tunes, such as *Oleo* and *Anthropology*.

In the key of G,

Chord I is GMaj7

Chord VI is Em7

Chord II is Am7

Chord V is D7

We'll look at how these chords can be altered later, but for now let's begin by learning these chords as *guide tone* voicings in their most basic form on the neck. Pay attention to the fingerings; a couple may feel unnatural at first, but there is a reason for playing them like this that will become apparent. Make sure the notes marked with an X are muted.

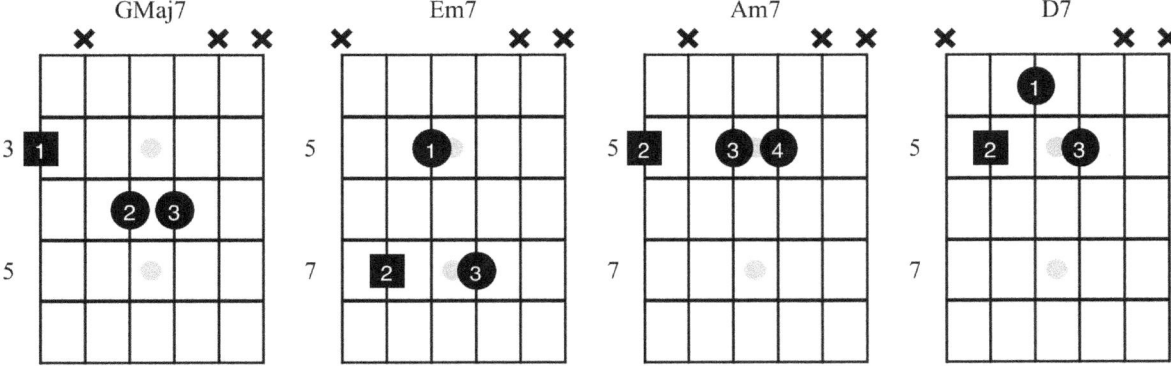

Let's play these chords as a simple jazz progression. Use your fingers and be sure to mute the unwanted strings.

Example 1a:

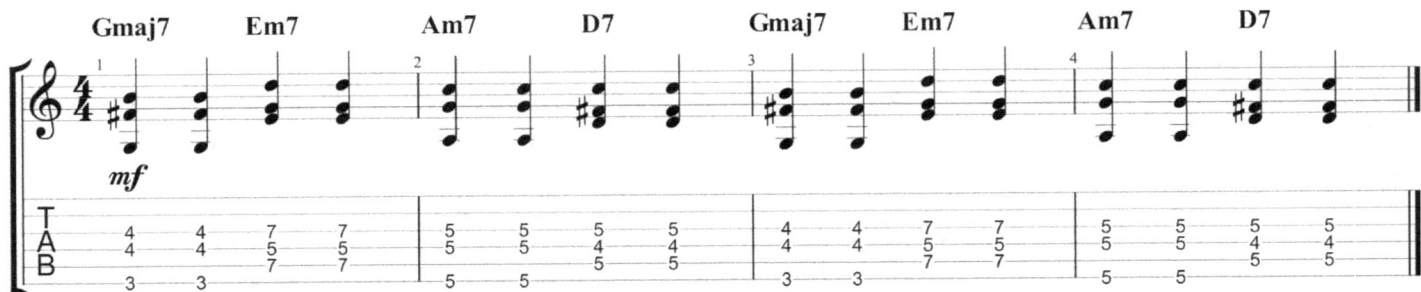

These chords are *diatonic* to the key of G Major. This means that every note in every chord is contained in the G Major scale. However, jazz musicians like to mix things up a bit and often they will play a G7 instead of a GMaj7, an E7 instead of the Em7, or an A7 instead of the Am7.

In fact, pretty much the only chord that's set in stone is the D7, and sometimes you'll see substitutions for that too. We'll come back to substitutions later in the book. For now, try playing the I VI II V sequence using the following chords.

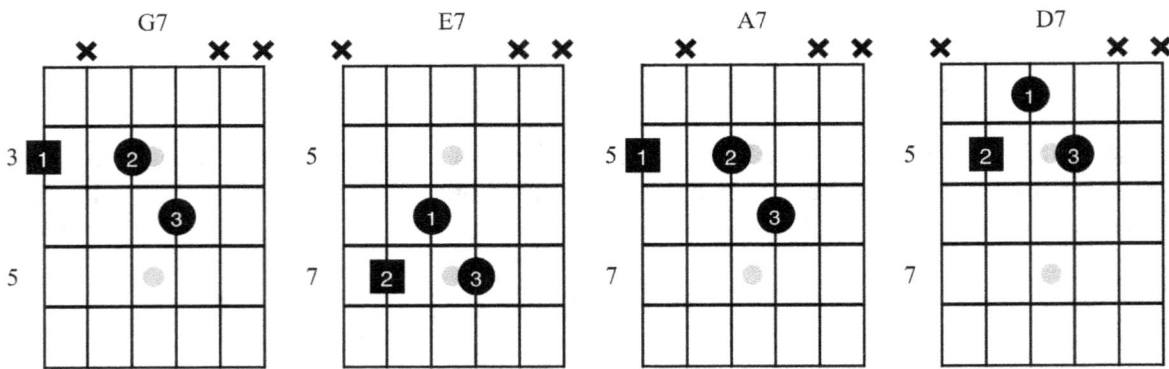

96

Example 1b:

When you can play Example 1a and Example 1b fluently, try combining them and getting the sounds of the different possibilities into your head. For example, you could try the following sequence:

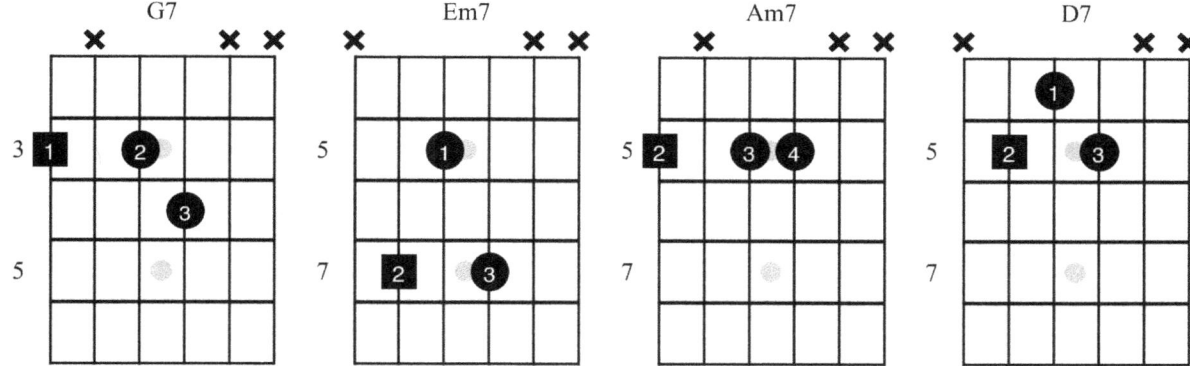

Example 1c:

Try looping the I VI II V sequence repeatedly and using different chord *qualities* each time around.

Next, I'm going to teach you an important chord *substitution*. Instead of the GMaj7 (or G7) chord, we will play a Bm7 chord. This substitution sounds great because Bm7 contains the guide tone (3rd and 7th) notes of GMaj7 and adds an extra note.

Compare the chord tones of GMaj7 and Bm7:

Chord	1	3	5	7
GMaj7	G	B	D	F#
Bm7	B	D	F#	A

When we play Bm7 instead of GMaj7, the only difference is that we introduce the note A. Normally, if a bassist or piano player is playing the original root note G, we hear the A as a beautifully rich note added to the harmony. Don't worry though, this substitution works beautifully whether there is a bass player or not!

Try playing through the following progression using this voicing of the Bm7 chord. The first time through I play a G7. The second time through I play Bm7 instead of the G7. Loop this sequence until you're confident before moving on.

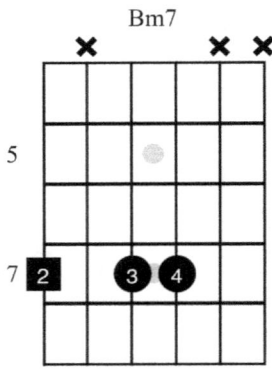

Example 1d:

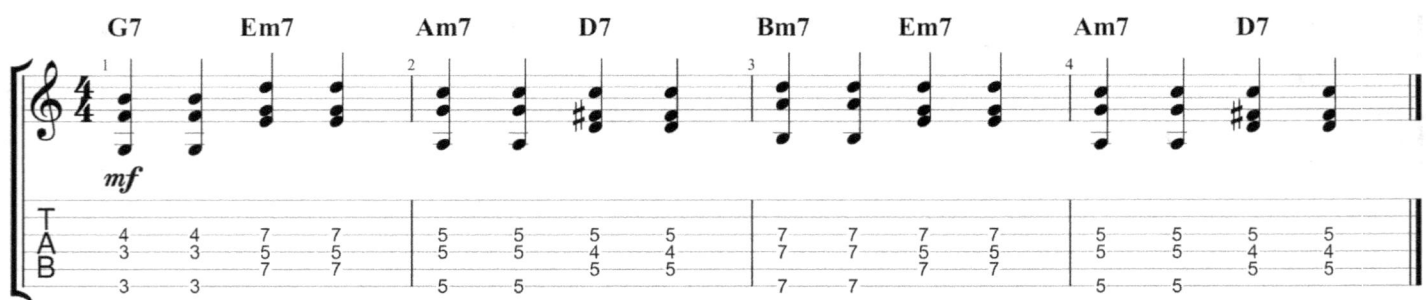

Using a Bm7 (chord III) instead of chord I is a very common substitution in jazz and the two chords are completely interchangable. You can use either and it won't affect the soloist or a singer.

We'll get to the walking bass section soon, I promise! But first we need to open up the neck a little more and learn some different ways to play around the I VI II V chord sequence in different areas of the fretboard.

How about starting up high on the neck and descending from a G7 at the 10th fret?

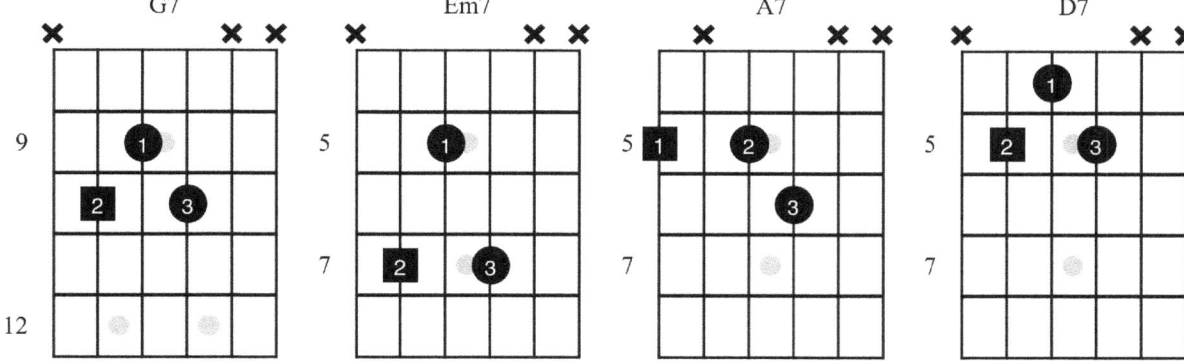

Example 1e:

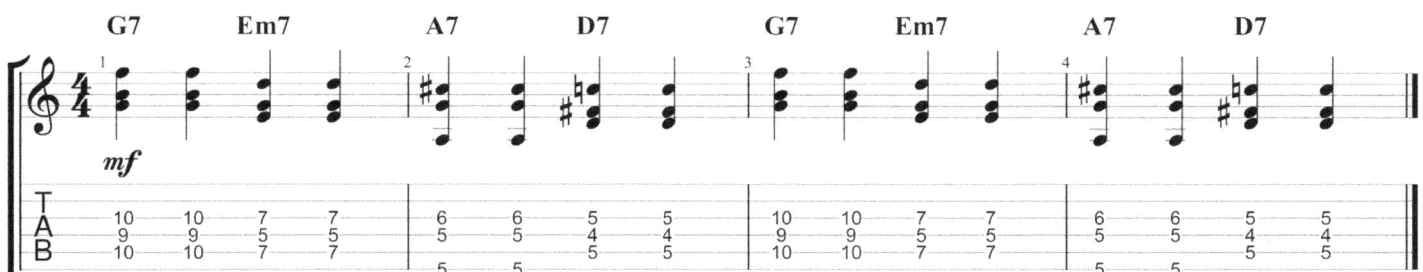

We could also descend from the lower G7 and play an E7 using some open strings.

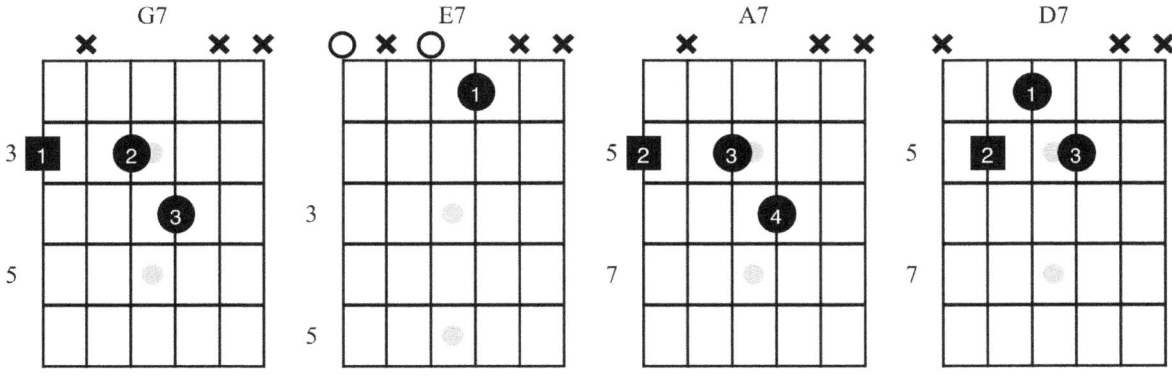

99

Example 1f:

We can relocate the Am7 and the D7 at the top of the neck. This works great if we begin with the Bm7 substitution.

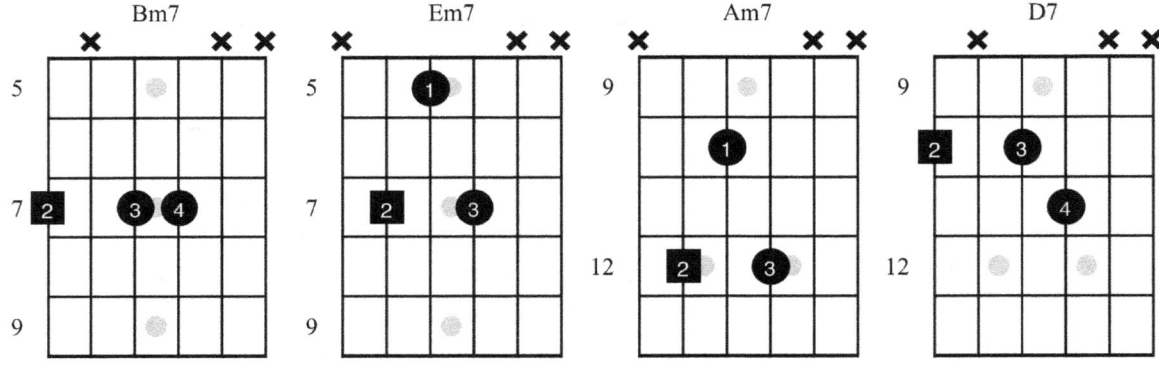

Example 1g:

Of course, we could begin with the G7 too!

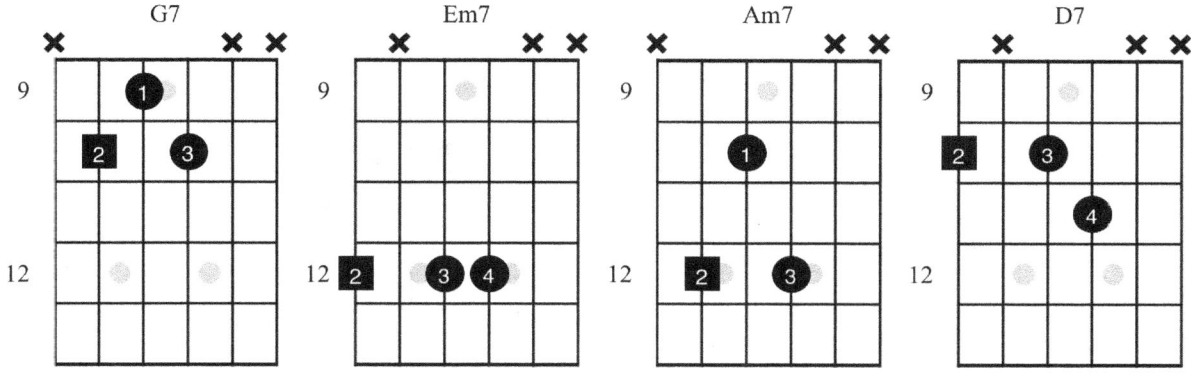

Example 1h:

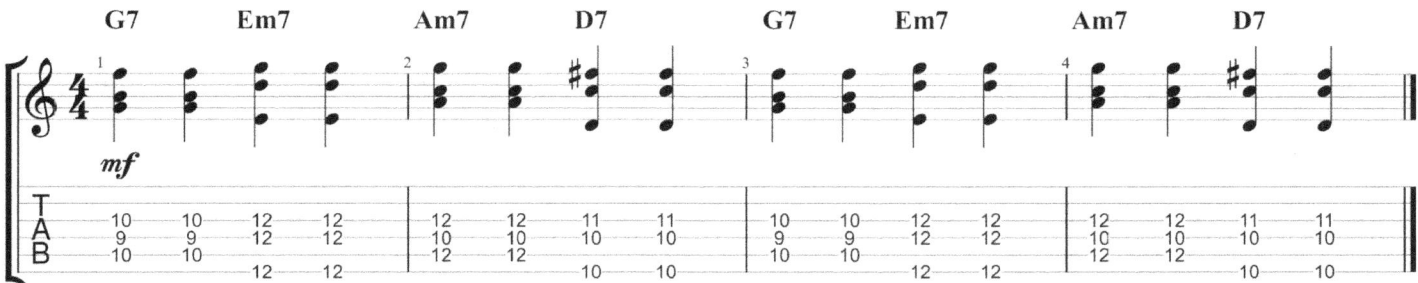

The most important thing to do is experiment and have fun with these progressions. In later chapters we will add walking basslines and more rhythmic interest, but for now explore this chord sequence in G Major and discover how it feels to play all the substitutions we've covered.

You can play:

Chord I	GMaj7	G7	Bm7
Chord VI	Em7	E7	
Chord II	Am7	A7	
Chord V	D7	(Top tip: Try Ab7 too!)	

Before we move on, I'd like you to learn this sequence in another key. This will help develop your understanding of the neck and make it easier to transpose these ideas quickly when working with a singer or brass section.

Begin by learning the I VI II V progression in the common jazz key of F.

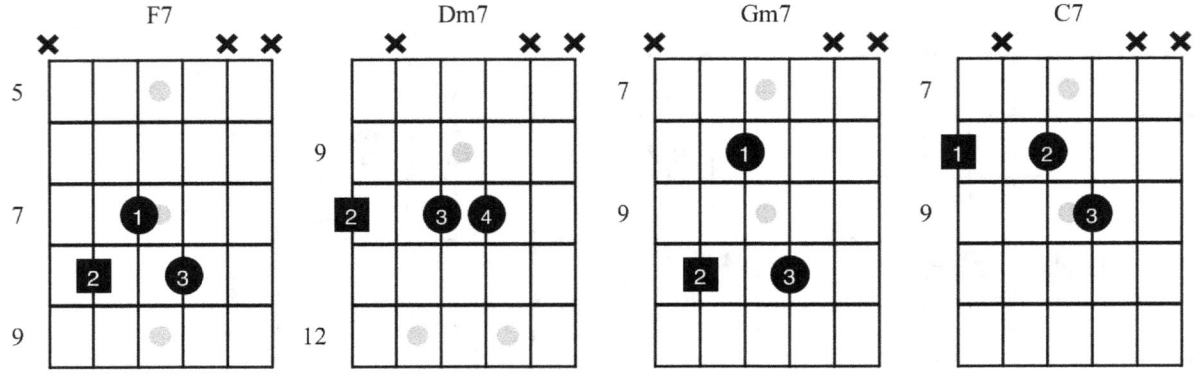

Example 1i:

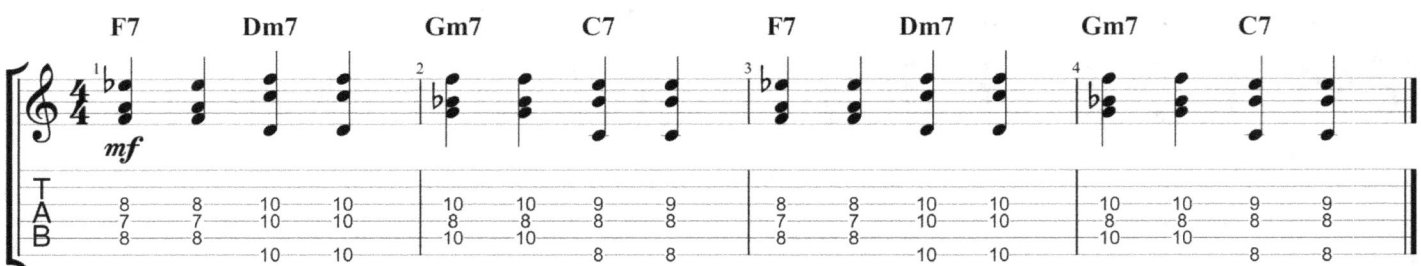

Chapter Two – Simple Walking Bass

Now we know how to voice the important chords and substitutions in the I VI II V progression, let's take a look at how to build a simple bassline. The first step is to play only the root of each chord. Even though you already know where the root notes are from Chapter One, play through the following exercises using your first finger to play each bass note.

Play the root twice on each chord, but pay attention to how I accent each note. The first note is longer and the second note is slightly *staccato* (cut off). Listen to the audio and try to copy my feel.

Example 2a:

Now, let's play the same thing, but starting from the Bm (the III chord) we used as a substitution in the previous chapter

Example 2b:

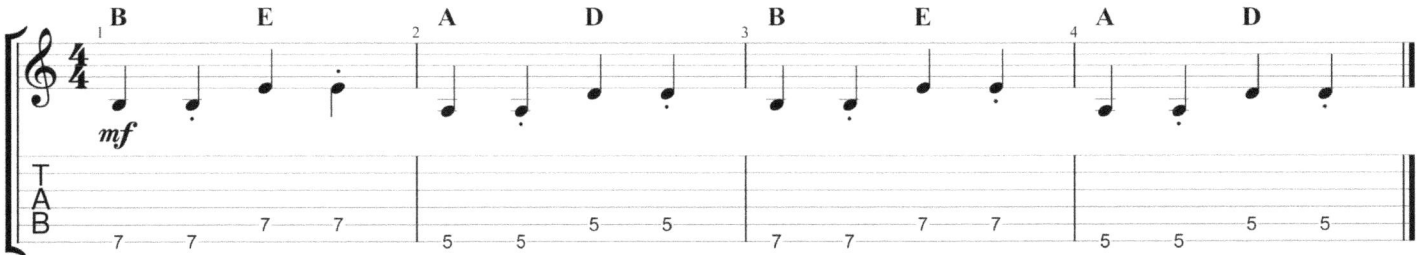

When you've got that down, link up the previous two examples.

Example 2c:

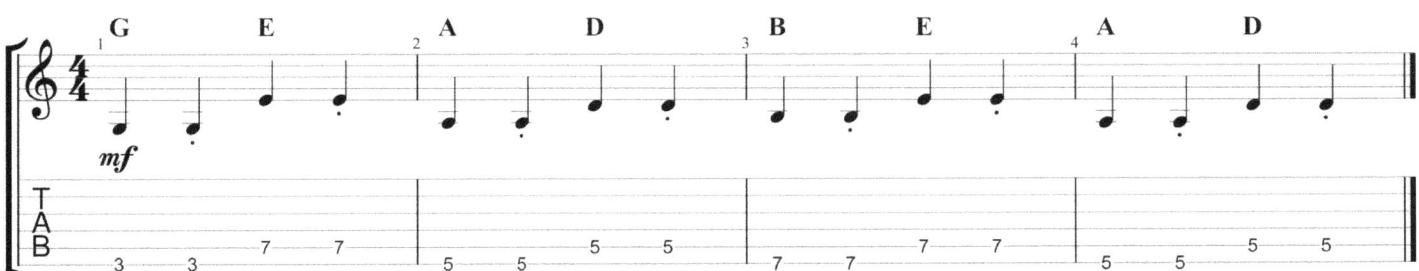

Finally, take some time to explore the other positions of the neck for both the I VI II V and III VI II V sequence. Here's one way you could play through the changes, but you should spend time exploring the neck yourself.

Example 2d:

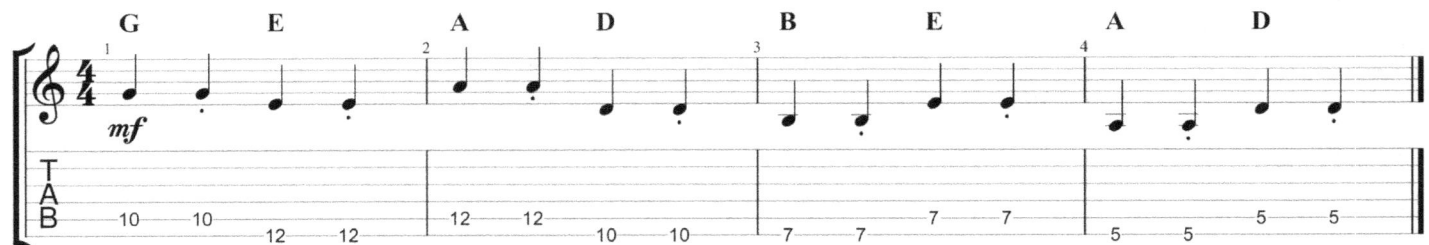

OK, now that we know where the important bass notes are, how do we begin to walk? Well, it's easier than you think!

To create a solid walking bassline all we need to do is add a *chromatic approach* note either above or below the target bass note. In other words, instead of playing two root notes on each chord, we replace the second note with a chromatic approach note a semitone above or below the *following* chord.

When written down this sounds a little more complicated than it is, so let's look at the first two chords, G and E.

When we played two notes on each chord, we had the following:

Example 2e:

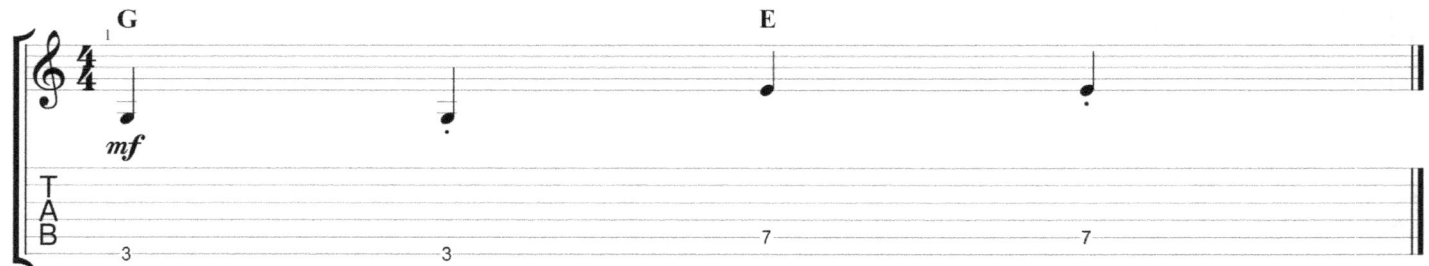

Replace the second G with the note a semitone above the E (F).

104

Example 2f:

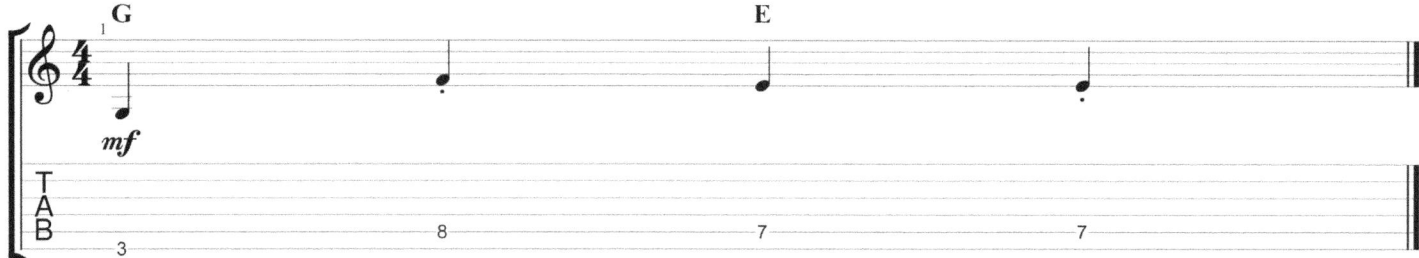

Let's repeat this process on every chord in the bar so that each bass note is approached from a semitone above. Use your first finger to play every note. It might feel a bit basic, but at this stage I want you to learn the sound, feel and location of the notes and not trip over your fingers.

Example 2g:

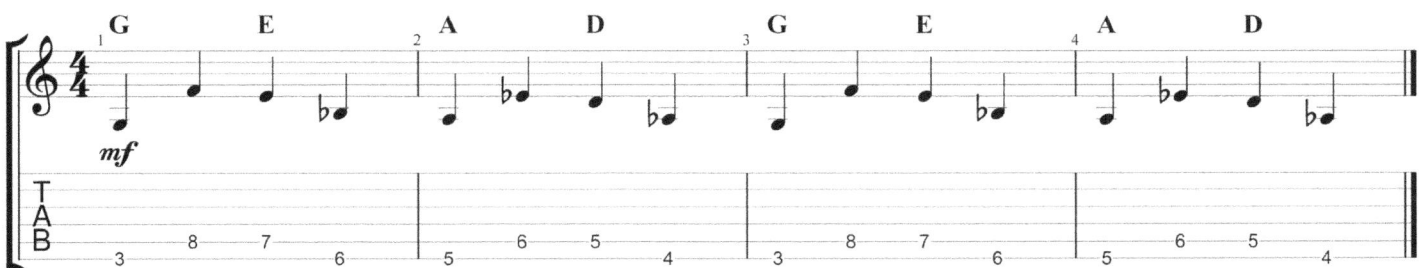

Can you hear how suddenly we've become bass players?! The root notes of the chords are all on the strong beats of the bar (beats 1 and 3) and the chromatic approach notes are all on the weak beats of the bar (beats 2 and 4) This means that not only have we created *movement*, we've created a *tension* that *resolves* when we move to the targeted root note.

These chromatic movements won't get in the way of any other instruments (apart from another guitarist or a bassist who is playing a walking bassline) because they all occur at weak points in the bar and resolve strongly to root notes.

It's the same process when we want to move to the root note from a semitone below. Begin on G then approach the E from the chromatic note below (D#). Use your first finger to play each note in the following example.

Example 2h:

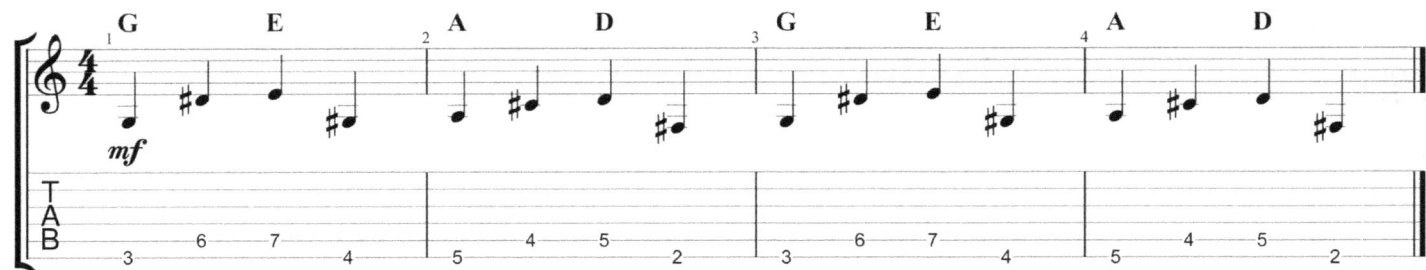

Approaching the root from a semitone below sounds just as strong as approaching it from above. Musically, it has the same effect, as once again the tension on the weak beat resolves to the root note on the strong beat.

Now begin on chord III (Bm) and play though the sequence adding a chromatic approach note from above.

Example 2i:

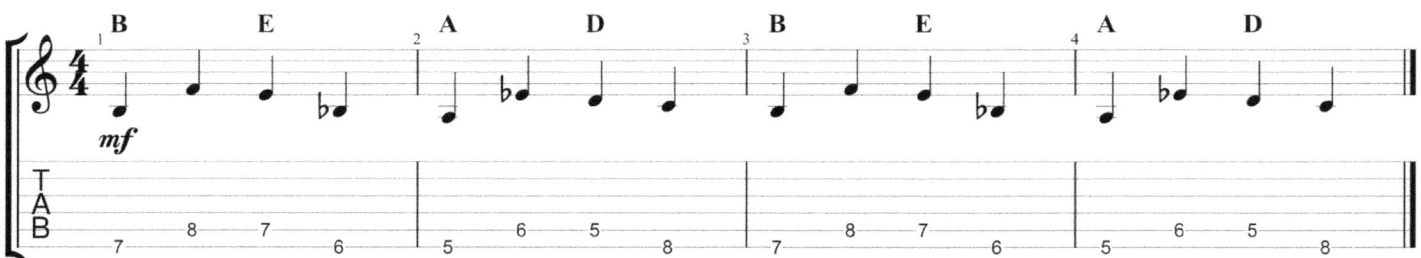

Repeat this exercise using chromatic approach notes from below each chord.

Example 2j:

When you're confident, link the I VI II V and III VI II V sequences together using chromatic approach notes from above.

Example 2k:

Repeat this example, but with chromatics approaching each chord from below.

Example 2l:

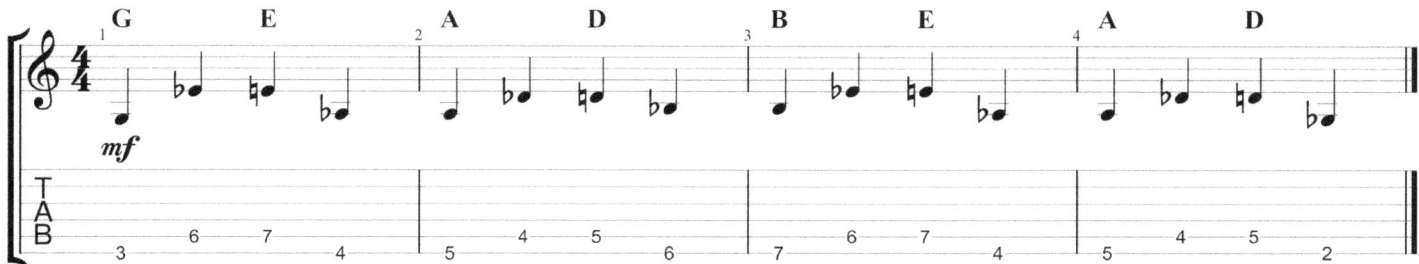

After you've spent some time on the previous two examples, it's time for you to get creative and mix up the chromatic approach notes. Combine chromatic approach notes from both above and below and play whatever you feel. I've given you one example below, but consider this a creative task – find as many ways as you can to navigate the progression. Stick to using one finger and try to create a musical feel that really sounds like a bass player.

Example 2m:

When you're confident creating a walking bassline, explore different positions of the neck. Here's one idea played in a low register.

Example 2n:

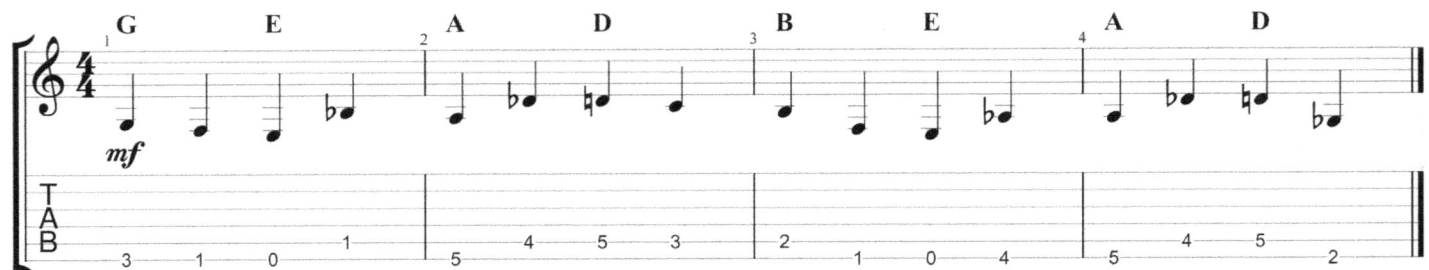

Now play high up on the guitar.

Example 2o:

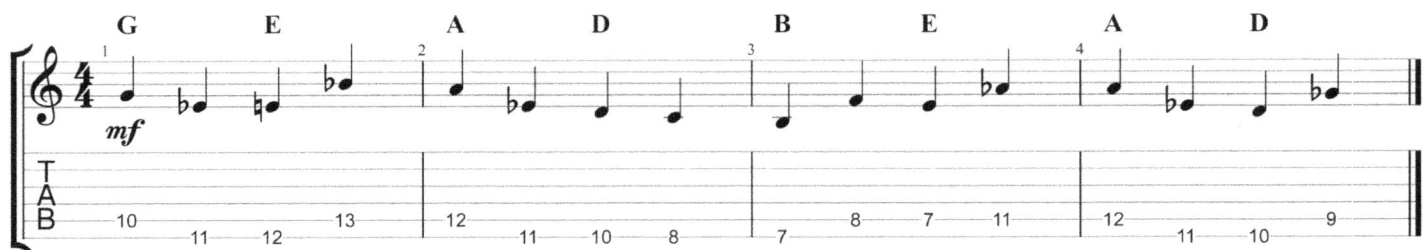

It's worth spending some time here, as really knowing your territory on the guitar neck will help you massively when we combine walking basslines with chords in the next chapter.

Before we move on, here's a creative challenge:

Set your metronome to 60 beats per minute (bpm) and see how long you can walk for on the I VI II V III VI II V sequence. Your priority is to always place a root note on beats 1 and 3. If you make a mistake, just keep going and try not to lose your place.

Always record your practice sessions and review your playing 24-hours later. Pay attention to your rhythm (are you playing in time?) and see if there are any places where you consistently struggle or lose your place in the progression. If there are, isolate those parts and work on the movements individually.

As your confidence grows, apply all the techniques in this chapter to the key of F. The chords you need are shown at the end of Chapter One.

In Chapter Three, we will reintroduce the chords and have some fun combining them with basslines.

Chapter Three – Chords and Harmonised Basslines

In the previous two chapters we learnt how to play chord voicings for the I VI II V progression and how to build a chromatic bassline. In this chapter we will combine these two skills and also *harmonise* the chromatic approach notes to create a self-contained chord and bassline structure.

As you saw in Chapter One, there are various *qualities* we can play for each chord, so to keep things simple we will stick with the following chords to begin with.

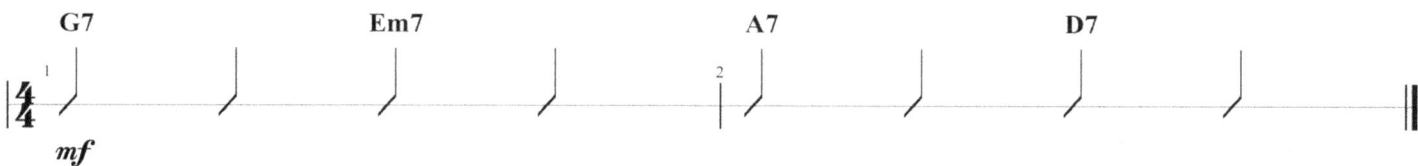

At the end of the chapter I will show you a few important variations and how to approach them musically.

The first step is to *harmonise* (add chords to) the chromatic notes we added to the basslines in Chapter Two. This sounds complicated, but actually it's very simple.

You'll remember that all we did to create our walking bassline was to add a chromatic note either a semitone above or below the target note. To harmonise these chromatic notes, we simply play a chord that has the same quality as the target chord.

For example,

- If we approach Em7 from a semitone above (F) we play an Fm7 chord.
- If we approach A7 from a semitone above (Bb) we play Bb7
- If we approach D7 from a semitone *below* (C#) we play C#7
- If we approach G7 from a semitone above (A#) we play A#7

We will learn some lovely variations later, but this approach is incredibly solid and will always sound good.

Let's take a look at this in action on the I VI II V sequence.

In the following example, I play each chord in the progression and create a bassline by approaching each one by a semitone from above. I then harmonise the approach note using a chord of the same quality as the target chord.

Example 3a:

Now repeat the process, but this time approach each chord from a semitone from below.

Example 3b:

This time, let's explore the III VI II V sequence, first by approaching chromatically from above.

Example 3c:

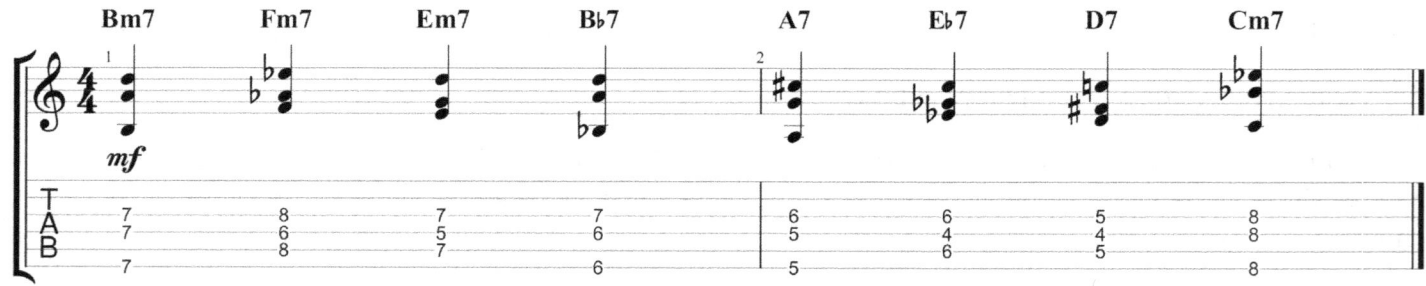

And now chromatically from below.

Example 3d:

When you've wrapped your fingers around all that, try combining both progressions. In the next example I've shown each chord approached from below, but you should also play it approaching each chord by a semitone above.

Example 3e:

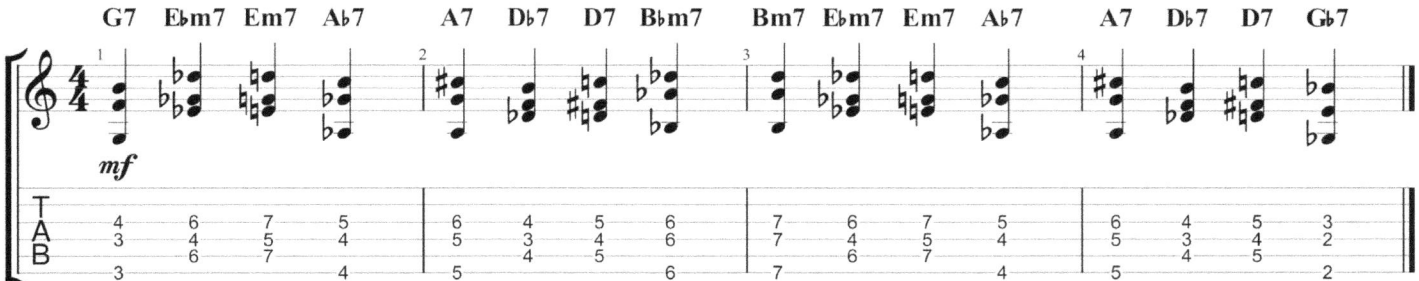

Just to get you started, here's an example that combines chromatic approach notes from both above and below.

Example 3f:

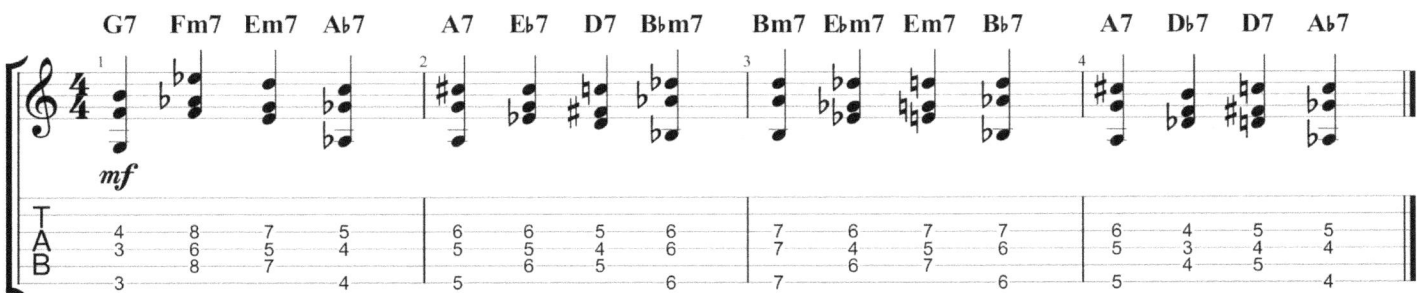

Before moving on to the second part of this chapter, explore the other regions of the neck that were covered in Chapter Two. It should be an easy job to apply the techniques in the previous six examples to other areas of the fretboard. Also, apply everything to the chord sequence in the key of F Major.

Now you're confident playing the chords and bassline around the neck, let's examine how to approach different chord qualities. As you might expect, the informal "rule" is that the approach chord should have the same quality as the target chord, but there are a few exceptions that sound great, so let's take a look at these now.

So far we've been playing a G7 as chord I. However, in quite a few tunes, the I chord needs to be played as a GMaj7. When this happens, I still *like* to approach it using a dominant 7 chord from above. In other words, the chord that precedes the GMaj7 is an Ab7. It is played in the following way.

Example 3g:

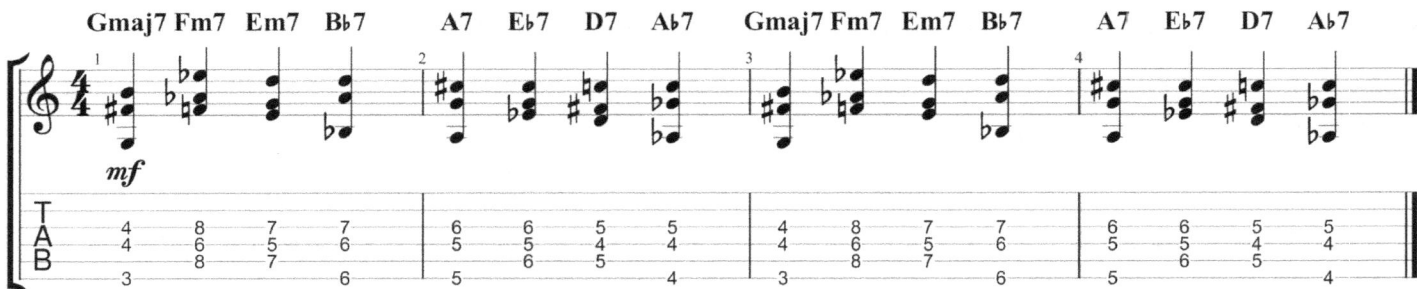

This "rule" also applies when you approach the GMaj7 from below – an F#7 sounds great.

Example 3h:

While this is my preference, playing an AbMaj7 chord before the GMaj7 still works well, so trust your ears and choose your favourite! You'll often find that they are interchangeable.

When we use the Bm7 (chord III) substitution, I'll also normally approach that from above using a dominant 7 chord, i.e., C7 in this instance.

Example 3i:

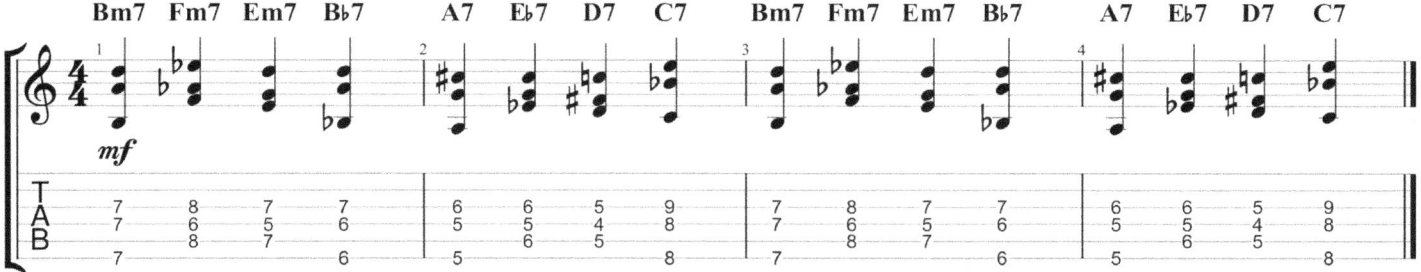

However, when I play a chromatic chord below the Bm7, I'll often play a minor 7 chord – in this case, an A#m7.

Example 3j:

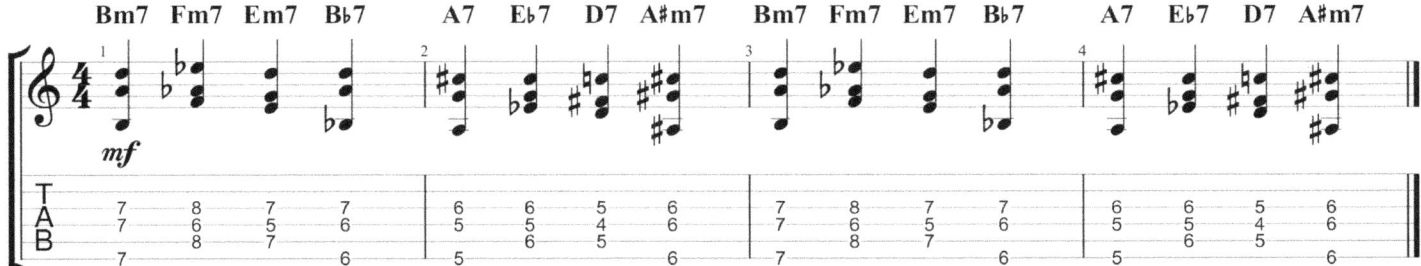

These are two of the most common variations I use, but you will find your own with practice.

Before moving on, here are a couple of longer sequences that combine the I VI II V and II VI II V chord progressions using the approaches in this chapter. Learn them carefully before improvising your own ideas.

Example 3k:

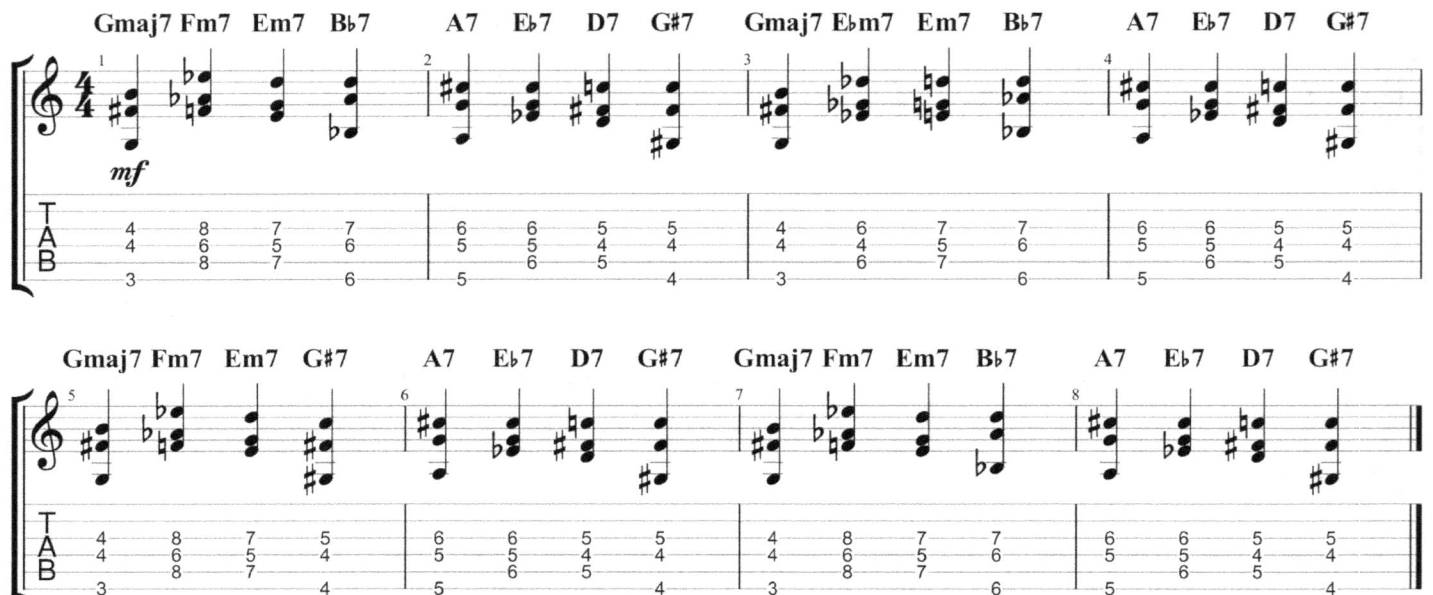

Example 3l:

Finally, expand these sequences to other areas of the guitar neck. Here's one idea in the higher register.

Example 3m:

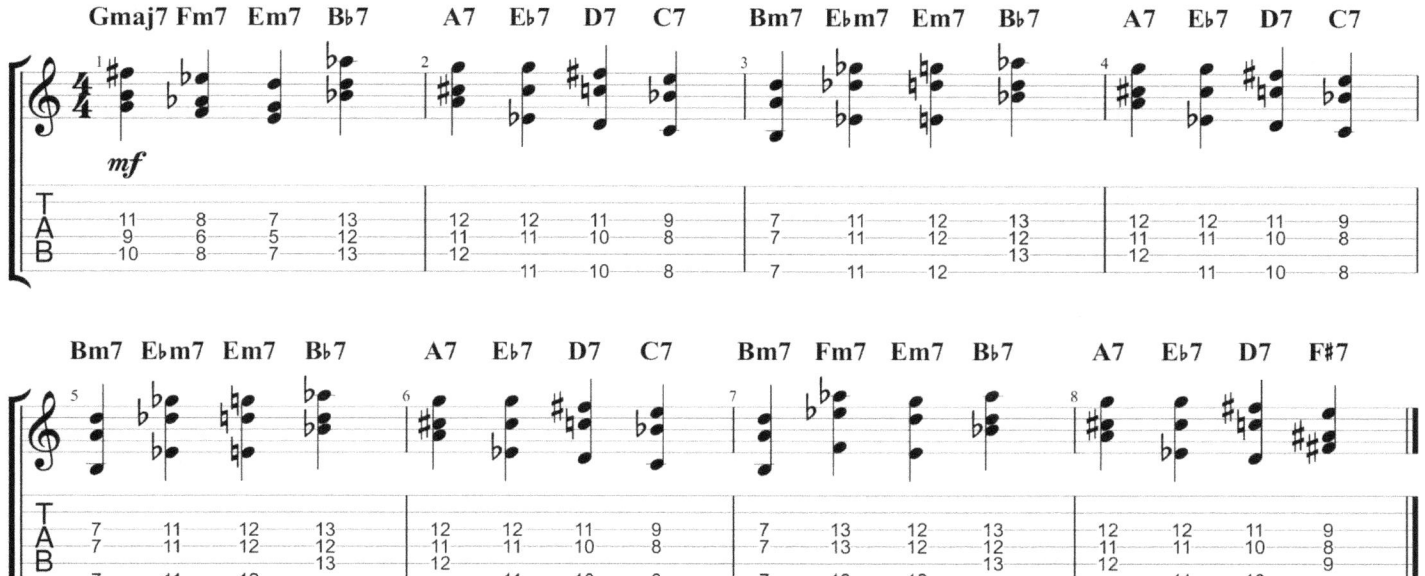

As always, use a metronome and record your playing. Listen back to yourself 24-hours later and pay careful attention to your rhythm and groove. When you're ready, learn everything in the key of F too!

OK, we've got a lot of the groundwork done now. We have learnt the chords, the bassline ideas and harmonised the chromatic approach notes. In the next chapter we're going to take a more detailed look at rhythm and syncopation. This is the stage where your musical feel will develop quickly and you'll really start to hear the bass and chords become separate voices.

Chapter Four – Syncopation and Separation

So far, we've studied the nuts and bolts of combining walking bass and chords on the guitar, and in this chapter we're going to learn how to "separate" the parts and make it sound like there are two instruments playing together. This is where the magic happens and your jazz feel can really develop.

Our aim here is to allow the steady 1/4 note walking bass pattern continue, while the target chords are moved and played on the off-beats of beats 1 and 3. For the moment, we will omit the chords played on the chromatic approach notes, but add them back in later for some variation and interest.

Let's begin by getting the fundamental rhythm of the two parts working together.

Play the bass note of the G7 chord on beat one, and with a slow and lazy swing, play the rest of the chord (the two notes on the middle strings) on the off-beat, before quickly jumping up to the F on beat 2, which is the chromatic approach note to the Em7 on beat 3.

Repeat the chord rhythm before playing the Bb chromatic approach note to A7 on beat 4. Repeat the rhythm and feel with the A7 and D7 chords in bar two. Approach each chord from a semitone above.

In the following examples, keep the chord stab short and staccato.

Example 4a:

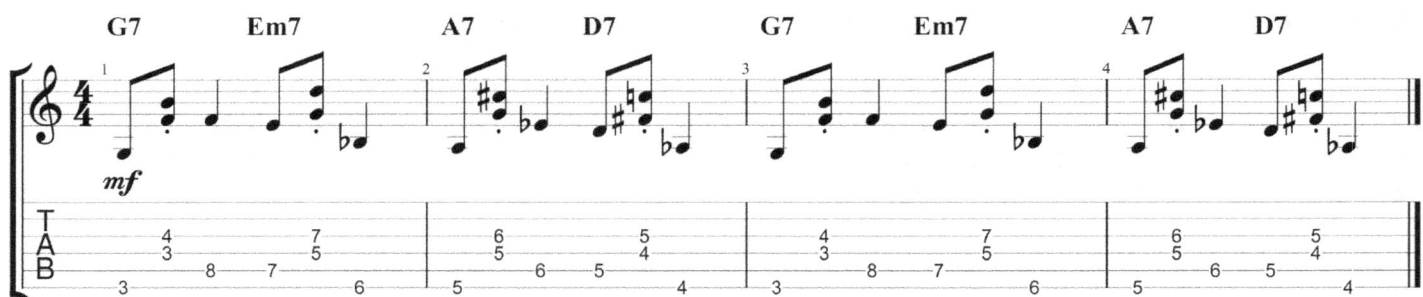

Try playing the same rhythm and approach every chord with a chromatic step from below.

Example 4b:

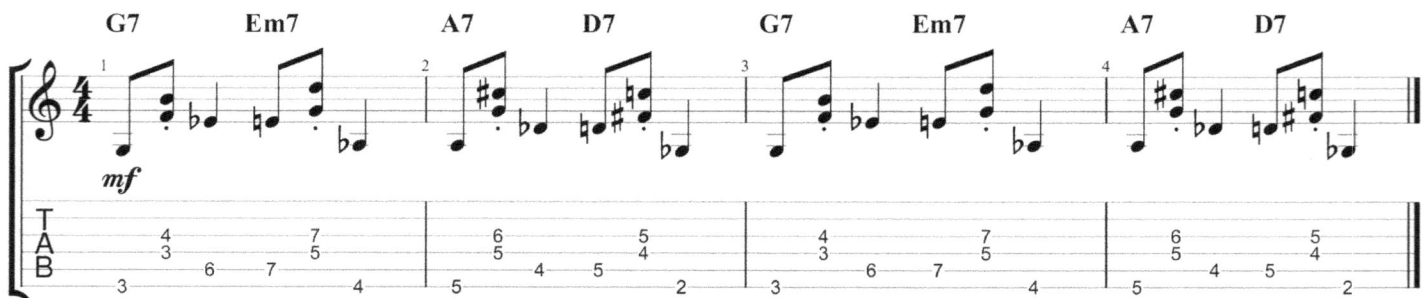

Repeat the previous idea using the Bm7 in the sequence. First, play chromatic approaches from above.

Example 4c:

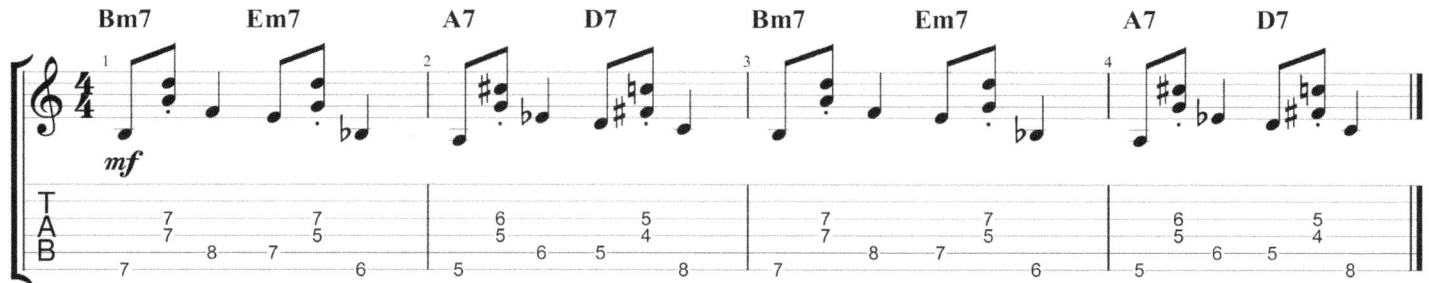

Now try the same progression approaching from the chromatic note below the chord.

Example 4d:

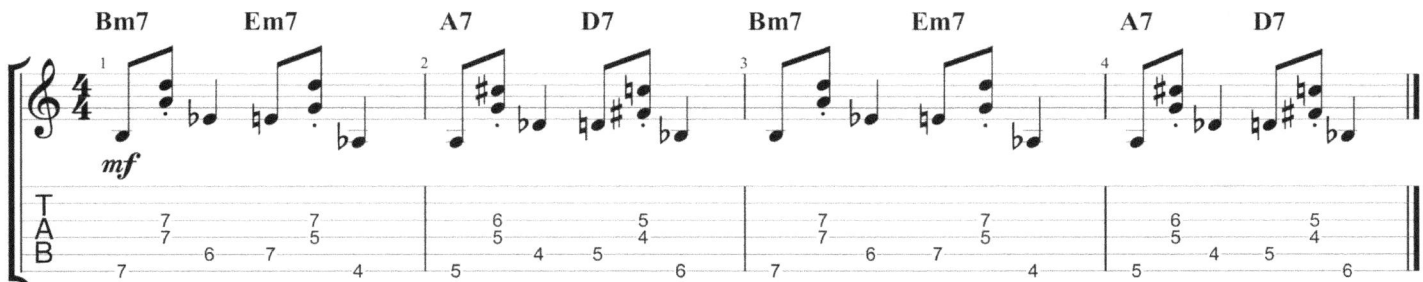

Finally, play the full I VI II V / III VI II V progression and combine chromatic approaches from both above and below. Here's one route around the changes, but you should be able to come up with many more!

Example 4e:

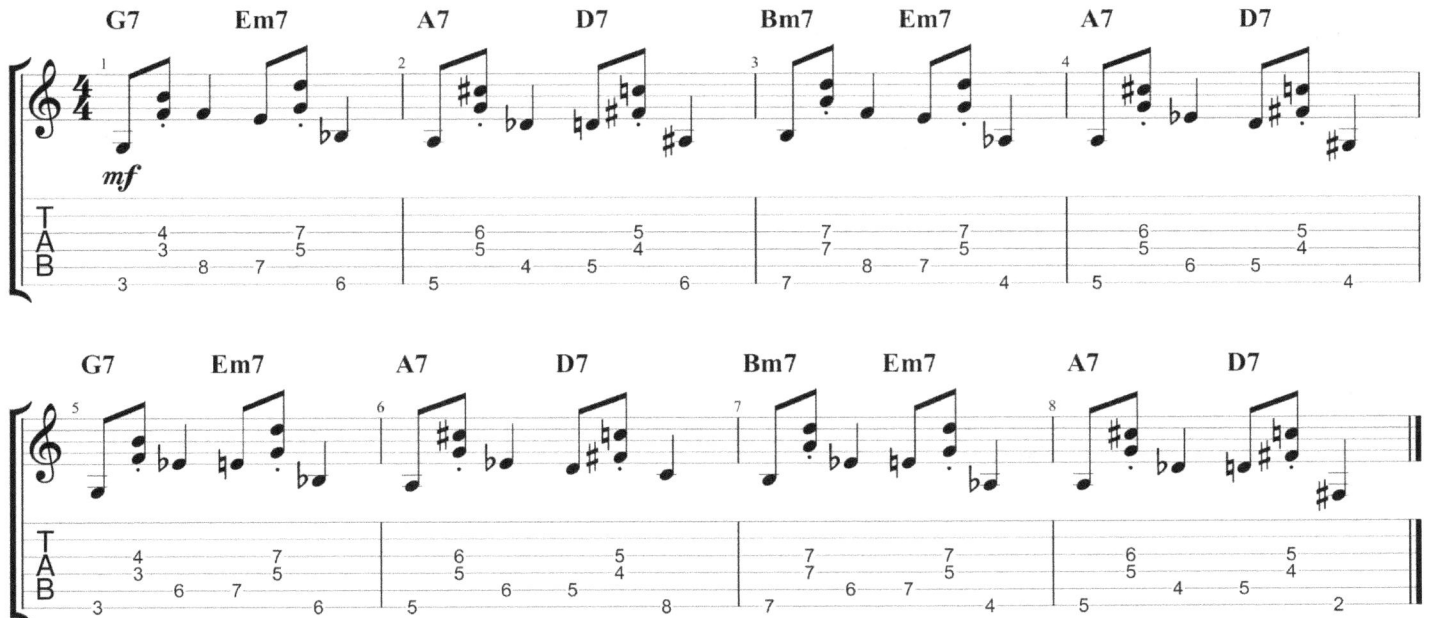

As I'm sure can hear, the bass and chord parts are starting to sound like two different instruments. This is perfect and exactly what we're aiming for.

The next stage is to try to accentuate that difference by playing both parts at different volumes. We want the bassline to be loud and proud, and the chord stabs to be quieter and less obvious.

In the next example all the chords are approached from a semitone above, and I've really exaggerated the volume difference between the bassline and the chords. It's a bit over the top, and I'd never play like this on a gig, but it's done deliberately to cause you to think hard about your volume levels. Separating the *voices* in this way is quite an advanced skill, and one that takes practice to make it sound natural, so to begin with, exaggerating the dynamics will help to build the independence between your thumb and fingers.

Example 4f:

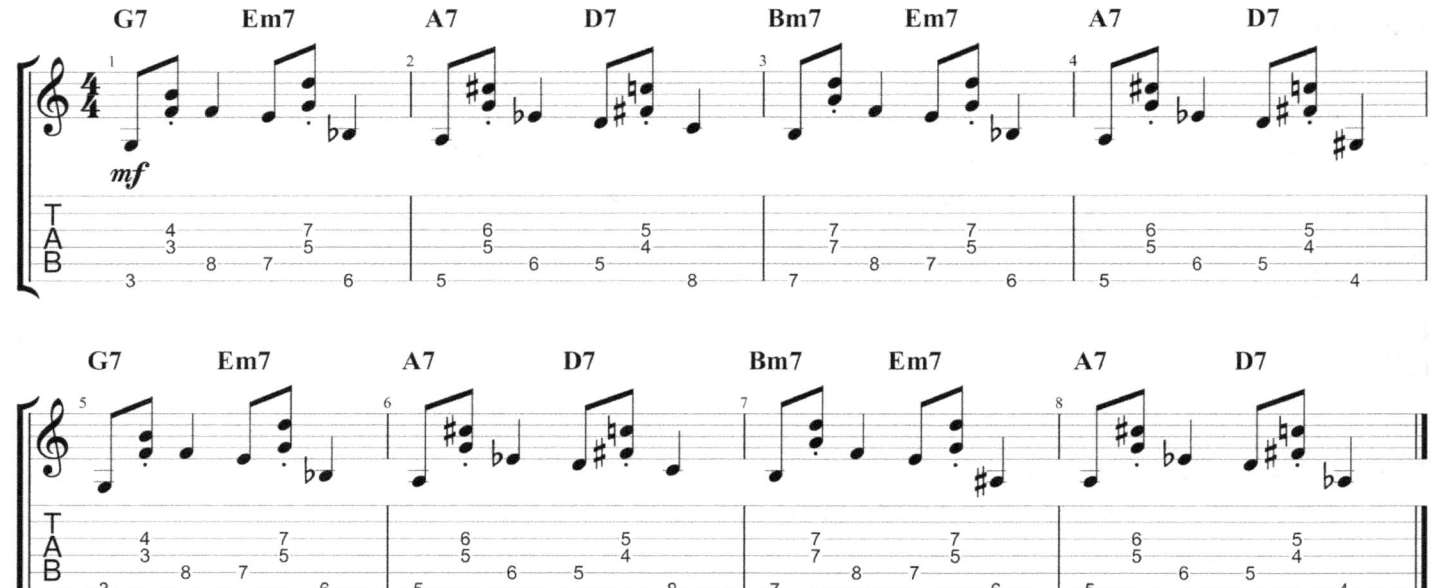

Working on the "volume controls" between your thumb and fingers is a real challenge for most students at first, but it gets easier with time. A little trick I like to teach is to get my students to play the bassline once through loudly *without* the chords, and on the repeat to add the chords back in as quietly as possible. It takes a lot of practice, but this additional dynamic adds great depth to the musicality of the guitar part. Try this on the I VI II V sequence.

Example 4g:

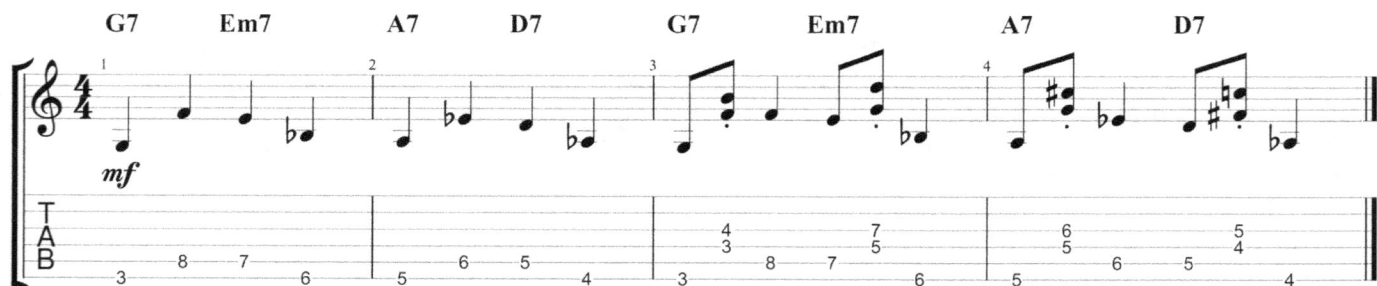

I will reiterate, this is an advanced skill, so keep coming back to the previous two exercises and practise them often.

Until now, all the chord stabs have been played *staccato* (short and detached). However, it's possible to let the occasional chord ring out, as a contrast to the stabs, by leaving the fingers on the higher strings while you play the next note of the bassline.

This is one of those things that's easier to hear than it is to explain, so listen carefully to the audio track before playing through Example 4h. On the I VI II V progression, play chords I and II staccato, letting chords VI and V ring for one beat. The trick is to leave the fingers playing the chord in position for as long as possible, while the spare finger plays the bassline. It's important to keep the bassline simple at first, so always approach the target chord by a semitone from above.

Example 4h:

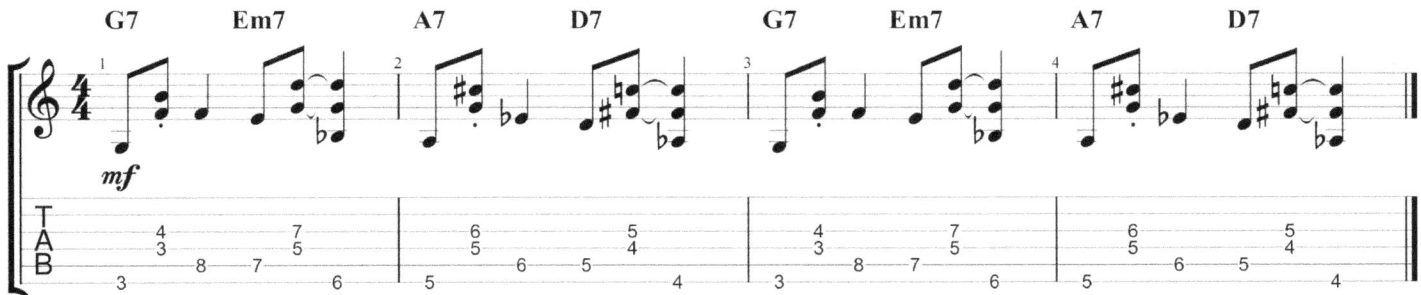

These types of variations keep the texture of the rhythm guitar parts interesting and break up any monotony.

Another way to add interest is to move the position of the chord stabs in the beat. Until now, we've played each chord on the "and" of beats one and three, but with a bit of practice we can move them on to the 1/16th note divisions of the beat.

To develop this rhythmic feel, forget about the whole chord sequence for a moment and just hold down a G7. Play the bass note with your thumb and quickly play the rest of the chord immediately afterwards. Let the chord notes ring for two beats and repeat this sequence four times.

Example 4i:

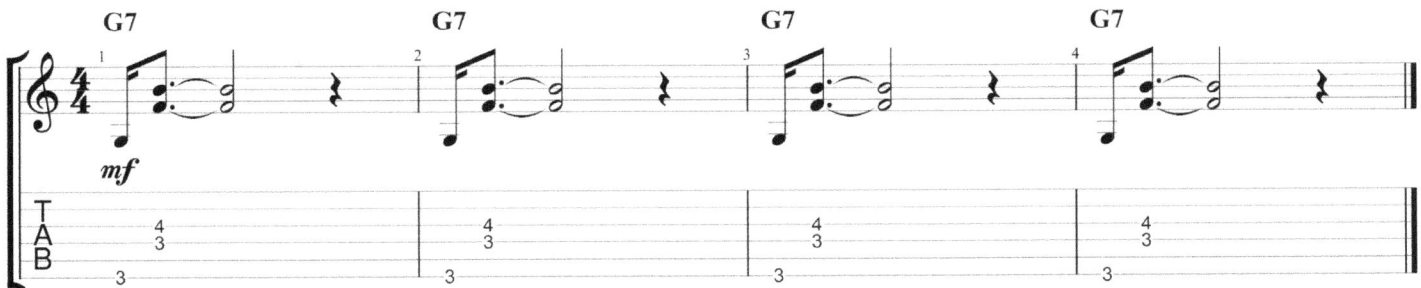

When you're confident with this rhythm, apply it to the four chords in the I VI II V sequence.

Example 4j:

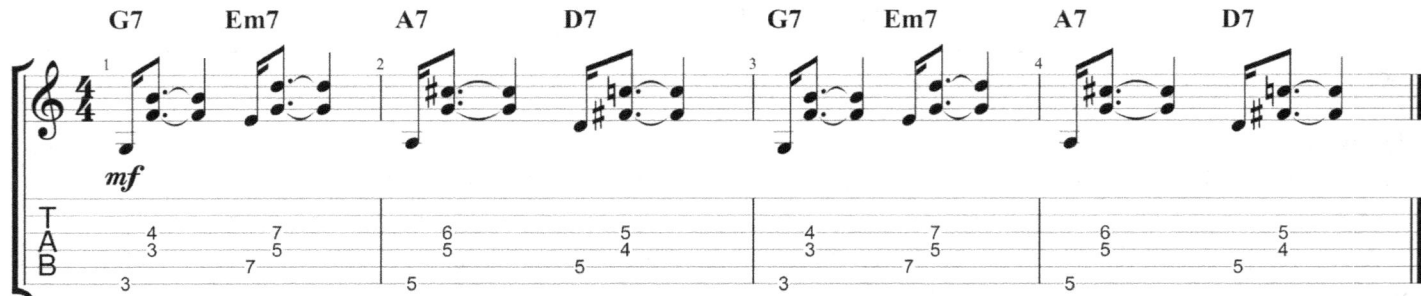

Now add the 1/4 note walking bass back in. I've notated the bass approaching from above, but when you're ready you can begin to improvise your own basslines.

Example 4k:

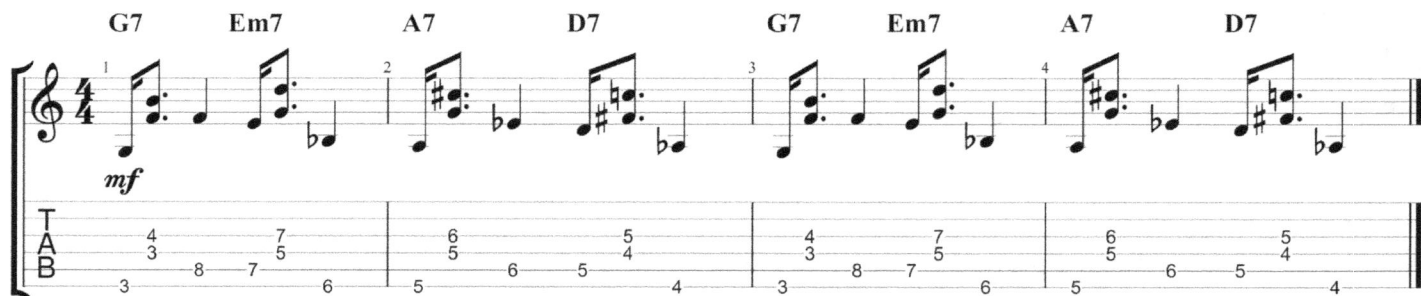

Finally, this 1/16th note stab can be played at any point in the bar and works beautifully on any of the harmonised chromatic bass notes. In the following example, I play all the chords with the normal 1/8th note syncopated chords, but on the chromatic bass notes *preceding* the A7 and the G7, I use the 1/16th-note rhythm to harmonise those approach notes.

Example 4l:

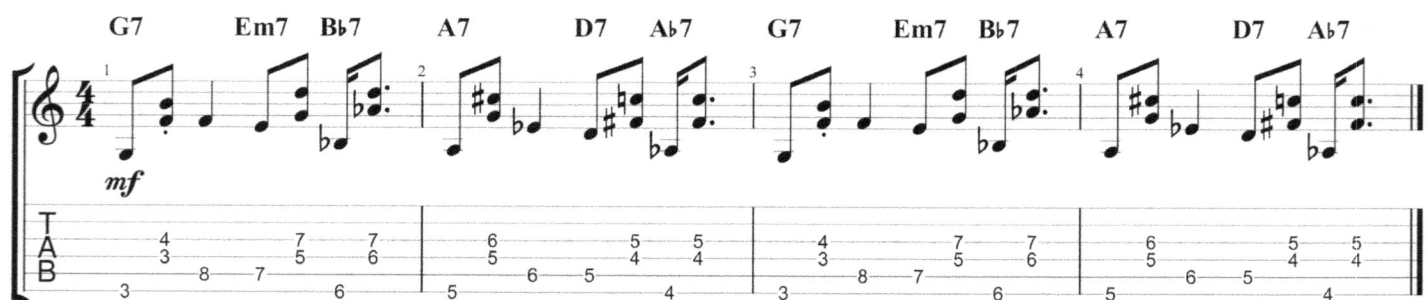

Try doing the same thing with the 1/16th note stab before the Em7 chord.

Example 4m:

We've now developed three chord rhythms we can use when playing a walking bass.

a) The first is to simply play straight, un-syncopated chords on every beat of the bar.

b) We can play 1/4 note bass notes with a syncopated chord on the 1/8th note off-beats.

c) We can also play the 1/16th note stab I taught you in the previous few examples.

There's also a "secret option D", however, which is to play the 1/4 note bassline without any chords at all. This provides a steady pulse for a singer / soloist to work with, while thinning out the texture of the music, should it be required.

The most common approach is option b, but by combining the four techniques it's easy to create an interesting, grooving part that adds to the music and doesn't become monotonous. When you combine these approaches with the different ranges on the guitar (playing up high or down low), and add in some substitutions, (like playing Bm7 instead of the G7), there are hundreds of creative options for you to explore while improvising a walking bassline.

The following example gives you 16 bars of me playing through the I VI II V sequence, putting together all the harmonic, rhythmic and substitution ideas we've learnt so far. I've added a couple of new ones, so keep your ears open! Learn this example note for note and use it as a basis for your own exploration.

Example 4n:

When you're getting to grips with Example 4n, get out the metronome and really concentrate on your rhythm. Set the metronome to click at about 80bpm and focus on playing all the bass notes on the clicks. When that's solid, add a bit of "snap" to the chords by digging in a little harder with your fingers.

One useful metronome technique is to half the speed of the click and "hear" it as beats 2 and 4. You must fill in beats 1 and 3 yourself. Set the metronome to 40bpm and play at the same speed as you did when it was set to 80bpm. You should hear every chromatic bass note fall on the click and the root notes fall in the gaps. Listen carefully to Example 4o and play along to develop the feel.

Example 4o:

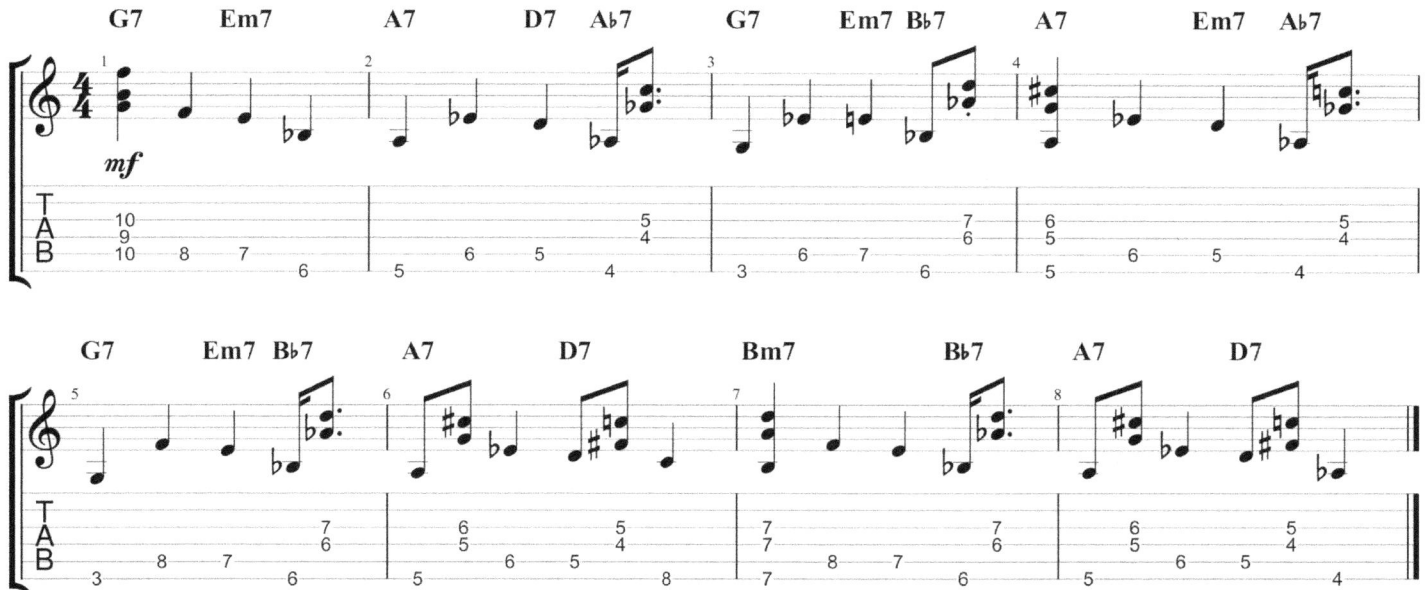

There's been a lot to learn in this chapter, but we've now covered the main components of an effective walking bassline on guitar. The key here is for you to practise these ideas as much as possible. Your bass should be loud and confident, and your chords should be quieter and snappy. Work towards the point where you have total control over the rhythms, chords, syncopations and volume you play.

It's OK to plan what you're going to play at first, as this will help you to develop discipline and control, but soon all the techniques will begin to combine naturally and you'll start to play what you hear.

Keep listening to bass players too, because this will quickly help to develop your feel.

In the next chapter, we'll look at how we can vary the dynamics of the guitar part by using a pick.

Chapter Five – Imitating Drums with the Pick

In this chapter I'll teach you something that will add a whole new feel and dimension to your walking bass parts.

Even with all the variations to the walking bass we've looked at in the previous few chapters, you may find that the music sometimes calls for another colour.

One of my favourite things to do is imitate a drummer by using my guitar pick instead of my fingers to create a more percussive effect on the strings. By holding the pick in a particular way, and playing with a relaxed, laid back rhythm, it's possible to create the effect of a drummer's brushes on the snare drum while still playing the walking bassline.

When you've learnt this technique, it'll sound like you're playing guitar, bass and drums all at the same time! As you can imagine, that's a great skill for an accompanist and it will turn you into an extremely versatile rhythm guitar player.

The trick to imitating the "swish" of a drummer's brushes it to *angle* the pick as it crosses the strings. I like to turn the pick so that its leading edge is pointing up to my left shoulder. In this position, instead of the flat edge of the pick striking the strings, the curved edge is the part that makes contact. Other guitar players turn the pick so that the leading edge points down towards their knee, so experiment with what feels best for you.

Let's begin by learning the strumming pattern and feel you'll use to mimic the drummer's brushes. With the pick angled as described above, play two 1/4 note down strums followed by a quick, light, soft up-strum on the second off-beat.

Begin by fingering a Bm7 chord, but don't press the strings all the way down to the fret wire. When you strum, be careful not to hit any open strings and you will create a deadened percussive effect. This rhythmic technique is one reason why I tend to use these little chord fragments and avoid full barre chords. Fingering chords in this way really helps to stop unwanted strings from ringing and gives me a great deal of control over my dynamics. Don't forget that everything is played on the bottom four strings!

Play a Bm7 chord and listen to the scratchy feel on the upstroke. You don't want to hear any of the muted strings individually. Instead, aim for a brush-like effect, so that the strings blur into one as the edge of the pick glides across them. Play softly until you can hear that swish and try to match my feel on the audio track.

Example 5a:

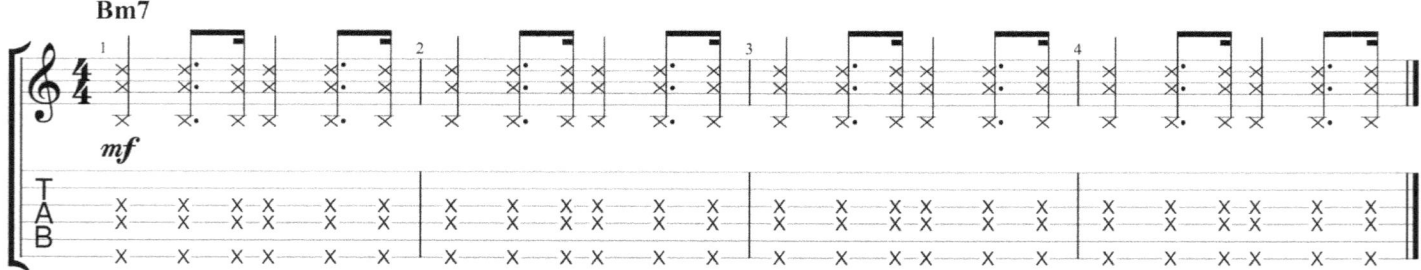

Now try this rhythm on a properly fretted Bm7. The chords on each bar should be strong, but release the pressure between each strum to make them staccato. Also release the pressure on the upstroke to play the muted scratch. Play softly!

Example 5b:

When you can match the feel on the audio track, apply the rhythm to the III VI II V progression.

Example 5c:

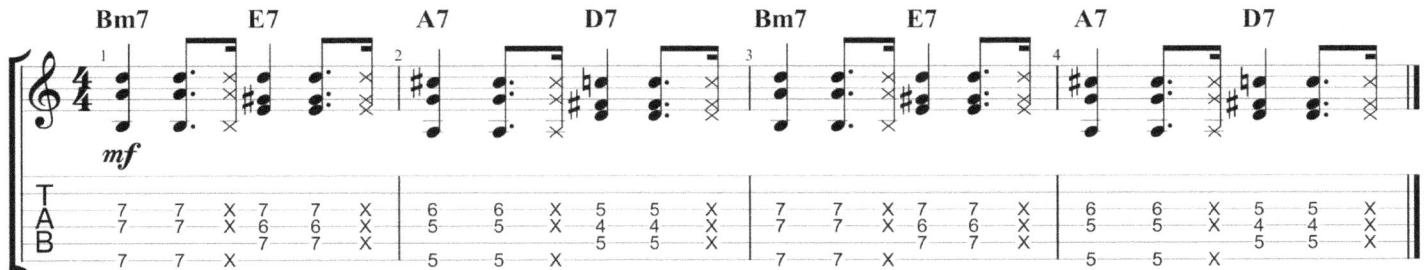

Now let's add the walking bass back in, along with the harmonised chords on the chromatic approach notes. Keep those up-strums going on the off-beats.

Example 5d:

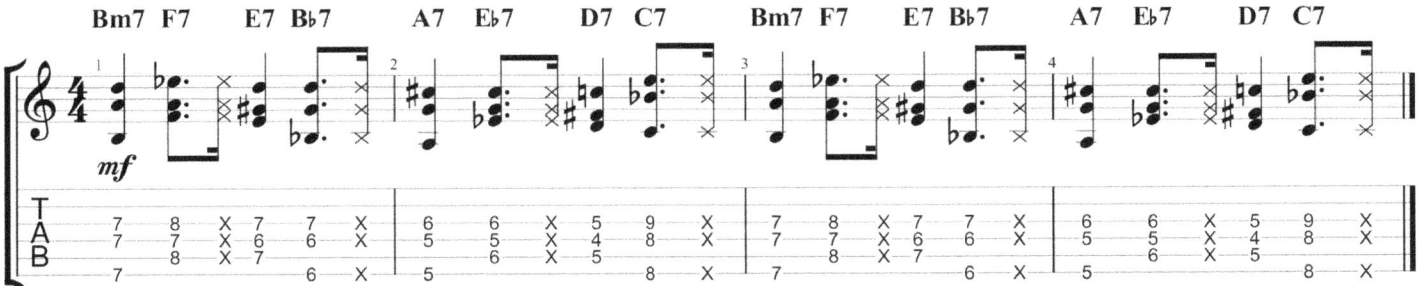

When you have that down, play the rhythm throughout the full sequence as shown below.

Example 5e:

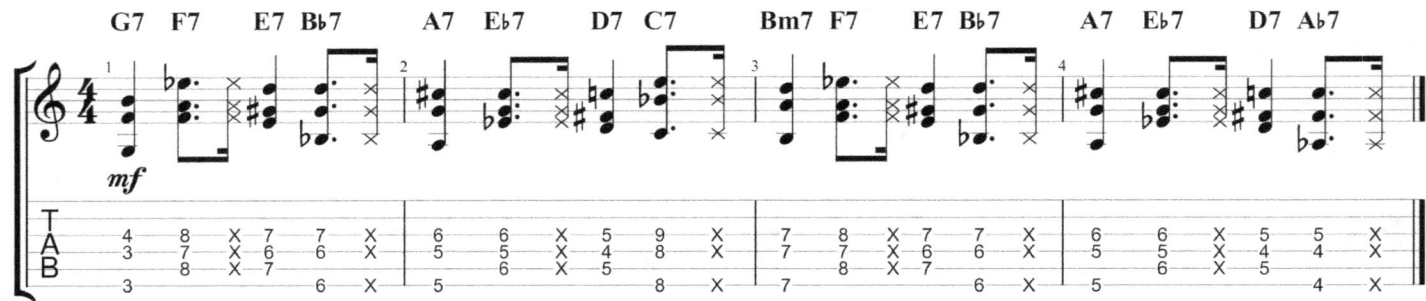

As you gain confidence, start to bring in some of the substitutions we've covered in earlier chapters. The following four examples apply the brush rhythm to other ideas we've covered.

Example 5f:

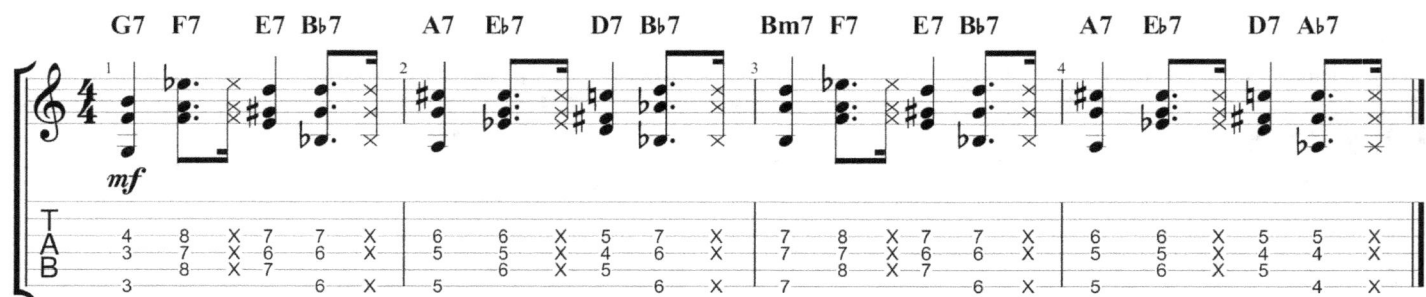

Example 5g:

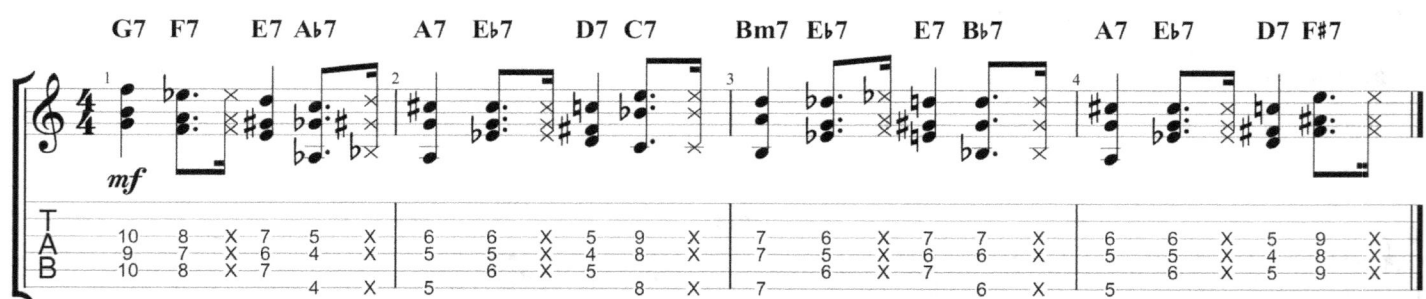

Example 5h:

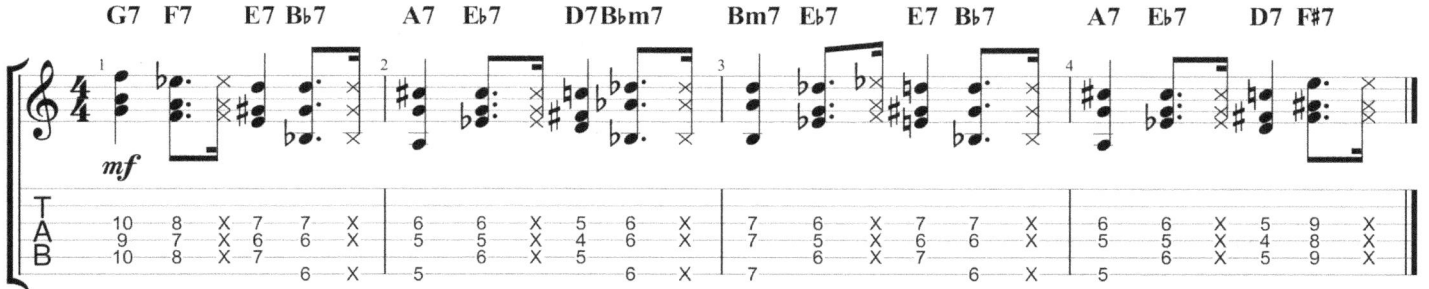

Example 5i:

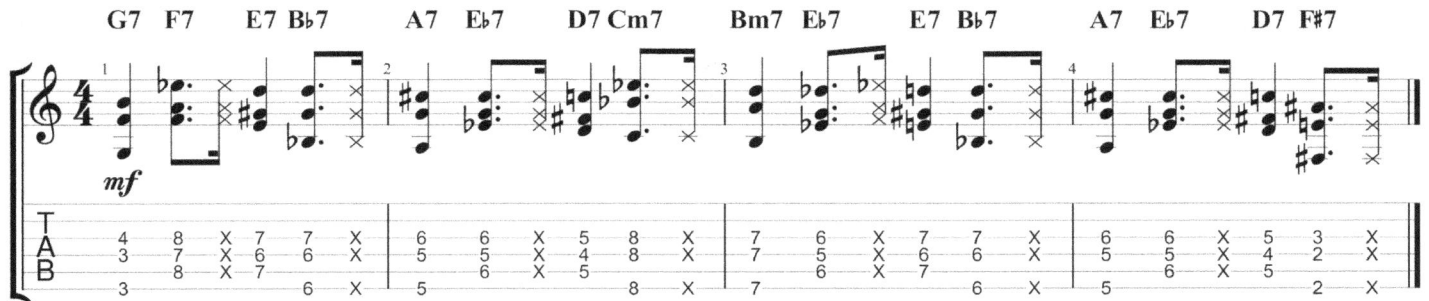

Now string some of these examples together into one longer piece.

Example 5j:

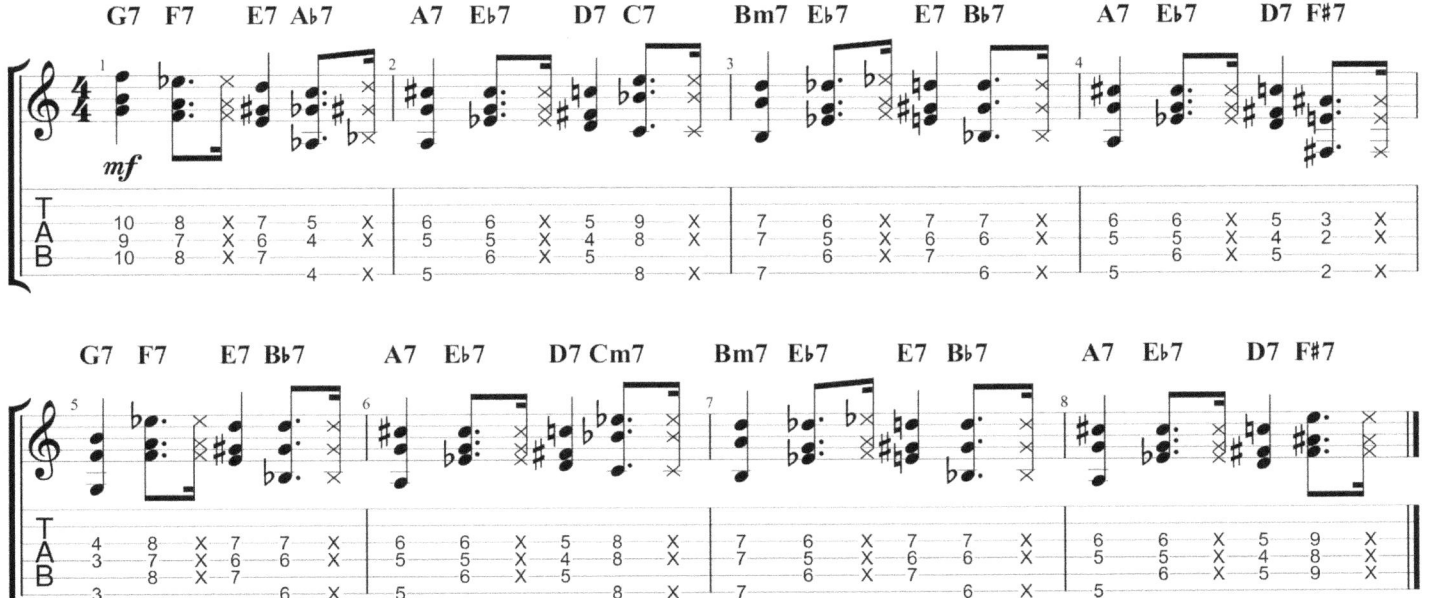

127

Finally, before we move on, transpose the chord sequence into the key of F Major to test yourself. I've shown it in its basic form here, but you should apply all the substitutions you've studied in the key of G Major.

Example 5k:

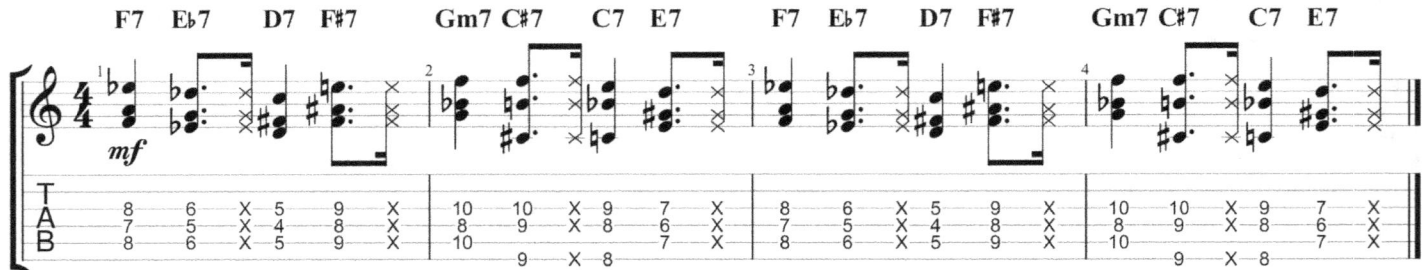

This has been a short chapter, but it's an important one. The brushes feel is essential to master, as this adds a distinctive rhythmic element to your playing that other instruments can't copy. When you've practised this feel, you'll sound like a guitarist, drummer and bass player all at once!

In the next chapter, we'll look at how to add some rhythmic interest to the bassline.

Chapter Six – Walking Bass Variations

We've now covered many of the elements of playing a walking bassline on guitar, and in this chapter we'll take a look at some of the ideas that will help you to get more creative with your rhythm and texture. We'll explore how to play walking bass with a "two" feel, how to play up at the dusty end of the fretboard, how to add a little bit of melody, and how to play the minimum of chords while still laying down the harmony of the tune.

Some of these ideas are less tangible than others and will develop more with practice. They are often about feel, which is something I can't teach in this book. The secret to developing great feel is to listen to your favourite musicians (especially bass players in this instance) and play with other people as much as possible.

We will begin with one of the most tangible elements of texture: playing in twos.

Until now, we have been walking with four even bass notes in each bar, but now we will vary that and use a different rhythm to accentuate the root notes on beats 1 and 3.

The trick is to delay the chromatic approach note until *just before* the target note. The listener begins to hear the bassline phrased in twos and it's almost like we've created a half-time feel. It's a great effect and all we need to do to achieve it is delay the chromatic approach note.

Listen to the audio track before playing Example 6a and you'll get the idea immediately. Begin with chromatic approach notes from above each chord and only play the bassline for now. We'll add the chords back in later.

Example 6a:

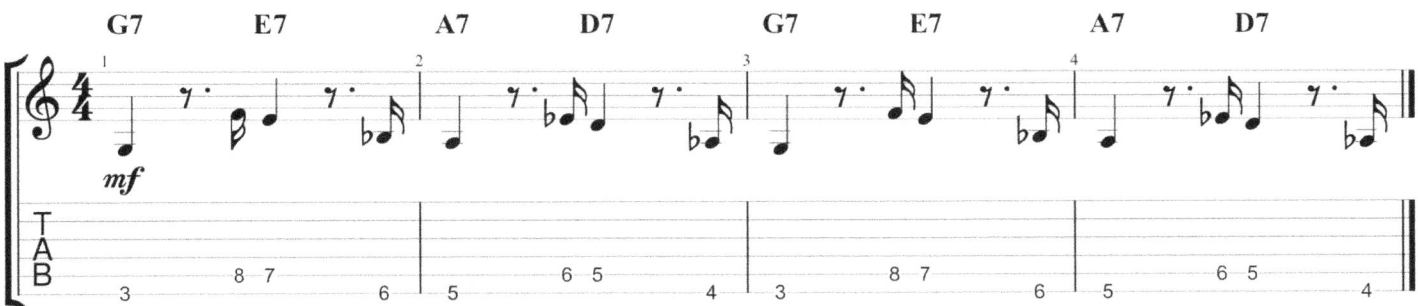

Now apply the same rhythm to the III VI II V sequence and use a chromatic approach from below.

Example 6b:

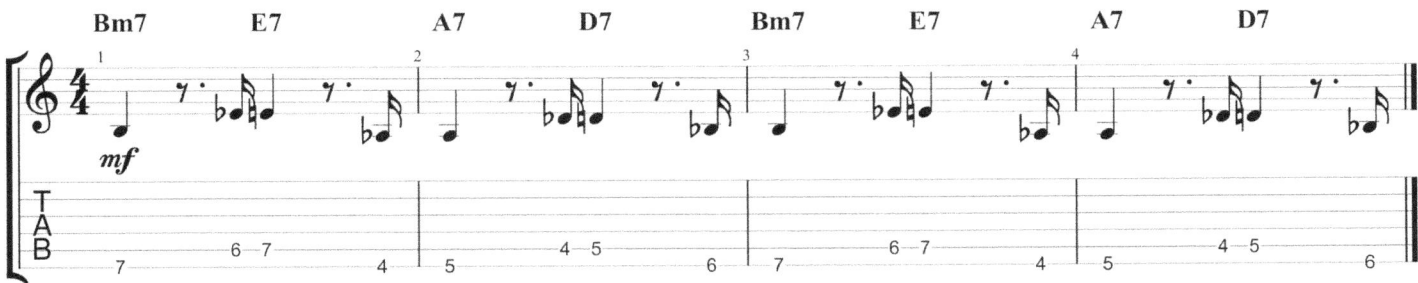

Let's link those two sequences together and harmonise every bass note, including the chromatic approaches.

Example 6c:

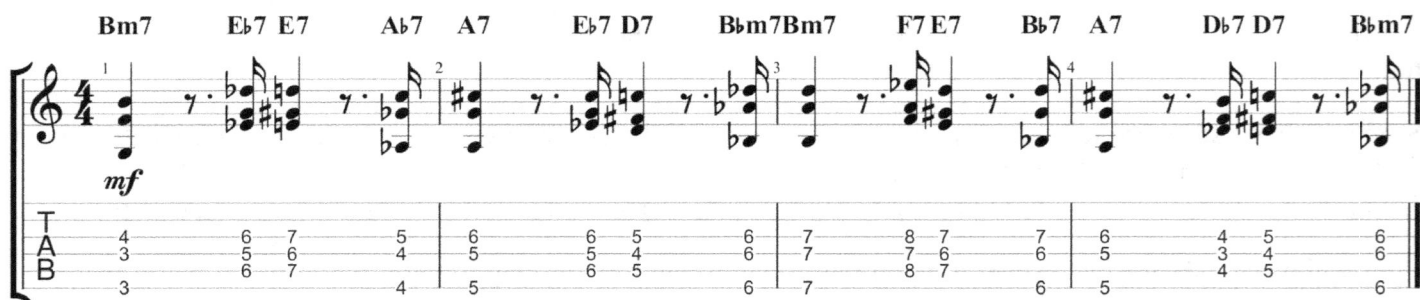

This time, don't harmonise the approach note, and syncopate the chord so that it falls on the off-beat. This creates a great feel and is definitive of the style.

Example 6d:

Now you've got the two feel under your belt, it's time to combine it with the four-to-the-bar walking bassline. For now, forget about chords and practise moving between twos and fours. There are infinite ways you can do this, but here are a couple of examples to get you going.

Example 6e:

The previous example gave you a predictable place to move from twos to fours, but I like to do it in the middle of the sequence too. Here's an idea that moves to fours on the Am7.

Example 6f:

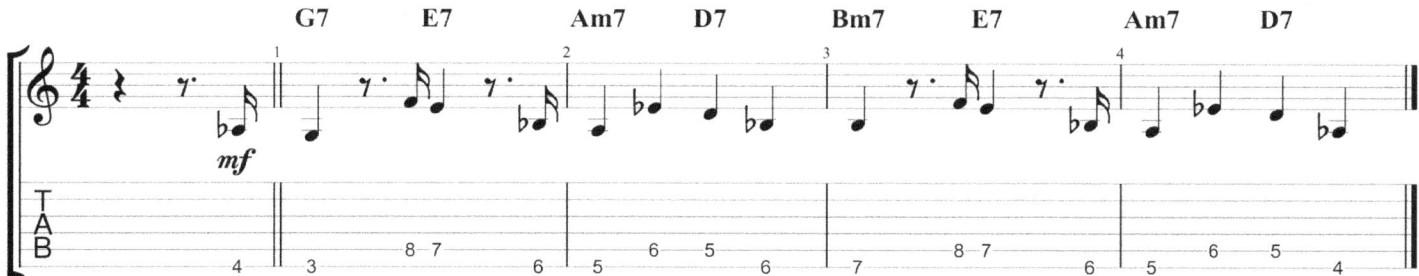

When you're confident with this feel, add the syncopated chords back in. Here's another way to move from twos to fours, now with the chords played on the off-beats.

Example 6g:

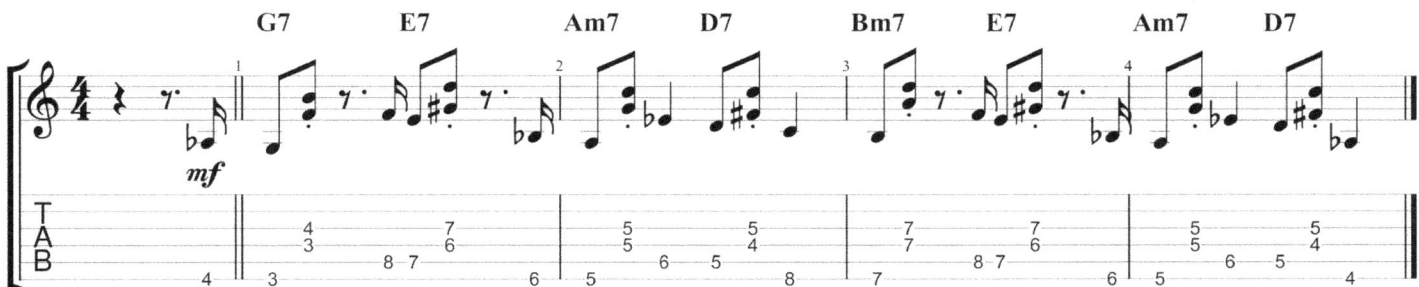

Of course, there are unlimited ways to combine chords on the beat, chords off the beat, playing in fours, playing in two, and playing unaccompanied basslines. It's up to you to get creative and try out as many permutations as you can. The following idea will get you started. It's an eight-bar phrase that mixes up all the approaches listed above. Use it as the basis for your own exploration and see how many ideas you can come up with. Set a metronome and focus on your groove.

Example 6h:

High Range Basslines

Every so often, it's great to explore the dusty end of the fretboard, so let's have a look at some ideas that work above the 12th fret. Of course, these ideas may be difficult to play depending on what type of guitar you own, but they should be doable on most jazz boxes.

One word of warning though: don't use these ideas all the time. You've got to pick your moment, because the high pitched "bassline" could start to interfere with what a singer or soloist is doing.

The following ideas are all based on the same I VI II V / III VI II V chord progression, but are played high up on the neck. They shouldn't need too much explanation by now, as they use the same concepts we've discussed in earlier chapters, so just learn them and explore each approach to make it your own.

The first idea starts at the 10th fret and gradually descends the neck.

Example 6i:

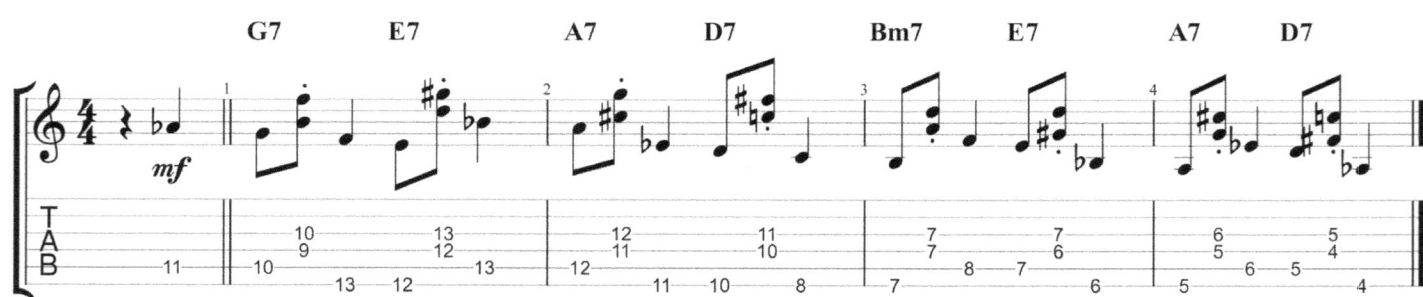

The next idea begins from the B (chord III) at the 14th fret and descends to the G at the 12th fret.

Example 6j:

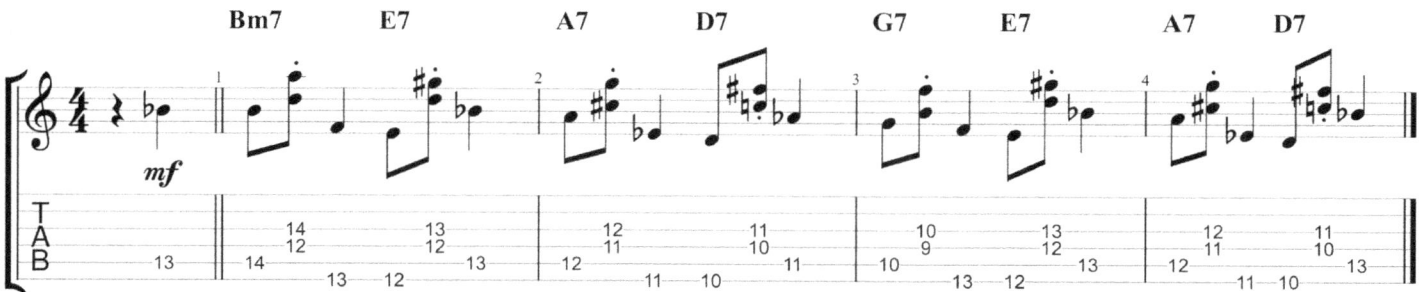

This route around the changes begins at the 15th fret and targets the E at the 19th fret. It might be easier to play it as just a bassline to begin with and add chords later.

Example 6k:

Root and Tenths

For a change of texture, it's possible to move away from playing full chords and instead play the root and 10th (3rd) of a chord. For a comprehensive guide to this technique, check out my book *Beyond Chord Melody* where I get deep into building melodies with these shapes. For now, here's a quick overview.

Instead of going deep into the theory, I think it's best to just show you a few practical examples of where I add some melody on the second string.

The first idea begins on the Bm7 chord and as the bass note moves to F (chromatically above the target of E), I add a G melody note on the 8th fret on the second string. This melody ascends a semitone to G# as the bass note descends to E. The two notes together form an E7 chord. I then repeat the process after approaching the A7 in bar two from a chromatic note above.

Pay particular attention to this example as it is a common feature of my playing and, while the fingering is a little awkward, this contrary motion is quite captivating for your audience.

Example 6l:

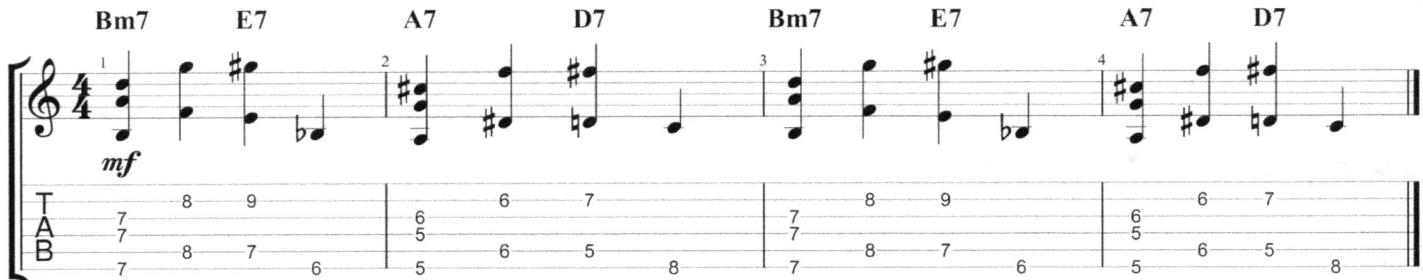

The following example is easier and played once again beginning on a Bm chord, this time at the top of the neck. Notice how I only play two notes on each chord. This tiny change helps to accent the melody and give the harmony part more space.

Example 6m:

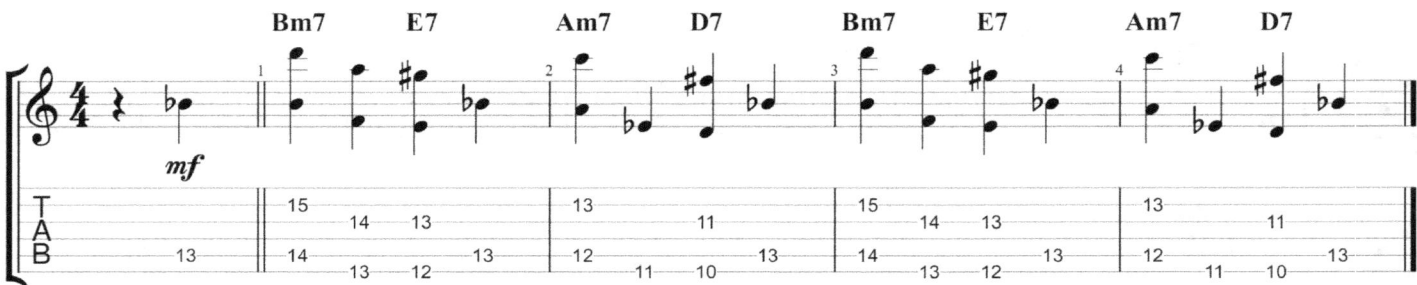

The final example in 10ths outlines the chords GMaj7, Em7, Am7 and D7, with the first three chords approached from a semitone below and all played with a root on the fifth string. The D7 is approached by a semitone above and is played off the sixth string. As you can hear, we don't need to play complex ideas to give the chords room to breathe and create additional interest.

Example 6n:

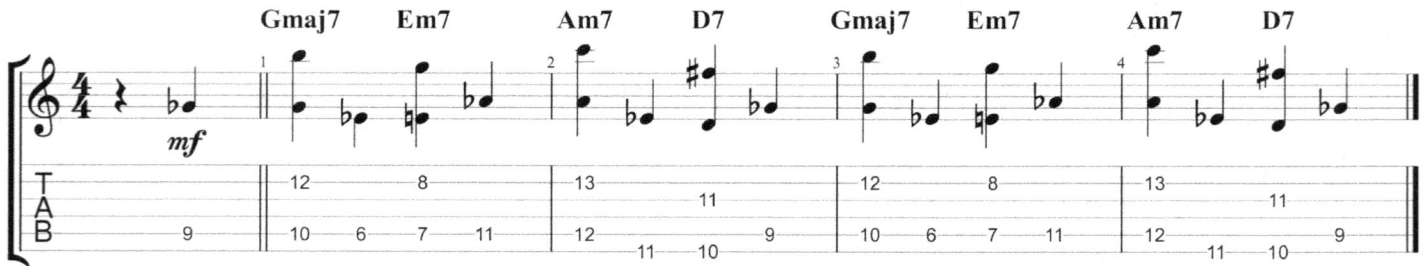

This root and tenth approach is a huge part of my chord melody playing style, so I do encourage you to check out my book *Beyond Chord Melody* which explains it in detail. However, in the context of playing a walking bassline, these voicings are yet another way you can break up the monotony of the guitar part.

Before moving on, try the following suggestion.

Plan out your entire walking bass part covering 32 or even 64 bars. Use some tablature and jot down the root notes you'll use and get your "geographical" positions fixed on the guitar. Then, above each four- or eight-bar phrase, write down which texture or rhythm you're going to use. See if you can build a part from an unaccompanied bassline, right up to a busy bass and melody part, and then bring it back down again.

The textures and rhythms we have covered are:

- Walking bass only
- Every bass note harmonised on the beat
- Only target chords harmonised on the beat with a walking bassline
- Every bass note with a syncopated chord
- Only target chords harmonised with syncopated chords and a walking bassline
- Harmonising with just roots and 10ths
- Playing in fours
- Playing in twos
- Playing with a pick to imitate brushes on the drums
- Loud Bass / Quiet Chords
- Quiet Bass / Loud Chords

Many of the items on the above list can be combined, so you should never be short of ideas. Grab a blank piece of paper and compose your walking bass part, learn it, then compose another one. Gradually, all of the ideas will become internalised and you will be able to improvise these parts unconsciously.

We're going to add a few more ideas into the mix in the next chapter, so make sure you're solid on these ones before moving on.

Chapter Seven – Jazz Skips

In this chapter, I'm going to teach you two beautiful rhythmic variations that I use when playing walking bass: jazz bass skips and picking thumb flicks.

Jazz bass skips are the one rhythmic idea I'm *always* asked about when I teach walking basslines. They are a specific triplet rhythm idea that upright bass players often add to their lines to create great groove and interest. They sound *fantastic* and, while most people think they're some sort of industry secret, the skip is actually quite simple.

The skip is a triplet *inflection* you can bring in to break up the regularity of the 1/4 note bassline. Most people think I'm doing something very clever with my note choice here, but as you will see, it's all a clever illusion! However, while the technique is uncomplicated, as with everything in music, this is all about feel. You *must* go and listen to jazz bass players and immerse yourself in the music to get that groove under your skin.

To perform a jazz bass skip, I simply add a *muted* triplet on the notes of the chord. In other words, I pick the bass note with my thumb normally, then relax the pressure with my fingers on the middle strings to mute the notes and pick them with the index and ring fingers of my picking hand.

As with learning any new skill, let's isolate the movement before reintroducing it into the turnaround chord progression.

Begin by holding down a Bm7 chord. Fret the root note normally and let the other fingers just touch the third and fourth strings to mute them. As this chord is played at the 7th fret, you might find that you accidentally create a couple of harmonic notes when you're trying to mute the strings. If this happens you'll need to press very slightly harder.

Play a triplet with your thumb, index and middle fingers as shown below. Repeat the triplet four times to complete a whole bar. Listen carefully – the bass note should sound normally and the middle strings should be muted. Adjust your hand if you start hearing harmonics. Loop this until you get it right.

Example 7a:

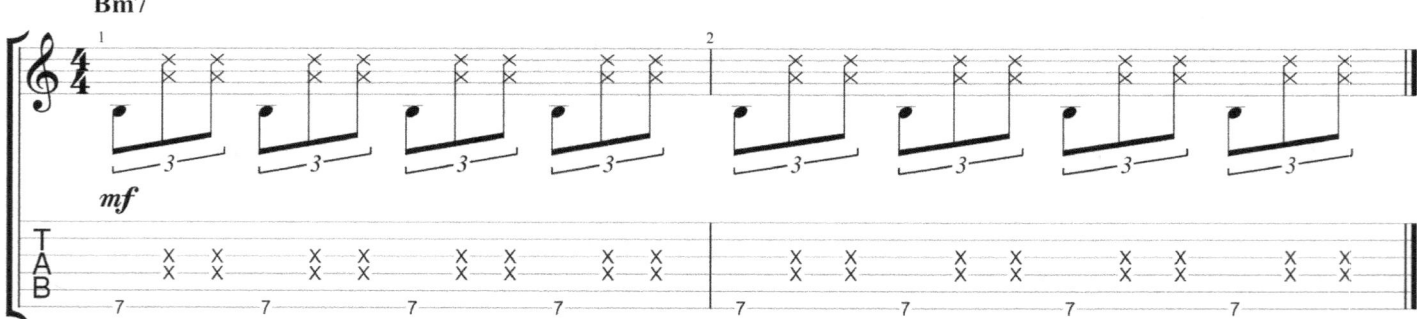

When you've got that down, let's learn how to move to the E7 chord via a chromatic F7. For now, the F7 and E7 chord ring for a full beat. Repeat this until it's comfortable.

Example 7b:

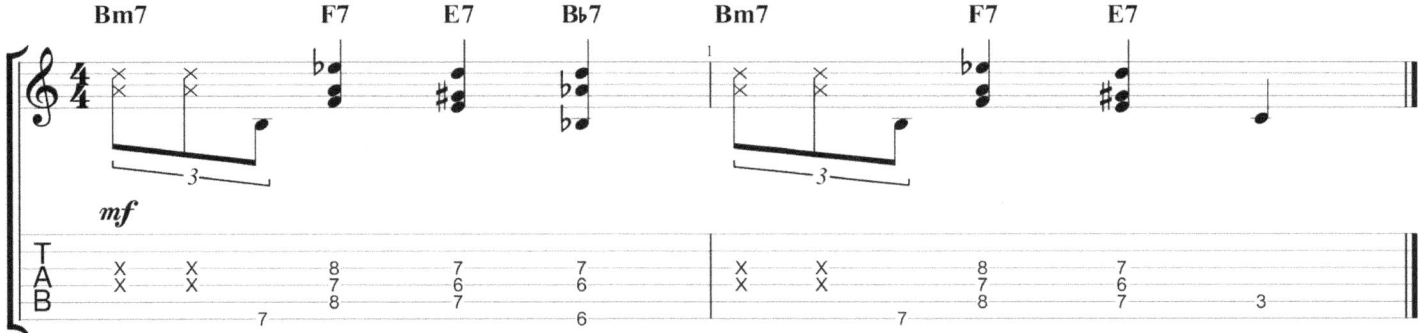

Next, play the same thing, but add the skip to the E7 chord and continue to play Bb7 immediately after.

Example 7c:

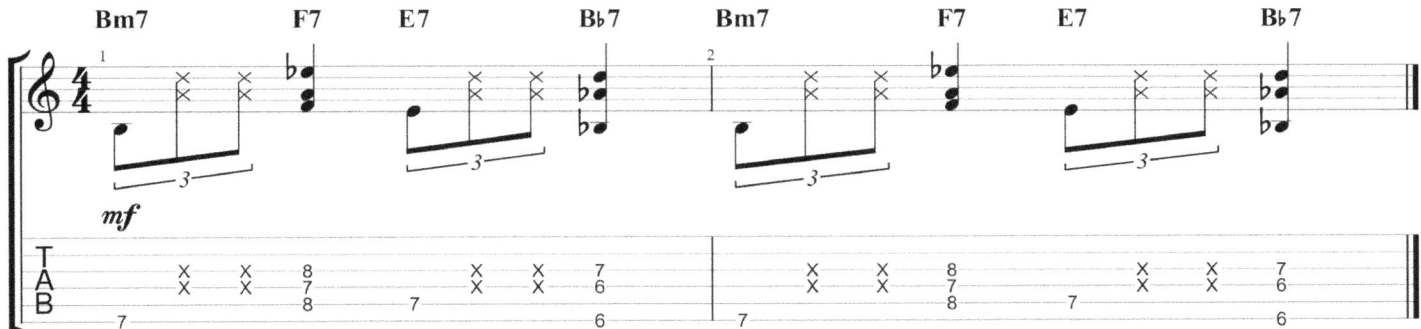

Now you're ready to take that pattern through the whole turnaround sequence. Play a muted triplet skip on each of the target chords, and play the approach chords as sustained 1/4 notes.

Example 7d:

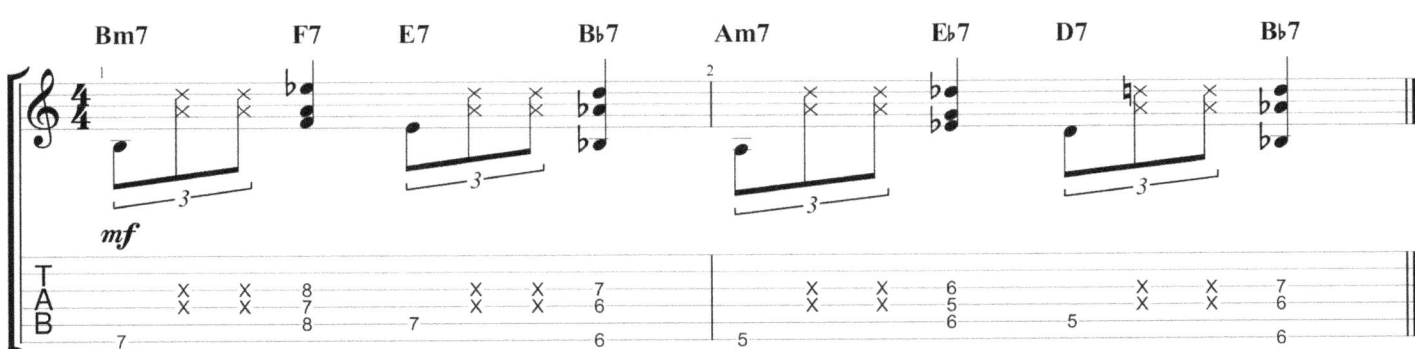

The previous few examples will help you master the feel of the triplet skip. Of course, we are overplaying it at the moment, to really internalise the technique. Soon we'll make these ideas sounds much more tasteful, but first let's try placing the skip in some different places.

First however, I want to introduce you to a picking technique I use when the music is too fast for the "Thumb and muted middle string" muted skips we used in the previous four examples. I frequently play the triplet as "thumb middle-strings thumb". The first bass note of the triplet is played normally, then the middle strings and final (thumbed) bass note are muted. We will use this technique for the next few examples and you will find it easier to play at speed.

In the previous example, we played the skip on the target chords. Let's now place it on the chromatic approach chords. Again, use fully held chords (no syncopation), but this time begin from G7.

Example 7e:

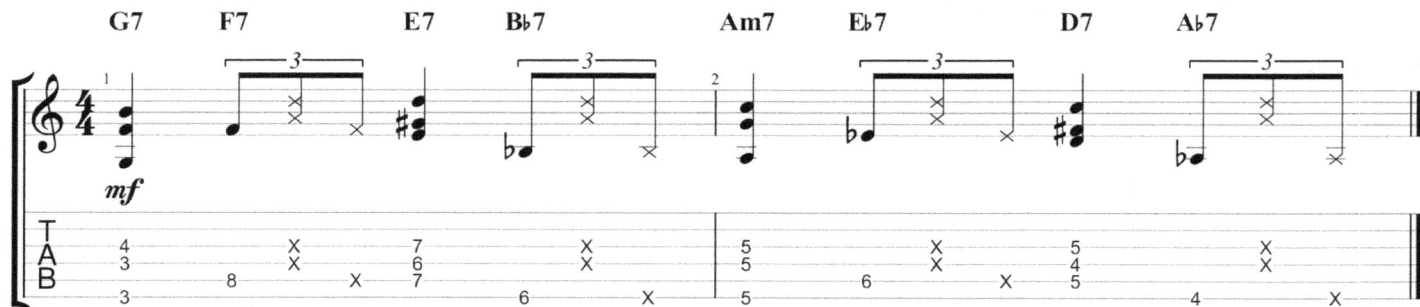

When you've got that, repeat the previous idea and reintroduce the syncopation so that all the target chords are playing on the off-beats.

Example 7f:

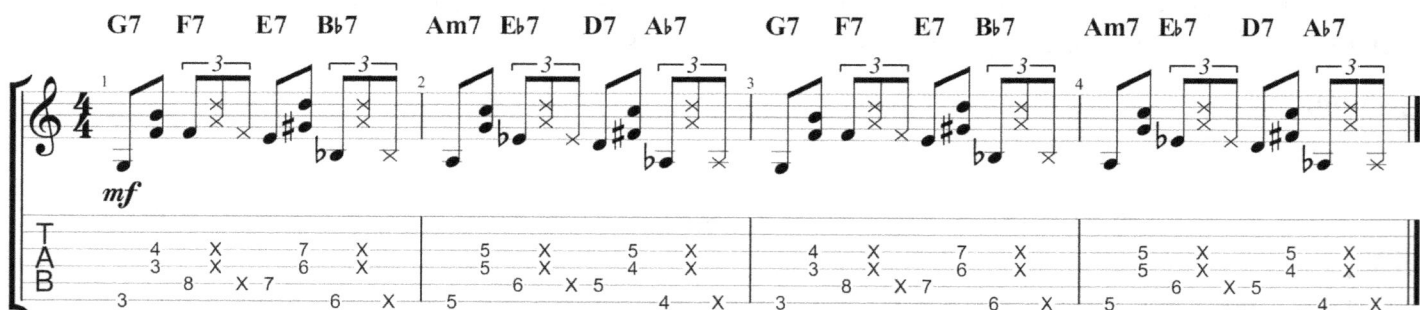

Finally, let's reverse that, so the skips are played on the target chords and the approach chords are syncopated. Play through the sequence from Bm7, and notice that this idea may feel a little more technically awkward. Ensure every bass note is consistent and has an even volume – it's easy to accidentally mute too many notes.

Example 7g:

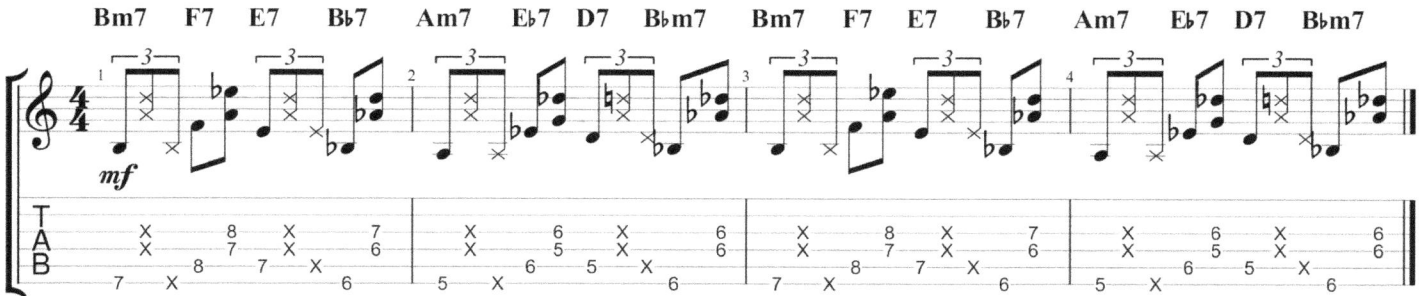

You wouldn't necessarily play the ideas in Example 7g too often, but it's a bit of a finger twister that is designed help you to focus on the clarity of the bassline. Take it slowly and pay attention.

It's also possible to play two skips in a row. In the following example, I add the skips to the Am7 and Eb7 chords before landing on the D7 chord. Practise this with and without syncopated chords on the off-beats.

Example 7h:

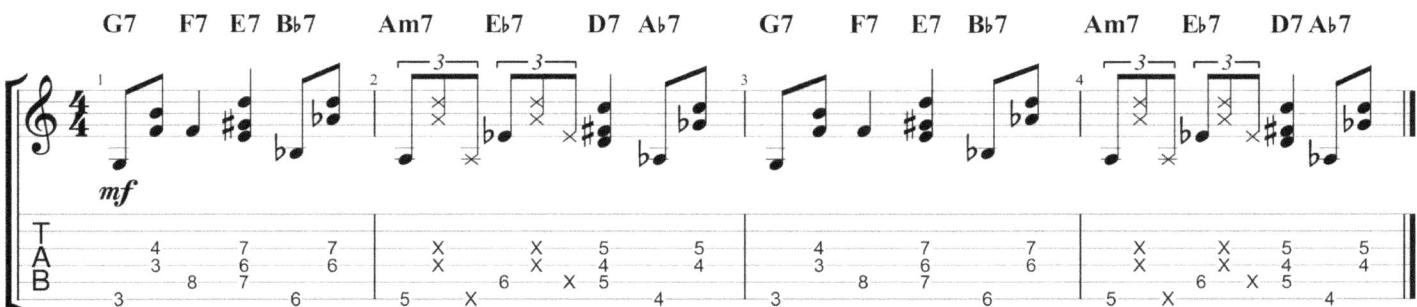

By now, you're starting to get the idea. Skips can be added at any point in the sequence to break up the rhythmic monotony of the bassline and draw in the audience. They also help to inject some energy into the rhythm part and will help to inspire the soloist.

As with most things, less is more, so don't overplay these ideas. They'll be much more effective if the listener isn't expecting them.

The following three ideas add skips to different chord textures to show you some different ways of introducing them. The first is introduced while playing an unaccompanied bassline.

Example 7i:

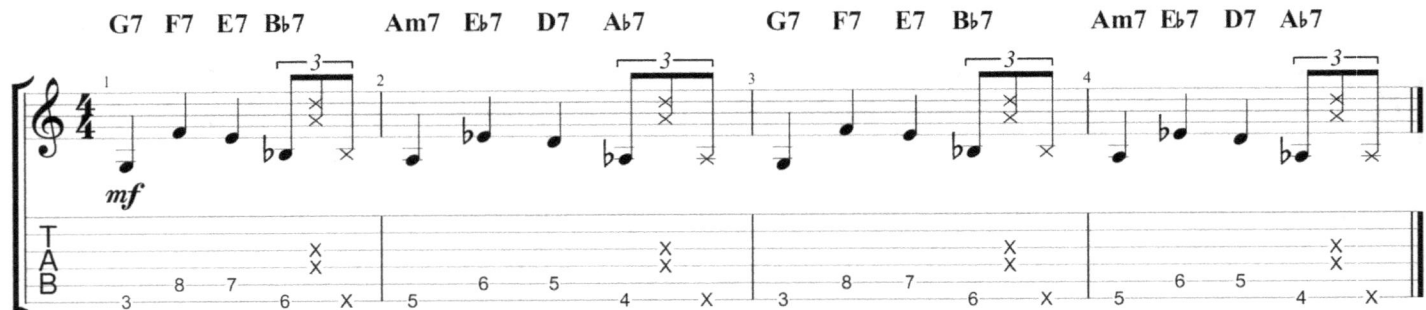

Here's an idea that's 90% bassline. I play a skip late in the sequence on the Am7 and follow it with a single syncopated chord on the D7.

This example also teaches you one final picking pattern I use to play the muted triplet skip. This time I play the first note of the triplet with my thumb, then play the second note on the muted 3rd string, and the final note on the muted 4th string. This technique is much like the way a classical guitarist would approach the technique and, when combined with the other two approaches I taught you earlier, gives you a very diverse way to approach playing walking basslines that creates a lot of subtle nuance.

Example 7j:

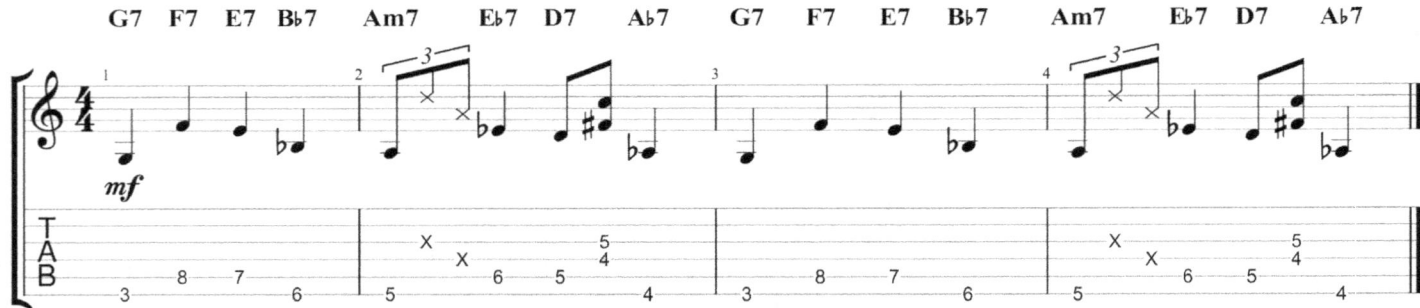

Finally, here's an idea that begins with un-syncopated chords until I add a skip on the Bb7. After that I play syncopated chords except for the isolated bassline on the note Eb. The skip helps to add a bit of energy and encourages the transition from 1/4 note to syncopated chords.

Example 7k:

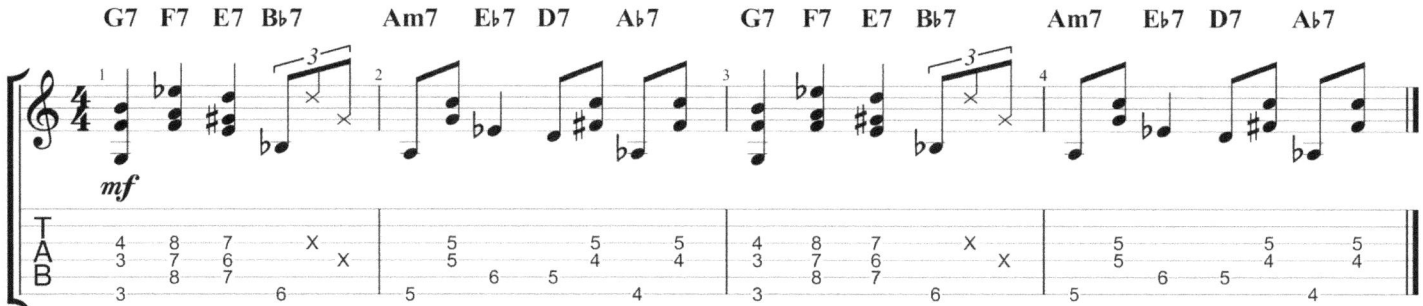

The key with all these techniques is to simply play them for hours. You need to internalise them and develop a feel for where they should be played. Listening to great musicians is the most important thing you can do, so check out the recommended listening at the end of this book. The ideas sound fairly pedestrian when you play them straight, but really come alive when you add a deep jazz swing.

Here's a 16-bar example of me playing these ideas with a strong swing. Try to copy my feel as much as possible.

Example 71:

In the next section, we'll look at a technique that seems to be unique to my style and is an effective way to add more percussive rhythm and melody to walking basslines.

Chapter Eight – Thumb Flicks

If you've played any fingerstyle or classical guitar, you'll probably have been told that you shouldn't ever play an upstroke with the picking thumb. Well, I'm going to teach you how to break that rule right now! I've been doing these thumb flicks for years and it's become an integral part of my sound.

All it involves is a little upward flick of the thumb onto a muted string to create a percussive effect, just before landing on a properly fretted note. It helps a lot if you have a bit of thumb nail, as you'll be able to dig into the strings a little more and create a real "snap" sound.

To learn this technique, listen to Example 8a before playing it. Play the G at the 10th fret and the F at the 8th fret normally, but before playing the E, relax the fingers of the fretting hand to mute the 8th fret, and flick your thumbnail upwards into the 5th string.

This works better if your picking fingers are pointing slightly into the guitar, like a classical guitar player. If you have a flat wrist, like a rock guitarist you may struggle a bit.

Example 8a:

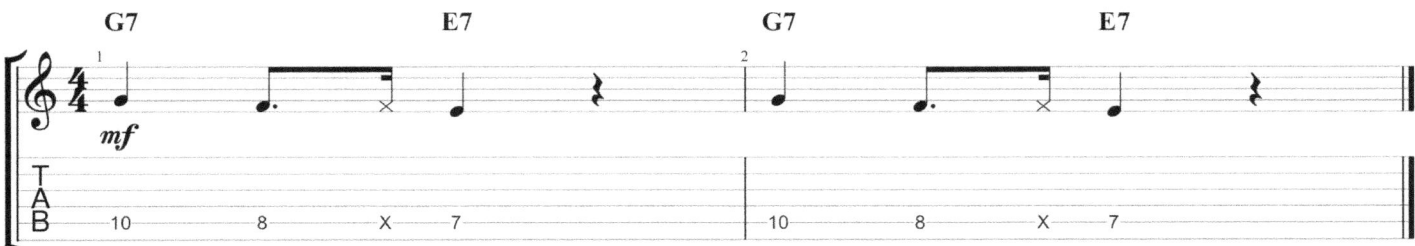

Now add the flick after all three of the notes.

Example 8b:

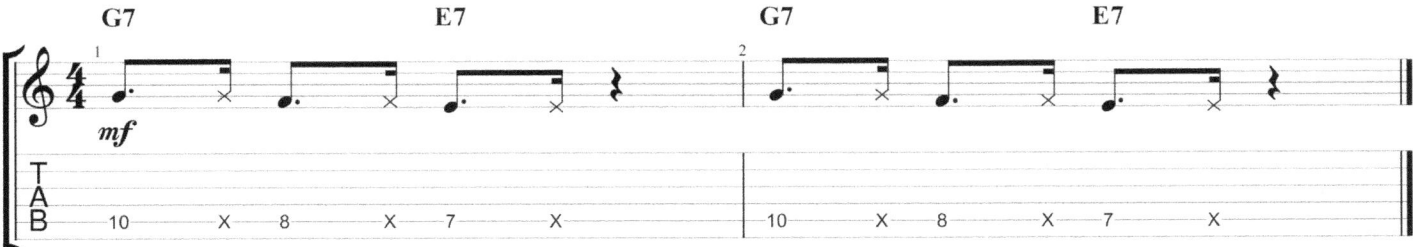

Expand the exercise and play the thumb flick before every bass note in the sequence. Don't add chords just yet, stick to the solo bassline.

Example 8c:

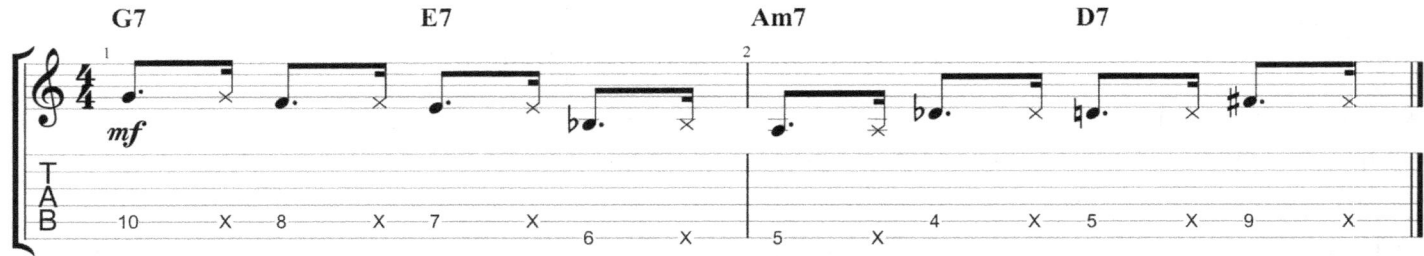

Before moving on, try the exercise again, but this time only play the flick after a target chord tone. i.e., after G, E, A then D.

Example 8d:

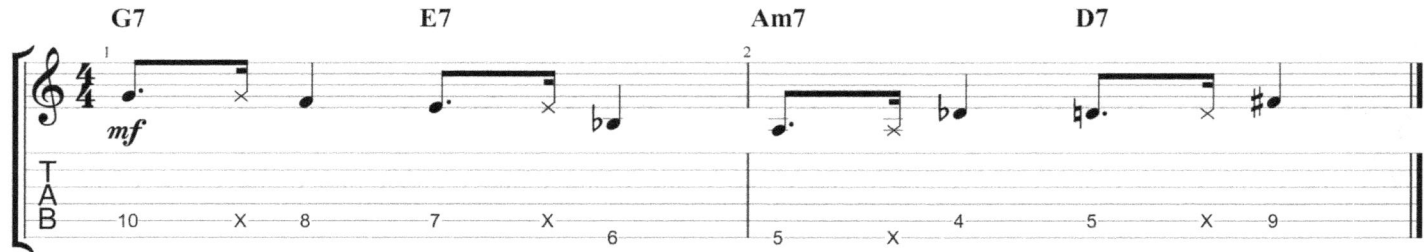

You'll notice that if you need to change string from the fifth to the sixth after playing a flick, it can be a bit of a challenge. The answer is to flick your thumb far enough so that it actually crosses the sixth string to leave you in position to play the bass note with a down pick. It also helps to keep your thumb very loose.

To help relax your thumb, place the fingertips of your picking hand on the higher strings, and see how fast you can "tickle" the sixth string with the nail of your thumb. The more you relax, the faster and louder you'll be able to play.

Now you've got the hang of the flick, let's add the chords back in. In the following example I play straight chords (no syncopation) on the G E A and D, but notice that I don't harmonise each approach note and follow it with a thumb flick, just before landing on the target chord.

Example 8e:

Example 8f is broadly similar, but now I syncopate some of the chords while keeping the thumb flicks on unaccompanied bass notes.

Example 8f:

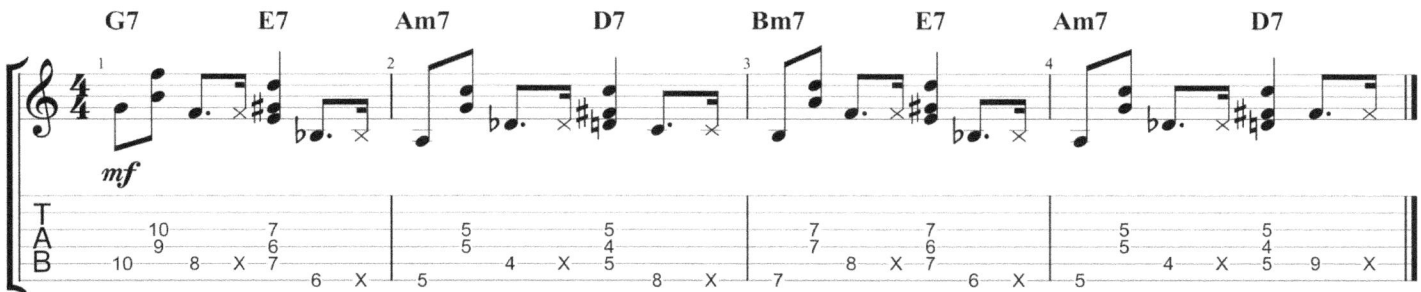

Like jazz skips, it's easy to overplay thumb flicks when you first start, but it's a tricky little thing to introduce so a bit of overplaying is probably a good thing when you first learn it. As you've discovered, there are many routes around the chord changes and many different textures you can use, so think about all the different rhythms we've covered and go back through the previous chapters to apply the occasional thumb flick where you think it's appropriate.

Just as we performed a triplet skip with the fingers in the previous chapter, we can also play it using the thumb. It feels a bit awkward at first and it's important to get the "picking direction" correct. After careful analysis, I've discovered that I nearly always play the triplet with the sequence "down up down" and play another down pick to land on the beat of the following bass note.

This is easier to show in a notated example, so pay careful attention to the picking directions below and listen closely to the feel of the audio track.

Example 8g:

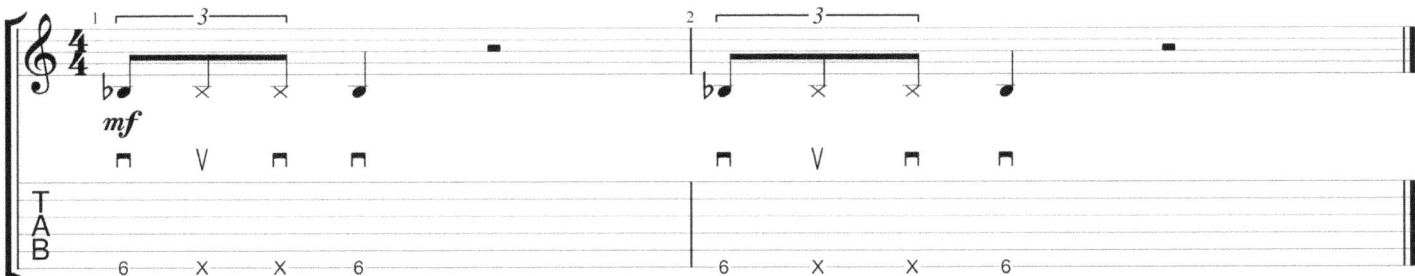

It's important that you always play the note on the beat with a down pick, so even if the picking suggestion above doesn't work for you, make sure you land on a down stroke when you come out of the triplet.

Try adding the triplet thumb skip to the notes E and D in the I VI II V progression. Pay attention to your picking.

Example 8h:

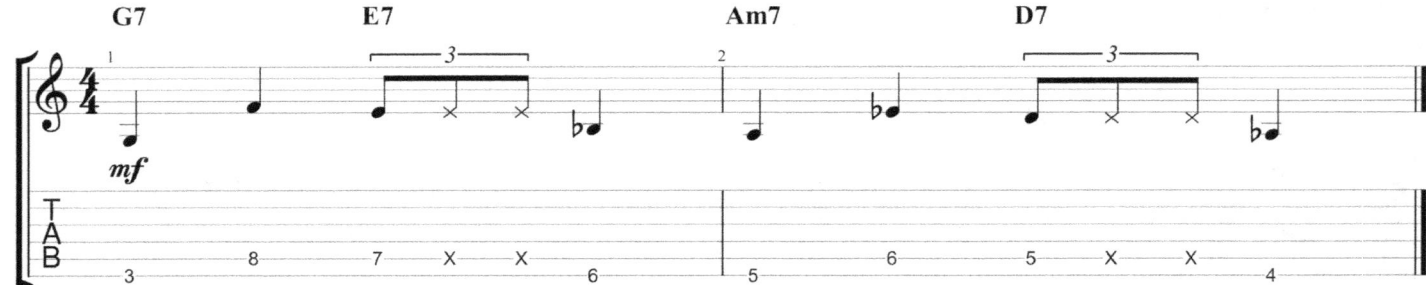

An advanced idea you might like to try is to combine the thumb flick with the triplet skip in the picking fingers from the previous chapter. Here are three ways you can approach this to get you started.

Example 8i:

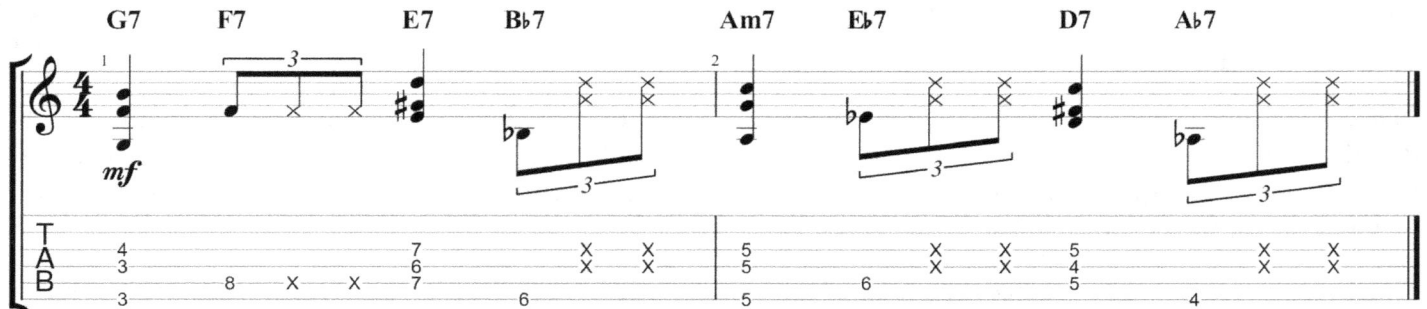

Example 8j:

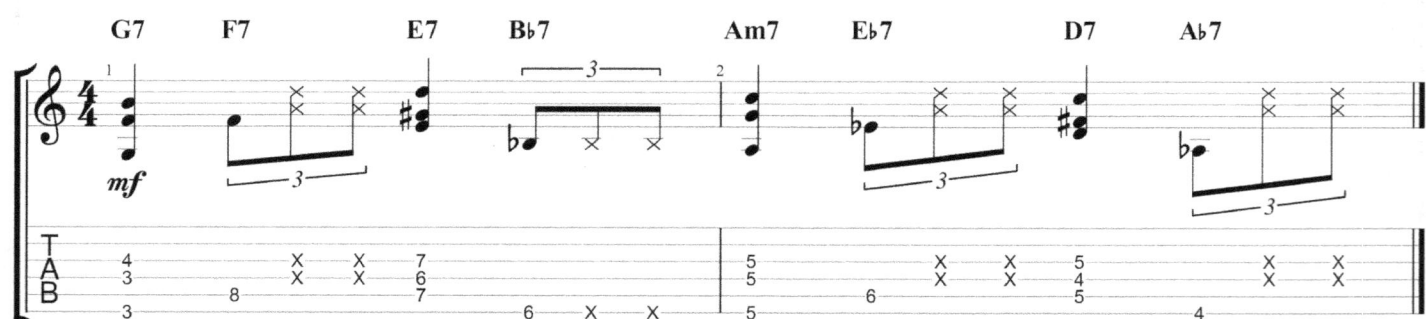

Example 8k:

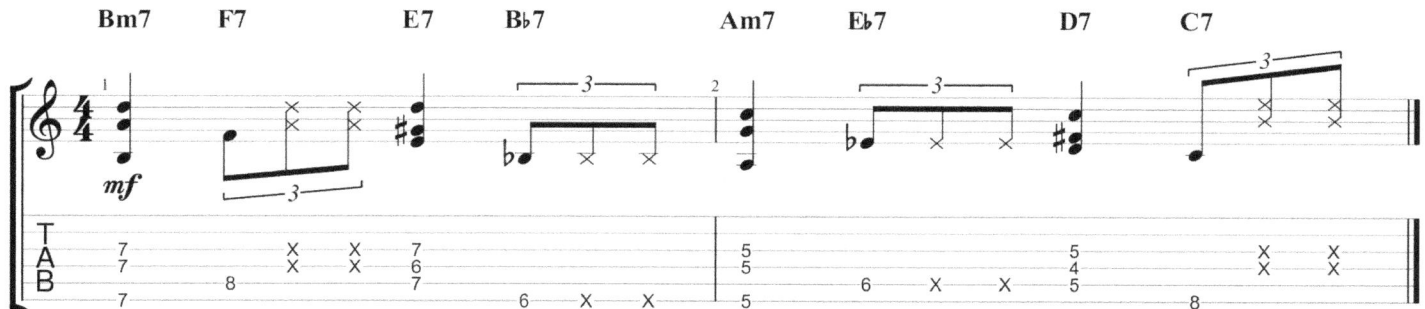

There are many different ways in which you can place these rhythmic ideas, so it's important to get creative. I like to be very logical when I'm playing, so I'll cycle through where I place the triplet skips and flicks. For example, I might first play a skip on chord I and work on that for 5 minutes. Then I'll place the skip on chords I and VI and work on that. Next, I'll place a skip only on chord VI, before adding a flick before chord I.

You get the idea!

You don't need to work through every permutation, otherwise you'd spend a lifetime on this, but what you'll find is that after a few hours of focused practice, you'll simply be able to play what you hear. This is the goal for all musicians, but it does take some serious "wood-shedding"!

In the following chapter, we'll look at some new bassline patterns we can use to add a different dynamic and feel to the music.

Chapter Nine – Decorated Basslines

Until now, we've approached every target note by step in 1/4 notes, either from a semitone above or below.

In this chapter, I'll show you some patterns you can use to break up the 1/4 note rhythm and approach the target bass note in new ways. These ideas are called *chromatic approach note patterns* and are commonly used by jazz players to decorate arpeggios when they solo.

We've covered the two most common chromatic approach note patterns – the semitone from above and semitone from below – but there are many more ways to target the root note. These patterns normally contain more than one approach note, so quite often they will be played in 1/16th notes and "crammed in" the available space before the target note. To execute these faster phrases, I tend to use a thumb flick.

The first chromatic approach note pattern we'll learn is to begin one tone above the target note and descend in semitones.

Example 9a:

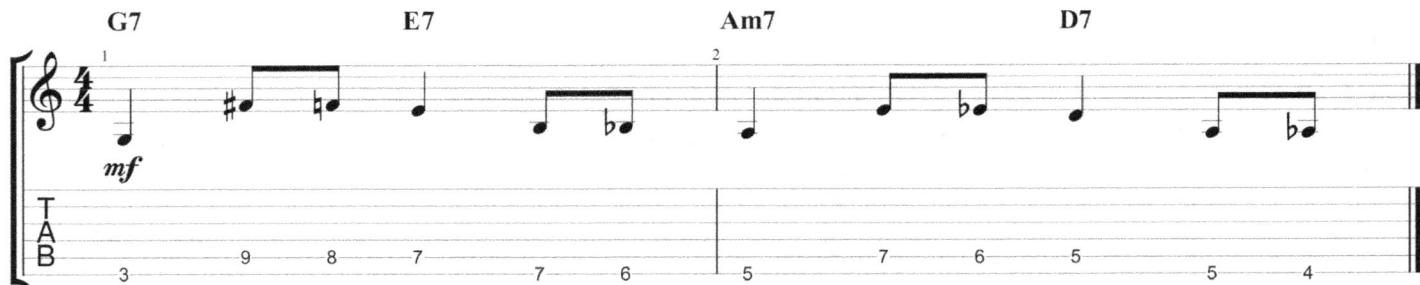

Similarly, you could ascend using the same pattern and rhythm.

Example 9b:

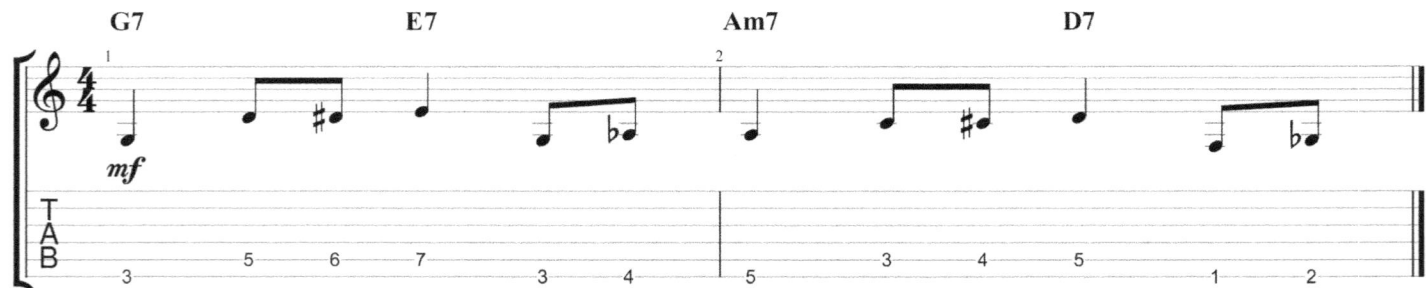

And, of course, you can combine both directions.

Example 9c:

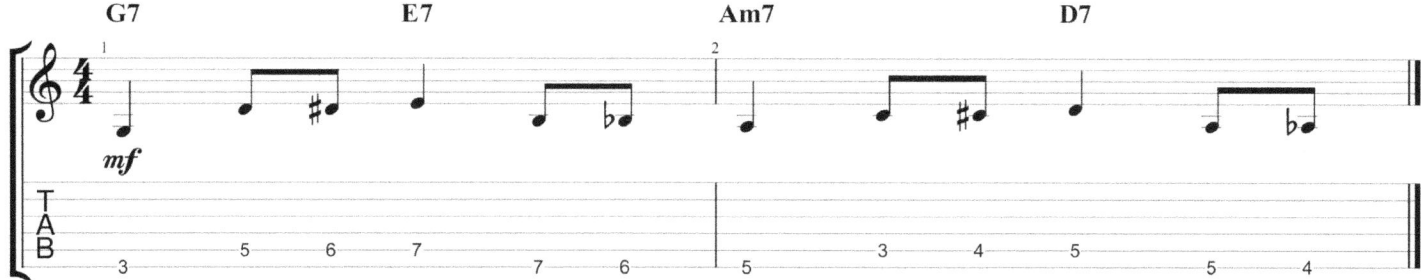

Try adding a harmonised chord to the note immediately preceding the target chord. Spend time experimenting with which notes you harmonise. You can harmonise all of them or none of them! Here's one example with ascending approach notes.

Example 9d:

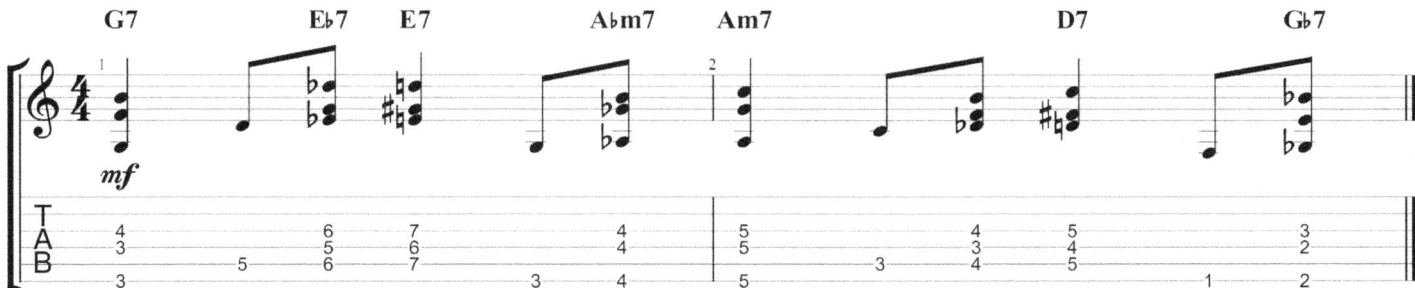

Here's a different chromatic approach note pattern that begins on the tone above the target, then moves to the semitone below, before resolving to the root. Play it first without chords:

Example 9e:

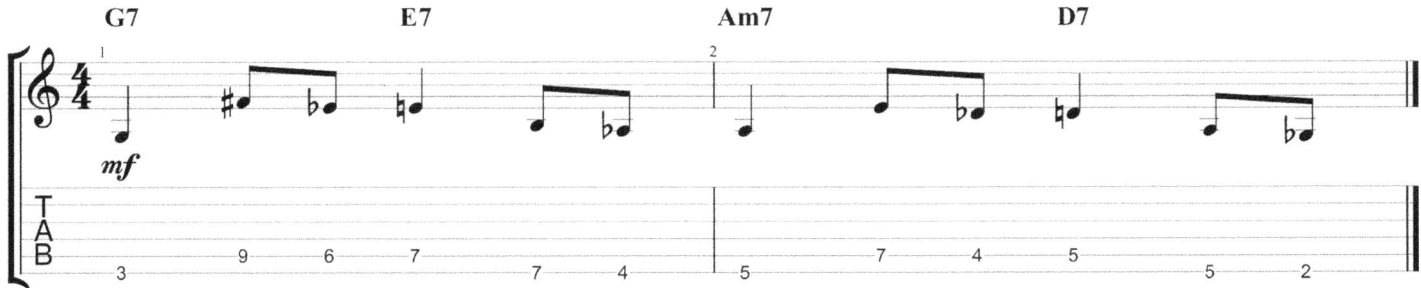

149

Now add chords on the target notes.

Example 9f:

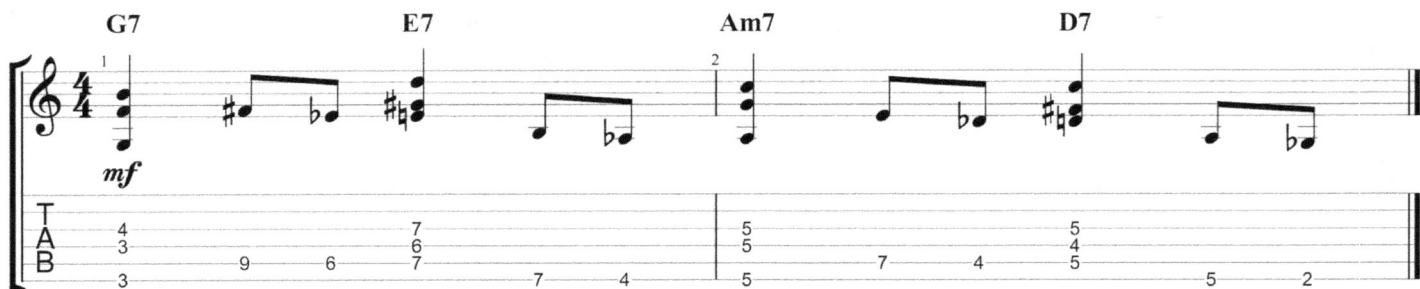

Let's reverse the pattern to play the semitone below the target note, before playing a tone above. Learn this as a solo bassline first.

Example 9g:

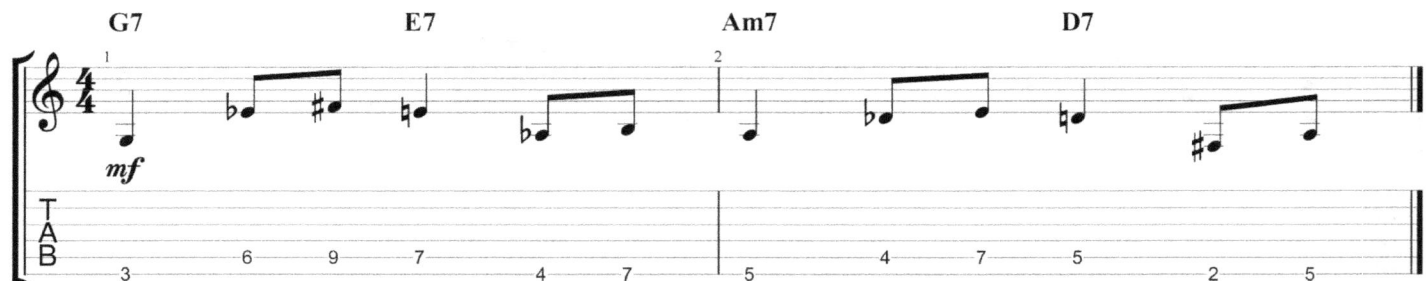

Once again, introduce the chords back into the sequence.

Example 9h:

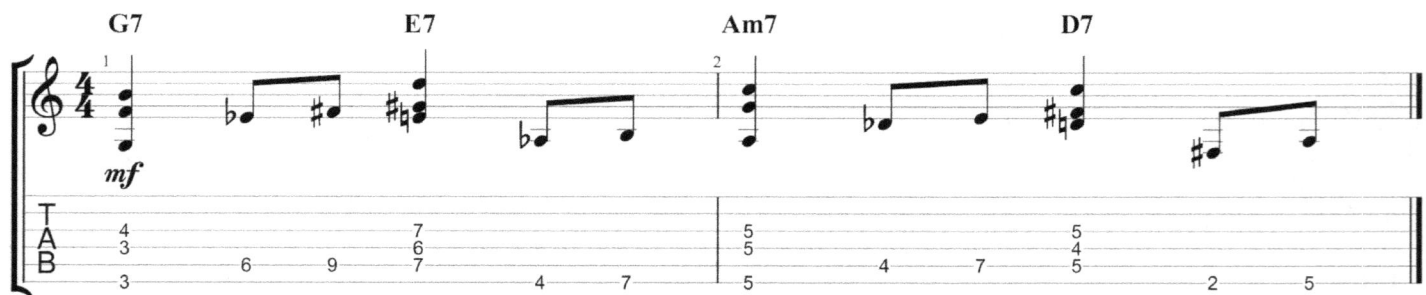

The next "level" is to play chromatic approach notes in constant 1/8th notes, and there are a couple of important patterns you should know.

The first is "tone above, semitone above, semitone below" This is easier hear and see in notation than it is to describe, so listen to the following audio track then play along. As always, learn the bassline first before adding chords.

Example 9i:

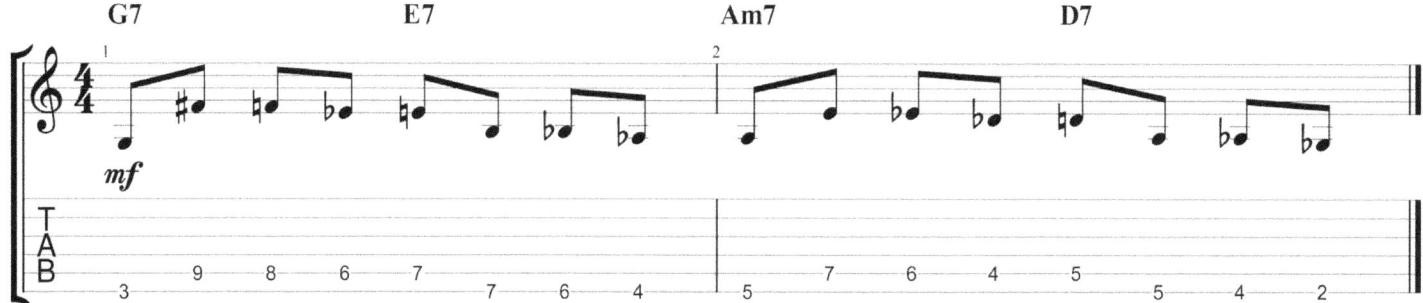

Now add the chords in appropriate spots.

Example 9j:

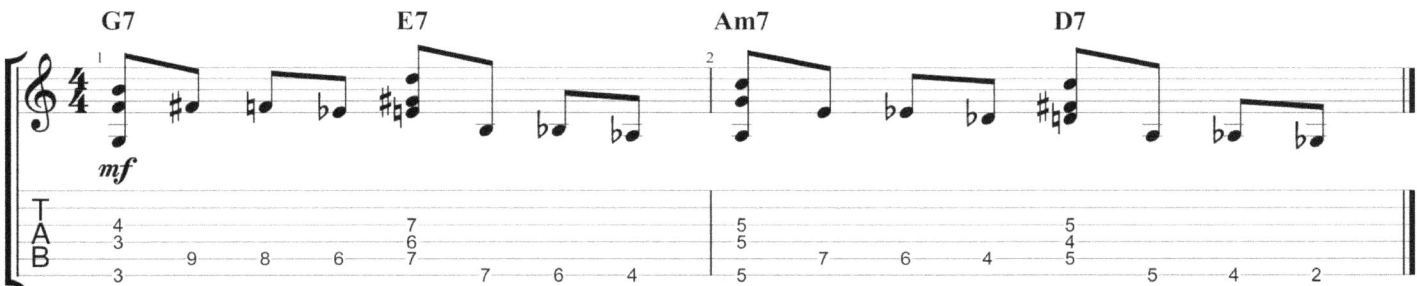

The final important pattern to know is "semitone below, tone above, semitone above". Learn it on a solo bassline before adding chords.

Example 9k:

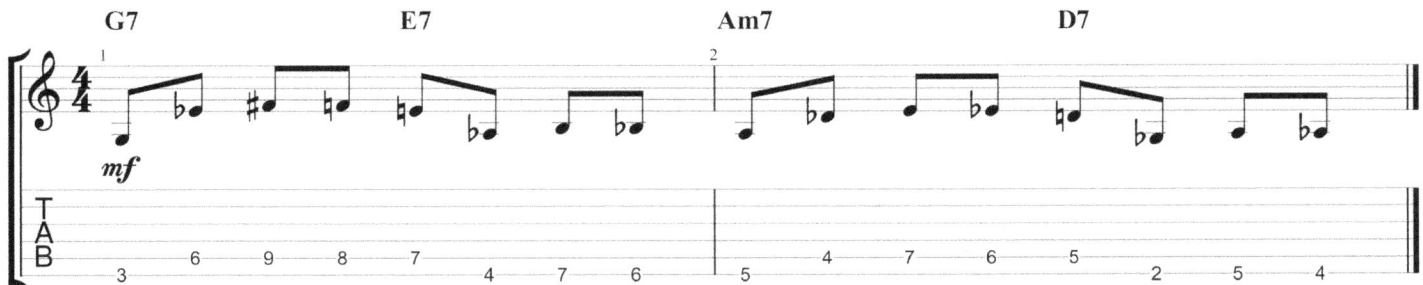

Example 9l:

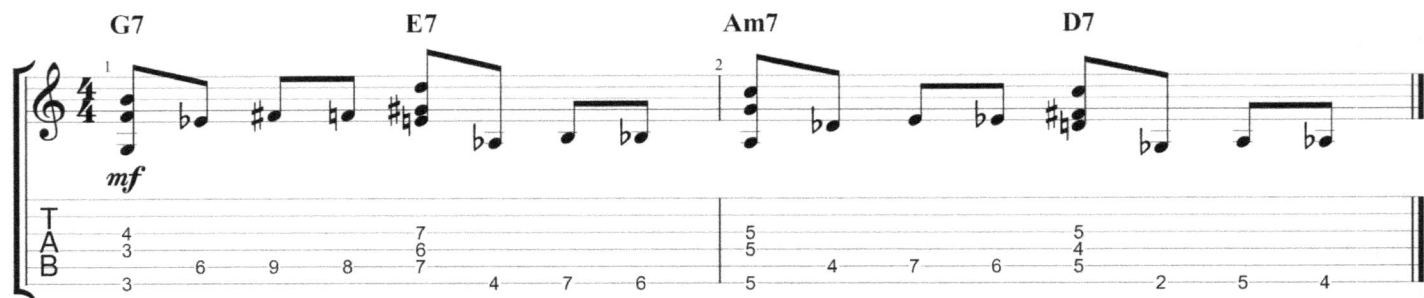

As you can probably hear, these basslines get very "busy" so it's important not to use them too often. To really make them work, it's all about adding them subtly to a bassline that is walking naturally in 1/4 notes.

In the following three examples I play standard walking basslines using both syncopated and un-syncopated chords, and occasionally I add in a chromatic approach note pattern. Notice that if I play a syncopated chord, there's no time to use a 1/8th note idea.

Example 9m:

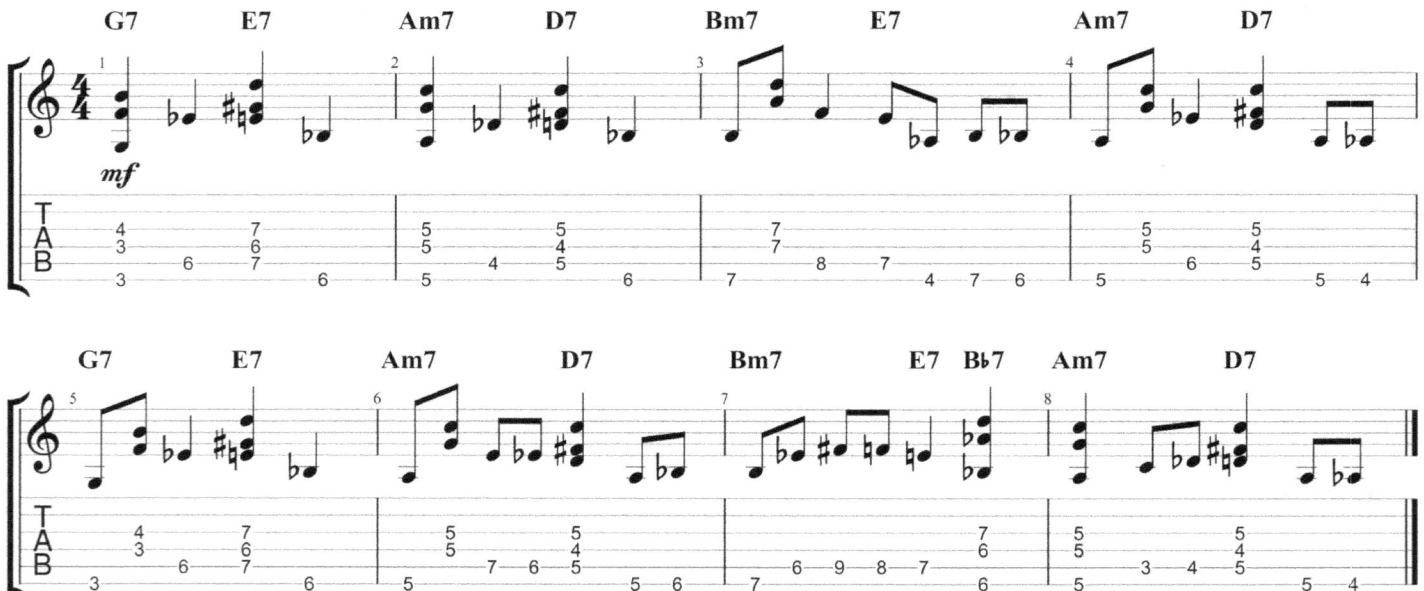

Example 9n:

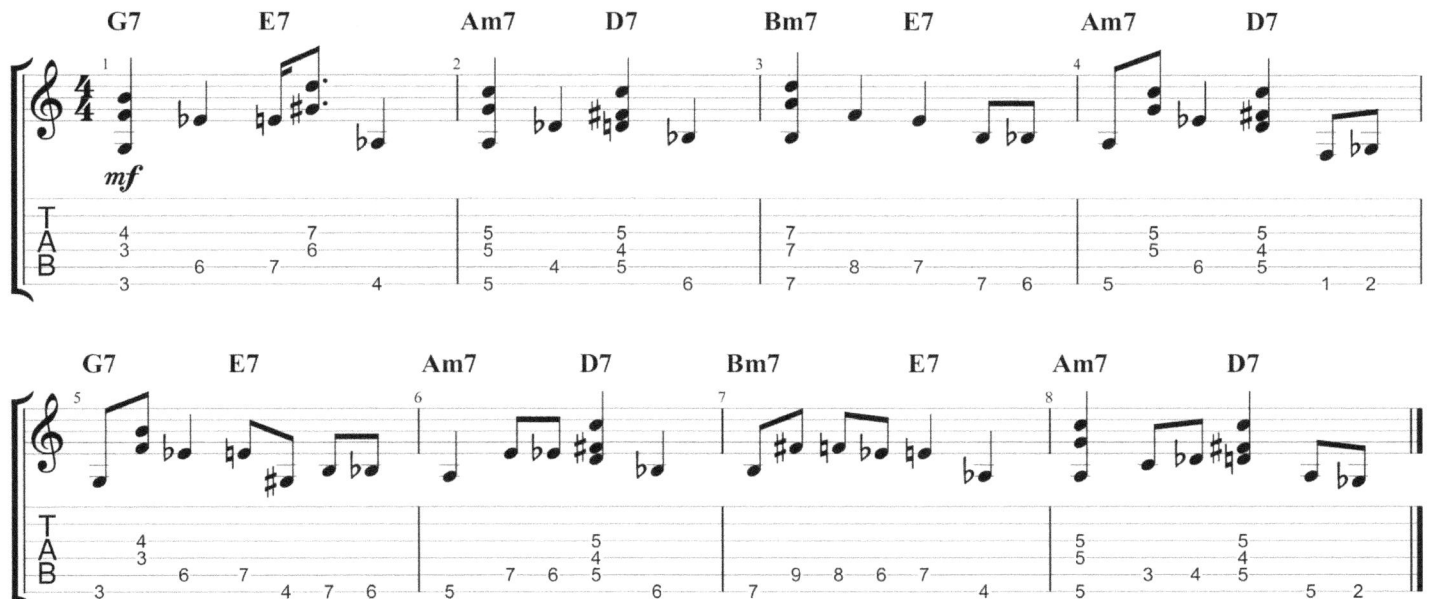

Example 9o:

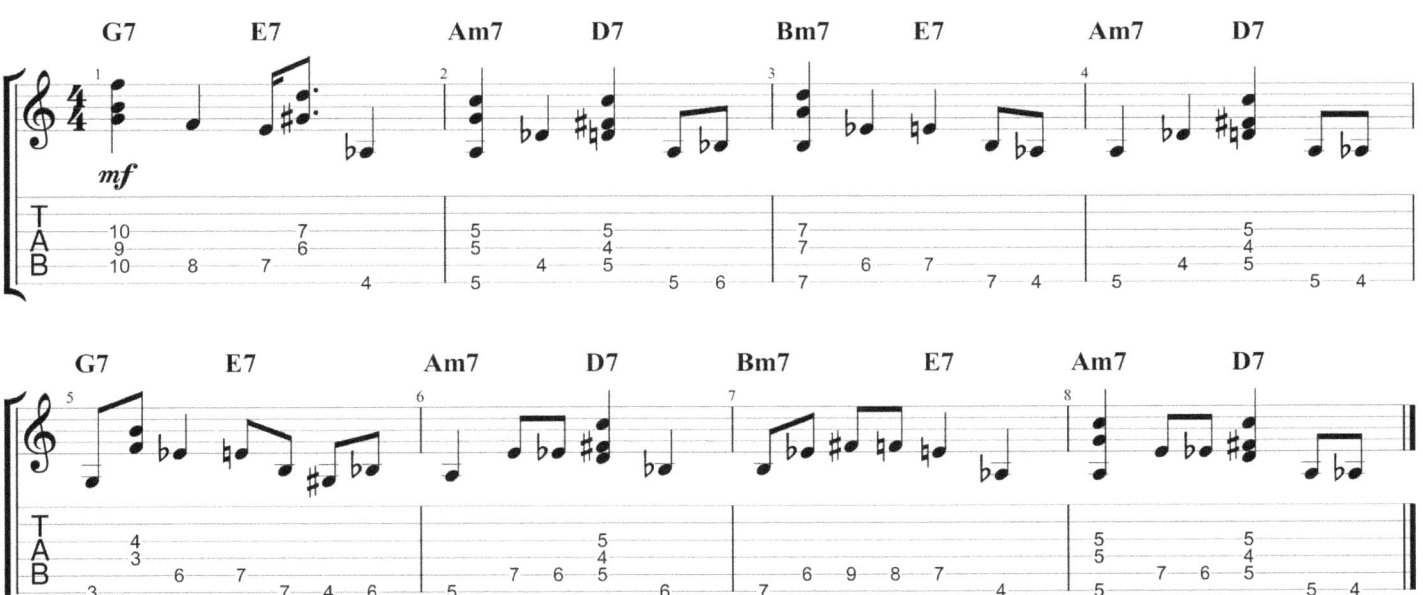

Spend time getting creative with these basslines and think carefully about the options available to you. You can play syncopated or off-beat chords, add skips and flicks, or any other technique we've covered in the book. Think about whether you will harmonise only the target chords, or whether you will harmonise the approach notes too.

While the faster chromatic approach note patterns are used as an effect when we play two chords in a bar, they are a great basis for forming walking basslines when we play chords for longer durations.

In the next chapter I will teach you some new approaches to use when we play walking bass on a chord that lasts for a whole bar.

Chapter Ten – Walking into the Bar

We're covered a lot of ground in the past nine chapters, from the basics of rhythm changes to some exciting rhythmic feels and chromatic ideas. Until now, everything has been based on playing when there are two chords in the bar. Well, what happens if there's only one chord in the bar and we need to walk for four beats?

In this chapter, I'm going to show you how to expand our ideas to cover any chord that lasts for four beats and show you some different ways to walk between some of the most important chord sequences in Jazz.

Let's begin with moving from chord I to chord IV – the first chord change in a blues. In the key of G, that's G7 to C7.

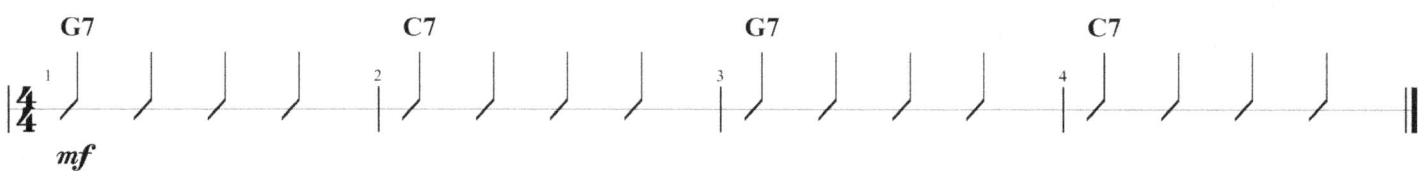

The good news is that everything we've covered so far works as we move between these chords, and the easiest way to begin is to add a chromatic "sidestep" idea to the G7, then approach the C7 by a chromatic approach note from above or below. You can play a similar idea when moving from C7 back to G7.

This is much easier to understand when you play it.

Example 10a:

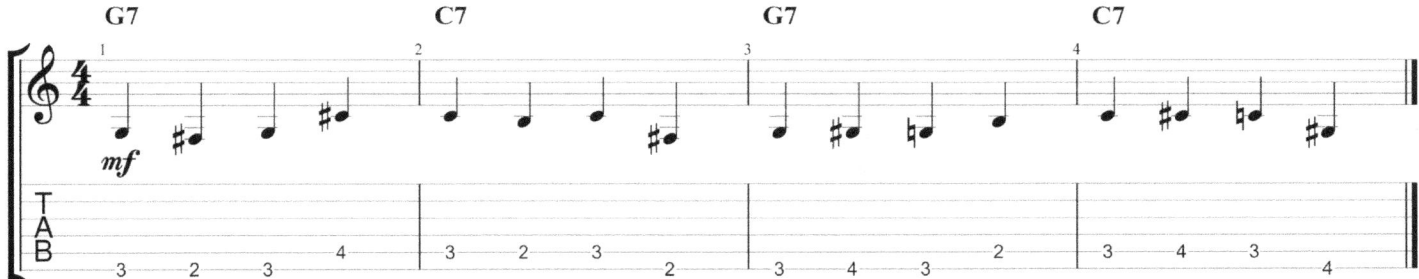

When you're confident with this idea, harmonise both the target chords and the approach notes immediately preceding them. Use the same chord quality for the approach chord as the target chord. In the first two bars I play un-syncopated chords, but in the second two I use off-beat chords.

Example 10b:

This kind of movement is the basis of playing longer walking basslines, but of course there are almost unlimited paths we can walk between just these two chords. The key to finding these lines is to listen to great bass players and copy their pathways, but to get you started I'll show you some of my favourite movements.

Notice which bass notes get harmonised and which bass notes don't. These are by no means hard and fast rules, but they should give you a good insight into my style, and the stylistic considerations of the genre in general. Joe Pass was a master of these ideas and people often think he's playing extremely complex chords while walking. However, more often than not, he's using the same three-note voicings as me. Listen carefully to his playing and watch him on YouTube. It's quite an education.

Here are a few more ways to move from G7 to C7 and back. Memorise them and come up with your own variations.

Example 10c:

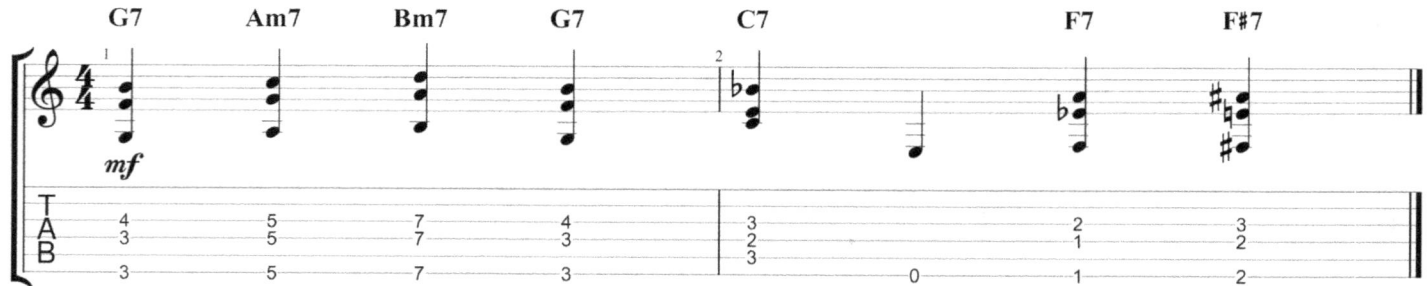

Example 10d:

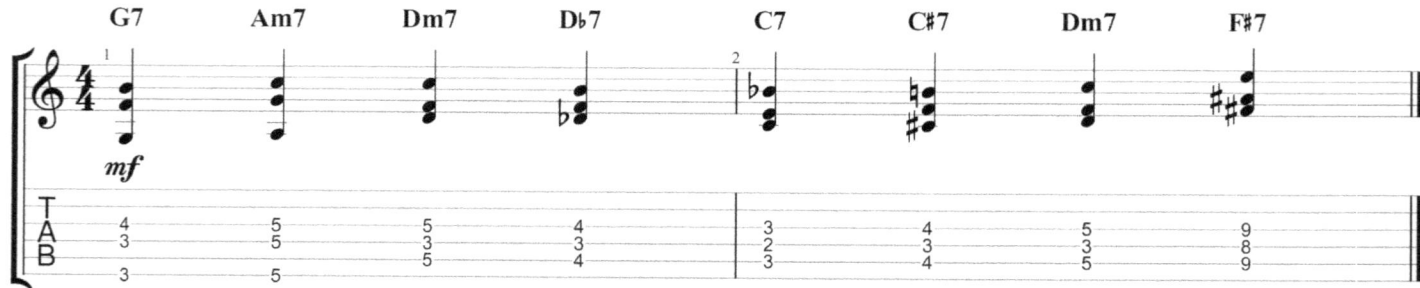

Example 10e:

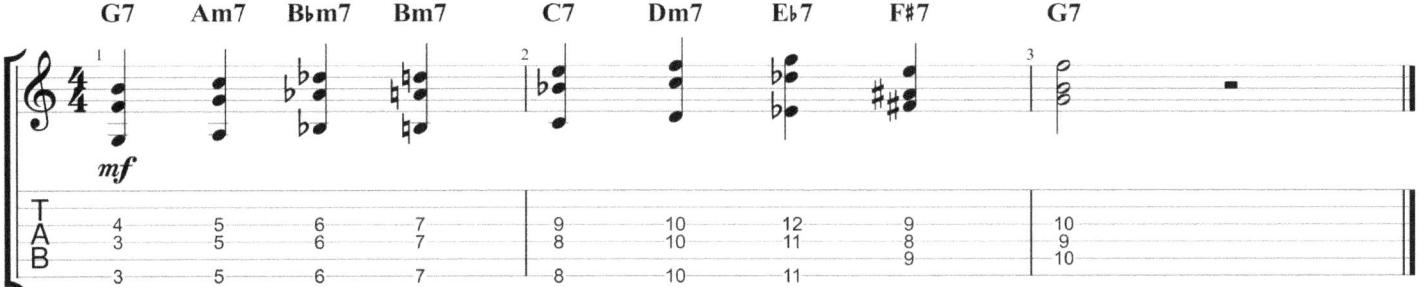

The next line is a common idea to use when you have two bars of G7. Notice how it moves to a Bm7 chord – an inversion of G7 at the beginning of the second bar.

Example 10f:

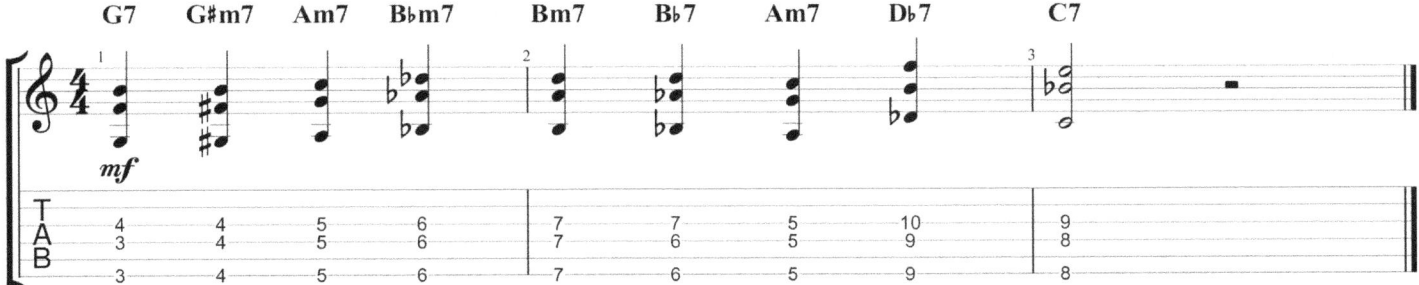

The following example shows how I like to substitute an F7 chord when I play two bars of C7 in a blues.

Example 10g:

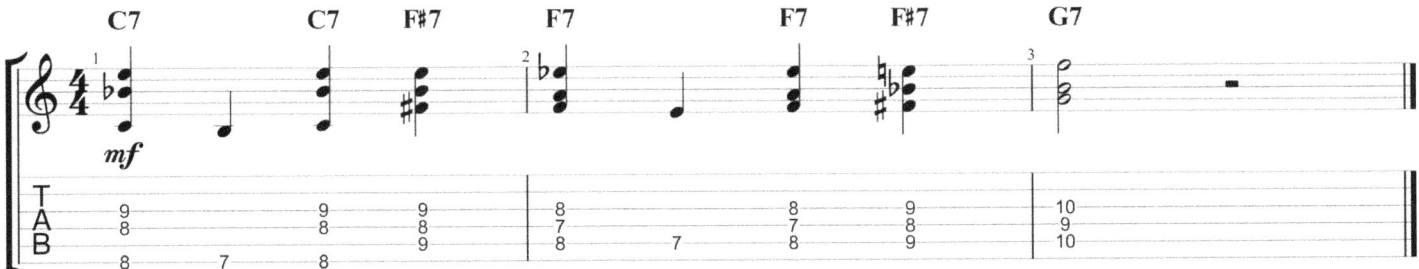

Now let's take a look at some ideas I play when tackling the "slow turnaround" section of a blues. It's the same as the I VI II V sequence we've been studying for most this book, but now each chord lasts for a whole bar.

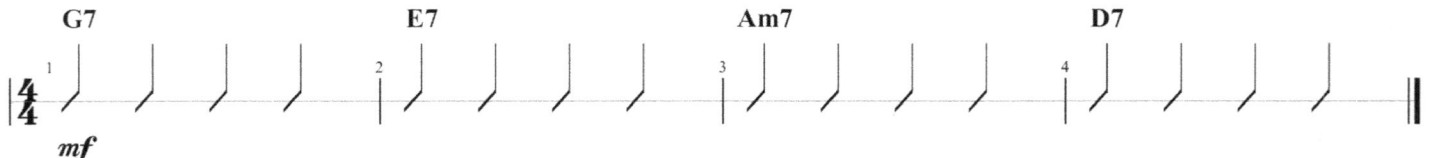

Example 10h:

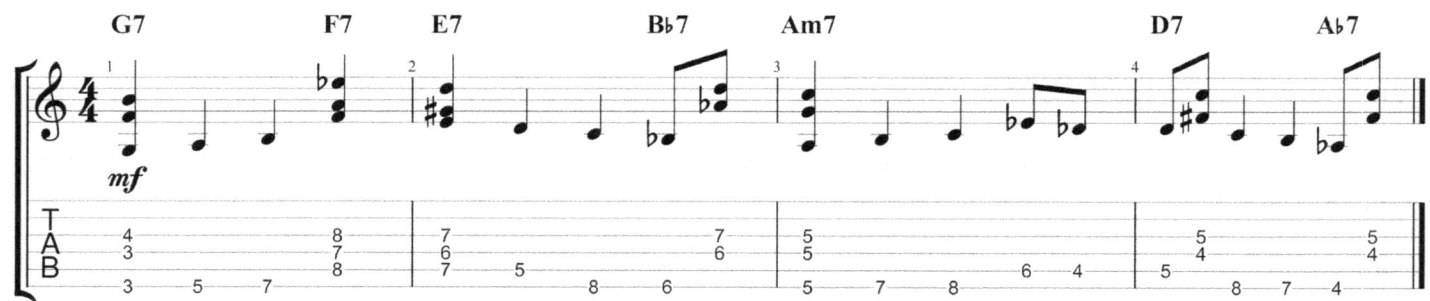

Example 10i:

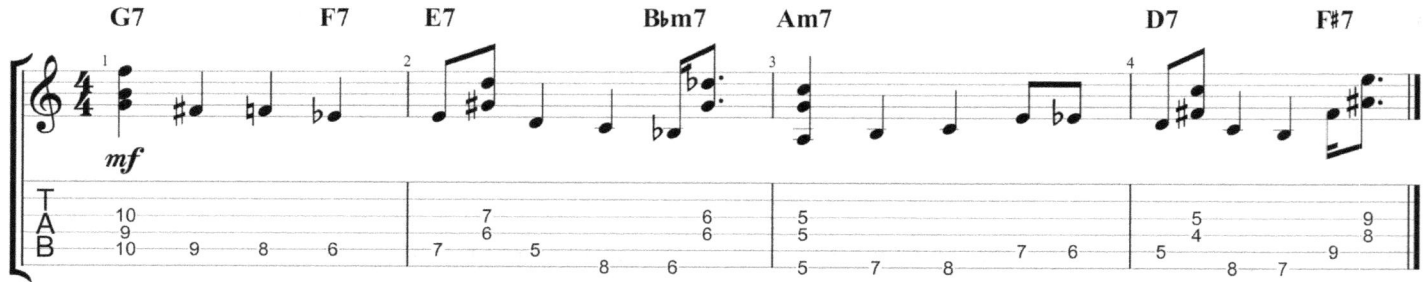

As you can see, there are limitless ways to move between one chord and another. What it really comes down to is keeping the target chord as your "goal". As long as you hit it on the right beat, then you won't go too far wrong. The rest is a combination of scale steps (normally taken from the tonic key), chromatic approach notes from above or below, and chromatic approach note patterns.

Some notes of the bassline are harmonised. If you're harmonising the chromatic approach note above or below the target chord, you'll usually harmonise the approach note with the same chord *quality* as the target.

When harmonising a scale step, you'll normally use the appropriate chord from the harmonised parent scale. For example, in the key of G Major, the chords are

GMaj7, Am7, Bm7, CMaj7, D7, Em7 and F#m7b5.

However, as we've seen, almost any of those chords can have their quality altered. For example, GMaj7 is often played as G7 and Am is often played as A7. Keep experimenting and listening to great jazz so that your ears begin to guide you.

The best way to learn these skills is to write out a bassline for your tune in advance and try harmonising different bass notes. If you try a minor 7 chord and it doesn't work, try a dominant 7. As I have stressed throughout this book, the only real answer is to listen to the great jazz musicians like Joe Pass, Bill Evans and all the bass players I've mentioned, and listen closely to how they do it. Borrow (steal) their basslines and see how you can harmonise them.

Of course, there are some walking basslines that are tried and tested, which have become part of the jazz guitarist's arsenal of licks. These are a great starting point and will help to teach you what a good bassline should sound and feel like. We learn to speak a new language by using stock phrases to begin with, and the same is true in music.

In the next three chapters, I've transcribed three recordings of my playing. The first is a *rhythm changes* sequence (like *Oleo* or *I Got Rhythm*), the second is a jazz blues (such as *Blue Monk*), and the third is me playing the chord changes to *All the Things You Are* to show how this technique can be applied to any jazz standard. Each piece contains sections with one chord per bar. I want you to learn them and see how I tackle each one. You'll learn more from this than I can possibly show you by giving you hundreds of isolated options.

I've recorded two choruses of each tune, and the first time through I keep things simple. On the repeat, I throw the kitchen sink at it and go to town. Please take my ideas and analyse them to see how they work.

Good luck on the journey!

Martin and Joseph.

Chapter Eleven – Jazz Blues

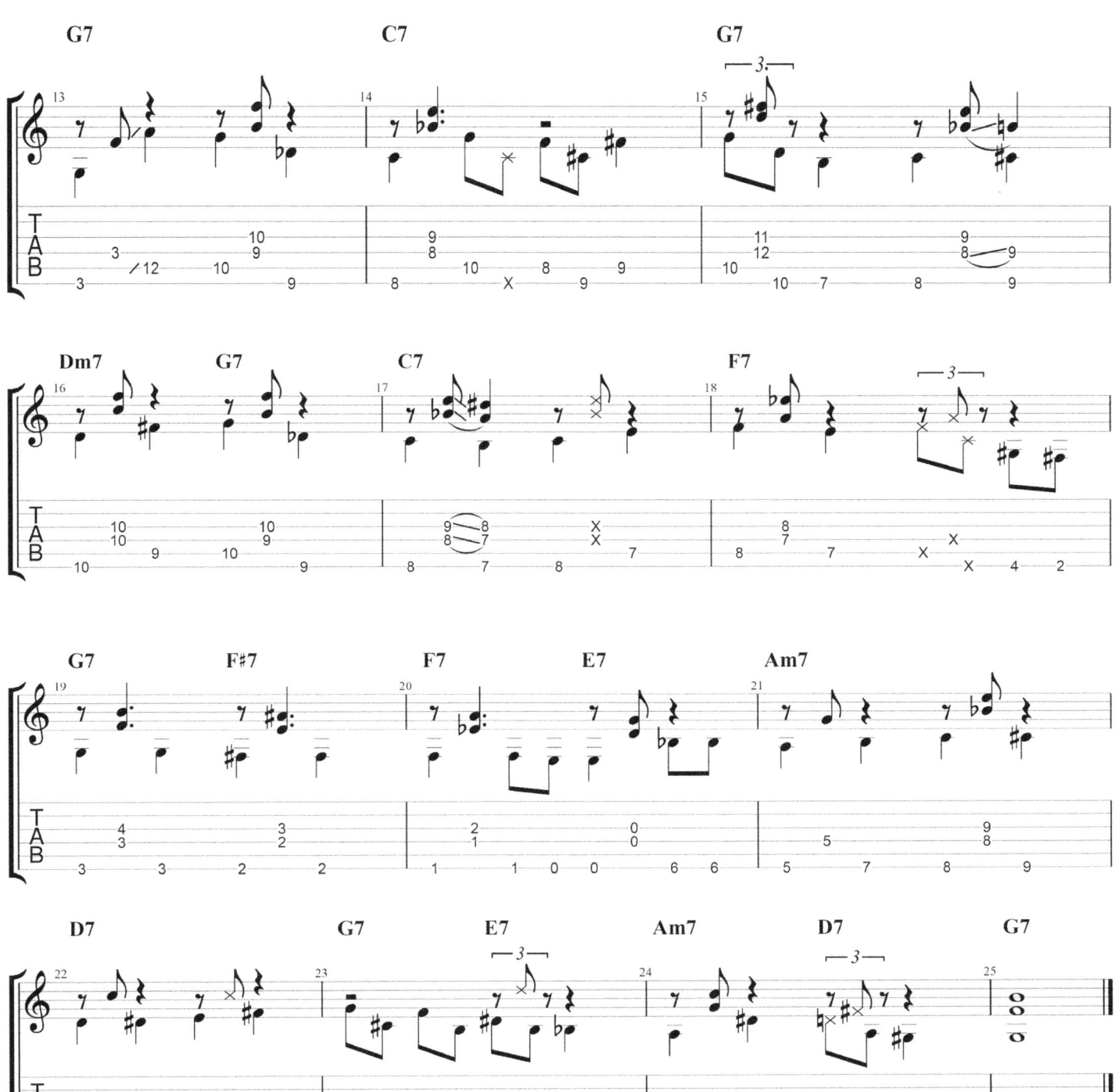

Chapter Twelve – Autumn Leavers

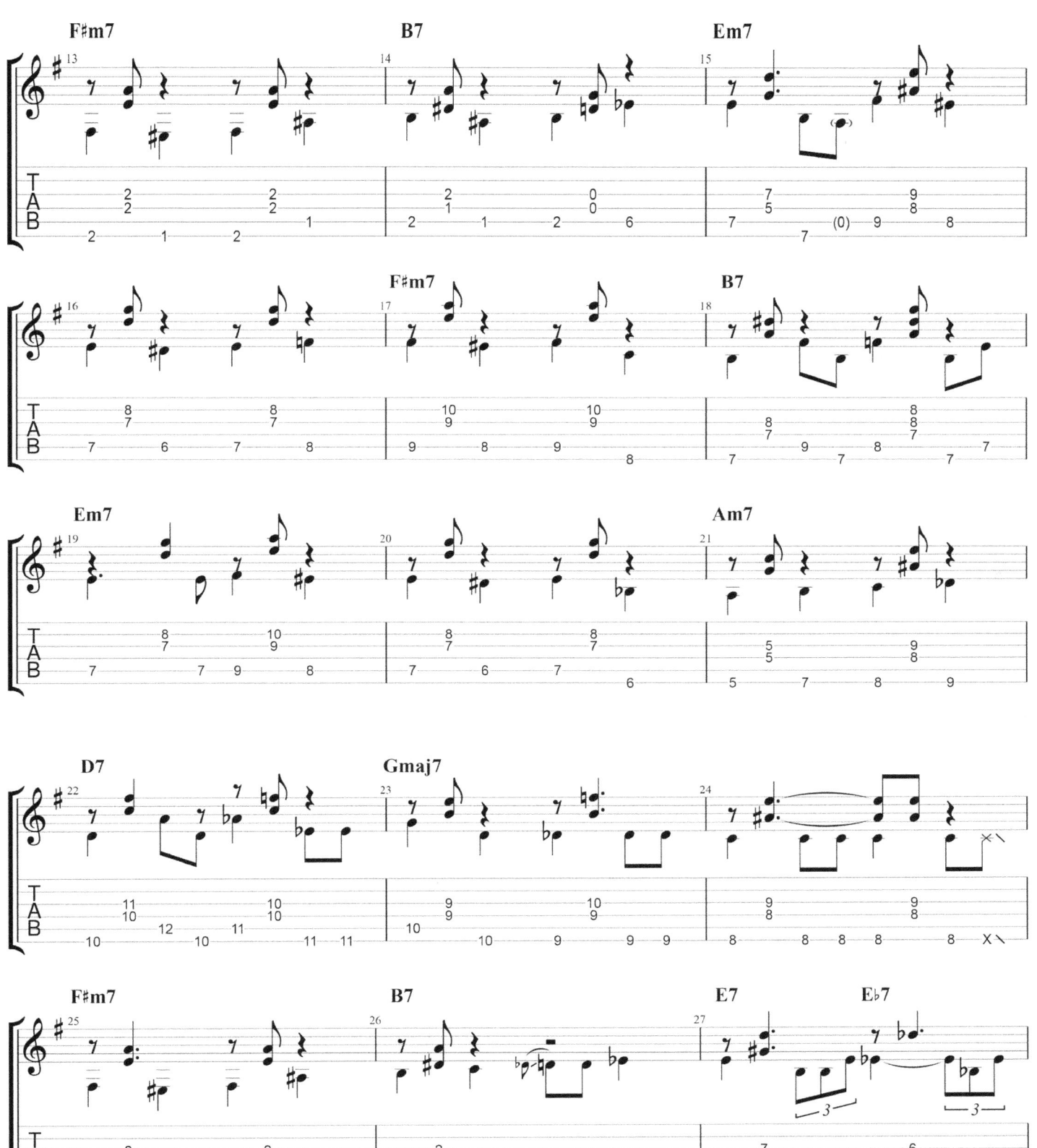

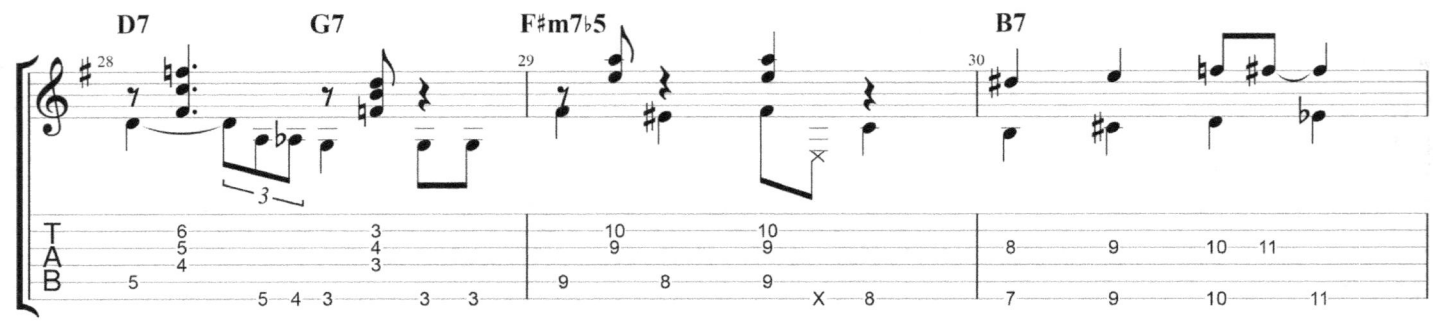
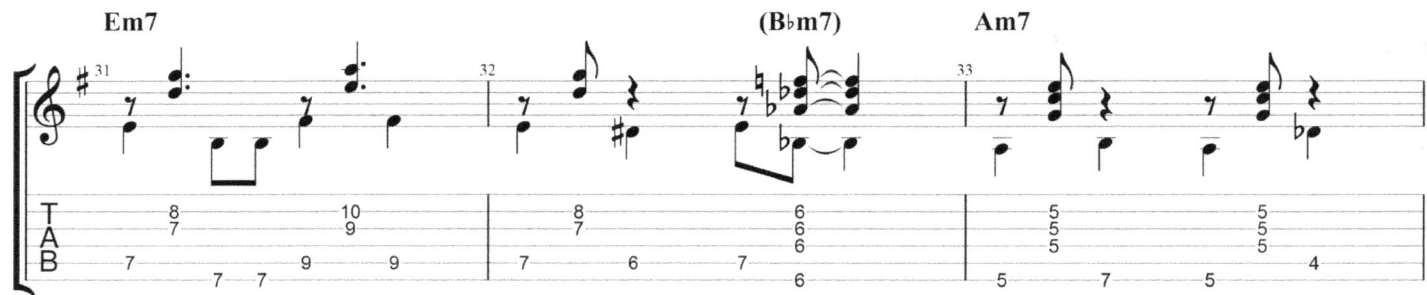
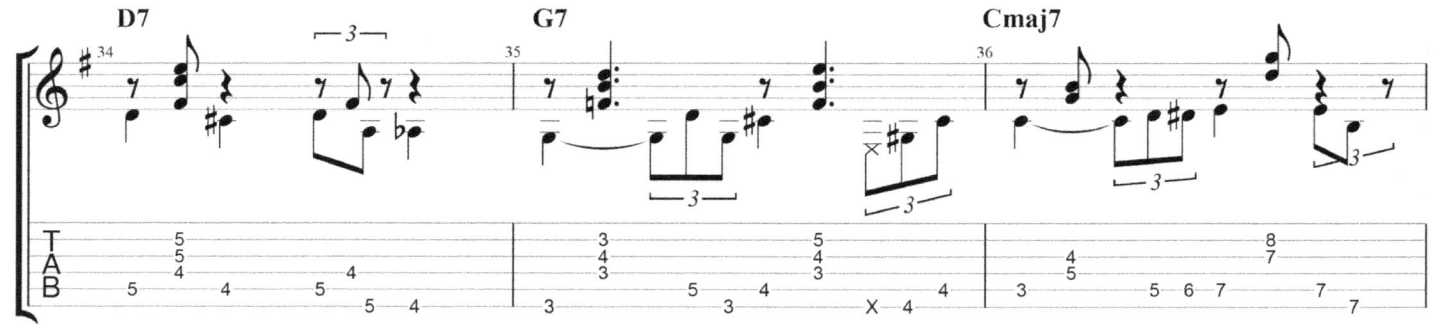

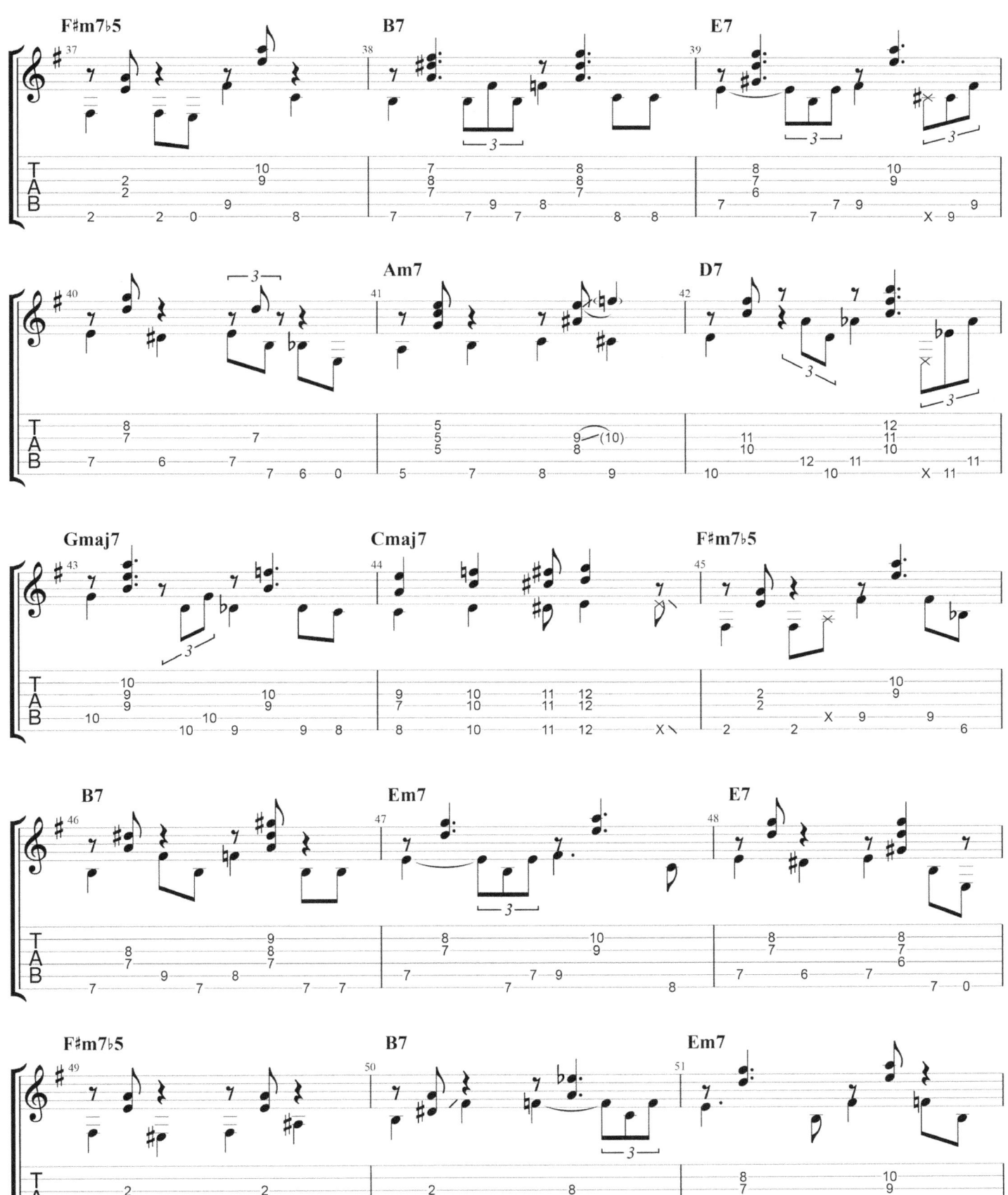

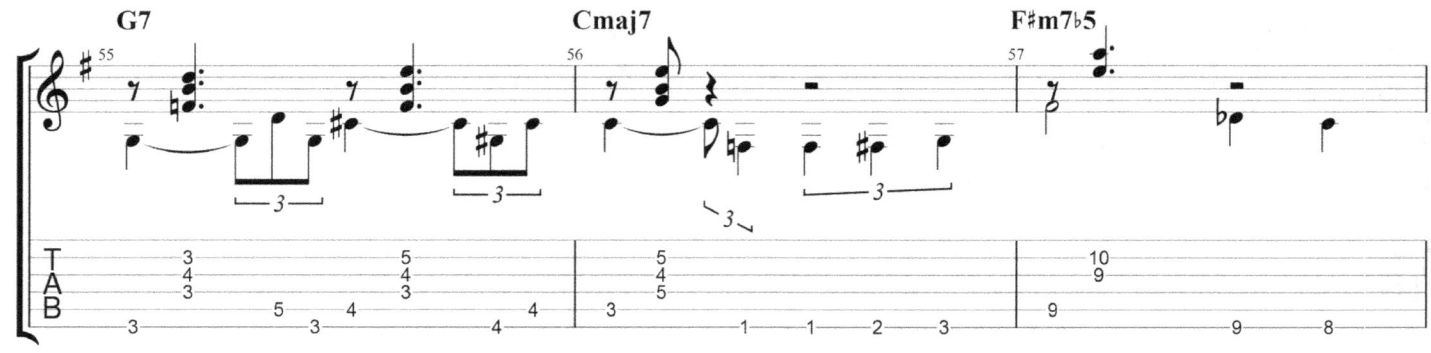
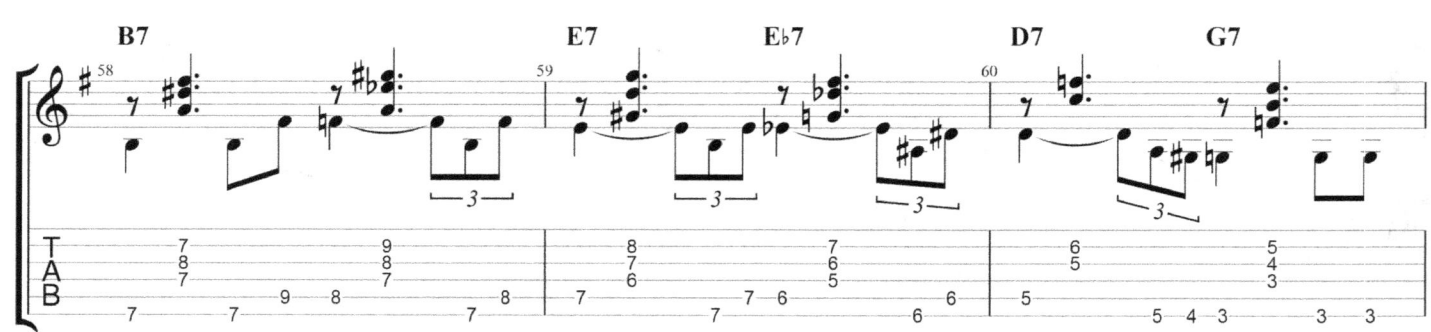
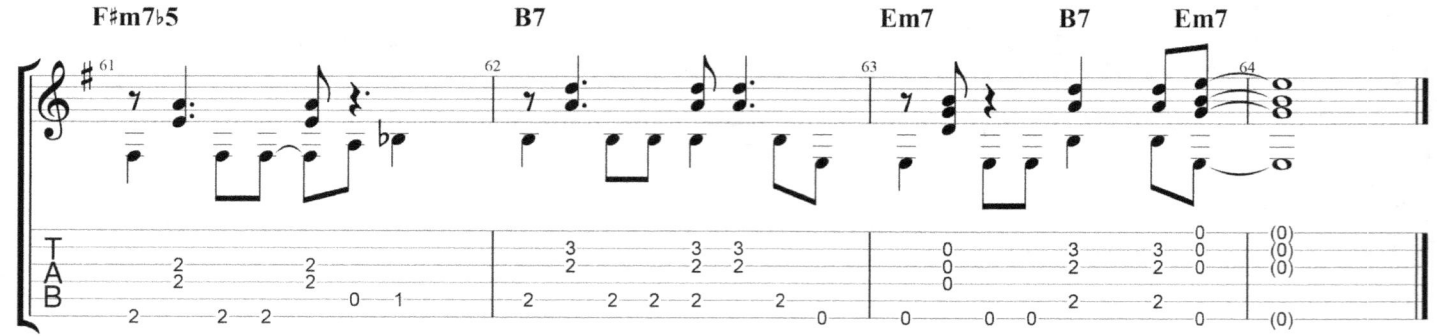

Chapter Thirteen – All The Things You Aren't

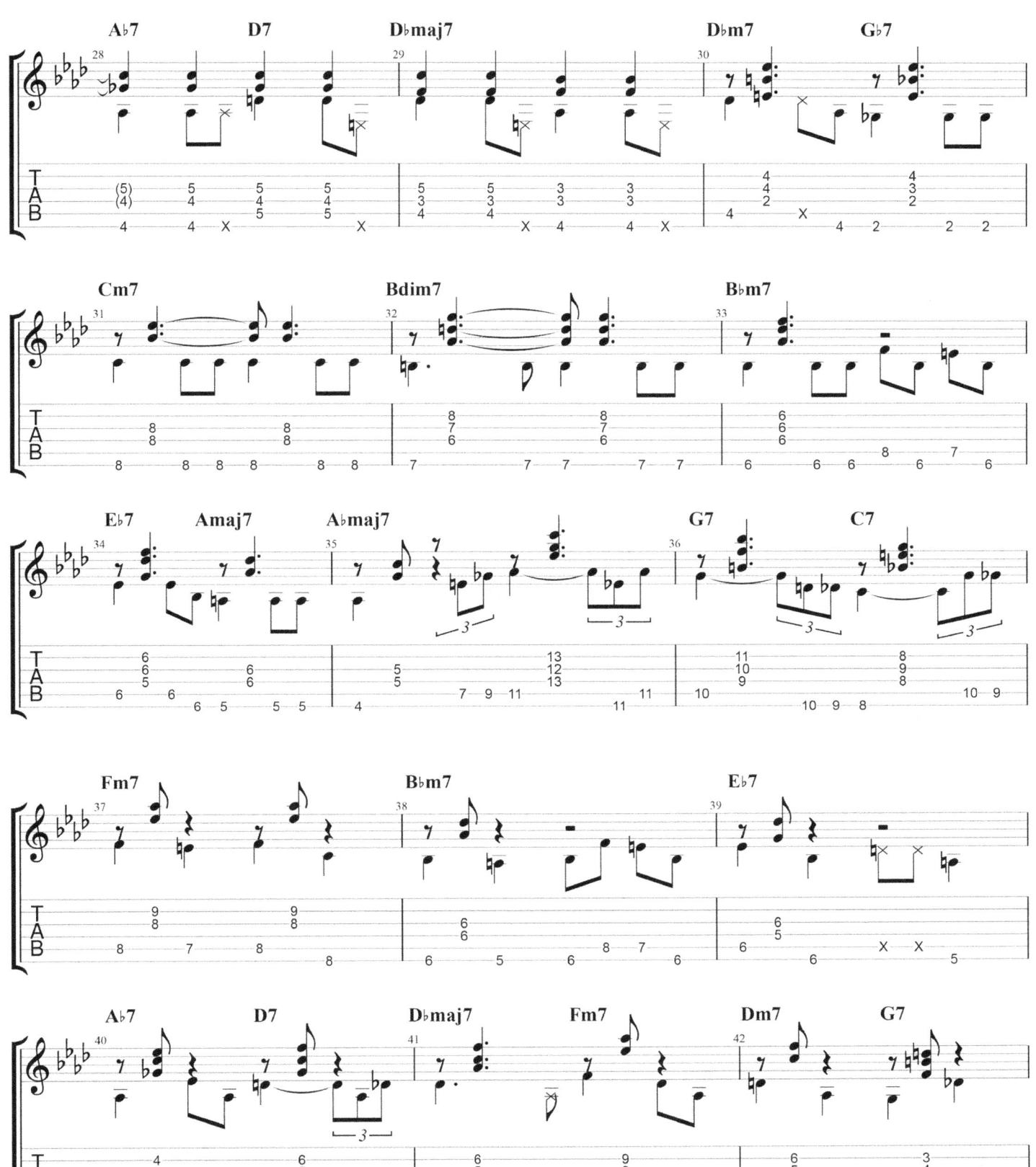

Conclusion and Further Listening

Well, we made it!

Congratulations on making your way through this entire book and coming out the other side unharmed. I hope it's given you a detailed understanding of how to improvise your own basslines and a real insight into the way I approach playing them on the guitar.

The next step for you is simply practice and application. Play walking basslines over your favourite tunes and use them as the basis of your own arrangements. The most important thing you can do is to listen to other musicians, particularly bass players and chord melody guitarists. Joe Pass was a great influence on me and I've borrowed a great deal of his approach in my style.

As I mentioned in the introduction, the following bass players are some of the biggest influences on my music, so please do listen to them and try to match their feel and phrasing.

- Niels-Henning Ørsted Pedersen
- Ray Brown
- Oscar Pettiford
- Jaco Pastorius

Practise without backing tracks and keep the metronome click on the 2 and the 4. This will help you to develop musical independence and great feel. It's important to be able to lay down a solid bassline without hearing any other instruments, so make sure you always know which bar you're on, and where you are in the tune.

Over time, you'll develop your own bassline "licks" that you'll be able to rely on in a tight spot. Please do steal mine and transcribe those played by the great jazz guitarists.

Finally, one overlooked part of guitar playing is the use of dynamics. Try to develop independent volume controls for each of your fingers, or at least between your fingers and thumb. By varying the volume of the different parts, you breathe new life into basslines that may otherwise sound pedestrian. Your control of dynamics really can inspire soloists and the musicians around you to better things.

Remember, you're now combining three instruments – guitar, bass and drums – the rhythmic backbone of any band. Be solid, dynamic and groovy to provide a dependable rhythm section for the other musicians.

Above all, have fun and keep exploring!

Best wishes,

Martin Taylor

MARTIN TAYLOR
SINGLE NOTE SOLOING
FOR JAZZ GUITAR

The Complete Guide to Melodic Jazz Guitar Improvisation

MARTIN **TAYLOR**

FUNDAMENTAL**CHANGES**

Introduction

Whenever I start to talk about jazz improvisation, I often see my guitar students get nervous, and it's no wonder when you consider how jazz soloing tends to be taught these days. There are so many "rules" and "proper" ways to do things that people can feel intimidated – faced with an incredible mass of theory that they're somehow supposed to play musically.

Many of you will have been taught that the route into authentic jazz soloing is through learning theory and somehow instantly knowing the correct scales and arpeggio substitutions you should play on a Gb7#9b13 chord. (Then, of course, turning all that knowledge into a hip-sounding musical idea for two beats at 180bpm!) I don't know about you, but I break into a cold sweat and feel nauseous just thinking about music that way.

What I want to do in this book is teach you a more musical way to improvise, using a method that grows organically out of the melody of any song and is tightly woven into the tune's structure.

We've all been gigs where it seems as though the melody of a tune is a mere formality. It's gotten out of the way as quickly as possible, so that the cerebral jazz solos can begin – and we've lost all sense of the tune in seconds. I want to show you another way. A way that uses the melody of the tune as the *source* of the solo; a way that doesn't require mind-boggling quantum physics to understand; and, above all, a traditional way of soloing that's been handed down through generations of jazz legends and that I feel privileged to pass on to you now.

Modern music institutions seem to be very concerned about teaching *what is possible* to play. Because of this approach, students leave thinking that they *should* cram as many of these theoretical options as possible into their solos. But the truth is, *the music comes first*. Theory is just a way of explaining what happened afterwards. When I play, I very rarely think about theory. In fact, it only really gets a look in when I'm in a tight spot! Over the years, the musicians I've played with have shown me a few great concepts, but most of my ideas come from mimicking the great players I grew up listening to.

Normally, my soloing ideas are quite simple and begin as *variations* to the melody. I have developed a simple way to target the most important notes in the melody and then build short *motifs* around them. These motifs start simple, then I use my jazz vocabulary and language to embellish them and grow them into fully improvised solos. This not only helps to develop a cohesive solo that tells a story, it helps the audience to understand and engage with what is happening.

The beauty of this approach is not just that it is instant, or that it requires a minimum of theory, it's that the solos you create are tightly linked to the melody and therefore *naturally musical*. I'll say it again, your audience will thank you! They will be able to follow your musical ideas easily and enjoy an improvised performance that relates strongly to the tune they came to hear. Many of them won't know *why* they enjoy your music more than other, more cerebral solos, but they will definitely relate to it more strongly and engage with your solos on a more profound level.

Ultimately, this book is about simplifying your thinking and building beautiful jazz solos. I hope you find it refreshing, but most of all, remember to have fun and enjoy the music!

A Note from Joseph

Once again I can't believe my luck! I'm sitting here writing a book on Jazz guitar with one of my musical heroes. I feel very privileged and honoured to be working with Martin on this book.

This book is the culmination of sitting in Martin's Scottish studio, firing as many awkward questions as I could at him in an eight-hour period. The difficulty for me as a writer is that Martin's virtuosity and fluency on the guitar is very much like the way you and I speak English. When I said to Martin, "Stop!... why did you play that note?!" I may as well have asked him, "Why did you just use the word 'hat'?" His response is, "Well, that's just the right word for the thing on that guy's head!"

For Martin, music is simply another language with words, phrases and vocabulary that is used when appropriate. As such, there's often no theoretical answer to the question, "Why are you playing that?" – it's simply a case of him applying a vocabulary that's been learned, invented and honed over half a decade of playing.

I've spent time around a lot of great guitarists, and out of all of them, Martin's soloing is the closest to someone simply sitting you down and telling you a story. For him, soloing is another form of speaking and is created in much the same way as asking a great novelist to spontaneously write a book. The words and music just flow and create something new and beautiful every time.

That said, I did ask Martin a lot of awkward question and squeezed as much information out of him as I could. There's a definite structure to what he plays and a wonderful logic behind his music. The main emphasis is on *developing the melody* and taking the tune of the music to somewhere new. There's very little reliance on "jazz theory" and he certainly isn't thinking "OK, this is a bar of A minor, I need to play such and such a scale…" Martin's approach is entirely about using the melody as the driving force to build the solo.

Despite Martin's music sounding incredibly complex, his whole approach is to simplify everything. For instance, he doesn't think G7b9b13, he visualises a two-note G Major chord. All the complicated chord extensions can be added later if desired. In addition, Martin knows and *feels* the sound of every chord tone. He understands what *mood* is created by adding a 9th, a b5 or a 13th. It's a very pure, musical approach.

As you can probably already tell, this book is light on theory, but we will discuss concepts like the intervals of a chord, such as the root, 3rd, 5th, 7th and 9th. If you're not familiar with these terms then you would probably benefit from doing some preparatory work before diving in. May I humbly suggest my book **Chord Tone Soloing for Jazz Guitar** as it will quickly get you soloing and develop your understanding of these essential elements of music.

So, if not "formal jazz theory", then what are you going to learn from this book?

The first thing is that it will grow your jazz vocabulary massively. There are hundreds of notated examples of Martin's playing that give logical insight into how to actually build a musical jazz guitar solo. We'll begin by learning how to vary a tune's melody to inspire and structure your solo, then teach you how to develop your improvisation just as a master jazz guitarist would do.

You'll discover how to break down the harmony of a jazz tune into its simplest elements and use it as a framework to underpin your creativity.

You'll study how Martin develops a musical jazz solo in real time, using an unexpected melody that you already know.

You will understand and master great phrasing and how to "swing" on your guitar

You'll discover how to create interest in your playing and, finally, piece it all together with transcribed etudes of Martin's solos.

This is the most practical, musical and above all hands-on jazz guitar book I've ever written and I'm very proud to be a part of it. All the answers to how to play jazz guitar are here.

Oh, and we talk about musical colours quite lot, and we're English so we spell it with a U!

Get the Audio

The audio files for this book are available to download for free from **www.fundamental-changes.com.** The link is in the top right-hand corner. Click on the "Guitar" link then simply select this book title from the drop-down menu and follow the instructions to get the audio.

We recommend that you download the files directly to your computer, not to your tablet, and extract them there before adding them to your media library. You can then put them onto your tablet, iPod or burn them to CD. On the download page there are instructions and we also provide technical support via the contact form.

For over 350 Free Guitar Lessons with Videos Check out:

www.fundamental-changes.com

Over 10,000 fans on Facebook: **FundamentalChangesInGuitar**

Tag us for a share on Instagram: **FundamentalChanges**

Get the Video

As a special bonus to buyers of this book, Martin Taylor has two videos that explain every key element of his walking bass and chords technique, that are not available anywhere else. Follow this link to view/download the content:

https://fundamental-changes.teachable.com/p/single-note/

Or use the short link:

https://geni.us/singlenote

If you type above link into a browser, please note that there is no "www."

You can also scan the QR code below to view the videos on your smartphone:

Chapter One – Melody and Variation

Throughout my years of teaching I have noticed that many guitarists struggle with jazz improvisation. Often, excellent guitarists who are well-versed in rock and blues will come to me for jazz lessons. When I ask them to play a jazz tune and take a solo, however, they often clam up and start "playing theory" as soon as the solo begins. When I ask them what they're thinking about when they play, their answer is often along the lines of:

"Well, that's a minor II chord, so I need to play a Dorian scale on that. Then the V chord moves to a minor I chord, which means I need to play the Altered scale there. To do that, I used a substitution and played a Maj7#5 arpeggio built from the #9 before resolving to the Lydian mode on the tonic chord."

I get anxious just typing that, never mind trying to play it!

It all sounds very academic and clever, but almost without exception, when students think like this during their solos, they don't sound great. When the melody stops and the solo starts, you can *hear them playing theory*. What's worse is that any sense of melody disappears as they try to "chase the chord changes" in their solo.

In this chapter, I want to offer you a better way – an older method of jazz soloing that is easier, sounds better, is more relatable to your audience, and will simplify your whole approach to playing. This is the *traditional* way to build a jazz solo and is a more authentic, musical way to approach the art. Just like most secrets, once the smoke and mirrors are removed, you'll see that it's really quite simple to get started.

The truth is, all the great musicians you've listened to and admire, who can play astonishingly advanced music, have all been through (and continue to work on) the process I'm about to teach you. Their cutting edge theory is built on these solid foundations. That's why they sound great. It's not advanced theory that makes a fantastic player, it's developing a jazz language based around the melody of the tune.

This is the first step of your new jazz soloing journey, because what I'm about to share with you will show you what jazz musicians *actually* do when they improvise. Are you ready?

Secret Number One: Replace the word "improvisation" with the word *variation*.

Being forced to "improvise" immediately puts pressure on you. It describes the daunting task of having to create great music from nothing, in real time, in front of an audience. What a terrifying prospect!

I promise you that I don't get struck by a lightning bolt of inspiration every time I solo. Instead, I begin every solo by playing *small variations to the melody* of the tune.

Think about this for a minute.

The melody is the strongest part of the tune. You don't leave a concert humming the chord progression! Almost all jazz standards were originally vocal songs, which is why they have such strong, memorable tunes. This means you can create a strong, meaningful solo by staying close to the melody and adding small variations. Even if the audience don't understand what's going on musically, they'll feel that your variations are related to the melody they've just heard. It will be a strong, tangible experience for them.

If you solo by varying the melody, you not only bring your audience along for the ride, you also have ready-made melodic material you can develop naturally – you're not starting from scratch.

Not only that, soloing by varying the melody gives you an entire *structure* and *framework* for your solo to exist in. You'll never get "lost in the chord changes" and, most importantly, you won't have to magically create a whole new musical theme on the spot.

By thinking of "melodic variation" rather than "improvisation", you get melodic ideas for free and you give your solo a meaningful structure.

The secret to strong jazz soloing is to learn how to vary a melody and develop it. Once you can do this, everything else falls into place.

Let's begin to learn how to vary a simple melody I've composed over a set of very familiar chord changes. You may recognise this melody from my previous book, **Beyond Chord Melody**.

The chord changes can be played on guitar like this:

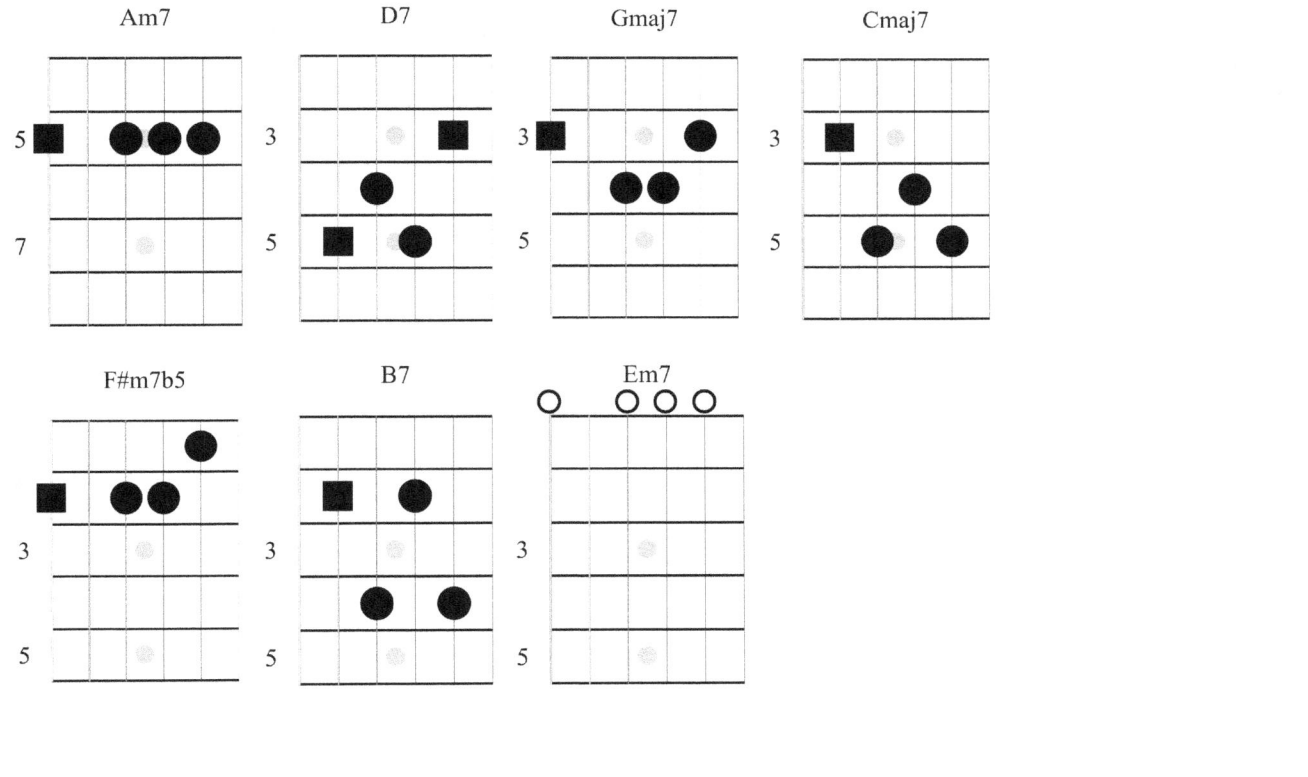

Memorise the position of each chord because this will form a geographic structure for your variations – something we'll discuss in greater detail later.

Now learn and memorise the tune that'll be the workhorse for the rest of this chapter.

Example 1a

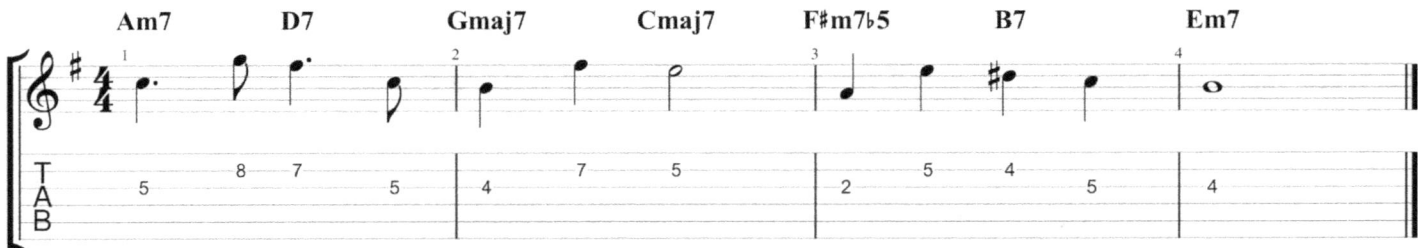

When you're comfortable playing the melody over the chord changes from memory, play it through again and really pay attention to which notes you feel are the strongest and most important in the phrase. To my ears, the most important notes in this melody are the ones that fall on the first beat of each chord. I call these "hit points" – they are essential in defining the shape of the melody.

Learn them now in this reduced version of the melody. Notice that I've added the bass note for each chord. First play the hit point notes on their own, then add in the bass note below them so you can hear and locate them in the context of the chord.

Example 1b

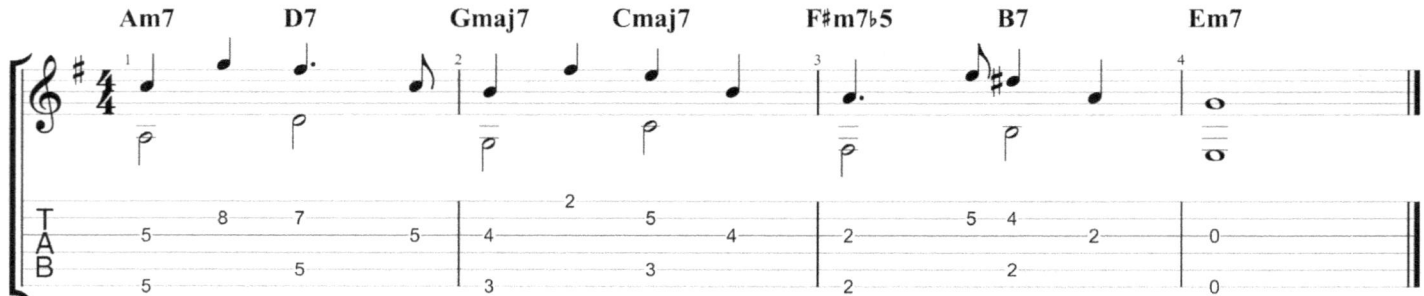

When the hit points are strong in your mind, go back and play the full melody a few times to hear how the hit points relate to the tune. When you're confident, it's time to start adding a little variation to the tune.

As mentioned, very often improvisation is taught in a way that says, "You can play this scale over this chord…" but this is too far removed from what actually happens when jazz musicians start improvising. The more intuitive, melodic approach is to *vary the melody* and that's what we'll do now. Learn the following variation to the melody, then compare it to the hit points in the previous example.

Example 1c

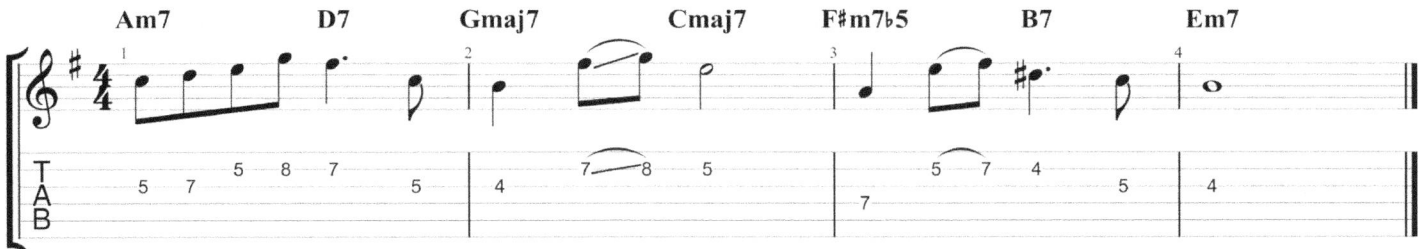

What am I thinking when I create little variations like this?

The first thing is that I keep those hit points strong in my ears. Each short variation I play is aiming for the next hit point in the sequence. In the previous example, I began on a hit point, then added a variation that led to the next one, then repeated this structure throughout. You don't have to begin on a hit point (and we will look at that in more detail later), but for now, beginning on a strong melody note will really help to anchor your variations to the melody.

The next thing to understand is that all these variations tend to fall quite nicely under the fingers when I play the root notes shown in Example 1b. These root notes help me "map" out the fretboard and I have lots vocabulary in each position. These days everything I play is led by my ears, but they have been trained by years of listening, copying, experimenting and playing – just like how you learned to speak English.

The bass notes and melodic hit points are like an early pencil sketch of an oil painting. Once I have the sketch in place, I gradually fill in the colour. By seeing the chord structure and melody like this, I am stripping the tune right down to its basics. I can then find different ways of moving between each hit point while keeping the chord structures in mind.

Play the hit points from Example 1b again, then try this new variation. The bass notes are shown in brackets. Don't play them at first, just learn the melody.

Example 1d

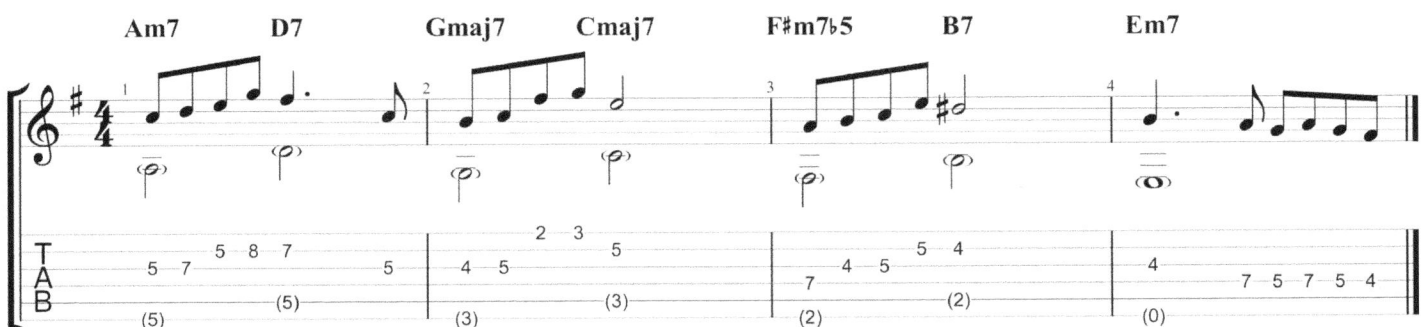

When you're ready, try playing Example 1d again, but add in the bass notes on each chord.

Remember, the bass notes and melodic hit points are an early sketch of the finished painting. I also visualise a simplified version of the chord structure in my mind when I play. I do this by adding the 3rd (or 10th) of the chord on one of the middle strings. The 3rd of a chord tells us whether it has a major or minor quality and is incredibly useful for guiding our ears. Most of the time when it comes to chords, especially when I'm improvising, all I think about is the root and 3rd. They are the bare minimum needed to define the harmony and once they are in place, we can add the different colours of extensions and alterations as we wish.

I love this approach because instead of thinking about how to play over complicated chords like B7#9b13, I'm really just thinking about the root and 3rd.

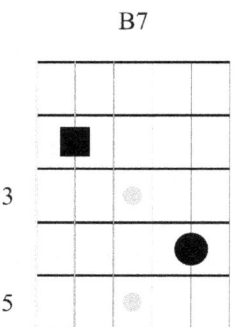

I don't have complicated harmony going on in my mind, I just have this simple outline of each chord shape. Anything that sounds complicated in my solos comes from variations to the melody that are built around the root and 3rd (tenth) shape.

Play through the "root and 10th" chords of our tune.

Example 1e

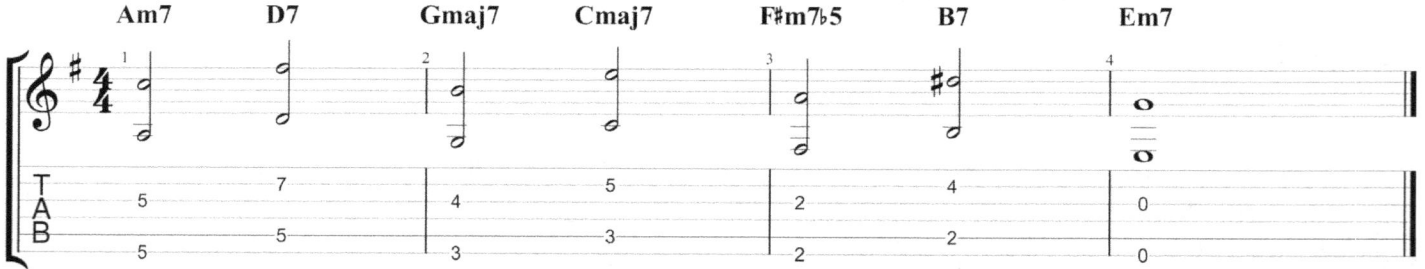

It just so happens that the melody of our tune is built around the 10ths of the chord. You can probably already hear this in the previous example, but of course this won't always be the case.

This reduced sketch of the song's harmony means that we are not keeping too much information in mind while we use melodic variations to colour-in the melody. Instead of thinking in terms of complex chords, we are reducing them down to simplify our thinking. We can add the other colours later.

These 10th structures are easy to move around the neck and they're also very recognisable to us. Our tune is in the key of E Minor, so learn the root and tenth voicings up and down the E string and A string.

Example 1f

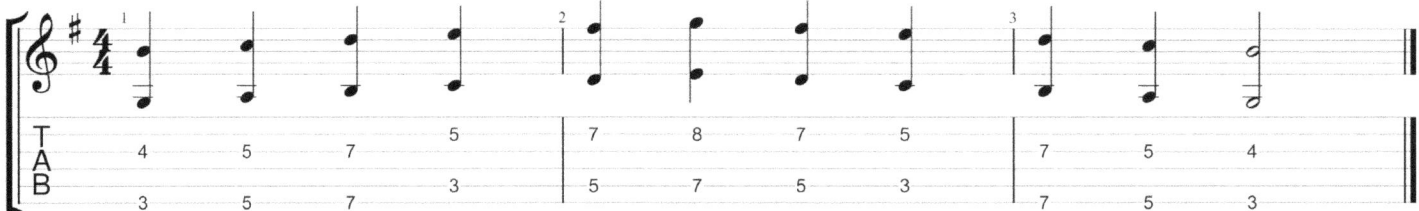

Now we have the neck mapped out in root and 10th chords, let's return to our melody and look at some more variations we could create. If you are new to this, there are a couple of common *approach note* patterns you should know. The first begins an 1/8th note before the beat and approaches the target note from a scale tone below.

Example 1g

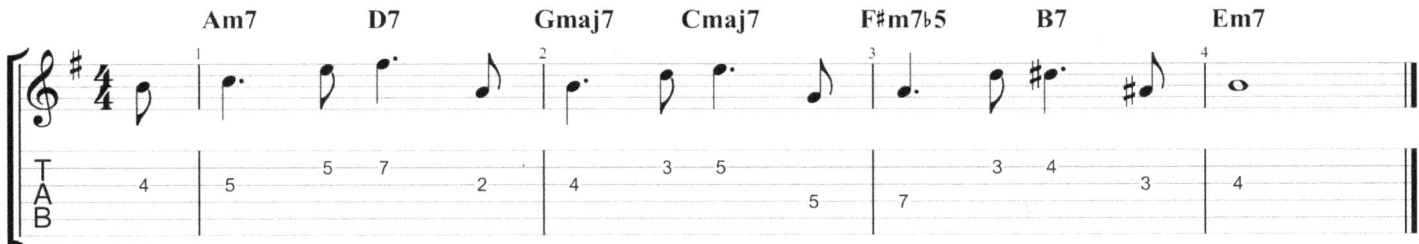

The next begins a beat before the target note and approaches the target note from the scale tone below, then the scale tone above.

Example 1h

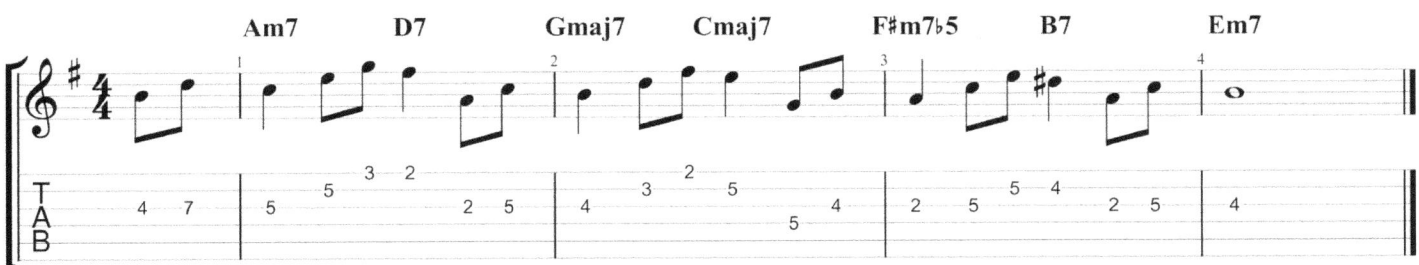

When you have got these ideas under your fingers it's worthwhile practising these approach notes patterns on the root, 3rd, 5th and 7th of each chord as it will help train your ears to hear some strong melodic shapes. For a complete guide to this technique, check out Joseph's book, **Chord Tone Soloing for Jazz Guitar.**

Let's begin to create some simple variations to our melodic hit points by approaching each target note from a scale tone above. It's a simple idea, but you'll quickly start to hear some new melodic variation possibilities.

Example 1i

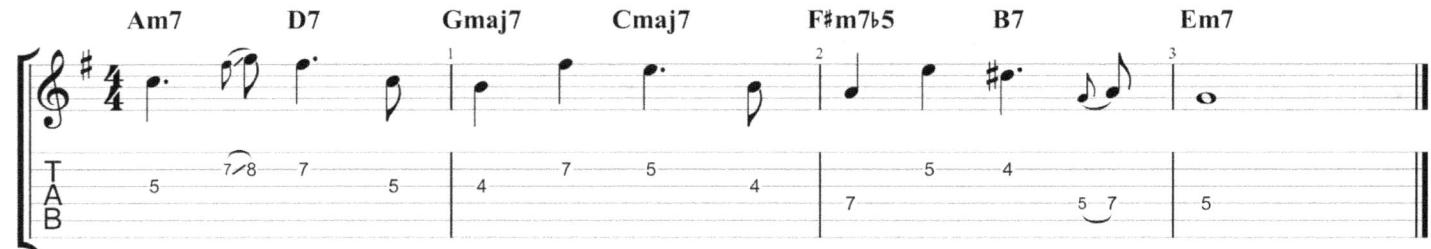

Now here's a slightly longer phrase that targets the hit points.

Example 1j

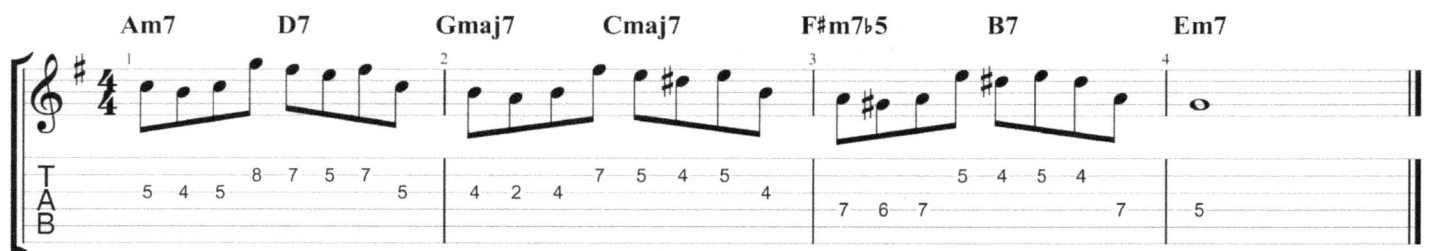

Next, we can introduce some rhythmic variation.

Example 1k

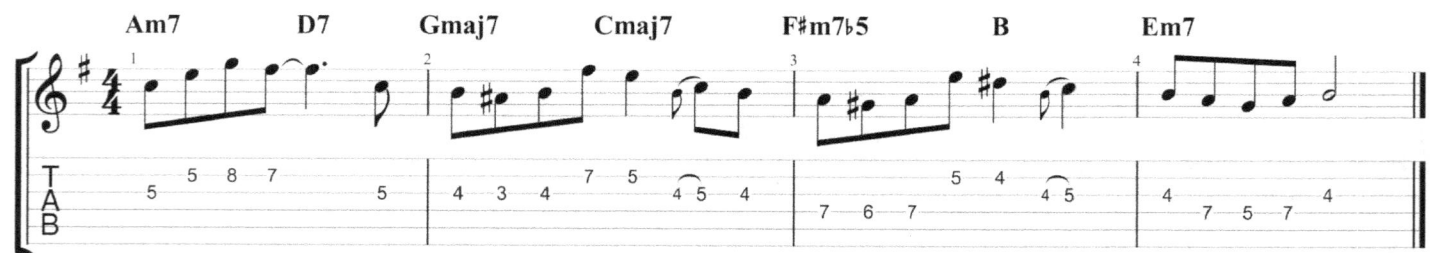

So far, all these variations have used scale notes (from the E Harmonic Minor scale if you need to know!) but of course, jazz musicians love to use chromatic notes to link up the hit points in the melody too. A chromatic note is any note that doesn't exist in the scale, so when you start to understand how they work, *every* note in music becomes available! Don't panic though… we're just adding a few more variations to the melody.

Example 1l

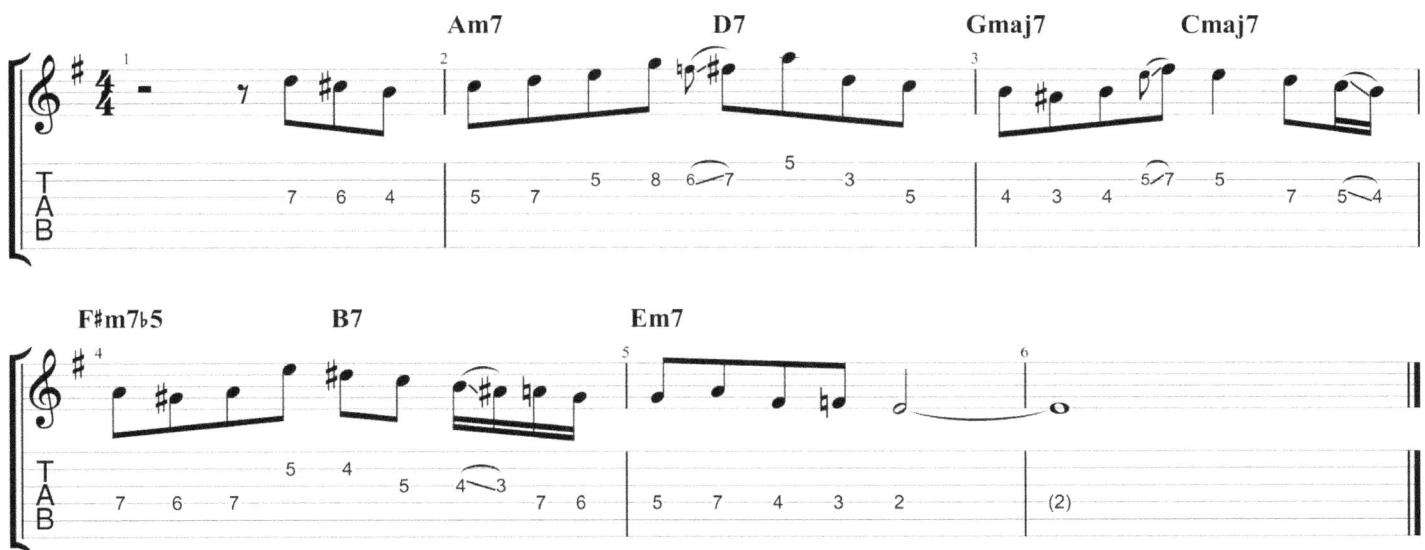

Here's another chromatic idea. Can you hear how the melody has influenced the line, but the simple addition of a few chromatic notes starts to make this sound quite jazzy?

Example 1m

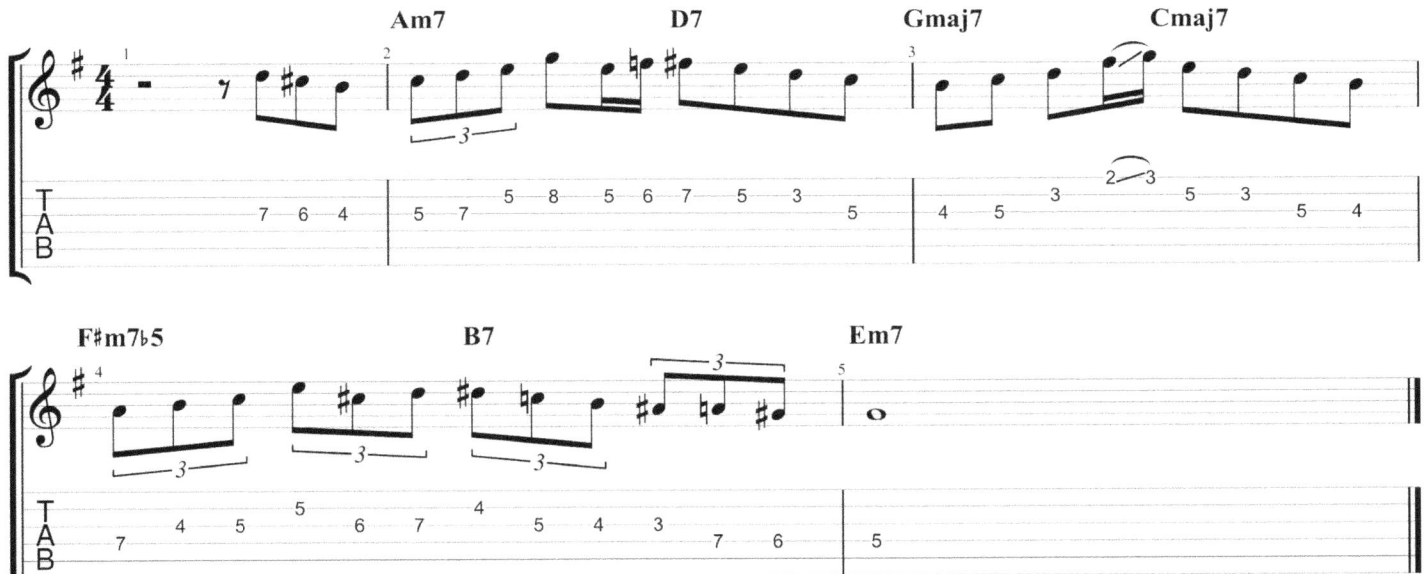

Playing with chromatic ideas is a lot of fun! Here's another longer idea, played in free time, that continues to target the hit points of the melody.

Example 1n

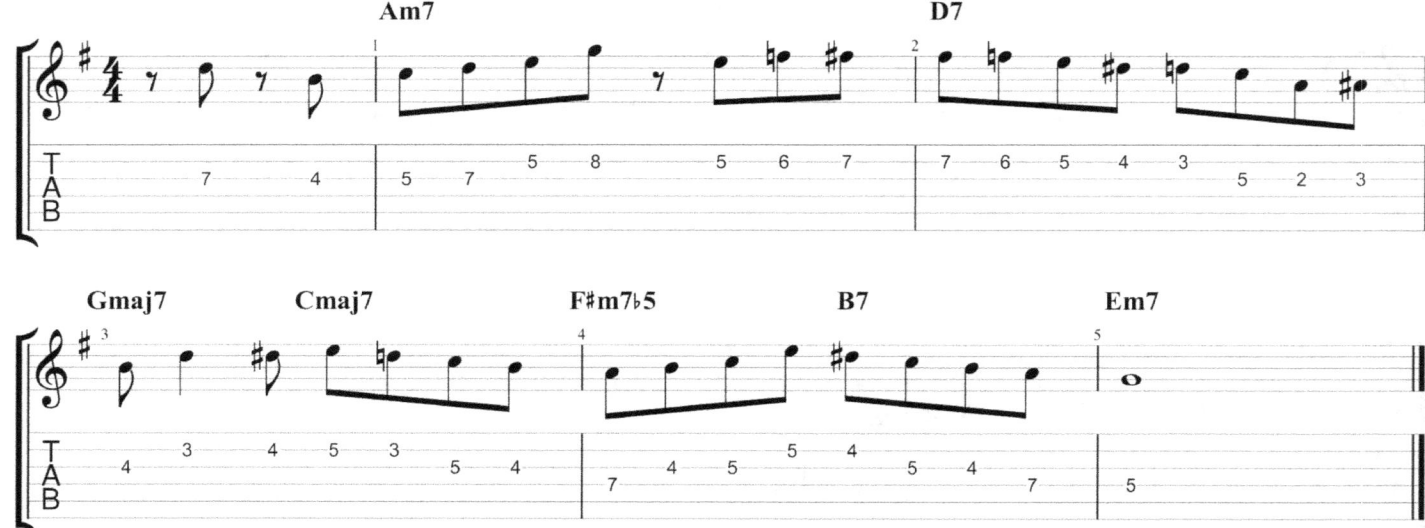

Now it's over to you for a while, to spend some time exploring different ways to approach the hit points of the melody using scale notes and chromatics. The best way to learn this is to listen to great musicians playing and recycle their ideas (I always joke with my students that we're helping the planet by recycling!) These approaches are used all the time and now you know what you're listening for, it should be easier to pick them out. Even if you don't copy their idea perfectly, listening to how other musicians approach this will help you understand the melodic shapes and rhythmic possibilities you can use.

As you get better at decorating the melodic hit points, you might stumble on an idea you really like. When you hit upon a variation, you can develop it into a *motif* – an idea that can be transferred around the chord changes and adapted as necessary to develop it into something new. For example, here's a little melody I came up with based around a trill. Notice how I take it around the chords and change it up slightly at the end.

Example 1o

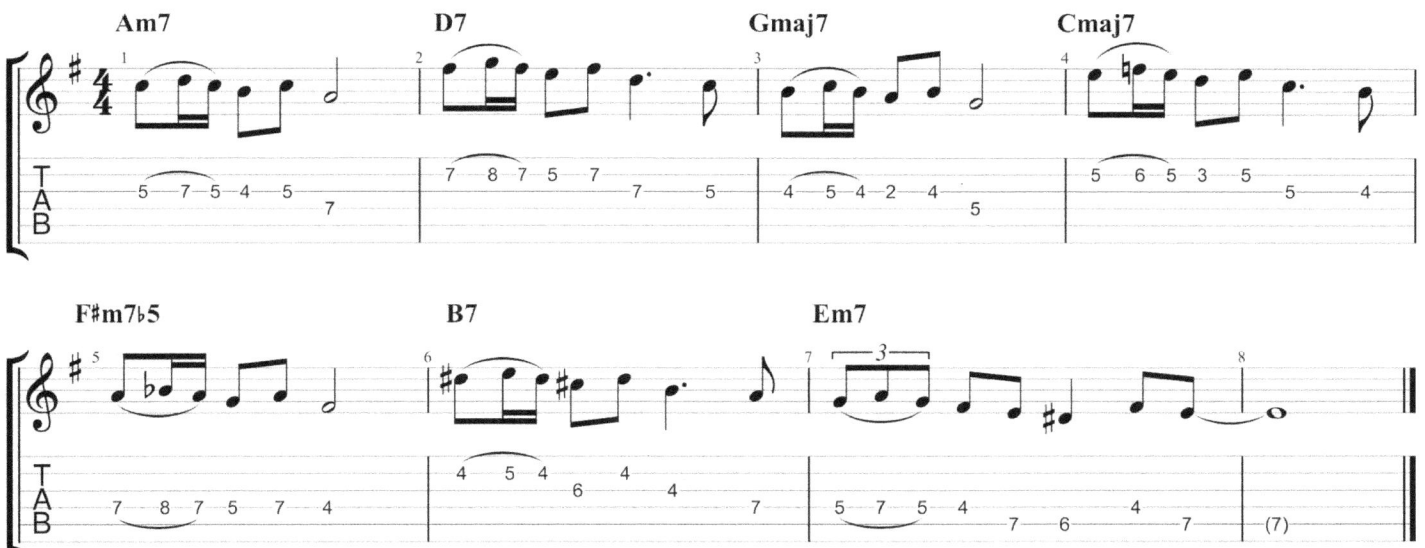

Here's another motif that I could take around the chord sequence. Again, you can hear how it starts early and targets the hit points of the melody

Example 1p

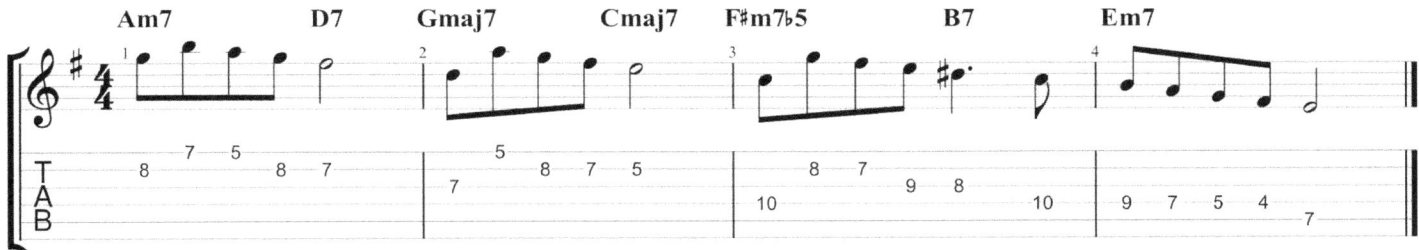

As you get more confident, you can begin to move away from the hit points of the original melody and create new motifs around your own hit points. This will happen naturally as you spend time practising. While these hit points will probably be arpeggio notes of the chords, they don't have to be, in which case the possibilities become endless. The only thing limiting you right now is your vocabulary of ideas. The secret is to listen to as much music as possible and steal the little motifs that stand out to you, then immediately use them in your playing.

Example 1q

As good as it is to practice a single motif around the whole chord progression, it's more musical to *develop* it as your solo progresses. This could begin as simply as practising different motifs on each chord, but when you've learnt enough musical ideas you'll begin to organically develop them on the fly. The next example is more of a free idea that begins by targeting a hit point but then grows into a more musical phrase.

Example 1r

Here's a longer idea that develops quickly. It's a more advanced idea, but break it down and play it slowly to understand how I target the strong notes of the melody. You might want to learn small fractions of this idea at first and explore them individually.

Example 1s

The next stage is to introduce some gaps in your variations and begin to think in phrases, just as you would when talking. This next example is split into clear phrases based around each pair of chords. Notice that I've stopped limiting myself to the hit points of the melody. This is a natural stage as your variations develop and means that you're beginning to trust your ears.

Example 1t

The next idea goes a little further out again and introduces more chromatic notes for you to play with and learn from. I played it freely and you'll probably hear me making comments as I play!

Example 1u

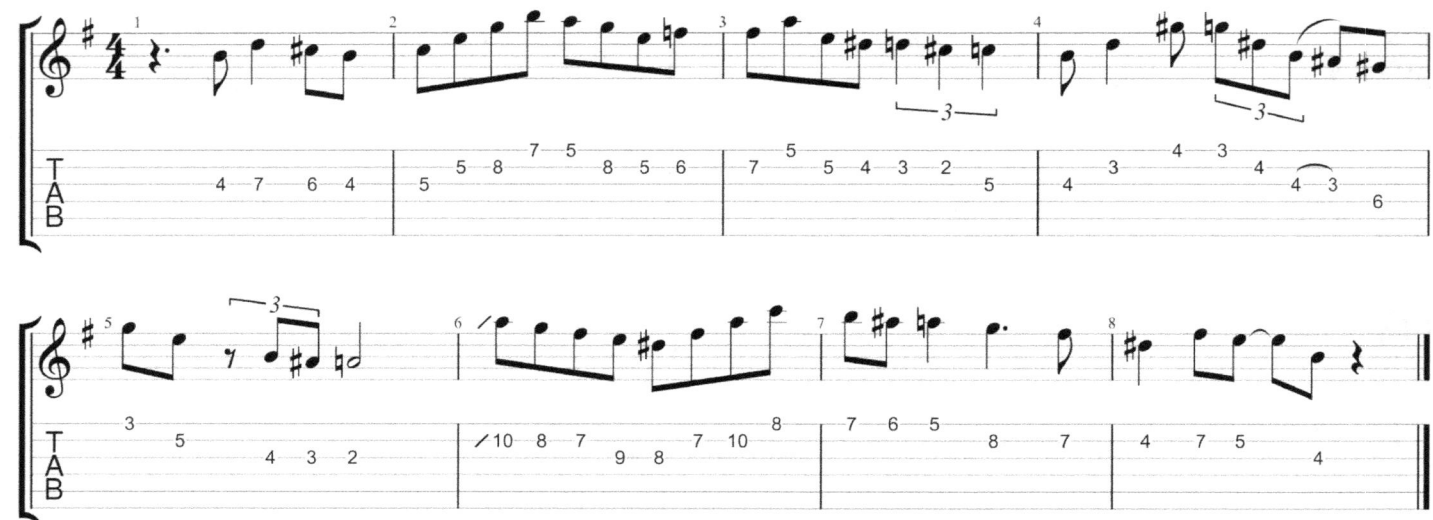

Finally, here's a fairly diatonic idea that really develops the line and is a long way from the original target notes of the melody. However, because the music developed naturally and your audience were brought here in simple logical steps, it is still a strong melodic idea.

Example 1v

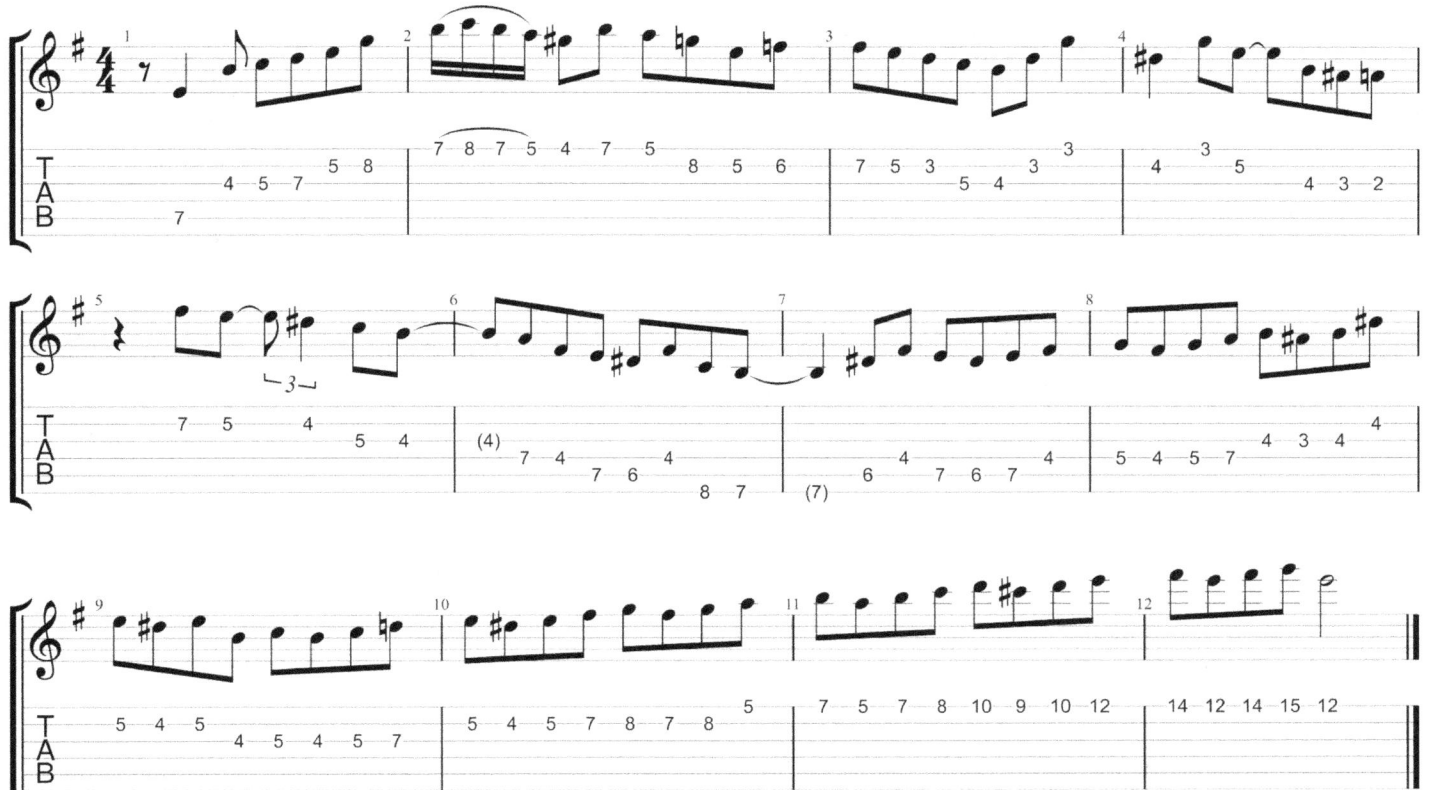

It's time to move on, but it's important to say that what you've learnt here is a massive part of the puzzle when it comes to creating well-conceived, improvised jazz lines. The solos of the greatest guitar players all retain a strong connection to the melody. There is a process to this:

- Learn the melody
- Define the hit points
- Vary the melody around the hit points
- Build motifs and decorations around the hit points
- Create your own hit points
- Build on these and develop them

Think of your improvisation as storytelling. Your strong connection to the melody (or main theme of the story) will take your audience with you.

Chapter Two – Other Target Notes and Colour Tones

In the previous chapter, we began our journey of melodic variation by creating hit points based on the melody, which was based on 3rd intervals. But what if the melody was built around 9ths or 5ths or 13ths? In this chapter we'll discuss the idea that it's not just chord tones that can form hit points for our solos. In fact, we can target pretty much any note we want on any chord to add colour and depth to the music.

As we saw at the end of the previous chapter, as we improvise variations on the melody, we naturally begin to target different notes related to each chord. And each of these notes has a different "colour" and adds a different mood to your solo.

There are no rules for how quickly you introduce these other colours. You might want to introduce 9ths and 13ths straight away, or maybe you want to stick to targeting "safer" chord tones when you first begin to vary the melody. The only way to judge what works is to develop your ears, and the only way to do that is to do a lot of listening, practice and *playing*!

I've been doing this professionally for 50 years, so I've experienced a lot of music. My ears are the boss now and I play 9ths, 11ths, 13ths and other intervals without really thinking about them consciously – my fingers simply play what I hear in my head.

That said, in this chapter I'll give you many starting points for your explorations of musical colour and hopefully set you on a path to your own sonic discovery.

Let's quickly recap the melody and hit points of the tune, which happens to be based on 3rds.

Example 2a

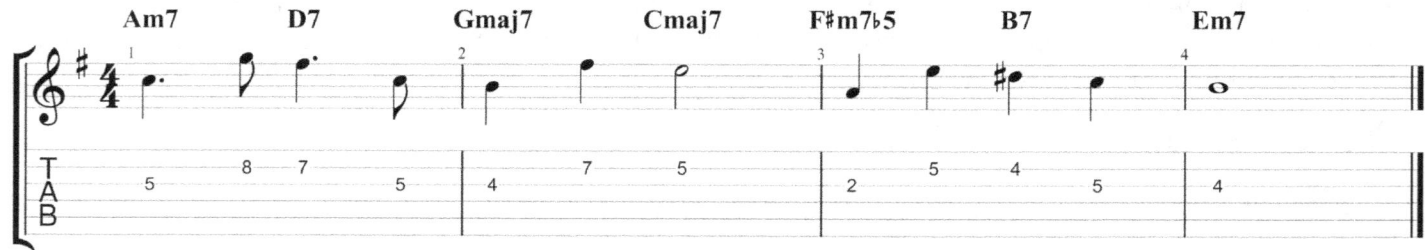

We also learnt that we can embellish those hit points by adding little variations around the melody, as in Example 2b.

Example 2b

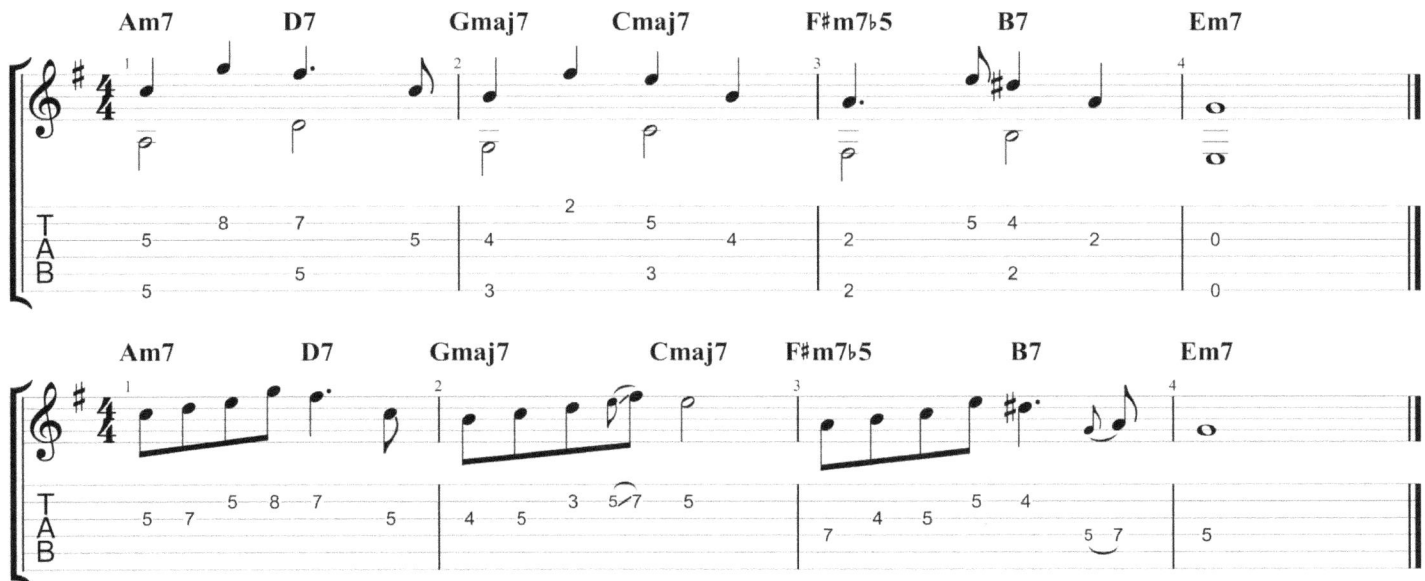

Instead of targeting the melody note (in this case the 3rd), however, I could target the 5th of each chord. The 5ths are located here. (Notice that I'm reducing down the complex F#m7b5 chord to simply an "F minor" sound).

Example 2c

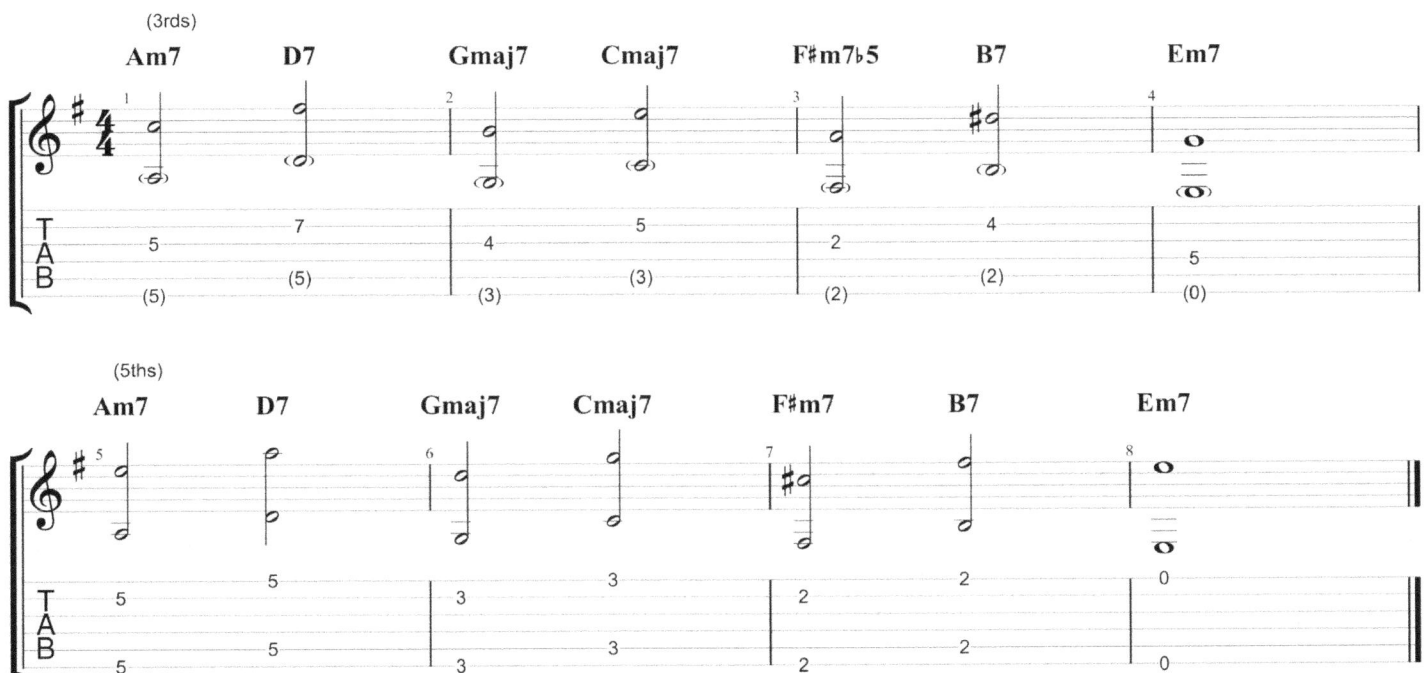

193

Once we have located the 5th interval of each chord, we can play a little motif that targets them. (In this example, I finish on the *root* of the final E minor chord to resolve the line, because that's where my ears take me).

Example 2d

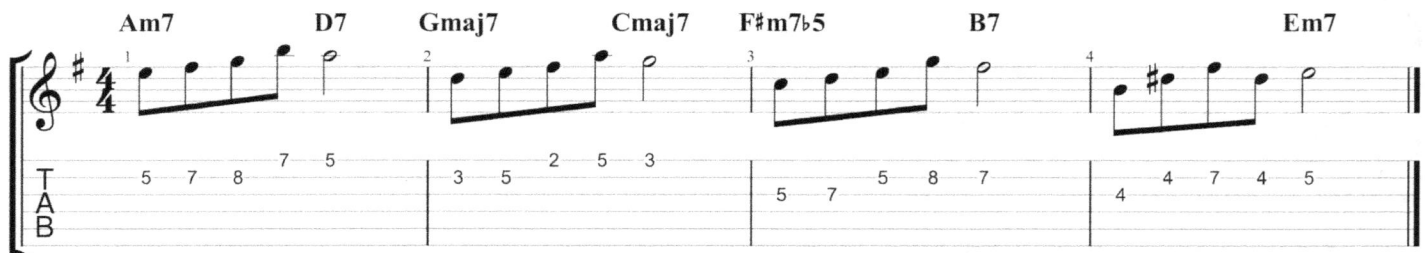

Now it's your turn. I want you to come up with five different ways to approach the 5th of each chord. Remember, you can use scale notes and chromatic ideas. Refer to the previous chapter and see how I targeted the 3rd to give you some ideas. Don't worry about playing the "correct" scale. You've used all these notes before in Chapter One. Your ears will tell you if there's a sound in there that you don't like.

Next, try combining ideas so that sometimes you target the 5th and sometimes the 3rd.

This line begins on the 3rd of Am then targets the 5th of D and continues alternating the target notes throughout the phrase.

Example 2e

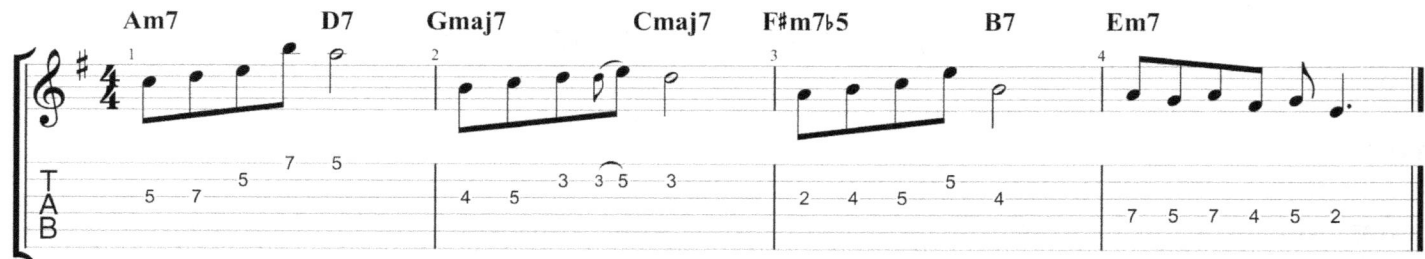

When you can confidently target both the 5th and the 3rd you're really cooking with gas! Put down the book for a while and begin freely targeting whichever note you feel like in your melody variations. You can use the original shape of the tune to help you, or just see where your ears take you.

This is a great time to simply have fun and explore the guitar. Do you see now why establishing the geography of the chord shapes is so important? All these phrases just begin to fall under your fingers as you learn where the strong target notes are in the relation to the chord.

Now go and invent five short melodies that target the root of each chord, and five that target the 7th. You already know where the root of each chord is, so here is a chart showing the location of the 7ths.

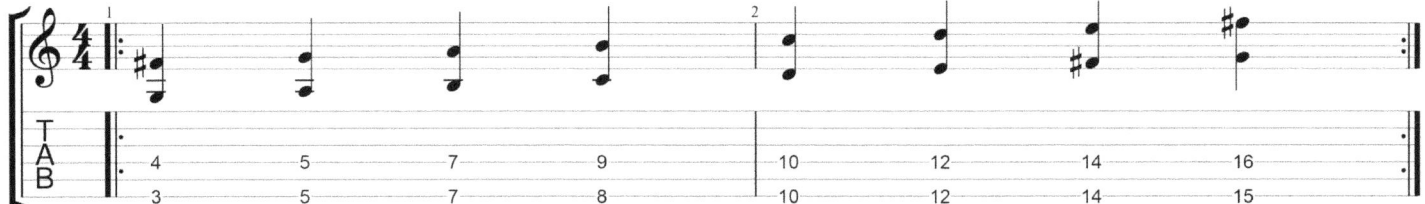

7ths are harder to hear at first but are an important note to know in each chord.

There are always new melodic ideas to discover. It's a lifelong pursuit, but if you listen to a lot of jazz you will quickly start to recognise and use these melodies in your own playing.

Spend time now combining lines that target whichever chord tone notes you feel like (1, 3, 5 or 7). Be aware that becoming fluent at this will take time. It's a slow process but don't be discouraged. You'll gradually begin to hear the phrases form under your fingers. To begin with, include the root note of each chord, so you can hear the effect of the other notes you're targeting.

In addition to the chord tones of the triad (1, 3 and 5) and the 7th, the 9th is a beautiful colour to target. It adds a richness and lightness to the chord. In Example 2f, I hold down just the root, 7th and the 9th of each chord, then play a simple motif that bounces between the 9th and root on the sixth-string. The chords are A minor, G Major and F# minor.

Example 2f

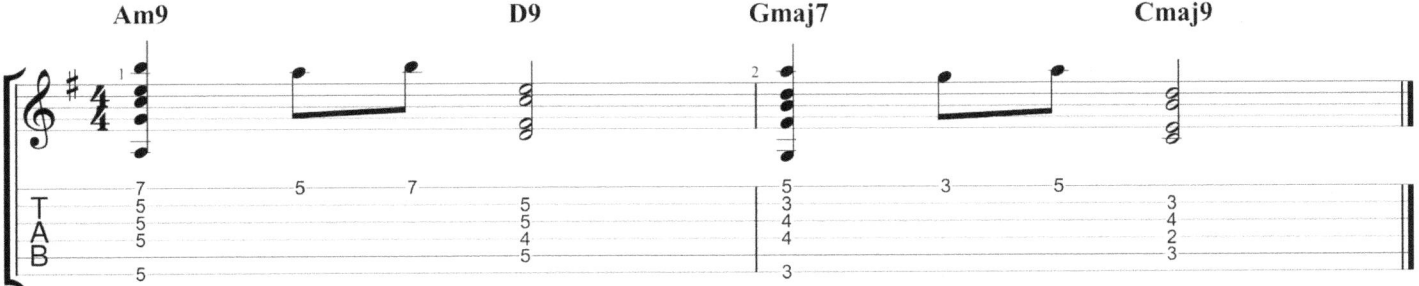

It's not always appropriate to target the 9th on every chord, but it sounds fantastic on the tonic G Major chord.

Example 2g

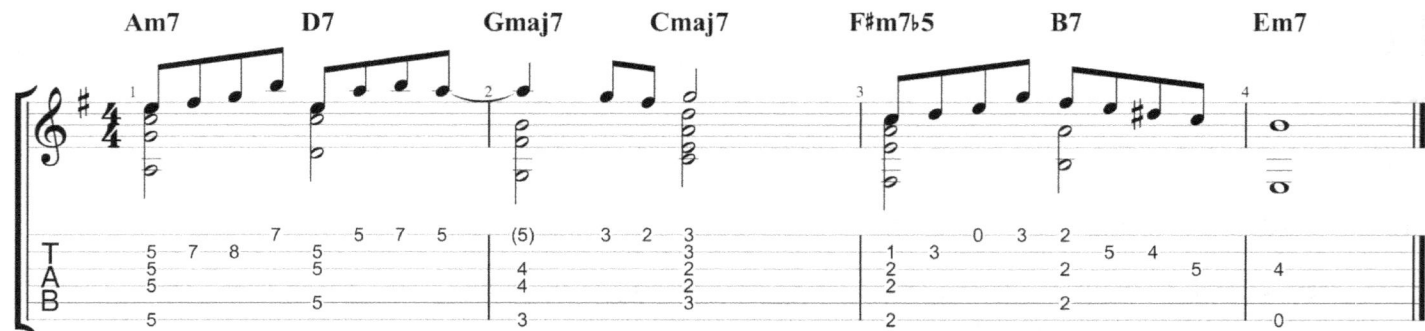

Once you have worked through the process of targeting the chord tones we've discussed so far (1, 3, 5, 7 and 9) and you have your geography figured out, you can mix and match these ideas, targeting the intervals freely. In Example 2h I jump up the neck and target different notes on each chord. However, there's a very important lesson I want you to take away with you here: *the chord position I choose follows the melody I want to play.*

Melody always comes first, so if I hear a jump in the melody, I'll often voice my chord higher on the neck. That's why it's so important to know the root and 10th chord voicings up and down each string.

You can analyse the following line to see which intervals the melody targets on each chord, but also use your ears. Can you pick out the sound and *feeling* of a 9th, a 3rd of a 5th? Hearing these intervals as colours and feeling their moods is so important for your musicality.

Can you see how I use chromatics to link together some of the target notes? These lines aren't composed, this is just me playing what I hear in my head.

Example 2h

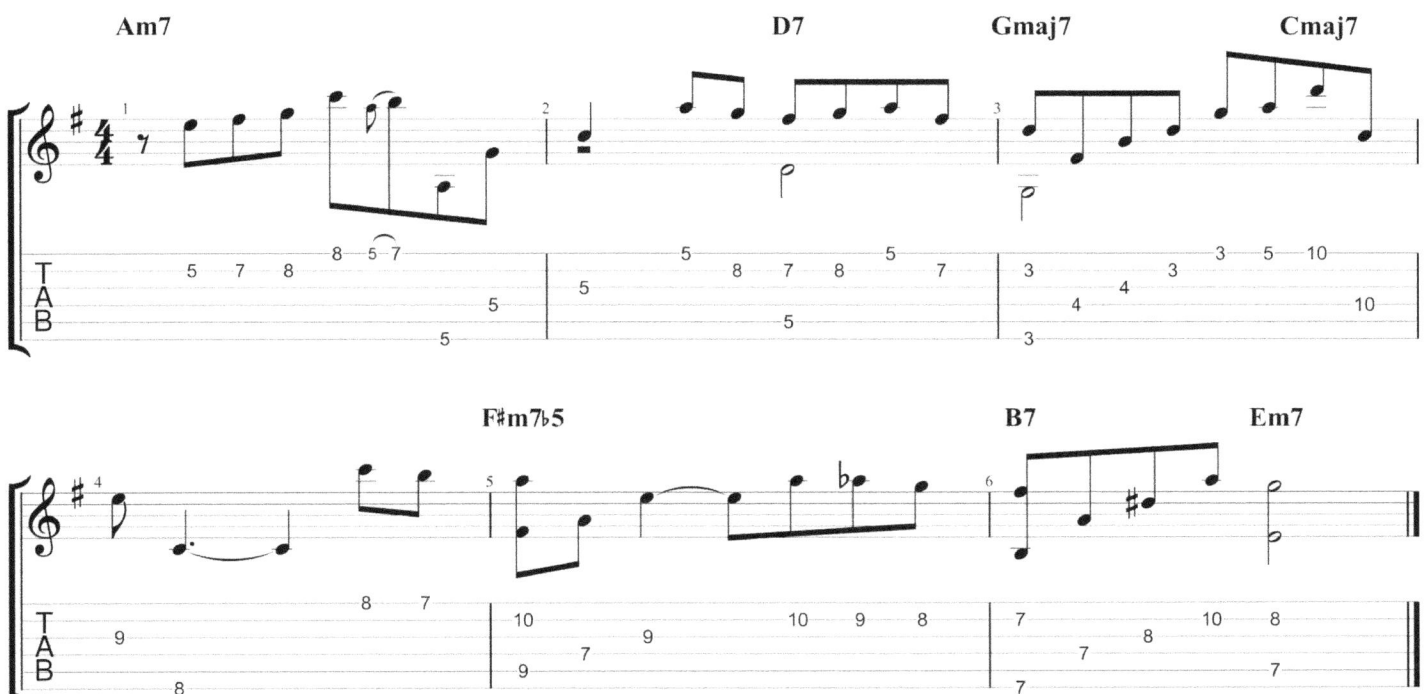

While you're up at the higher end of the guitar, here's a useful line to link together the Am7 and D7 chords.

Example 2i

Another lovely warm interval to target on the Gmaj7 chord is the 6th. Here's one way you could do that, but explore your guitar and see how many melodies you can make that end on this note. The 6th sounds like it wants to resolve to the 5th, but it doesn't have to.

Example 2j

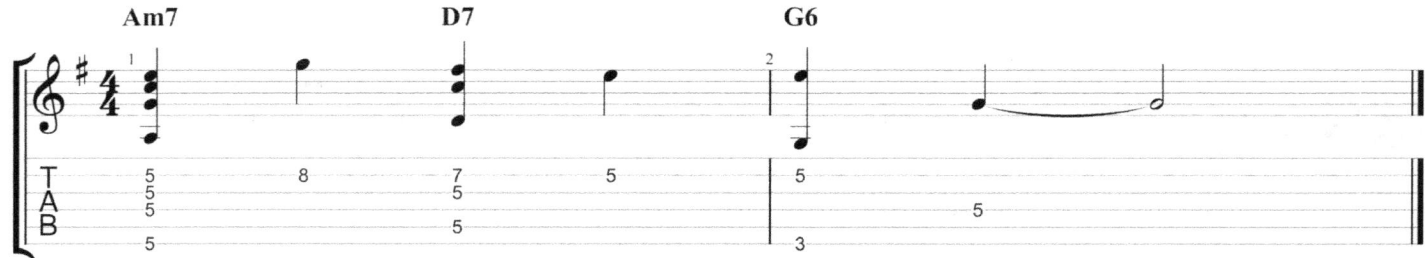

It's important to note that the F#m chord is a little bit different, so instead of playing a 5th here (C#), it actually sounds much better to play a b5 (C). I won't go into the theory behind this now – I just want you to hear the effect of the note, rather than it be an academic exercise. This example teaches you to hear the sound of the b5 in context over the F# bass note. Use your second finger to play the bass note.

Example 2k1

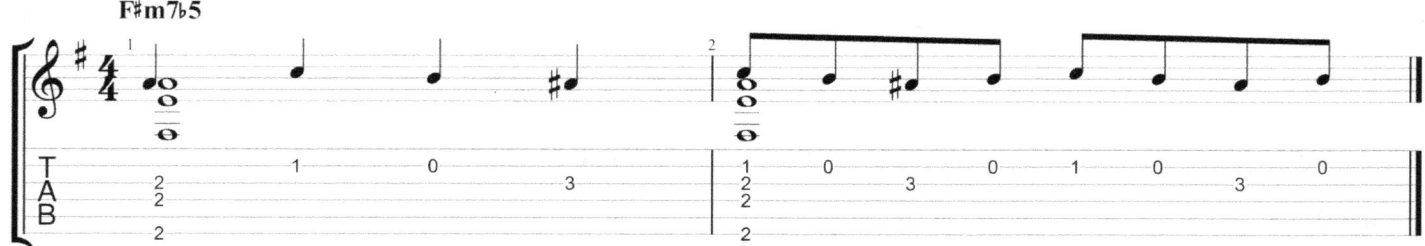

The b5 note really wants to resolve to the 5th on the B7 chord.

Example 2k2

Here's a line that highlights the beauty of the b5 over F#m, resolving to the 5th of B7.

Example 2k3

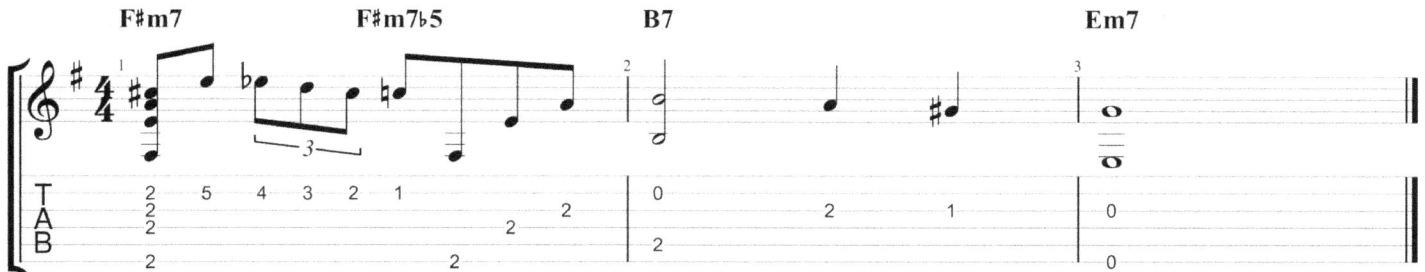

This line is also very pretty and targets mostly 9ths, with a b9 played over the B7 chord.

Example 2l

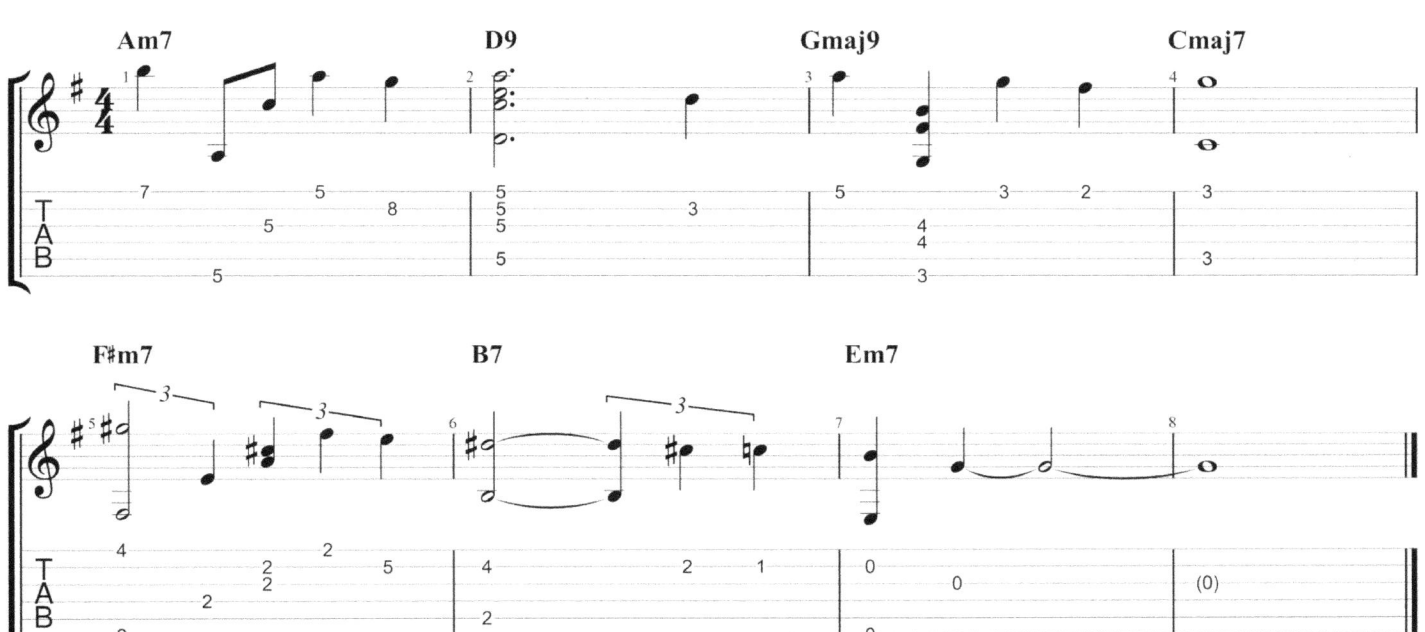

An Important Substitution

Before we move on, I want to talk about a very important chord substitution idea that I often use in my playing. A chord substitution is simply playing one chord instead of another. This means that when we think of a substitution as a chord, we can target its chord tones in our solo, just as we have been doing so far.

I want to keep our discussion about this concept as simple as possible. When we talk about substitutions, students often reach for the theory books and come up with some complex ideas. My way of thinking for chord substitutions (and knowing when to play them) is so easy it can be boiled down to a single sentence:

"You can approach any chord chromatically from a semitone above."

This means that instead of playing the following:

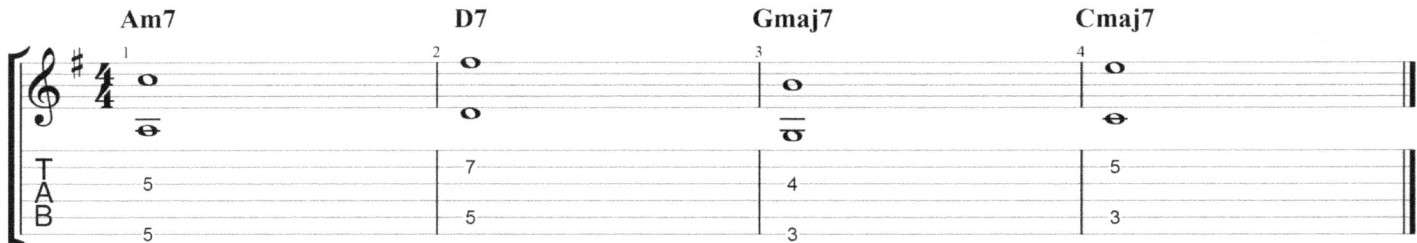

You could play…

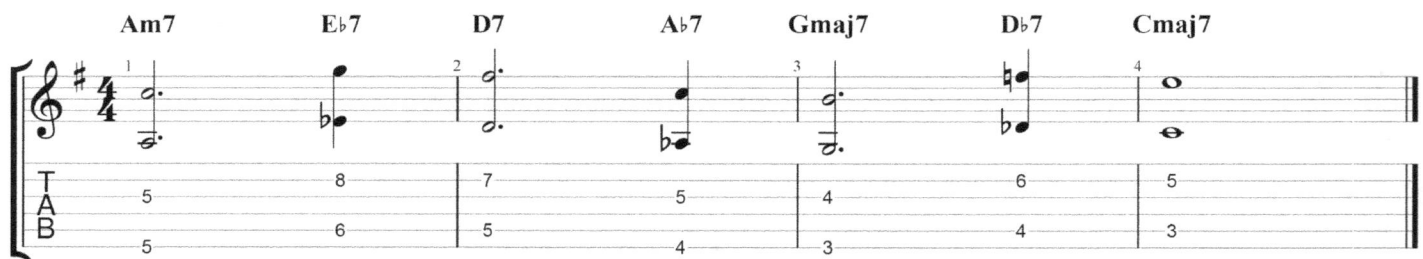

The series of bass notes illustrated in the second diagram is just like a walking bassline. We could play all of those substitutions all the time, but the music would start to sound heavy and complicated. Instead, we can pick and choose from them.

Let's explore the possibilities of just one of them – the Db7 chord that precedes Cmaj7.

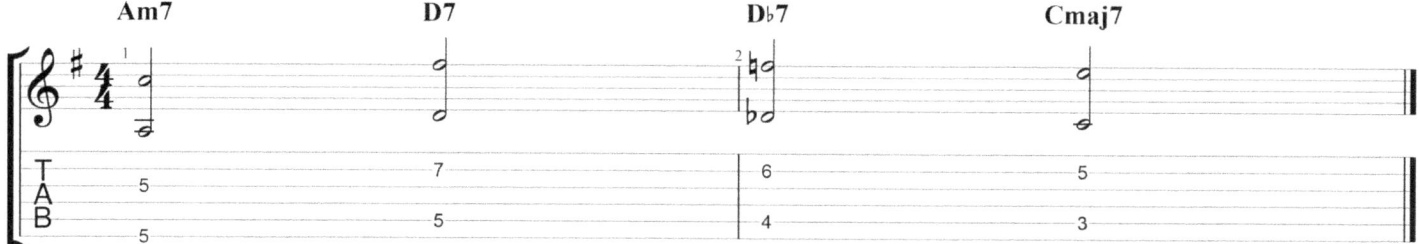

Now we have a Db7 in the first half of bar three, we can use its chord tones (and extensions if you like) as target notes in an improvised melody. The fingering of the following example will take a little bit of getting used to if you've not done this before, but I think it's important and a feature of my style to play the bassline as I play the melody.

Here I play a melody through the unaltered changes, then play the same thing with the Db7 substitution. I've chosen a richer colour here and played a Db9#11. You can hear how using just this point of tension makes the line a lot more interesting.

Example 2m

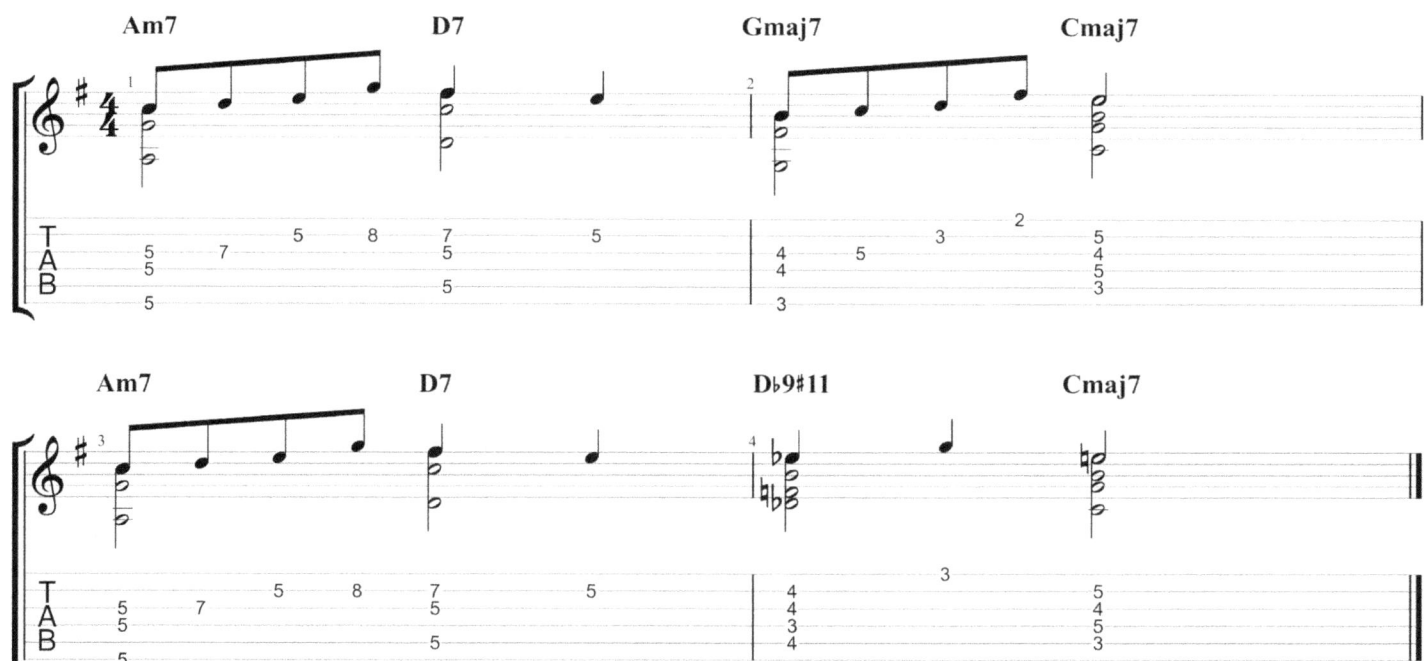

When I play these substitutions I don't really think about a separate scale choice I should be playing over the chord, but here's a line I use a lot that contains a great collection of notes from which you can create a melody.

Example 2n

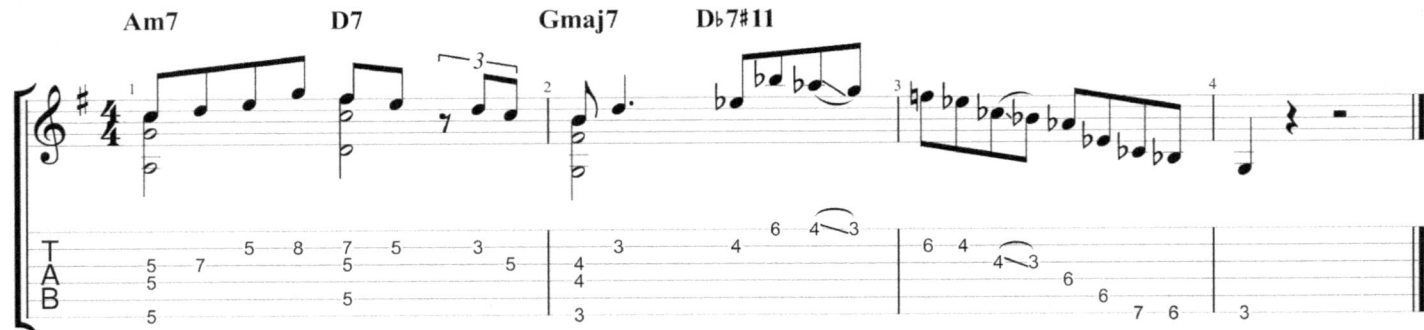

This concept can be applied to any chord you like, but playing it just before the Cmaj7 is a wonderful place to start. Even though you might play just one or two notes on that chord, it adds interest and sophistication to your solo. See how many melodies you can create with the notes of Db7 resolving to a chord tone of the Cmaj7 chord.

Which Colour Should I Use?

So far, we've discussed different ways of targeting the most important notes of each chord and also explored a simple substitution idea. The danger is that we use this information in an almost mathematical fashion, targeting one interval then the next and entirely forgetting that the aim is to create great music! The exercises have been useful to help you locate the chord tones, but want I really want you to focus on is the colours and moods each interval creates against the underlying chords.

How do they make you feel? And which interval should you use when?

I want to take a moment to describe how I think of the different notes in terms of their colour and mood. Like an artist, we have a broad palette of colours to choose from with many different shades – not just black, white and primary colours.

If I play a straight G Major chord it sounds solid, like a primary colour. But if I add the major 7th, now I've got a shade. Suddenly we're on a beach drinking Pina Coladas! It's a pretty sound that always reminds of me *The Girl from Ipanema*, especially when combined with the 9th.

If I lower that to the b7th, it quickly becomes more tense and bluesy.

Lower it again to the 6th and it creates a different feeling all together. What does it mean to you? Play the following example.

Example 2o

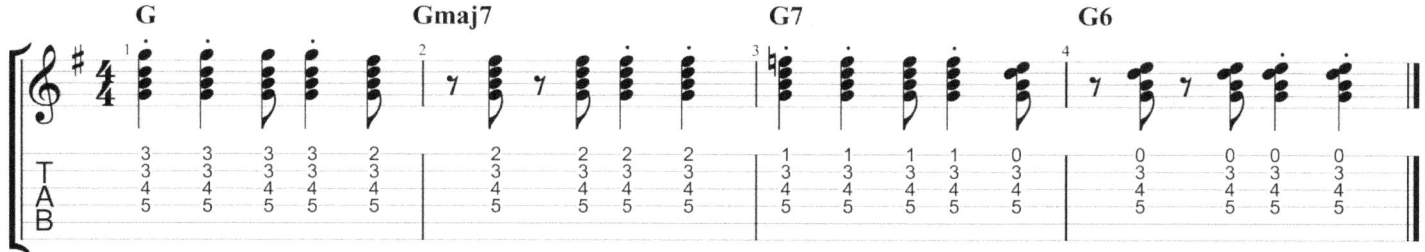

When you think more in terms of what mood you want to create (romantic, wistful, reflective, tense etc) it will affect your choice of melodic hit point. Here I've chosen to target the 9th on the Am chord, the 5th on the D7, and the 7ths on both Gmaj7 and Cmaj7. Notice how I roll my picking fingers through the chords to add another texture to the music.

Example 2p

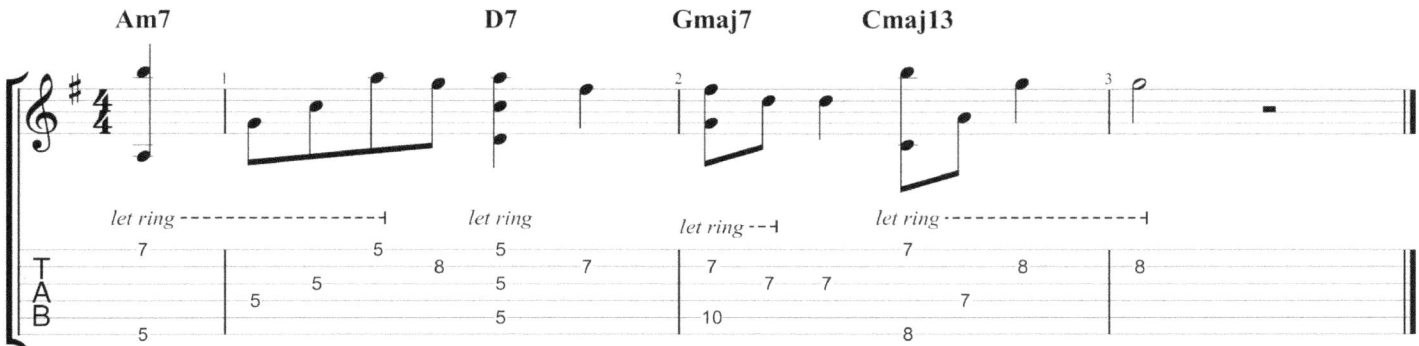

When it comes to deciding which tones to target, it all comes back to colours. Each chord tone or *extension* (9, 11 or 13) represents a different colour to me. Which one I choose depends on what kind of picture I'm painting.

To use a different analogy, it's like cooking. You wouldn't want to use the same ingredients in every meal. Adding chromatic notes is like adding some chili – it's only appropriate for certain dishes! So for example, while we can add the b5, #9 or #5 to any chord, you'll probably find that these work best (to begin with) on the dominant 7 chords.

I've added some spice in Example 2q. This is how the #5 on the B7 chord sounds moving to the 9th on the Em.

Example 2q

Work through the progression, focusing on each chord in turn, and listen to the sound of each tone against the root and 10th voicing. See how each one makes you feel. Internalise the sound.

This is an extremely worthwhile exercise, but a lifetime's work. The context in which you hear the intervals will often be different, so it will take time to absorb the sounds. However, there's nothing wrong with starting now. Listen to the roots, 9ths, 3rds 11ths etc at the top of each chord voicing. Try to take an organised approach. Sometimes you might want to play the bass note with your second finger to help you reach the desired pitch.

As you get better at choosing the notes that reflect the mood you're trying to convey, the next stage is to write lines that link them together. We looked at lots of lines that linked chord tones earlier in the chapter, but just for a bit of inspiration here's one that really pushes the boat out.

Let's say you're approaching the Am7 chord and the next note you want to target the b3rd of the D7 chord. Here's a creative line that links them together. It starts a beat before the Am7 and descends chromatically to target the b3 before jumping down a 6th and continuing. This line is a staple bebop idea, so get this important jazz lick in your ears and then try copying the shape beginning from the b3rd of the D7 to target the 3rd of the Gmaj7 chord.

Example 2r

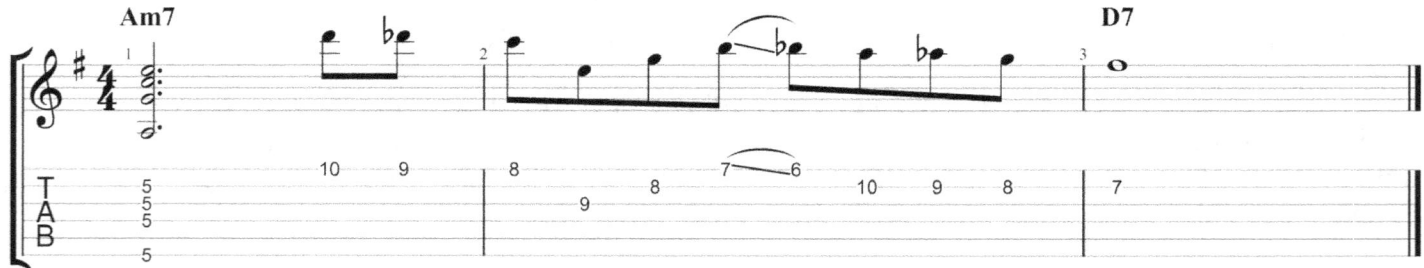

To close this chapter, I want to leave you with a short etude to study that combines many of the ideas we've discussed. Learn it then break it down to see how it links the chord changes together. You can analyse it if you like, but before you do that, I want you to listen to how the target notes make you feel.

The etude begins with me playing the melody to get the sound of the tune into your head, but immediately jumps into quite an intricate solo that misses out many of the variation and development steps I'd normally do. We've covered those – here I want to present a glimpse of where you can take the concept.

You should be able to hear that many of the hit points of the melody are surrounded by free improvisation that consolidates the ideas I've shown you so far.

Example 2s

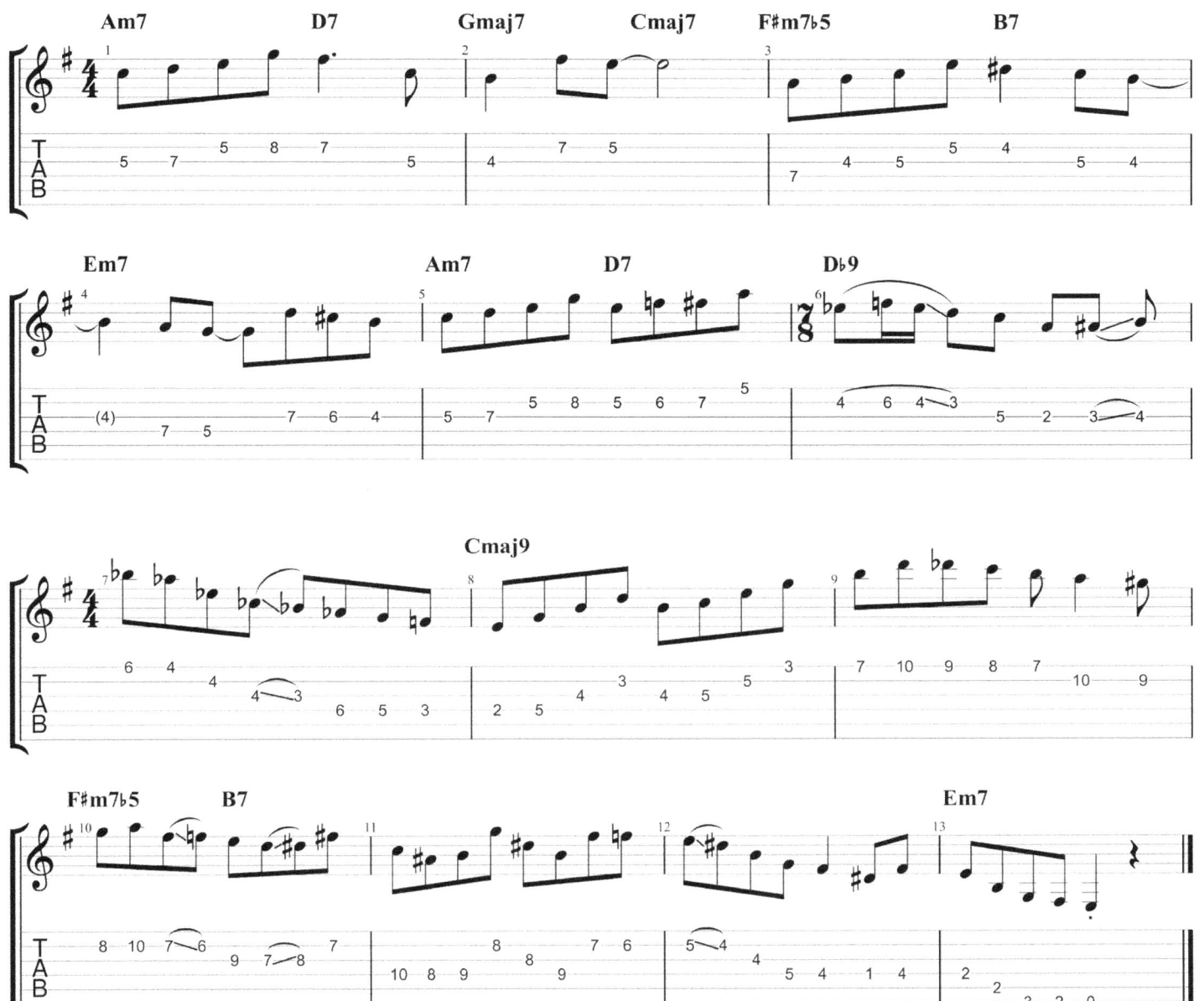

In the next chapter, I'm going to break down layer by layer how it's possible to vary, develop and build a solo on even the most basic of melodies. I think you'll like it!

Chapter Three – Baa Baa Black Sheep

In the previous two chapters, we've laid a lot of the groundwork for meaningful single note soloing, and I've shown you a great deal about varying the melody and targeting chord tones to build a solo. All this was done within the framework of a jazzy chord sequence and we looked at how playing different intervals on those chords affected the colour and mood of your solo.

In this chapter I want to show you just how effective *variation* can be in transforming even the most pedestrian of melodies into a jazz solo that has momentum and tells a story. I've often used this example in my guitar retreats, and it works because *everyone* knows this melody, even if they're not into jazz.

Baa Baa Black Sheep has a strong, simple melody based on the major scale. Because the chord sequence is not remotely jazzy, practising with this tune allows us to forget about the changes and concentrate on learning to develop variations. The goal here is to embellish the tune and build into a creative solo.

We will begin very simply and gradually expand the complexity of the variations until we're playing an exciting solo. You might think that this would result in the melody becoming unrecognisable, but when we underpin the improvisation with our new-found secret strategy of targeting melodic hit points, we will always retain a strong musical link to the melody. What's more, because we begin with simple variations, we can take the listener on a journey so they can hear, step by step, how the solo develops.

This chapter will teach you the art of melodic variation that goes back to the great classical composers like Bach, Mozart and Paganini. Despite our jazz phrasing and chromatic ideas, it's very easy to see how what we do as improvisers builds on the genius of the old masters.

Let's get started.

This chapter doesn't contain a lot of words as I want the music to speak for itself. If you don't already know it (though I doubt it!) here's the melody for *Baa Baa Black Sheep*.

Example 3a

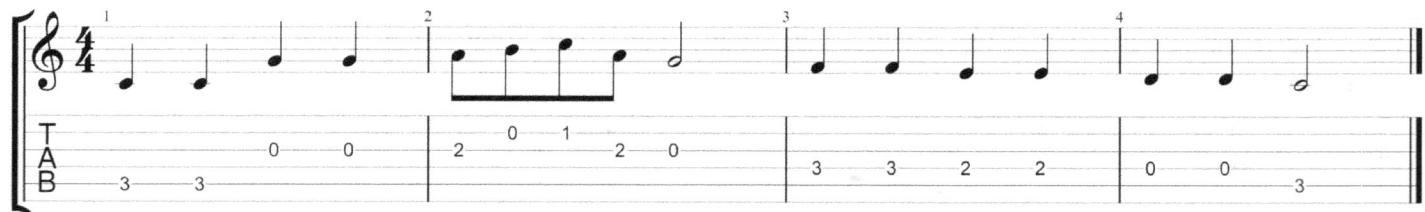

Hopefully it's pretty clear to you already which are the strong target notes of the melody, but I've highlighted the relevant words in the lyrics below, in case you're in any doubt.

Baa baa **black** sheep,

Have you any **wool**?

Yes sir, **yes** sir,

Three bags **full**.

All these notes are contained in the G Major triad, except for the F on the first "yes", which is the 4th.

Let's begin by adding a little motif to the melody to fancy it up a little bit! Notice how the hit points are the same. I just play a slightly different phrase to get to the next hit point.

Example 3b

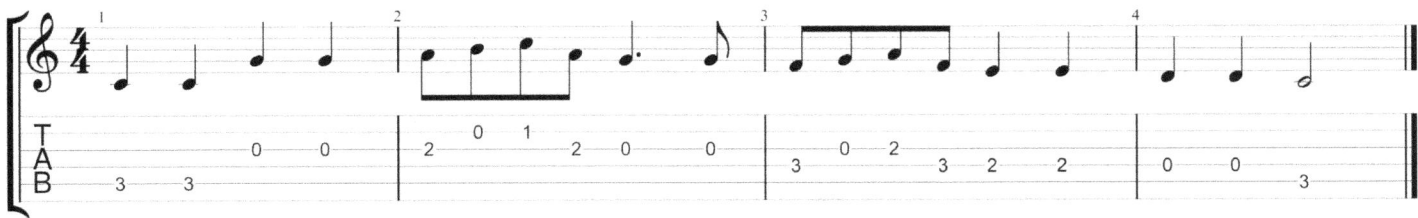

Here's another little variation.

Example 3c

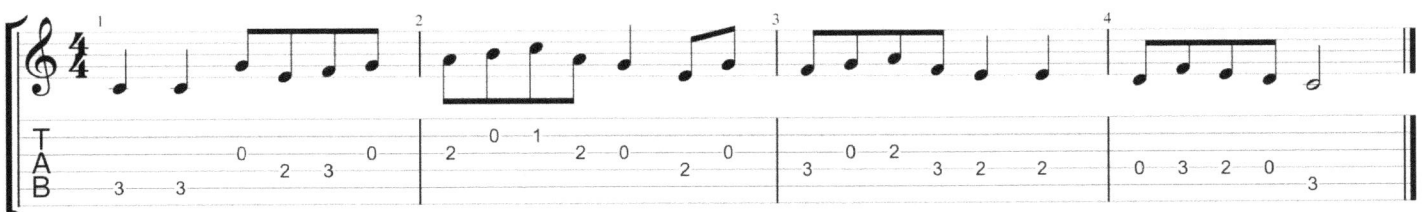

Here's another. I know I have to get to my target note, but how I get there is up to me.

Example 3d

OK, let's get a little more jazzy and use a motif with a little chromaticism.

Example 3e

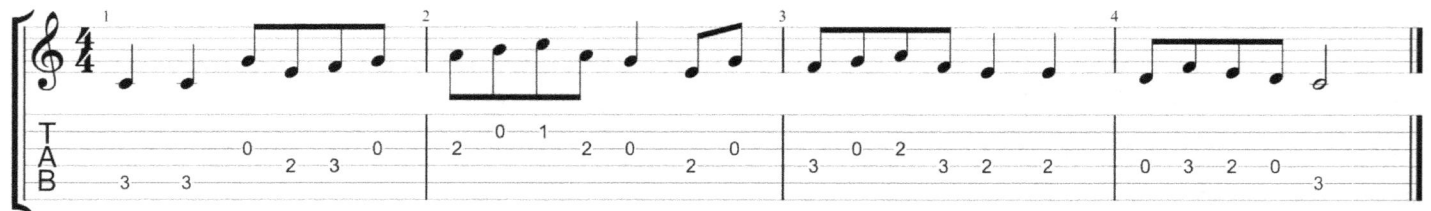

Example 3f is an idea that disguises the basic melody a little more, but it's definitely still in there.

Example 3f

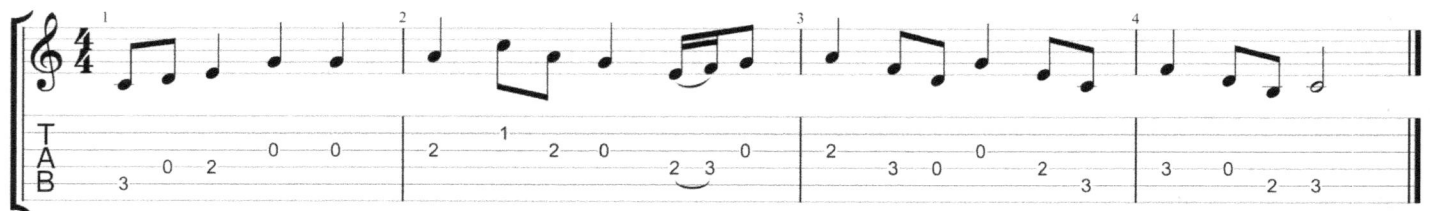

I've filled in some gaps in the next idea.

Example 3g

Playing with a different feel can have a dramatic effect on the overall effect of the music, so let's add a bit of swing!

Example 3h

Sometimes it's easier to get a jazz feel without using the open strings. In the next example I take the melody up an octave then add some jazzy embellishments.

Example 3i

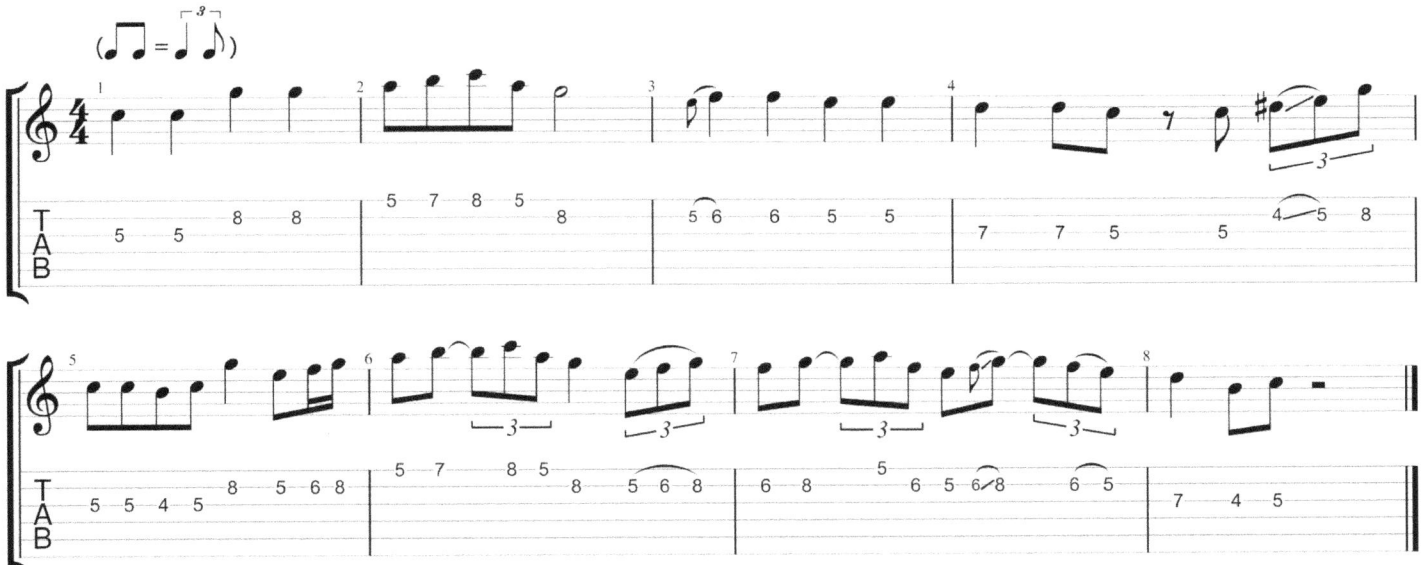

Here's a jazz/blues approach to varying the melody. Notice how my *feel* has changed. The notes aren't ringing out as much and I vary my articulation.

Example 3j

Now I really begin to pull out all the stops. There are chromatics, jazzy motifs and even the Blues scale creeping into my playing here… but you can still hear *Baa Baa Black Sheep* because I've led you to this point in simple steps and I still target the odd hit point.

Example 3k

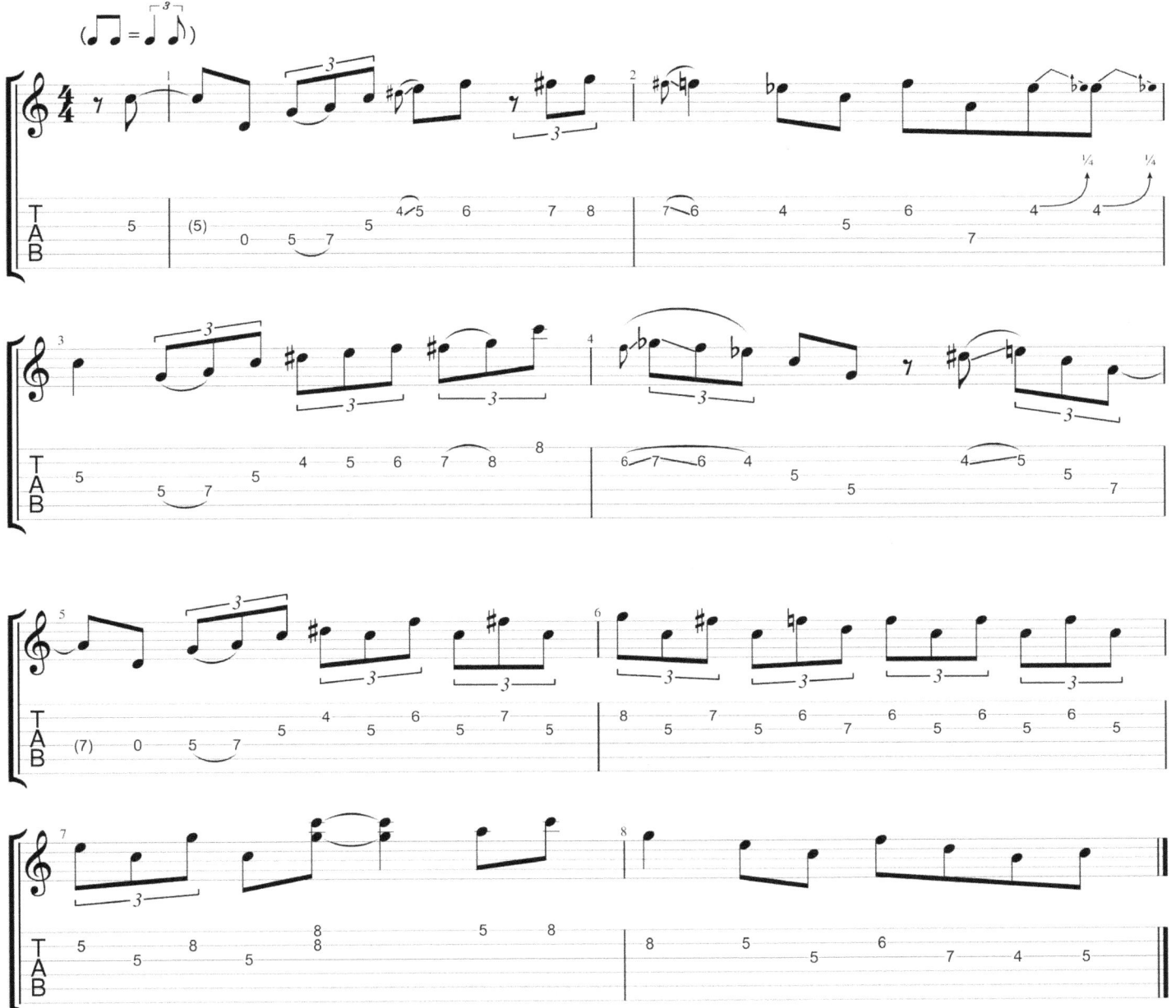

Now we're starting to take a few more liberties with the melody and things are sounding distinctly jazzy. I go twice round the tune here and keep building the variations.

Example 31

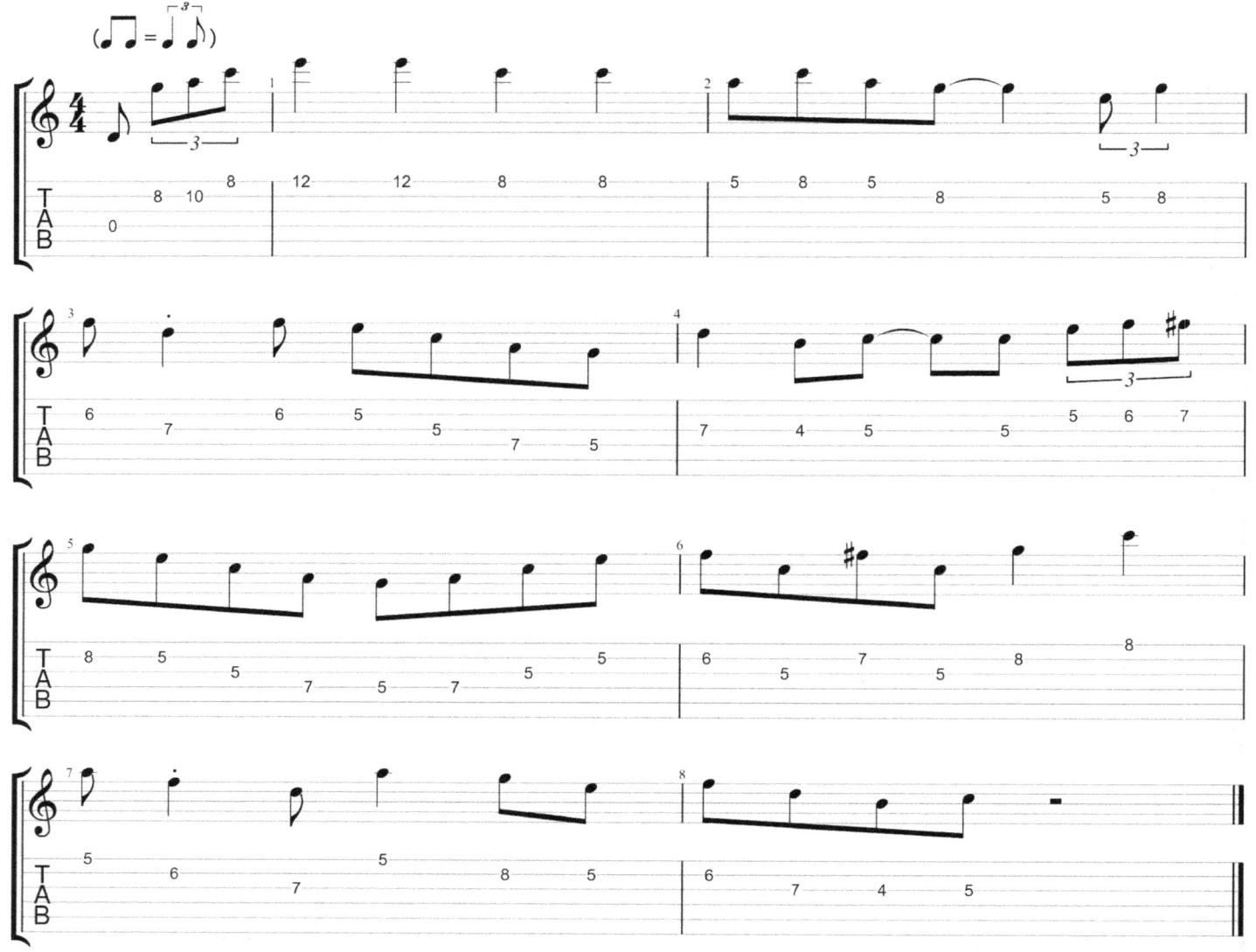

The next line begins sticking closely to the melody and introduces an important jazz pedal note idea that you should learn.

Example 3m

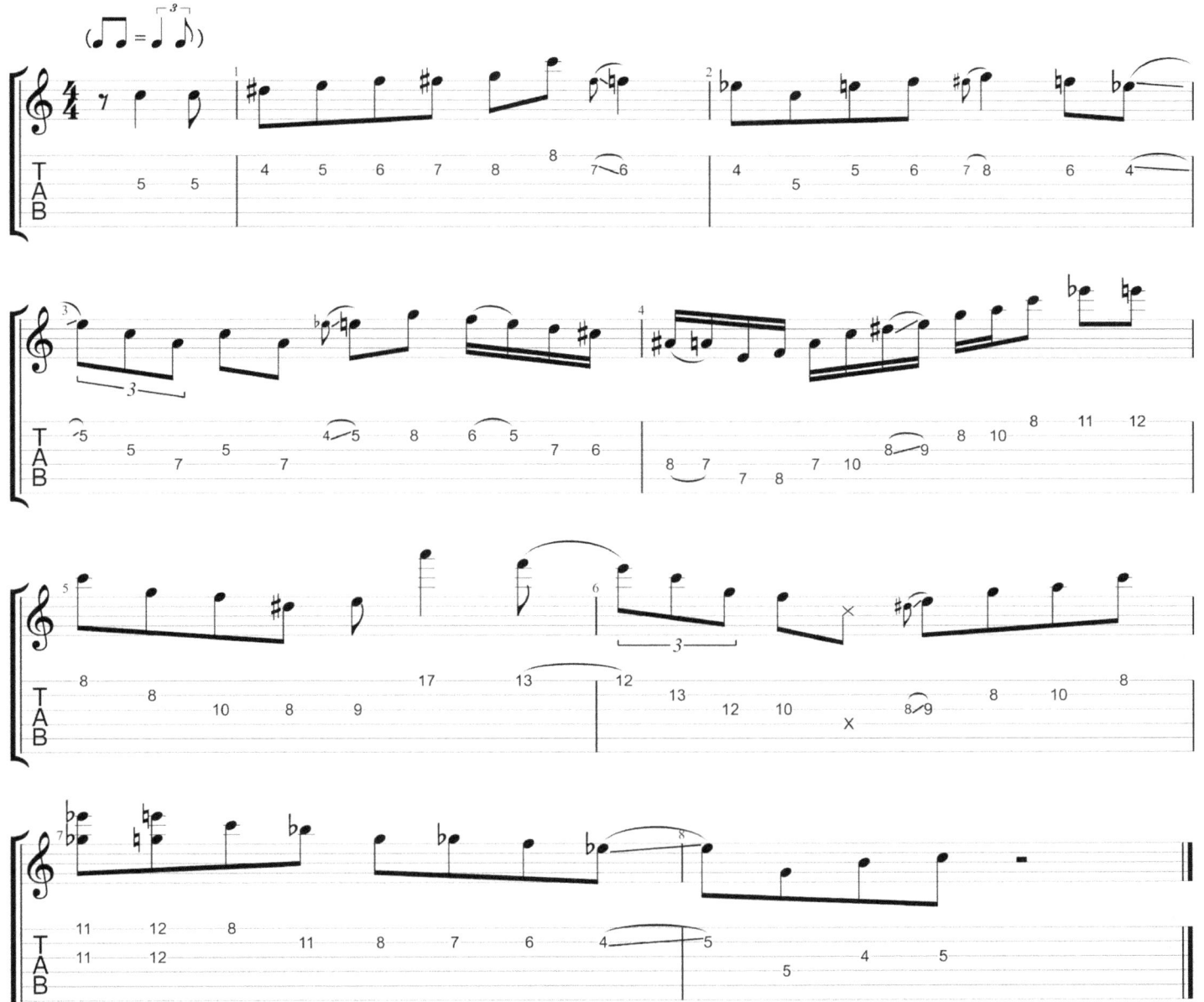

By now, the original melody has been developed so much that I can really play whatever I want. The only hit point in the next example is really the final note of the melody. I've gone "full blues", adding double stops and even a few bends.

Example 3n

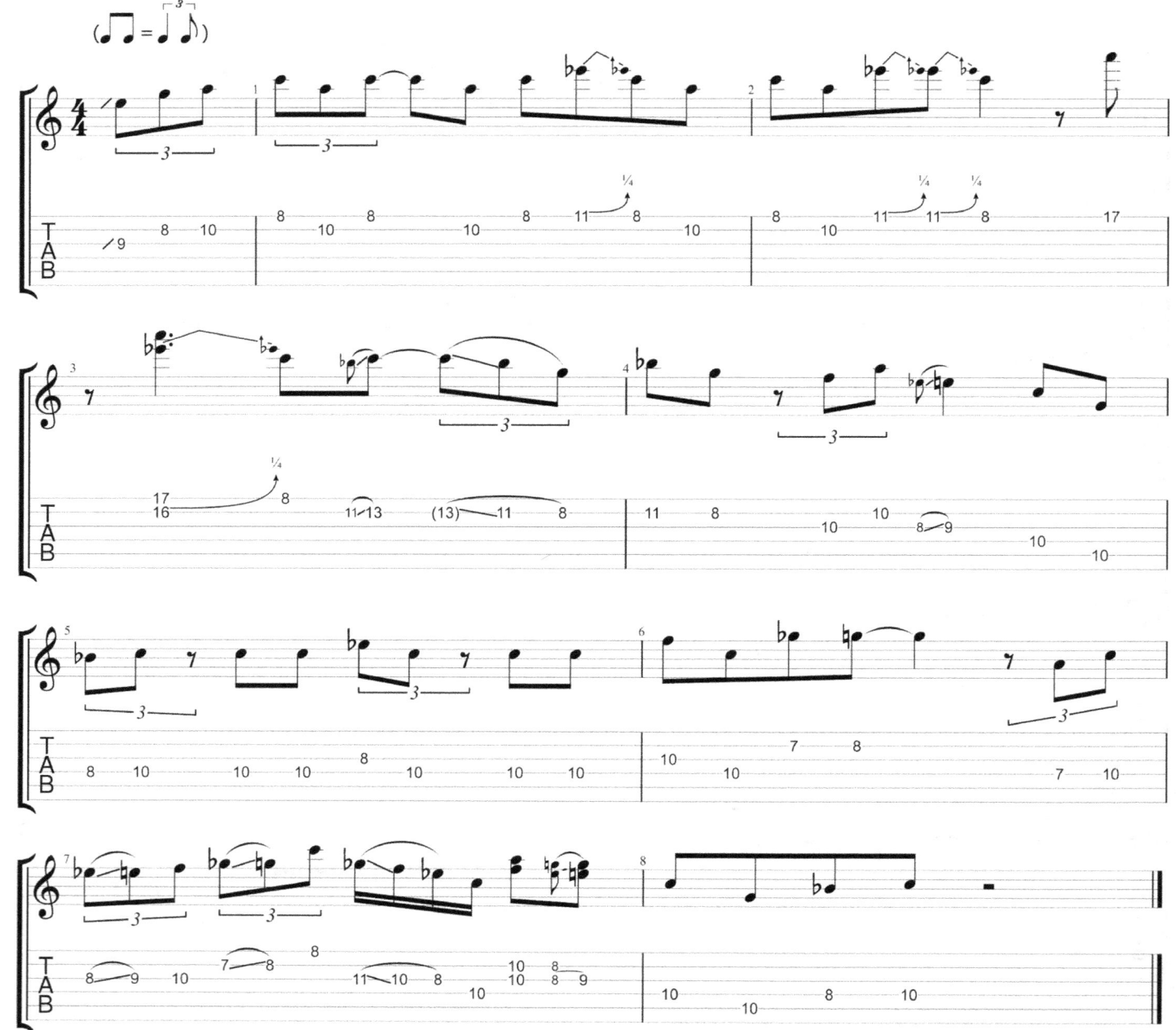

As you practise this approach more and more, some of your ideas will become licks you'll keep and reuse. This is how you'll develop your own language. Here's one final idea. A different take that really articulates the melody and sounds like an authentic early swing lick.

Example 3o

So there you have it: *Baa Baa Black Sheep!* Throughout all those variations I never deviated from the simple chords that underpin the melody. Even when the solo was getting quite advanced, I kept returning occasionally to reference the hit points, and so never lost sight of the melodic structure and strength of the tune.

When you first begin to learn this approach you might find it quite a challenge to come up with new ideas to vary the melody, so I recommend you learn my variations first and steal those ideas to use in your playing. It can be easy to lose the melody of any tune – even one you know inside out – so try humming the hit points as you play to keep in mind the notes you're aiming for. Gradually, your confidence will build and you'll be able to take more liberties with the rhythm and use fewer hit points to give you more freedom.

Don't forget, the secret is to use small variations that take the melody somewhere new. If you can do this, your audience with be right there with you. As you improve this skill, you will naturally become able to start your solos with more intricate variations and jazzier improvisations. Your only goal right now is to see how many ways you can find to vary the melody.

Chapter Four – Developing Vocabulary and Phrasing

After all the work developing your variations in the previous chapters, you might be starting to realise that successfully developing a melody depends on a few things.

First of all, you can create whatever melody you like as long as it is strong and reaches the target note at the right time.

Secondly, the more "connecting" vocabulary you have at your disposal, the more interesting your improvised lines become.

Thirdly, we all have the same twelve notes available to us, it's just how and when we play them that makes us different as soloists!

In this chapter, we will work to develop your vocabulary and get you thinking creatively about phrasing. This isn't a chapter about jazz guitar licks, it's about developing your own musical language on the guitar, which will begin to form your own unique voice.

How do we learn a language? Simple! We copy it from our parents and teachers before adapting it and learning to use it freely to express ourselves.

First, let me make one quick observation. There is a difference between "licks" and "vocabulary".

A lick is generally set in stone. It's a musical phrase that is always played in the same way and probably fits over a specific part of a chord progression. We all have our favourite licks, but they can be limited in their use. Licks are the equivalent of a phrase book when you're visiting a foreign country and don't speak the language well. You can pull out these stock phrases and read them aloud to achieve a desired but specific result.

Having *vocabulary* is different. Vocabulary is an understanding of the language, knowing the meaning of each individual word. Vocabulary is learned through study and immersion in a culture. If licks are a phrase book, vocabulary is an understanding of the how the language is constructed – the grammar and subtle nuances that are at your command when you've truly mastered the language. It's like knowing every available word in the dictionary and being able to combine them in any way you want.

You can, of course, learn vocabulary through learning licks – and this is the best way to begin – but ultimately, isn't it more creative and artistic to create licks that are personal to you through understanding the language?

In this chapter, I'm going to teach you some of my jazz language and you're going to learn it by copying my playing. As you begin to develop your own vocabulary (by using my ideas and taking them in other directions) you'll be able to use that language to connect the hit points in any tune you play.

One of the reasons that my style of guitar playing is very distinctive is that my vocabulary doesn't really come from jazz guitarists. I have always listened to a lot of pianists and horn players. That's nothing new, Django Reinhardt's favourite musician was Louis Armstrong. In fact, one of the challenges that jazz guitarists face is that the language of jazz was developed on horns and saxophones – and these lines are quite difficult to translate onto guitar. This is one of the things you first realise when you learn to play jazz on guitar – nothing really falls under the fingers.

However, it really is essential that you study vocabulary played on the traditional jazz instruments like trumpet, clarinet and saxophone if you want to develop an authentic jazz language. It's a little awkward at first, but you soon get used to the patterns involved.

Here's the sort of line that Django might have played, inspired by a trumpet. Imagine this being played by a trumpet and you'll hear what I mean.

Example 4a

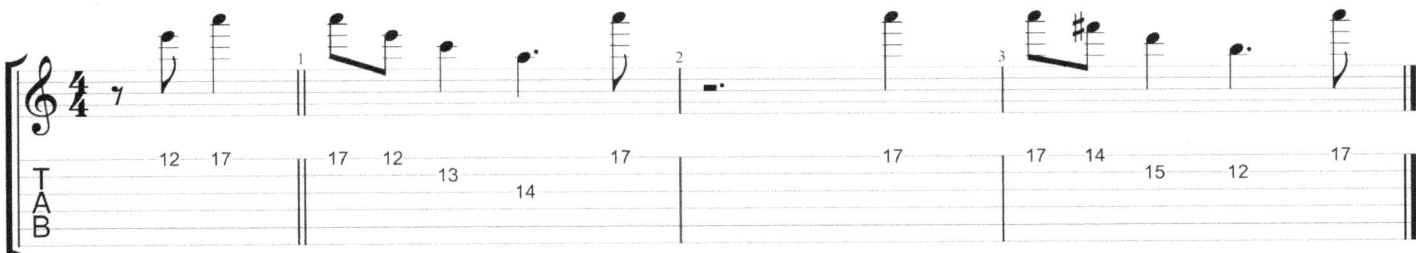

Here's another piece of Django vocabulary, this one inspired by a bugle call. Listen carefully to how I articulate the phrase because I'm copying the way a brass instrument would play it. This line jumps around the neck perhaps more than you'd like, but that's just part of the language. Don't learn this as a lick necessarily, just focus on the articulation and the shape of the line and see if you can use it as a variation to a melody.

Example 4b

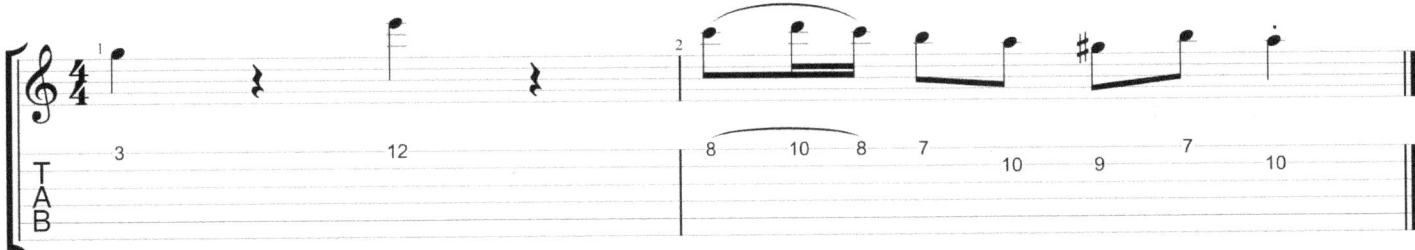

Here's another line that you could imagine Louis Armstrong playing. Again, pay particular attention to the articulations I use. Which notes are strong? Which are slurred? Which are short? Which are long?

Example 4c

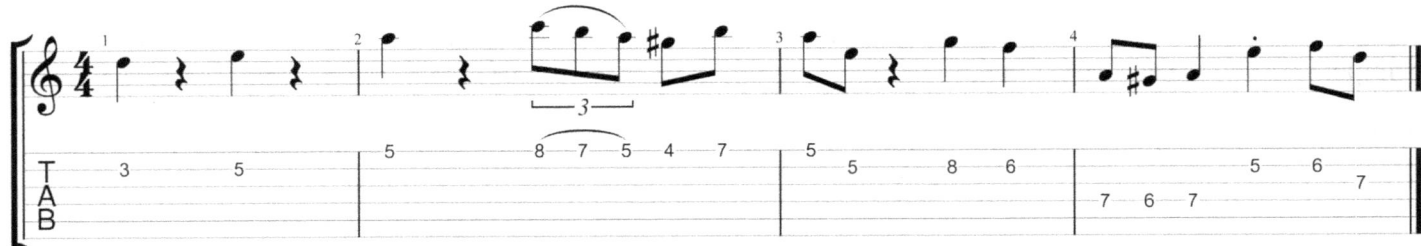

You could analyse the previous three lines to see which scales and arpeggios they're built around, but I think it's better if you just start to use them. One way you could do this is to focus on the final hit point of each phrase and use that as the target note in your improvised melody variation. You don't have to use the whole phrase, just the part of it that stands out to you. Then play it around the changes of our workhorse tune.

Spend 20 minutes using the phrase to target the root of each chord. Then spend time targeting the 3rd and so on. You might have to alter the notes slightly, but your ears will tell you when that needs to happen. What's important is playing these pieces of vocabulary with confidence and the same articulation you hear on the audio track.

You know where your hit point is, and you know the vocabulary works… so it's simply a case of getting in the "woodshed" and making these ideas work. One good tip is to see where the starting note of the phrase lies in relation to the target note. For example, is it a scale tone above the 5th or a semitone below the 3rd? Then fill in the gaps with the line. Not every phrase will work on every chord tone, but you'll quickly figure that out.

Use the backing track and explore what sounds these phrases create.

Let's move on and begin to look at some of my language. We've touched on this before, but chromatics are an important part of most jazz lines. Here's one way I can move between the chords in our tune. Each one of the movements between the chord tones is a little piece of vocabulary in its own right. Take the one you most like the sound of and move it around the changes. Why not take the phrase on the final few notes and use that to target one hit point on each chord?

Example 4d

Here are some other pieces of the chromatic puzzle. Again, they snake their way around the chord changes, but each transition is a little piece of vocabulary in its own right. You could spend days exploring just these ideas.

Example 4e

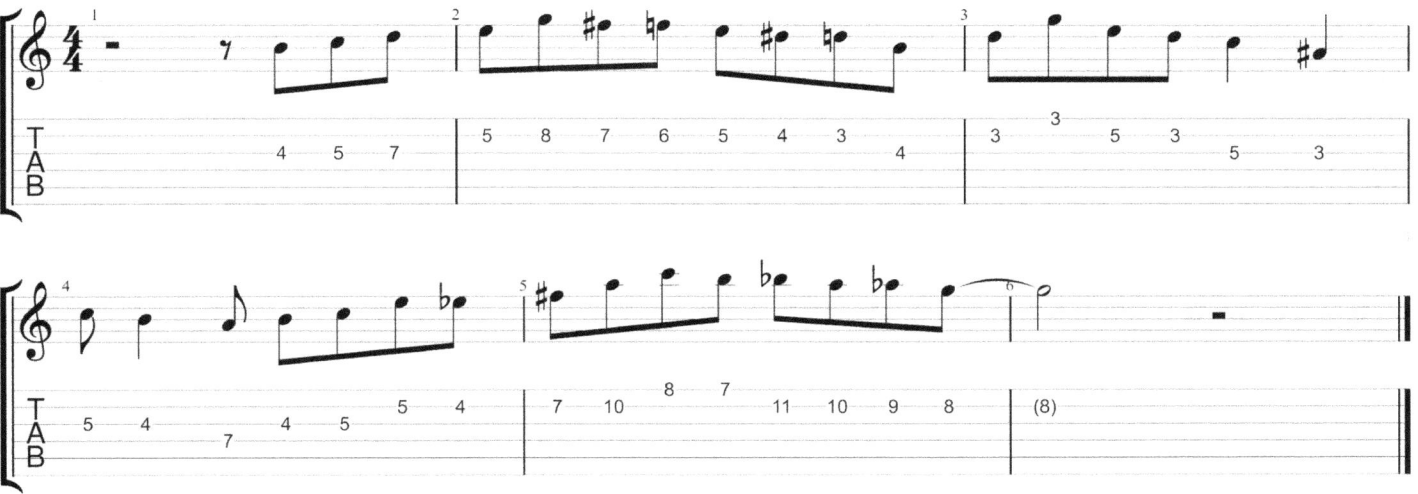

Now let's take add a little more complexity and take these ideas a bit further out.

Example 4f

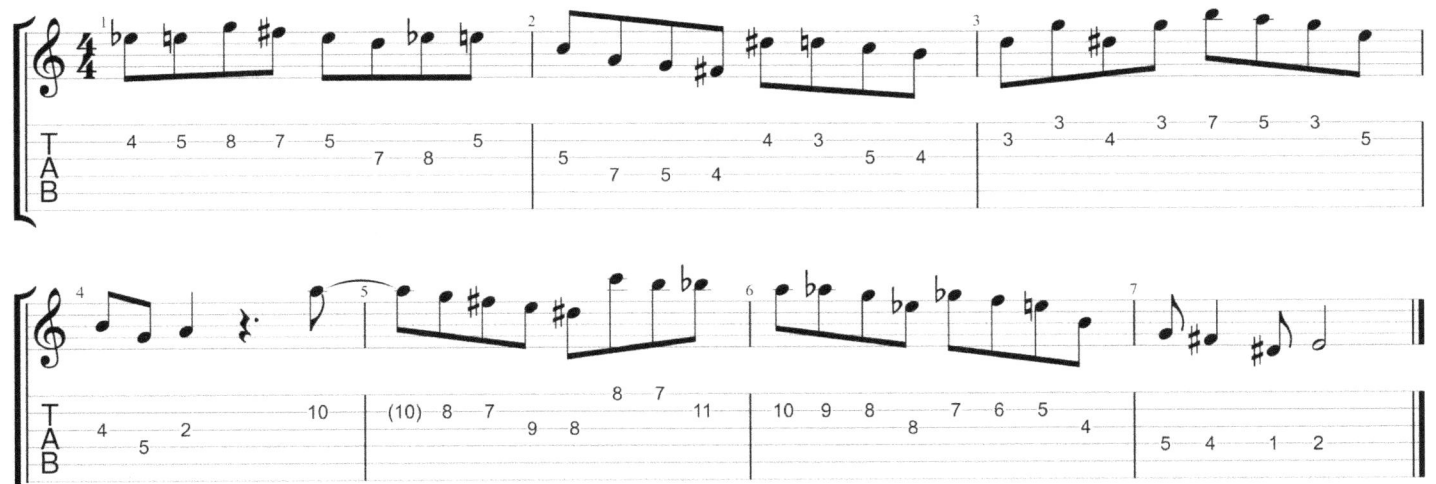

Here's a slightly longer improvisation packed with melodic ideas you can steal.

Example 4g

Finally here's another pass through the changes with some strong ideas based around trills. Notice how my improvisations led me to a little motif (the trill) that I locked onto and started to move around the chord changes. This is a very strong musical idea and you'll quickly start to develop themes in your solos if you do this. What's more, your audience will love you for it. Whenever you play an idea you like, repeat it and move it around the changes. This will help you to refine your melodic way of thinking and also sound great!

Example 4h

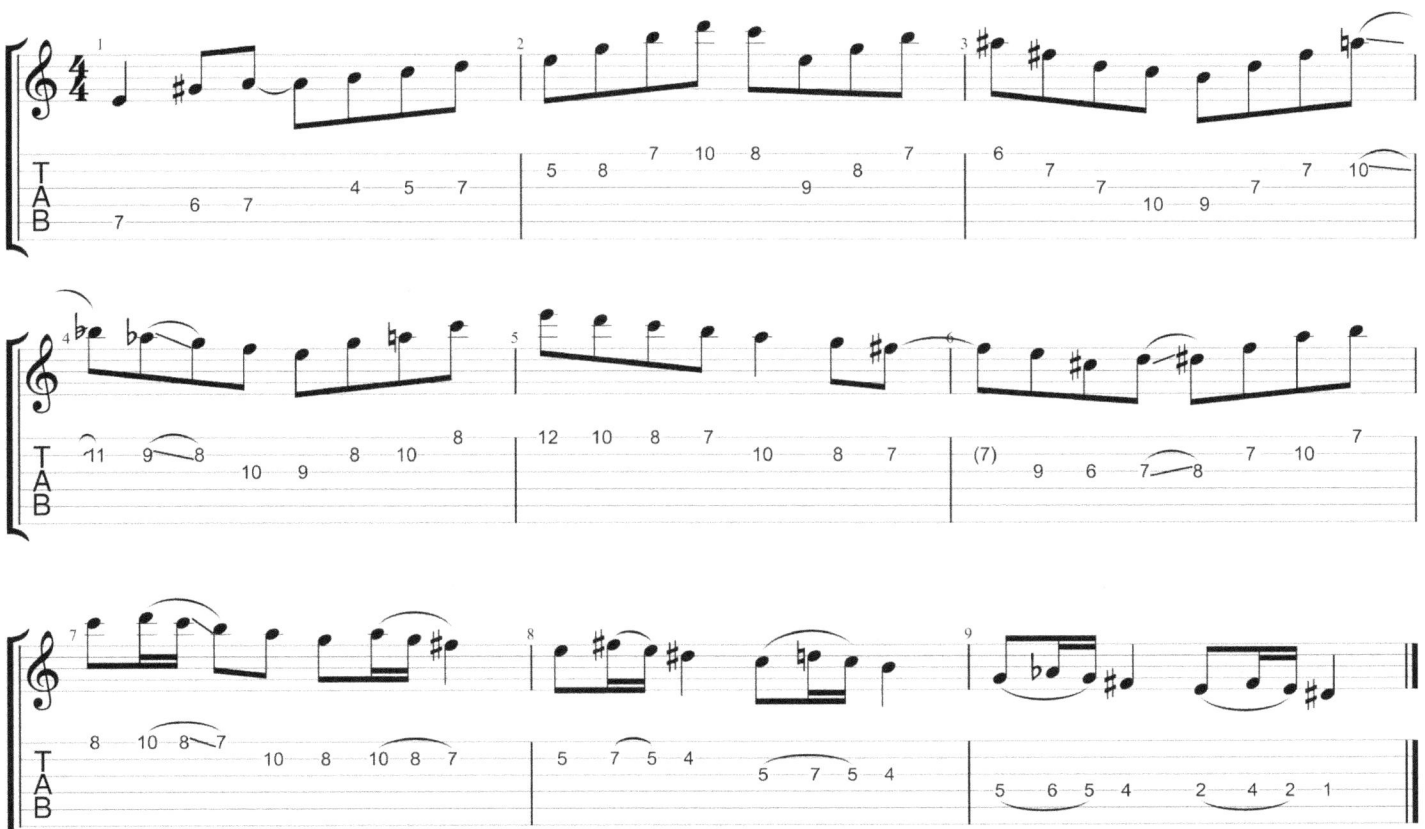

Think, Sing, Then Play

One of the dangers with the guitar is that our fingers take over when we play. This means we can quickly fall into playing pet licks that are part of our muscle memory and "programmed" into our body. It's common to hear my students' solos being led by the guitar, rather than them playing what they hear in their head, but this is like the tail wagging the dog!

The wonderful thing about jazz is that it works on any instrument because it is all about expressing the musical ideas we hear in our heads, and often a big part of my work when I'm teaching is to help the student take back control of the music. This is often a slow process because guitarists are so used to playing blues and rock licks they've memorised, rather than actually hearing the music first in their head and *then* playing it on the guitar.

For some reason, some people feel uncomfortable with the following set of exercises because they involve singing! I don't sing particularly well, but it doesn't matter – this isn't a singing exercise. Don't worry if you feel you can't sing, that's not the point.

This technique can make the biggest difference to your ability as a jazz soloist. It's about thinking of a melodic line, singing it, then playing it on guitar. This is a great discipline to develop. Not only will it help you to play the ideas in your head, it will dramatically improve your phrasing. Your lines will quickly take on a vocal quality that is missed by the majority of guitarists.

The following exercises will help you get started. (Feel free to change the key of the following exercises if they don't work for you at this pitch).

We'll begin with something simple and first of all, we'll flip the process around. Begin by playing the G Major scale and triad on your guitar. Then, without your guitar, sing up and down the scale and triad you've just heard.

Example 4i

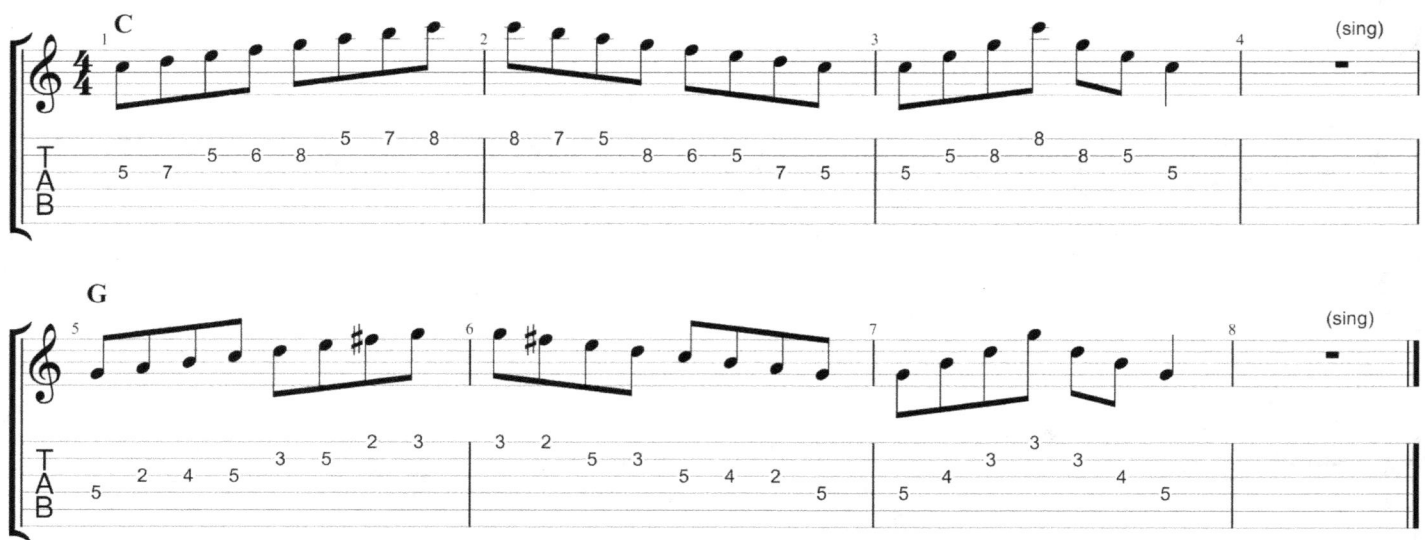

Now you're established your "territory", sing a very simple phrase of just a few notes and play it back on your guitar. Don't worry if you don't repeat it perfectly at first – it just means your ears aren't quite connected to your guitar yet. Figure it out note by note if you need to and the connection will come. Each note I sing in the following examples is taken from the eight note G Major scale, so you know the answers are in there somewhere.

Example 4j1

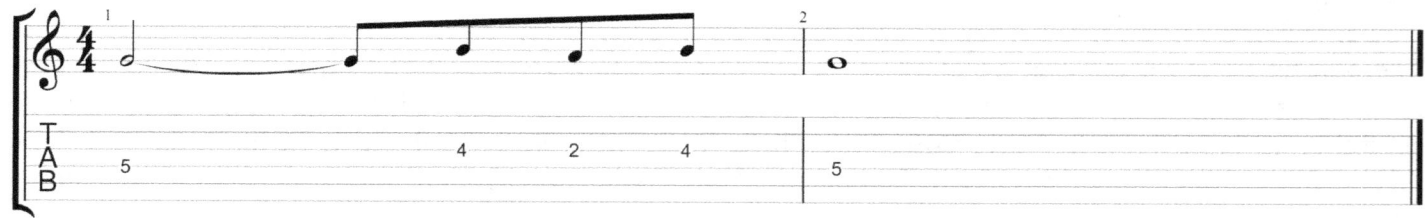

Example 4j2

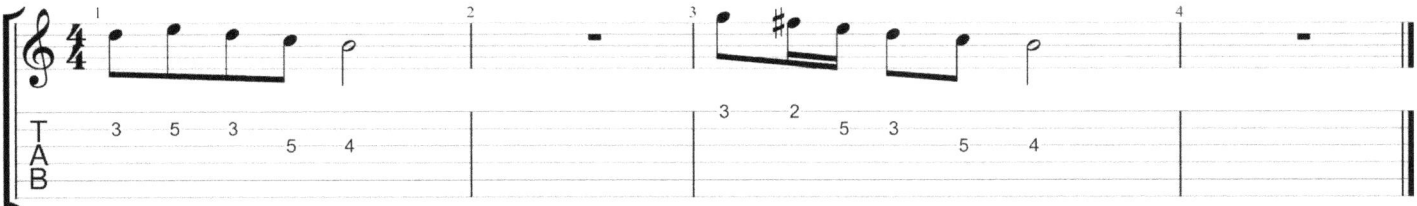

Example 4j3

Now it's your turn. You can spend hours doing this and it works as a great warmup every morning before you pick up your guitar. In your head, conceive some simple phrases using just the notes of the major scale, *then sing them,* then play them back on the guitar. You'll gradually begin to feel the connection between the music you hear in your head and what you play on the guitar grow stronger.

Soon, you'll want to get a little bit more adventurous and add slightly bigger jumps into your melodies.

Example 4k1

Example 4k2

This melody adds a chromatic note.

Example 4k3

Keep practising this exercise every day and very slowly begin to introduce bigger jumps and one or two chromatic notes. It's a lifetime pursuit and you'll learn to love it!

Remember the process: think what you want to play, *then* sing it, *then* play it.

Don't worry that when you begin there is a gap between what you sing and what you can reproduce on the guitar – you're working on establishing the connection between the melody you sing and where those notes are located. As long as you keep doing it, this gap will continually get smaller. Before long, you'll be able to play exactly what you hear in your head in real time.

When you combine this skill with all the vocabulary you've been learning, the vocabulary will begin to influence the lines you "hear" and your jazz soloing skills will quickly compound. In fact, at this point you can really stop worrying about scales and theory, because the lines you hear, sing and play will always work!

I've included a video of the next example to show you exactly how I think about singing and playing. Here's a transcription of what I play on the video but you should go and check it out here: **https://geni.us/singlenote**

Example 41

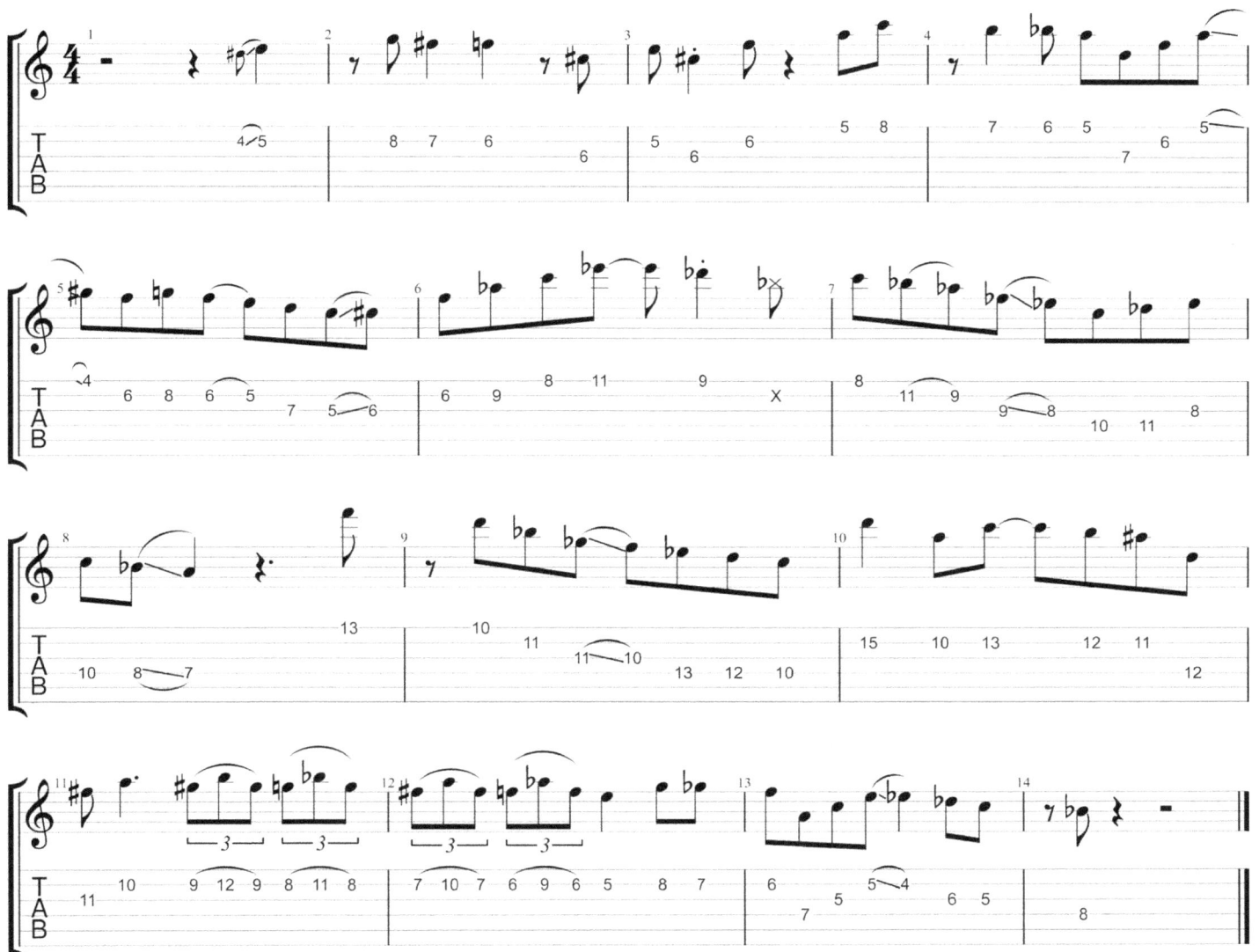

There are other ways to practise this skill. One great way is to find a vocal melody you like (it doesn't have to be jazz) and sing a phrase along with the record. Then turn the track off and sing the phrase again. Figure out the key of the song and play the phrase on your guitar. Again, you'll make mistakes, but don't worry, you'll make mistakes for the rest of your life – I know I do! The point is to hear the melody, sing it, then play it. If there are associated chord changes, you can figure them out too, but your primary goal is to sing, then play the melody.

A great bass player I worked with, Peter Ind, often didn't let his students get their instruments out of their cases and whole lessons were devoted to hearing then singing melodies to improve the student's vocabulary.

Another important approach is to transcribe parts of melodies and solos that you like, then sing them. This is a really good way to develop your own jazz vocabulary and again, links strongly to the way you learned to speak. I can't stress enough that *singing is the bridge* between the melodies you hear and actually being able to play them on the guitar in real time. It's called ear training because our ears *can be trained!*

Ultimately, the goal is to bypass the singing part and immediately play what you hear in your head. Singing is purely a device to close the gap. An old Buddhist saying visualises the process as crossing a river. We are on one bank (thinking) and we want to get to the other bank (playing). We can use a boat (singing) to get there, but once we're on the other shore, we've reached our destination – we don't need the boat anymore.

Phrasing and Articulation

Compared to many instruments, playing the guitar is a very mechanical process. What I mean by this is, unlike the saxophone, trumpet or voice, we can play the guitar constantly without any breaks because we don't need to take a breath to sound a note. While other instruments are *forced* to leave gaps in their lines due to their need to breathe, guitarists can go on all day! That's not really a good thing because there is a tendency to over-play.

This is another strong argument for learning to play jazz by listening to brass and woodwind players and bringing some of their phrasing approaches into our playing.

Think also about how a singer breathes. They sing a phrase, take a breath, then sing the next phrase. This naturally forms a two-line phrase which is often seen as a question and answer structure. It's something the listener naturally responds to and has the added advantage of helping you keep track of your place in the music. A two-bar question followed by a two-bar answer makes a four-bar line of music. If you do that eight times, it fills a 32-bar chorus. It might sound obvious, but guitarists often lose sight of that kind of structure in music, and this approach can really help you and your audience keep track.

When I learnt guitar I didn't really learn whole solos, I learnt phrases that I liked and that's something that has always underpinned my approach to playing. Thinking about *phrasing* not theory is vital, because when you think in terms of "these are the scales I can play on this chord" you really miss out on the musical, melodic aspect of playing jazz. Theory's useful, but not while you're improvising!

When you begin to think in terms of phrases to create melodies, you'll often find that one phrase you play suggests the next. Here's an example of a four-bar line split into two-bar phrases. Notice how the question phrase suggests an answer. Think about where a saxophone player would take a breath while playing this.

Example 4m

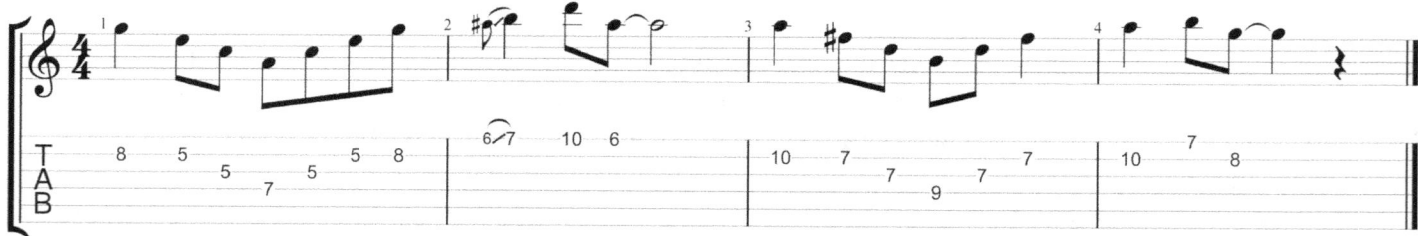

When I solo, I do actually breathe just like a horn player would. In fact, I only play when I'm breathing out. This stops me playing long "guitary" phrases without any break. Here's a short transcription of me playing that shows you where my breaths occur. (In the notation you'll see a * symbol which has been given a 1 beat rest. This is the pause for breath! I purposely overemphasise this pause on the audio example).

Example 4n

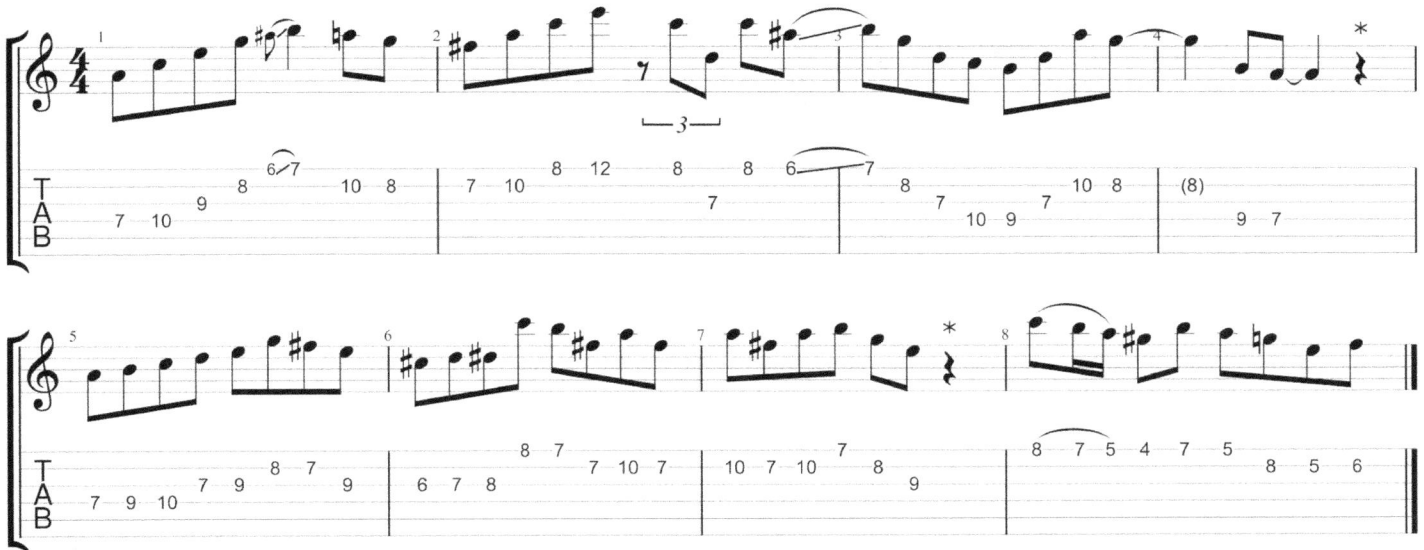

Breathing, thinking in phrases and learning vocabulary are all important factors in creating *poetic* phrases. When you focus on learning these skills you'll find that your jazz guitar playing quickly reaches a whole new level. When you speak, you breath. You use your vocabulary and talk in phrases to tell a clear story. The same is true in jazz soloing.

When you focus on phrasing, an unexpected benefit is that you automatically begin to incorporate *silence* into your playing. Sound and silence are two sides of the same coin. Think about when a seasoned actor delivers a monologue – their pauses create as much impact as their words. Silence in a story is essential because it allows the listener to process the information they've just heard. Don't forget to use plenty of silence in your solos to make your phrases stand out. You'll be a better player for it.

One final ingredient we must add to the recipe of good phrasing is *articulation*. Some guitarists like to give each note of their solo the same articulation by picking every note evenly. While that can work for some players, I prefer to mix up my articulation by picking some notes and using legato (hammer-ons and pull-offs) to give my phrases a smoother flow. The notes I do pick can really jump out compared to the legato notes, and this introduces a whole new textural dimension to my lines.

Here's a line that I first play by picking every note, then play with my normal style of mixing up the articulation. Each pick is marked and all the slurs are shown by the curved lines.

Example 4o1

Example 4o2

The key here is experimentation and finding your own approach to articulating your phrases. Listen to great horn players and the musicians you love. Listen to the dynamics of their lines and see how their articulation brings out the nuances of the music.

Chapter Five – Swing, Rhythm and Timing

When I first started working as a guitarist, I was lucky enough to get to play with some really great players. However, working musicians tended to be tough guys and they were quite hard on us youngsters. Playing the odd wrong note or forgetting your place in the tune were forgivable offences – but the biggest crime you could commit was not playing in time. It didn't matter how well you could play or what clever ideas you came up with, if you didn't play in time you didn't last long in the band.

While playing behind the beat was a little better – especially in jazz – playing too far behind was equally frowned upon.

Reflecting on this now, I can see these guys had a point. In real life, your audience will respond much more to groove and a strong rhythm than the actual pitches you play. It gives them an anchor for the music. No one leaves a gig humming a rhythm, but equally no one dances to just a melody. When the band is cooking, you can see the audience begin to move, sway, clap their hands and maybe even dance!

Time and feel is purely physical. This means that you shouldn't just count along to your metronome, you should *move* along to it too. Tap your foot, nod your head, sway, or do them all – but whatever you do, make sure you have a physical connection to the beat. After all, that's why musicians call it having great feel! When you've been playing music for a long time you can feel the rhythm in your body; it becomes like a heartbeat.

My advice is before you play a note, spend time setting the time and locking into the feel. Listen to the band or your metronome and physically feel the rhythm before you play. Also do something physical, like tapping your foot, so that the pulse isn't just something in the airwaves, it becomes part of your body.

Listening skills

Once you've developed the habit of locking into a rhythm before you play, the next most important skill to develop is listening – both to other musicians and yourself.

Listening to what your fellow musicians are playing in a band setting is important in any genre of music, but especially so in jazz, which relies heavily on improvisation and interplay. If you can open your ears and pick up on what other instruments are playing, you can mirror their rhythms and lock in with their ideas. Audiences love to hear the interplay between musicians, when the guitar begins to play the same rhythms as the drummer or pianist. They'll think you've rehearsed these ideas, even though you're just interacting on the fly!

I've also found, however, that we are often guilty of not listening to *ourselves* very much. Some musicians are guilty of not listening to every note they play and can quickly lose touch with the effect they are having on their audience. If we're not mindful of what we're playing, we can also lose our grip on that inner metronome and fail to lock into the groove.

The easiest way to combat this is to record your practice and performances and listen back to them later. You'll often find that you were rushing or maybe you didn't sound as good as you thought (although don't be surprised if you sound better!) Don't be down-hearted if you hear something you don't like in your playing, though. This is a positive step because it allows you to focus on and improve something you didn't even know existed.

Mastering swing

Playing with great time and feel in other musical genres (such as funk) is often called playing "in the pocket". Jazz has its own version of playing in the pocket called *swing*. You can consider it a great compliment if anyone tells you they enjoyed your playing because "you can really swing."

However, swing is notoriously impossible to notate in music, and it's even a little difficult to describe it in such a way that you'll immediately get it. Swing is more art than science. That said, I've created some exercises that will help you to move from playing "straight" to playing with "swing" in a great jazz feel. You will need to listen carefully to the audio of these examples to hear the swing feel develop. (If you've not downloaded it yet, you can get it from **www.fundamental-changes.com**).

Example 5a is a melody based on the tune you learnt earlier to the changes of *Autumn Leaves*. Here the melody is played with zero swing – it is completely straight.

Example 5a

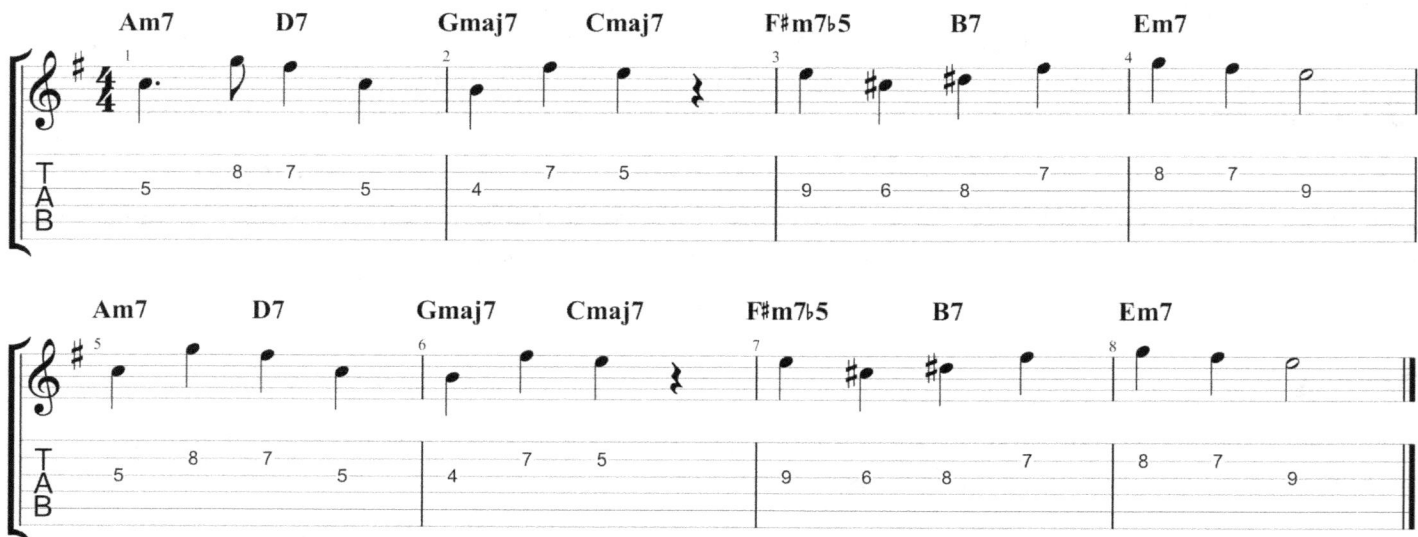

Here is the same melody, but now, quite subtly, I'm starting to swing. Notice that I'm not simply playing the same melody with a bouncy feel. It's the varied placement of the notes that creates the strong rhythmic feeling. Sometimes I'm anticipating the beat, playing notes slightly before it, and sometimes I'm playing behind the beat.

Example 5b

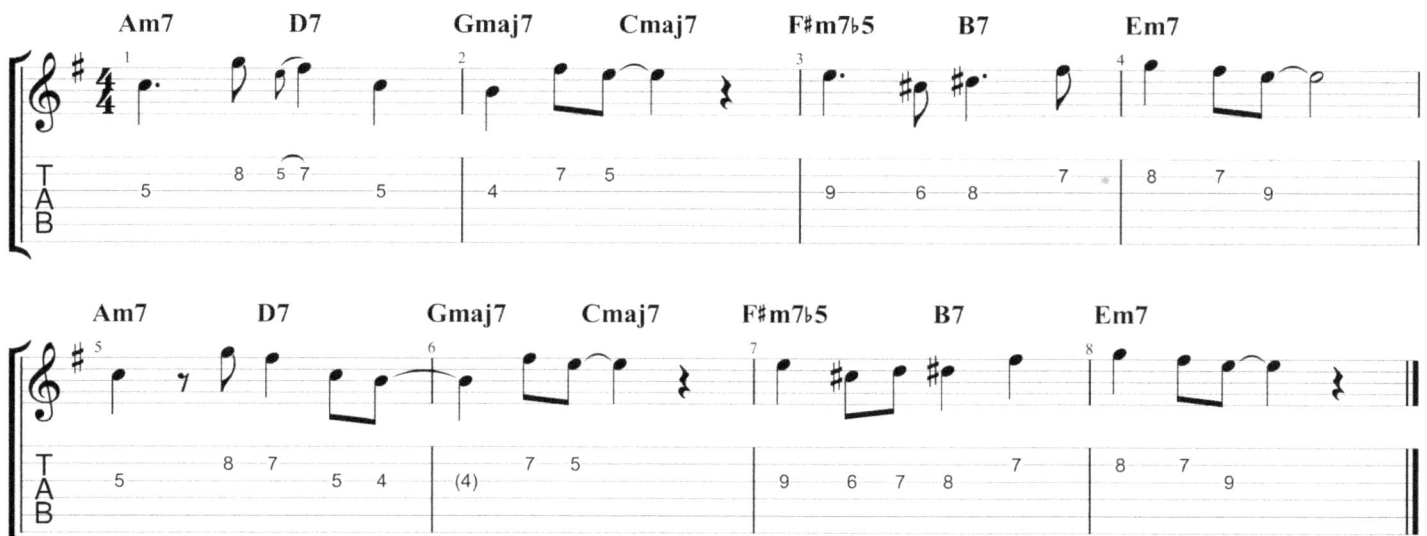

If I could describe it in one sentence, it's this pushing and pulling effect that is the essence of swing. In Example 5c notice that in the first four bars, I'm pulling the beat back by playing quite far behind it. It almost makes you feel awkward! But following this tension comes a release in the subsequent four bars, where the phrasing is still swinging, but the notes are played more on the beat.

Example 5c

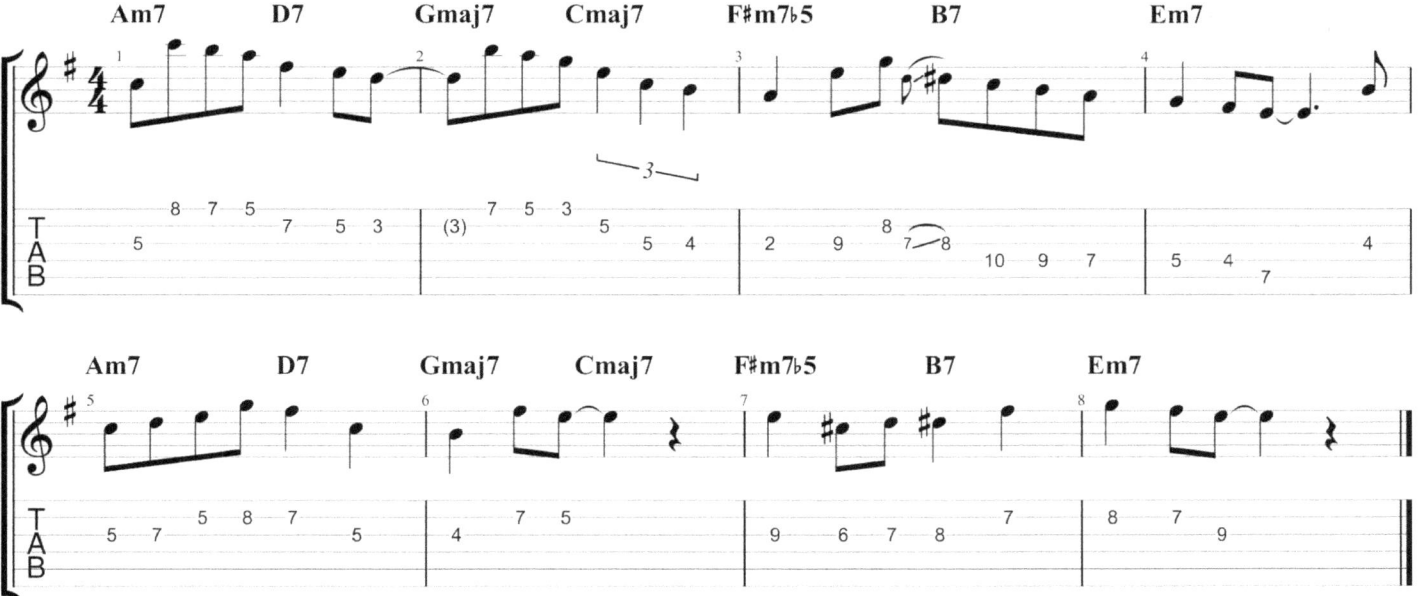

If you've been disciplined enough to record yourself playing to a metronome, you'll have noticed that the metronome is unerringly monotonous – it's supposed to be! It's perfectly in time. To create swing, you need to go a little off-kilter timewise and work around it. In Example 5d, I'm deliberately playing behind the beat in order to highlight what I mean.

Although the metronome is mathematically accurate, you can create the illusion that the time is swinging by pulling against it. Listen carefully to the audio example and you'll hear the interplay between the melodic line and the click.

Example 5d

I'm now embellishing the simple melody I began with by adding other scale and chromatic notes, and in the longer example that follows I'm illustrating how you might freely pull and push as you play to create a sense of movement and direction. Now we're not just playing notes, we're beginning to tell a story – and it's swinging.

Example 5e

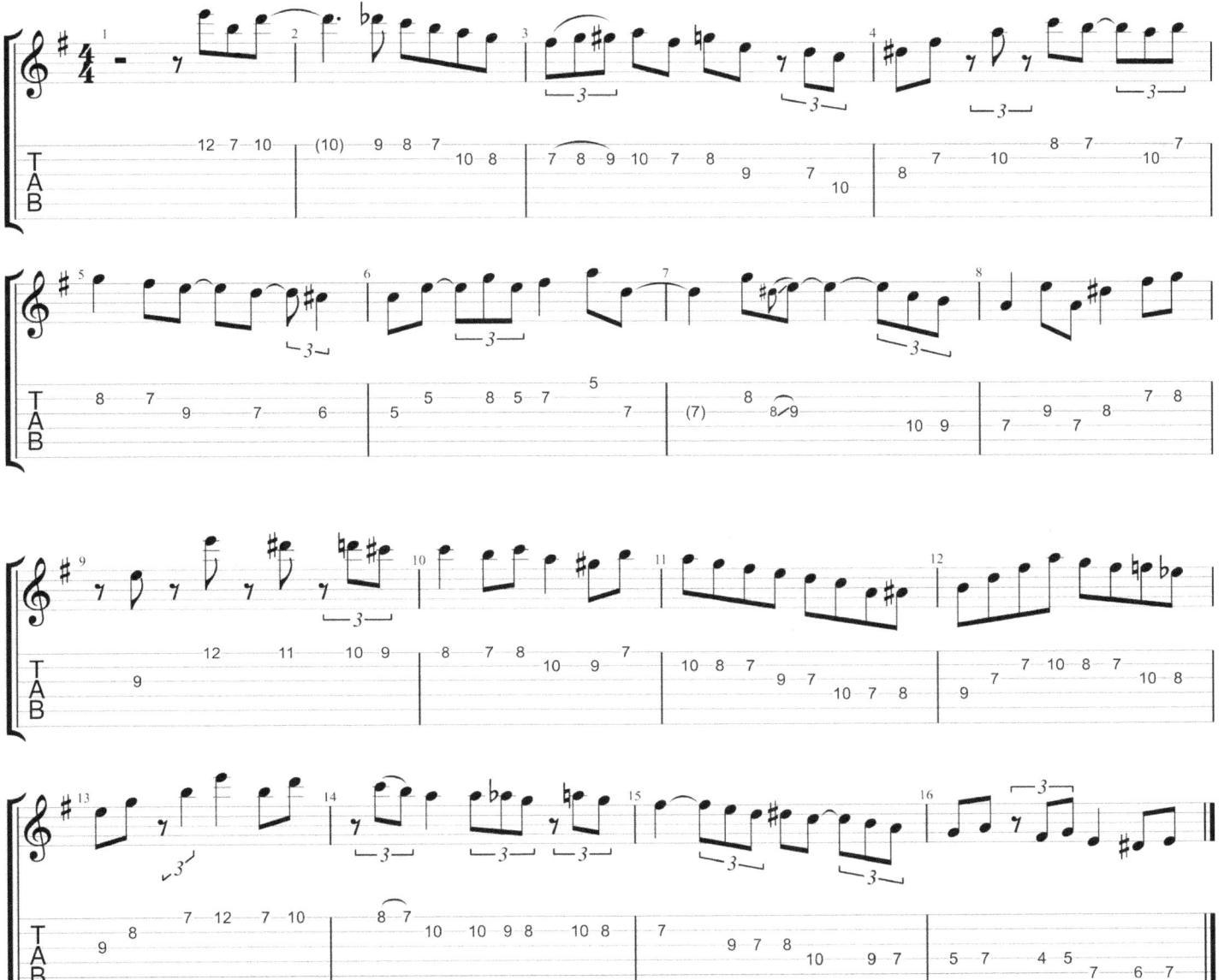

I'm sure you can hear the difference between something that's played totally straight and something that's swung, but how can one develop this skill?

When I play, I am consciously holding back certain phrases and playing them slightly late. When you first begin to practise this, it may feel like you're simply playing with bad time. Don't worry, this is normal! Record yourself and listen to where you are placing the notes. We guitarists have a tendency to rush and can often be straining against the beat. If you focus on playing notes just a fraction later than normal and listen back, you'll invariably find you're playing with a much better feel.

As well as consciously holding back, I also have target notes that I hit. This time I'm not targeting chord tones, I'm targeting *beats*. When I stretch time like an elastic band, pulling against the beat, I'll also hit certain notes dead on the beat.

When you are really comfortable and feel on top of the time, you can choose to target any beat you like, but in order to practice this skill, you should begin by targeting a specific beat over and over. In this short example I'm targeting the first beat of bar one and bar three.

Example 5f

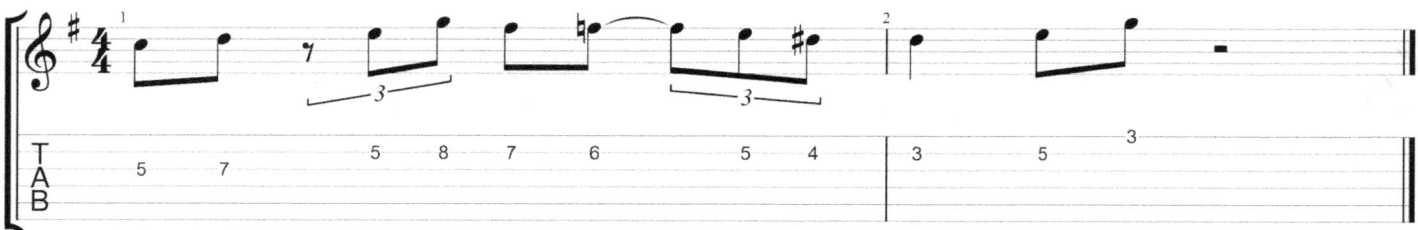

Set your metronome to around 60bpm and play any phrases you like, but ensure that you hit beat 1 of every other bar, dead on. For now, it doesn't matter what you do in between as long as you hit those beats perfectly. If you practise this diligently, eventually it will stop feeling like an exercise and begin to sound natural – and your time and feel will have improved dramatically!

Here is a longer example:

Example 5g

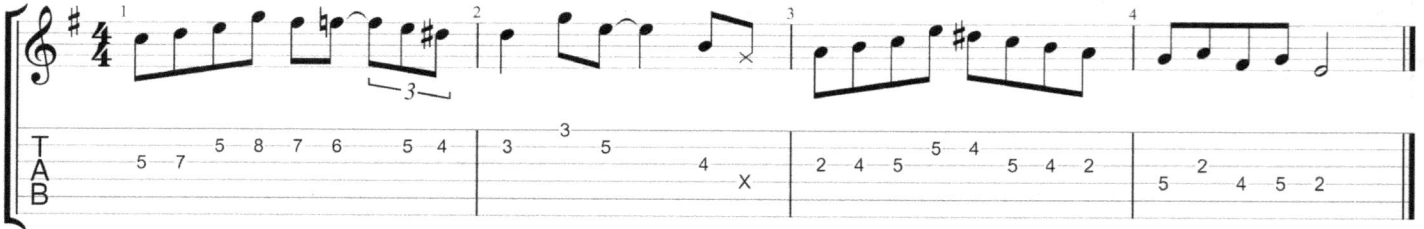

What I want you to take from this is that swing isn't just about playing the second 1/8th note later, it's about how you place the notes in the whole of the phrase. It's about relaxing and sitting behind the beat, making the pulse physical and listening to your rhythm section.

Here is one final example – a transcription of a spontaneous solo I played to demonstrate my swing feel and phrasing over a longer piece of playing. Work through it and pay particular attention to which beats I'm targeting and which notes are pushed or pulled.

Example 5h

Chapter Six – Playing Out of the Box

When you first learned scales on the guitar, you probably did so with "box" shapes across the neck. These are useful to get going, but one thing I've found over the years is that it's much more useful to play up and down the neck, rather than with my hand locked into a single position on the guitar.

Playing up and down the neck makes it a lot easier to follow chord progressions because there's always a root note on the sixth or fifth string we can move to, and it stops us getting locked into the same ideas and reaching for the same scale shapes. I find that I'm much more creative as a jazz guitarist when I can freely ascend and descend the neck.

In Chapter One, I showed you how to play root and 10th voicings up and down the neck, and the ground we'll cover in this chapter ties in closely with that framework.

Let me illustrate the difference in approaches. For example, here's a line played in one position. I feel quite "trapped" while playing this and my line feels a bit predictable and limited by range.

Example 6a

In the next example, I begin the line in the same way, but allow myself to change position on the neck to tackle some of the chords. Immediately I feel freer and you'll notice that the melody not only feels more comfortable, it allows me to access a much greater range of the guitar.

Example 6b

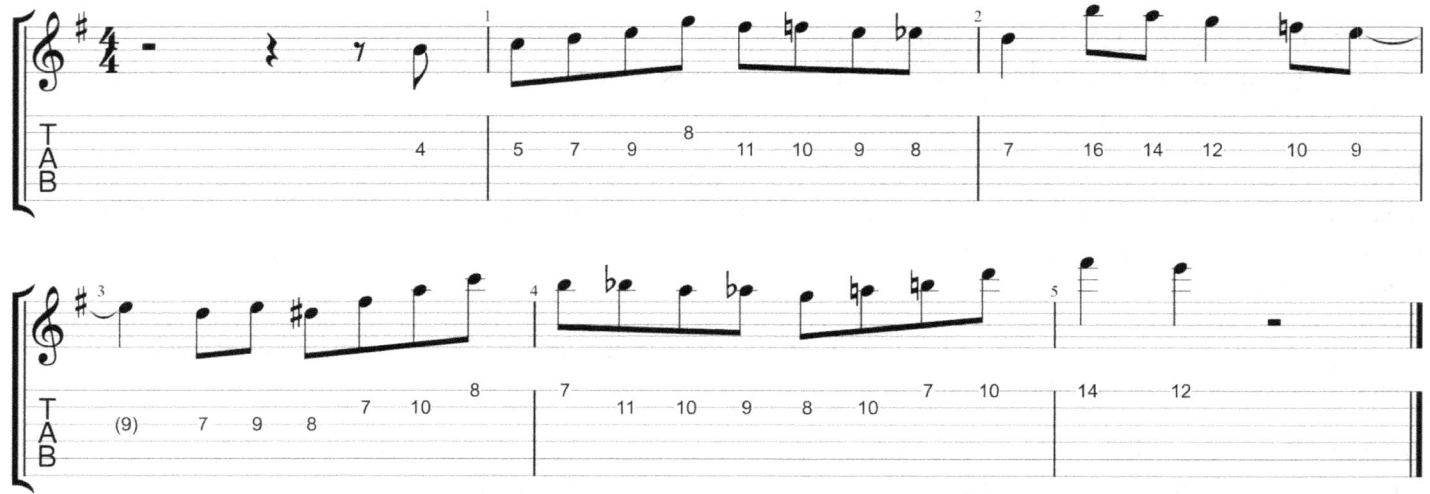

When I play the line above, I visualise the following chord shapes and build my lines around them. Of course, the shapes do jump around the neck, but the more you start to practice like this, the easier you will find it to join up these ideas and fill in the "no man's land" in between.

Example 6c

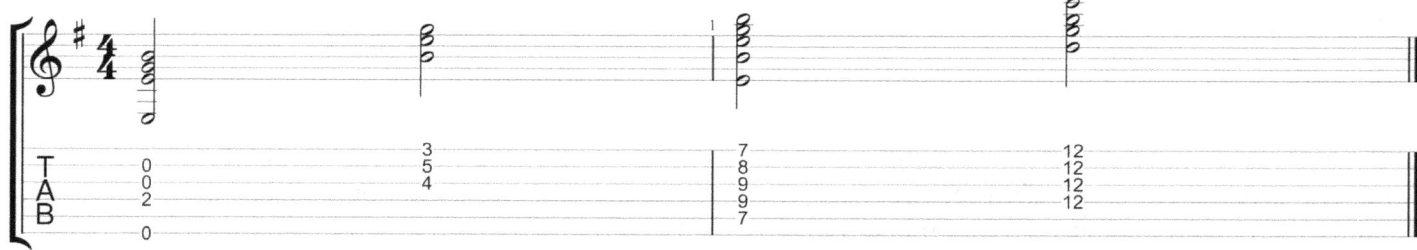

When guitarists play in one area of the neck all the time, one undesired result is that the music becomes quite one dimensional in its range. It's important to realise that the *register* we play in affects the *feeling* of the notes. Intervals played very low on the guitar are quite dark and dense, and intervals played high on the neck tend to be much lighter and brighter in colour. While the intervals are the same, playing them in a different range is like being able to paint in different shades of the same colour.

To demonstrate this idea, here is our tune played in three different registers. You'll instantly hear the difference.

Example 6d

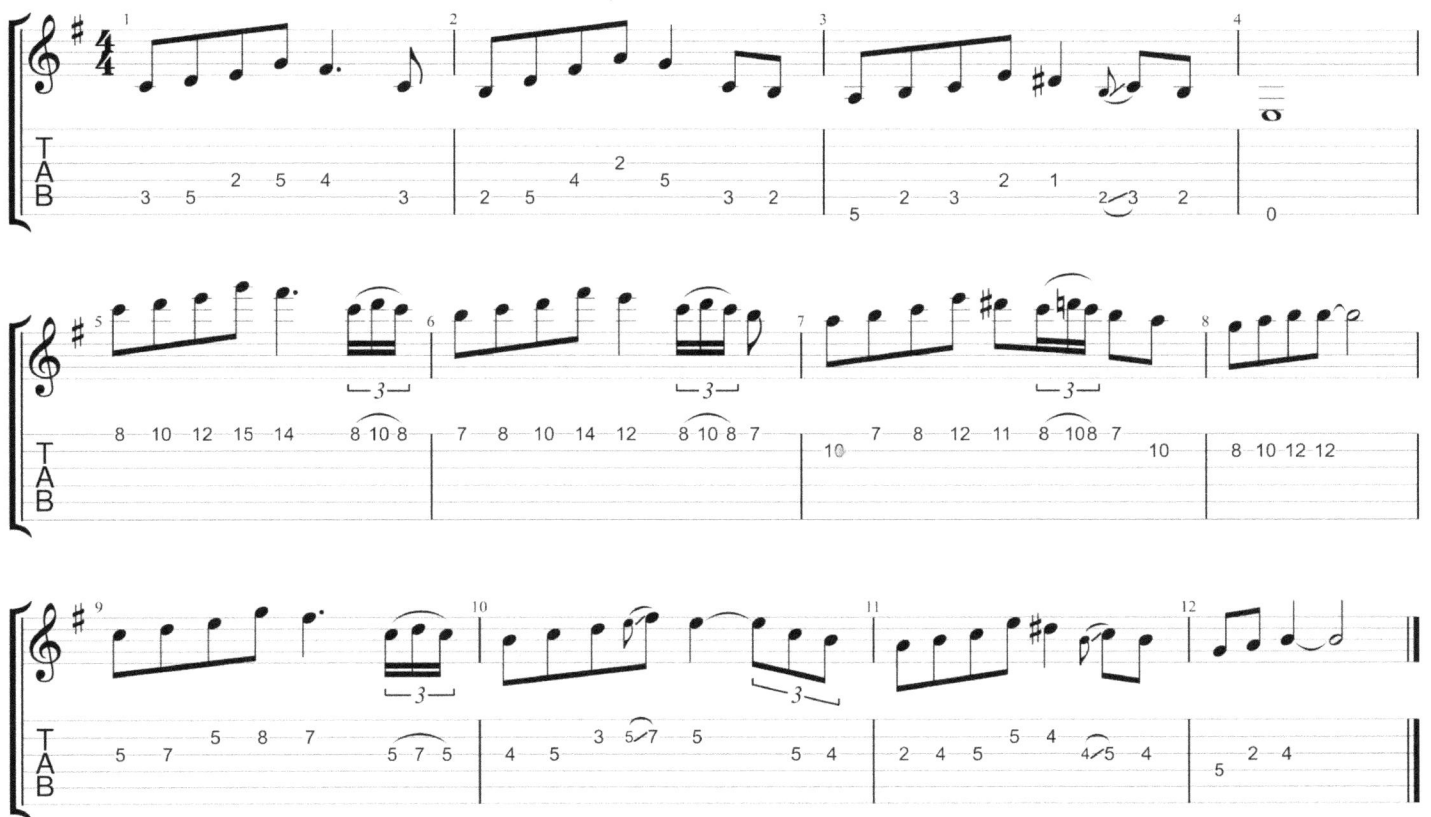

The dimension of colour is so important for both expression and for engaging that listener that I'm quick to notice its absence. Building freedom with range up and down the neck is a very important concept to practise.

I can use range deliberately to influence the mood of the solo. Here's a short example on that begins high, and then moves to a lower range to create a feeling of thoughtfulness and reflection.

Example 6e

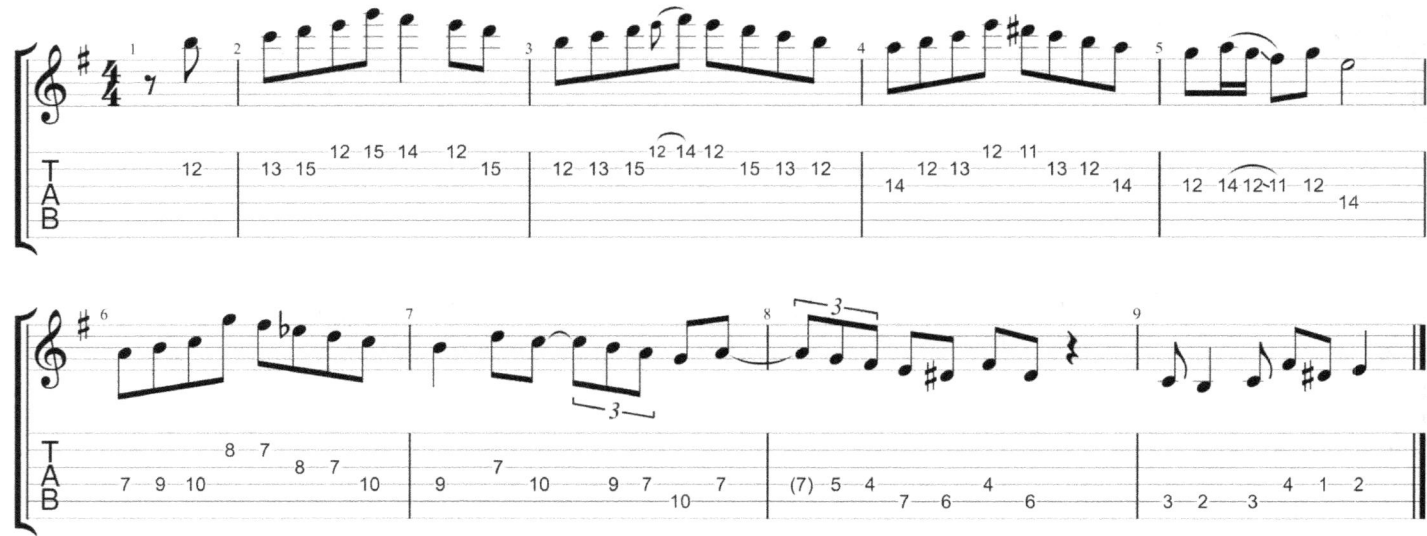

He's an example that achieves the opposite effect. I begin low and move to a higher register to add excitement and drama.

Example 6f

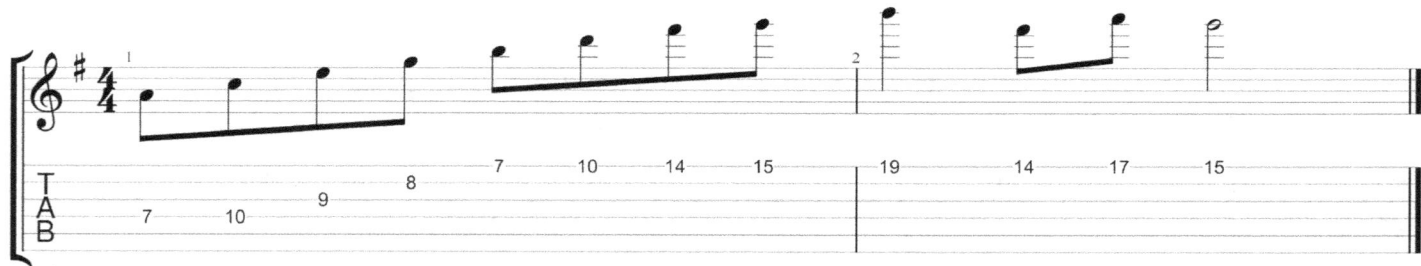

These colours are subtle, but they connect with your audience on a deep emotional level. They're an important tool in your musical kit box and are often forgotten in the pursuit of finding the perfect theoretical device to apply to a Bb7#9b13 chord!

Range is a valuable tool you can use to plan out your melodies and solos. As we've seen, it can be used to create a reflective mood or one of excitement. So, how can you practise using range? A wonderful exercise that will help you master it is to play a solo using *only one string*. This can be hard at first, but it will force you to do two very important things:

1. It will make you use the range of the guitar
2. It will make you think more carefully about your choice of note and phrasing

Here's an example of me improvising a solo played entirely on the B string.

Example 6g

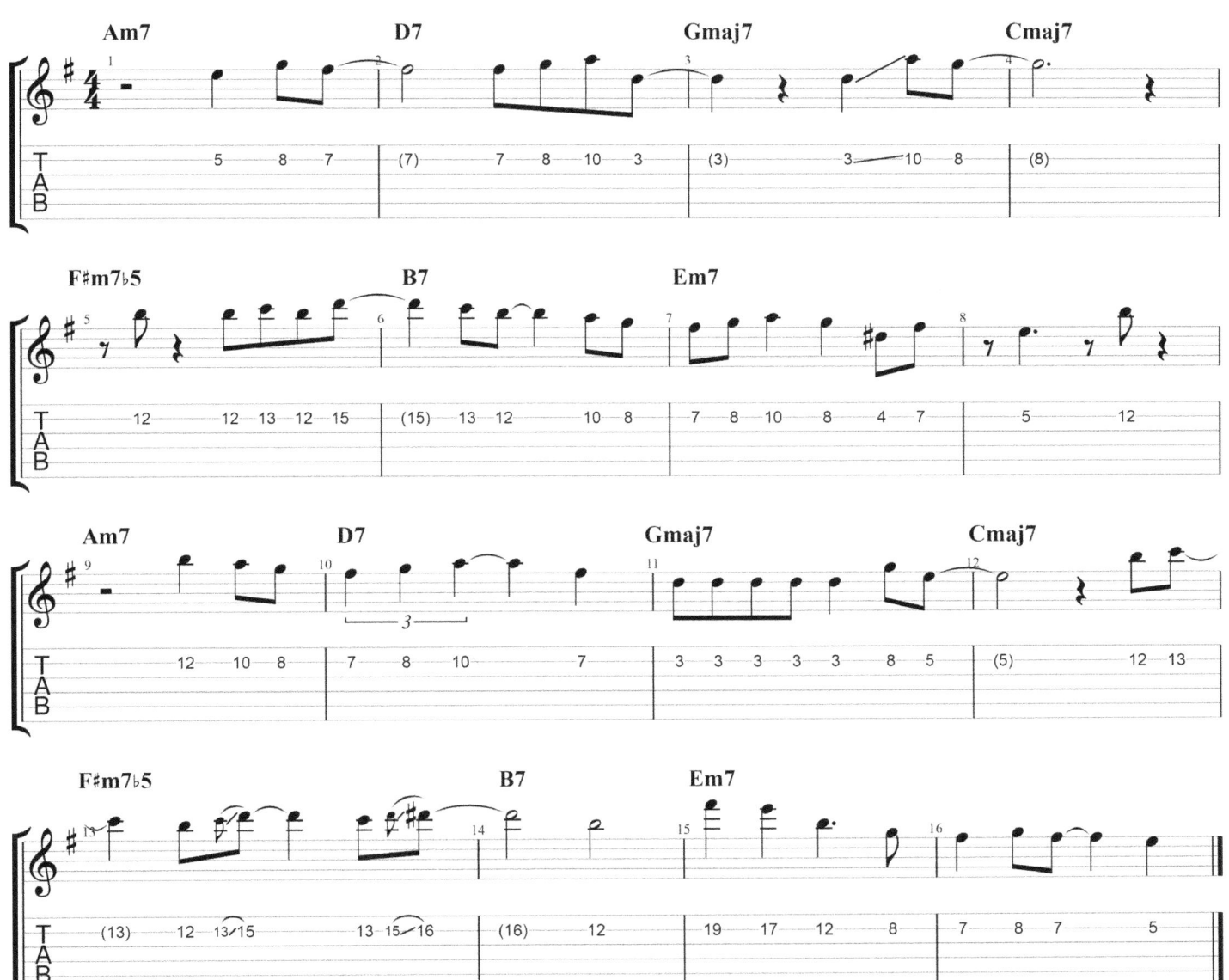

Here are another few passes around the changes using this approach.

Example 6h

You can apply the idea of playing one just one string to your *think, sing, play* practice. It's a great way of discovering where the notes are located if you sing a phrase, then replicate it on just one string. It frees you from the distraction of familiar scale patterns and arpeggios which are easy to fall into.

Here's an example of me singing and playing a melody, again on the B string.

Example 6i

You should, of course, do this on different strings, although it might be good to limit yourself to the top four to begin with. Here's me playing a solo on the D string to help you find the locations of the notes.

Example 6j

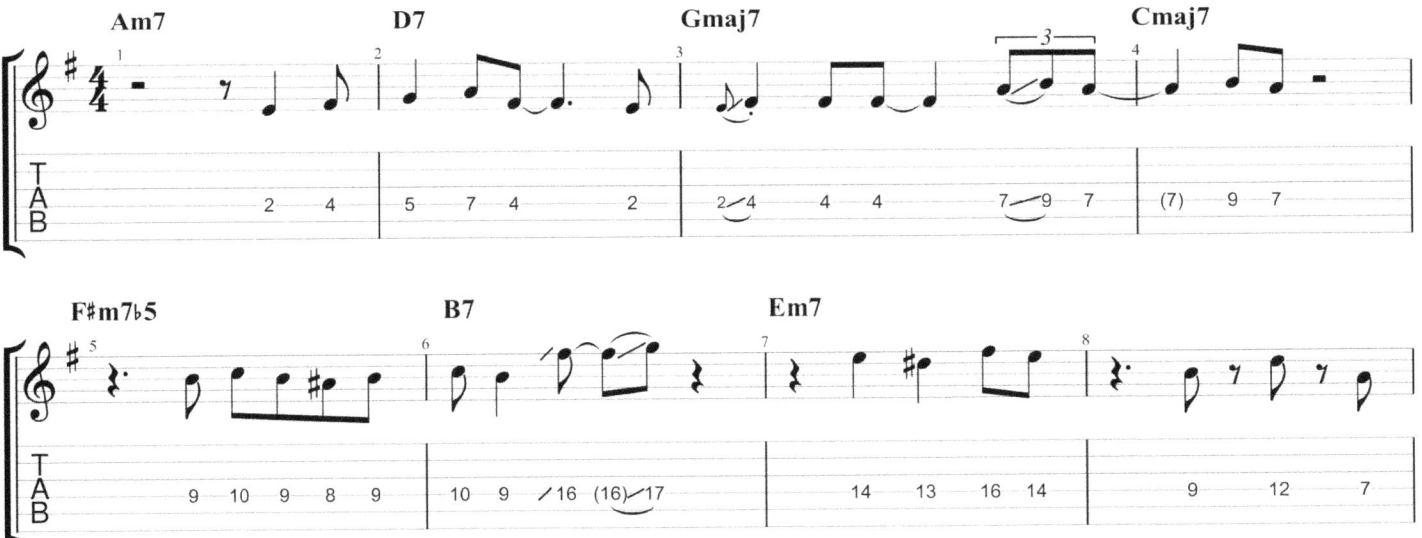

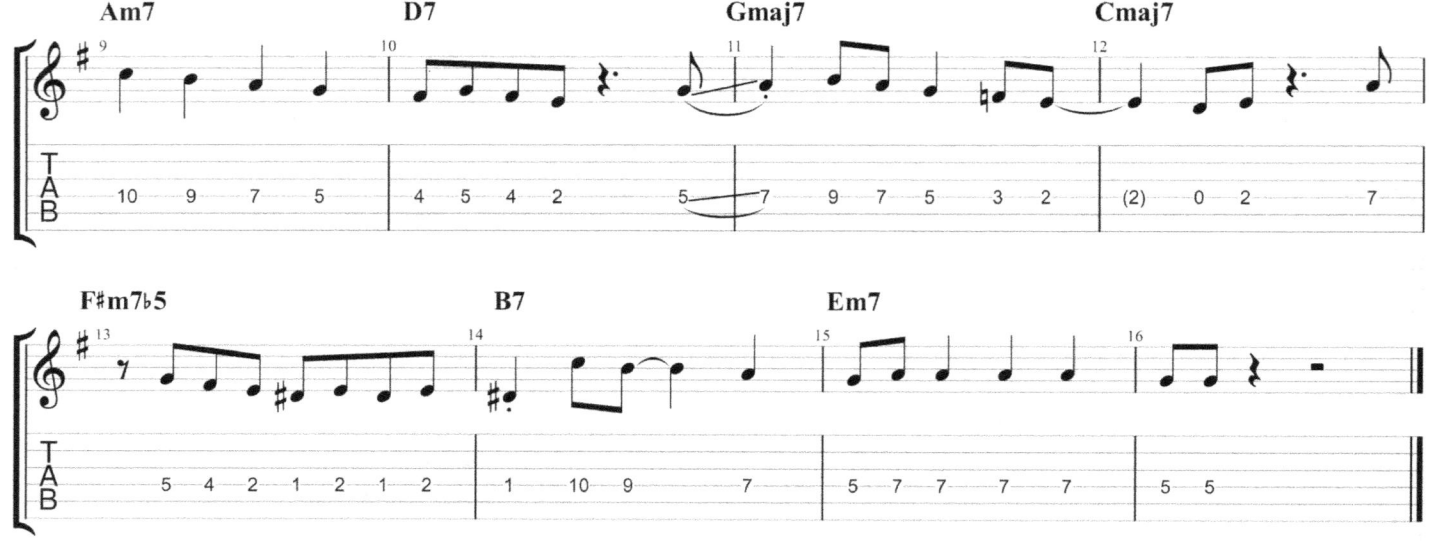

Try the *think, sing, play* method on the D string now. This is so important because you'll stop trying to find the scales and instead focus on finding the notes you hear in your head.

Example 6k

Ultimately, where I choose to play comes down to tone and feel. We know that there is more than one location to play a pitch on the guitar, and they all have a subtly different feel and texture. I learnt his from Stéphane Grappelli who did this a lot on the violin. He'd often repeat phrases on different strings to create subtle nuances in tone, like this:

Example 61

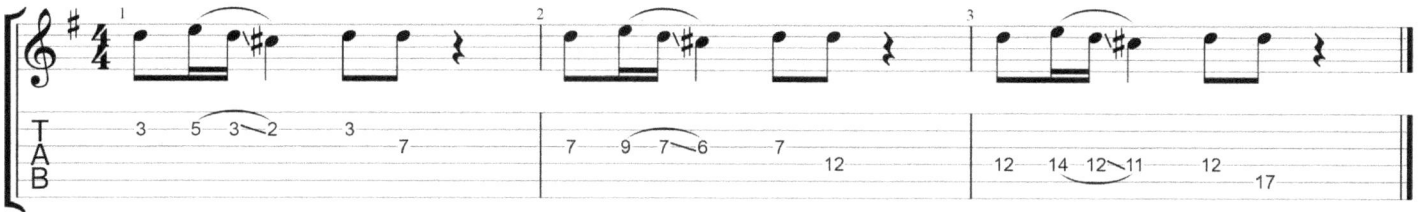

I'd like to make one last point in conclusion. As well as using the range of the instrument, the *key* you choose to play a song in is an important consideration. When I'm playing solo guitar, I'll often transpose tunes to more guitar-friendly keys. Not just because it allows me access to open strings for bass notes, but because of the over sound those keys convey.

Sharps keys, such as E, A and D, have a bright, happy sound, while flat keys such as F, Bb and Eb sound darker. The guitar is engineered to be play the sharp keys optimally, so it's no wonder they sound a little sweeter. This is another way of saying you should always bear in mind what mood, what colour, you want to communicate to your listeners. Think about which key really brings a tune to life or gives it the mood you're after, and use the full range of the instrument, so that your improvisations sound three-dimensional and are always going somewhere.

Chapter Seven – Creating Interest and Structure in your Solos

We've talked in great detail about different ways to create a jazz guitar solo. These have mainly focused on keeping in mind specific target notes and using creative ways of navigating between them. But there is another important dimension in jazz soloing that is often overlooked and rarely taught: how to *pace* a solo. *Pacing* is one of the key ingredients that will keep your audience engaged and eager to hear what comes next. What do we mean by *pacing*?

Let me use the analogy of a TV programme. A well-written TV show develops. It has a structure that gradually increases in tension, introduces new ideas and has emotional highs and lows. It has loud parts and quiet parts and other features that make it more than the sum of its parts. Pacing how these ingredients can be used effectively is the mark of a good storyteller. A good scriptwriter will know how they want the narrative to unfold: what emotions will be stirred 5 minutes; 10 minutes in; how the show will come reach its pinnacle before the credits roll…

This is exactly how to structure a great jazz solo. It sounds obvious to say it, but if you come out with all guns blazing, then you have nowhere left to go. A sound grasp of pacing will allow you to take your audience on a journey that has lows and highs and develops in an organic manner.

How does one learn to do this?

My advice is that just as we've focused on *melodic* hit points in our solos, we can target *dynamic* hit points. By "dynamics" I mean more than just playing loudly and quietly. For me, dynamics includes light and shade, but also the amount of space you leave, the density of notes you play, the speed at which you play, the intervals you target, and the intensity of your playing.

Just like the screenwriter, you can have these devices ready at hand and plan when you'll use them. Targeting a *dynamic hit point* is, for instance, knowing ahead of time that over the course of three choruses you will hit a peak where you are in the upper range of the fretboard and your note density will be high, as you place a fast, repeating motif. Knowing that you want your solo to peak here, you can gradually build the intensity of your improvisation over the choruses leading up to that hit point.

Having the "big picture" of the solo you want to play in your mind, rather than getting caught up in the minutiae of which notes to play or which scales to use is very freeing. It's a flexible approach. Some players think of their solos in terms of which licks/scales they'll use when over the chords. This can work, but considering the endless variables at work during a live performance, often things don't go to plan, and if you miss a note or lose your place, the entire performance can fall apart.

Dynamic hit points offers a simpler, more liberating approach. You might say to yourself, for instance, "I'll begin with a few spaced-out light phrases that gradually grow, then take it down towards the bridge. After that, I'll begin to build it up and really start revving it up towards the end of the solo. Instead of a big finish, this time I'll reduce the intensity to give the next soloist a platform to grow from."

Now we've captured the overall architecture and mood of our solo without getting bogged down in specifics. If you rigidly plan your solo around licks, you'll have no room for manoeuvre in a fast-moving, creative musical environment; no safety net. With dynamic targeting, you can always quickly adapt your approach to respond to what's happening around you.

Wrong notes?

Making mistakes can often throw musicians off course. If you're only playing licks, you'll probably have to stop if you make a mistake because you'll be locked into the phrase that has gone wrong. If you're not locked into licks, then if you make a mistake (I don't even call them mistakes, I call them "notes I didn't mean to play"), you can always adapt – even embrace the note you didn't mean to play and take the solo in a whole new direction.

Think of it this way: any note you didn't mean to play is just a tension note. It's only one fret away from a better note. If you can think of it like this, you'll begin to realise that "wrong notes" are another opportunity to be creative. If you resolve a "wrong note" strongly, then it will take your solo on a new, original path.

Often, I'll try to encourage myself to play notes I didn't mean to by playing songs in different keys, so I can't rely on my old patterns. Knowing that my new opportunities are endless, it actually helps me to relax when I solo. I embrace these notes and use them creatively.

The biggest mistake is to have your solo all figured out. It puts way too much pressure on you. When I play, I'm always thinking, "I don't know how this is going to turn out." I've got enough experience to know it's not going to be a total disaster, but embracing those notes is the secret to relaxing and being creative.

With all this in mind, let's look in detail at one way I structure a jazz guitar solo. The following examples break down a full solo transcription into small sections and begin with me just easing my way into the solo gently.

Example 7a

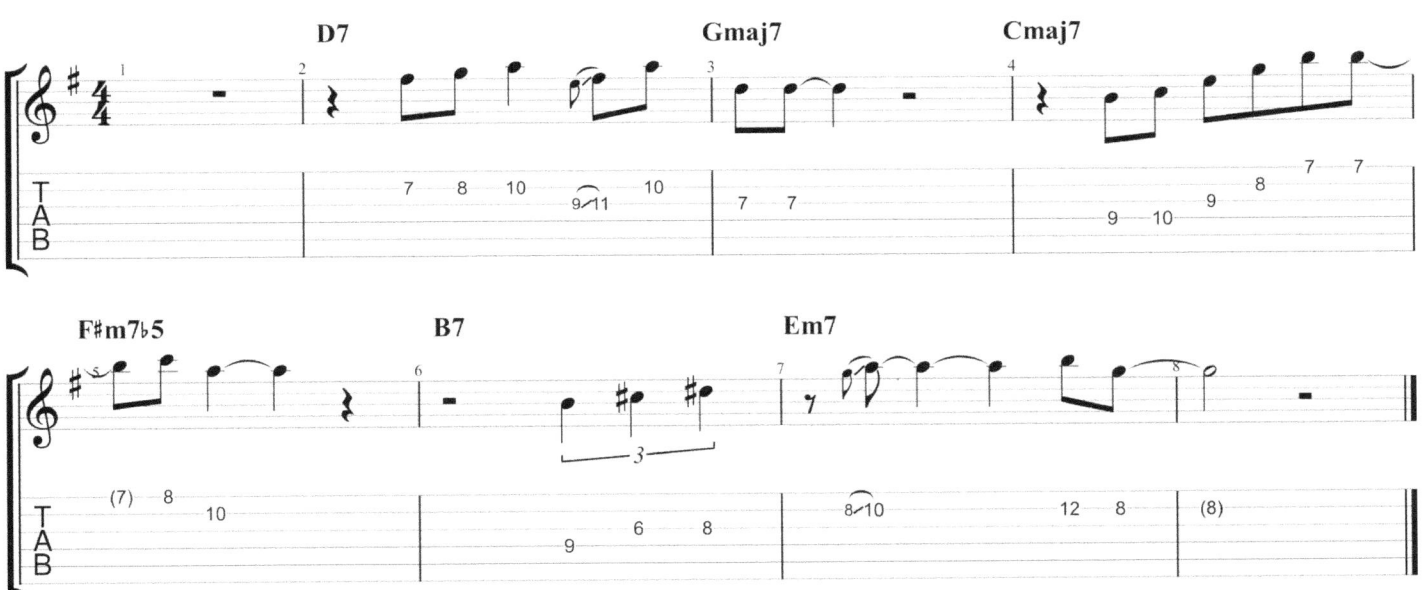

Here are the next few bars. Notice that I'm using a few melodic patterns already.

Example 7b

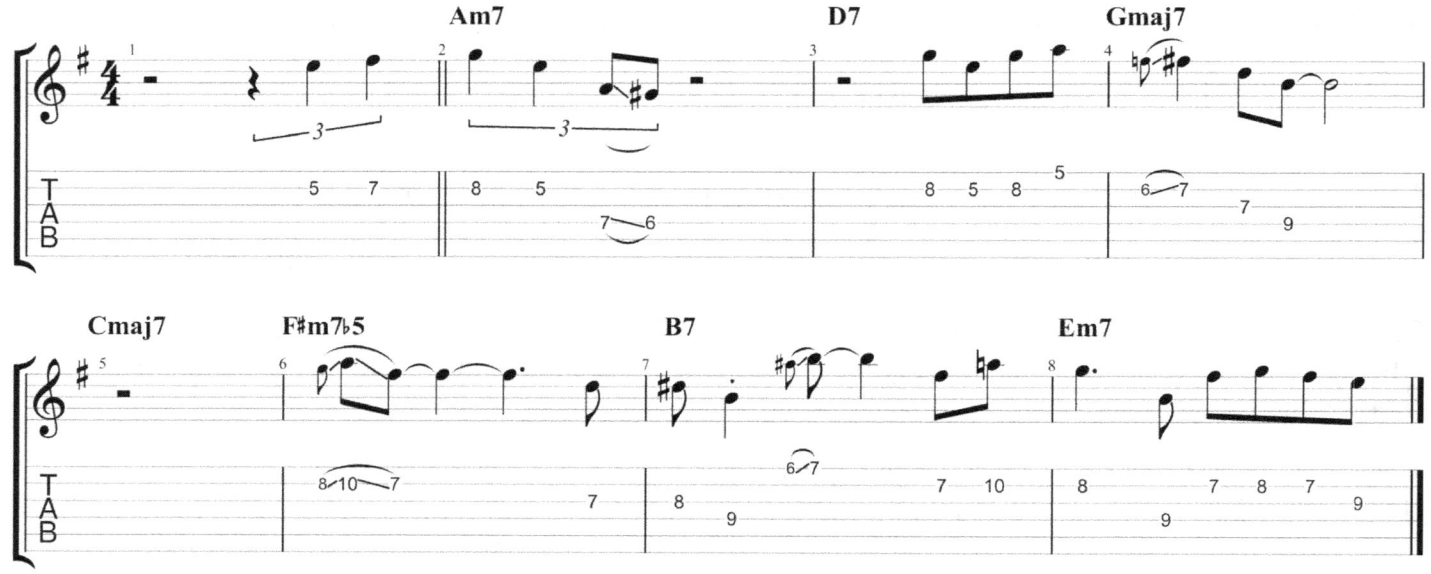

In the next example I lead with a strong motif that develops into a slightly busier phrase, using call and response.

Example 7c

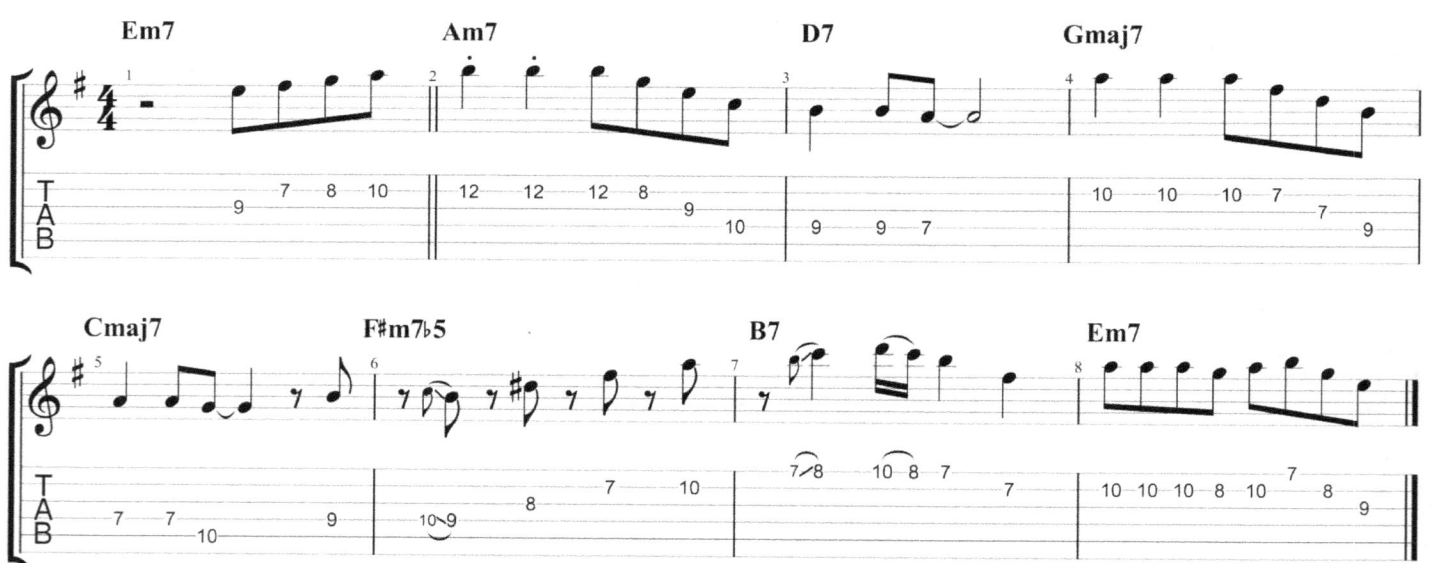

I start building the intensity with volume, flurries of fast notes and dynamics.

Example 7d

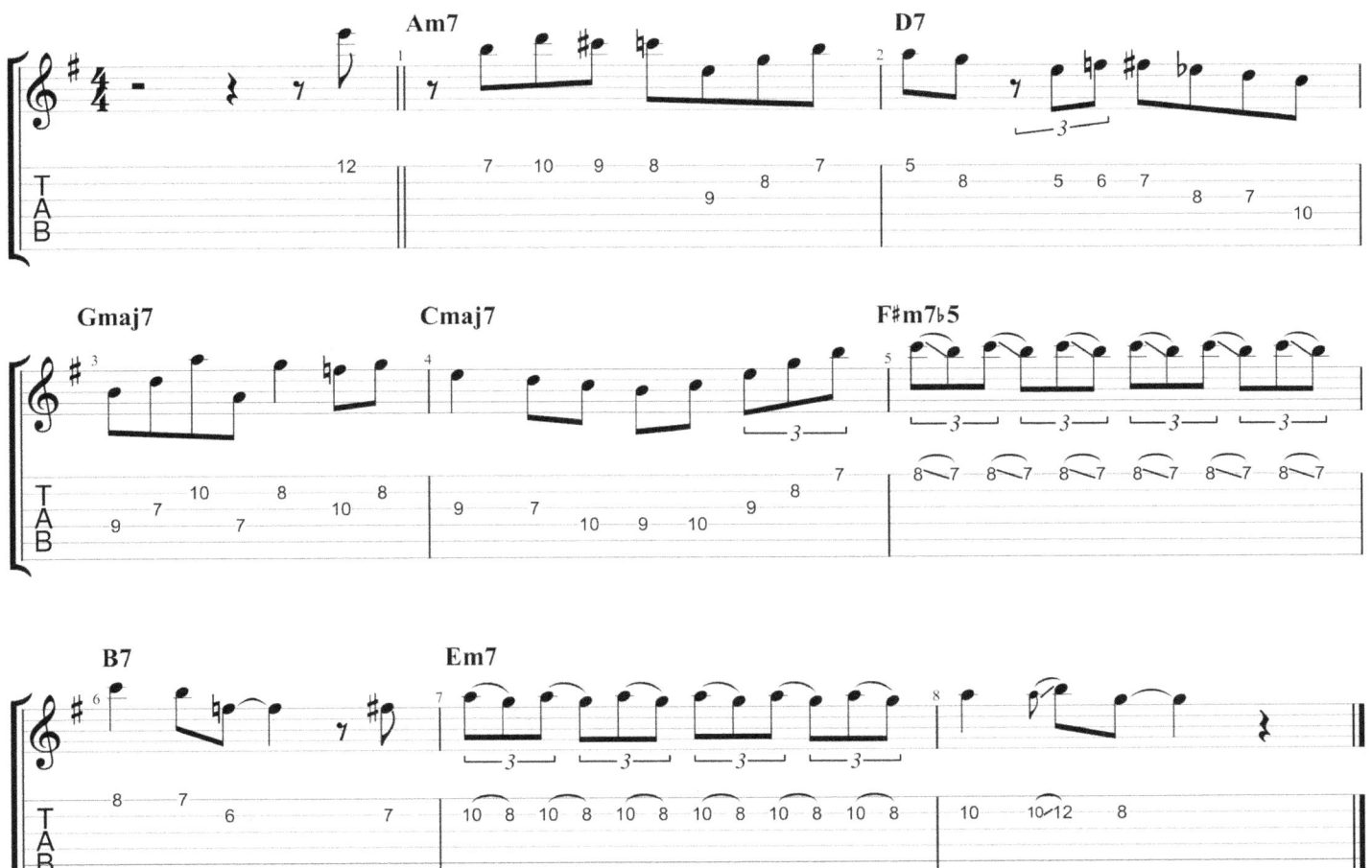

A strong motif sets me up to begin playing faster lines after a brief dip in intensity. The section ends with me reaching for some bluesy lines to balance out the faster phrases.

Example 7e

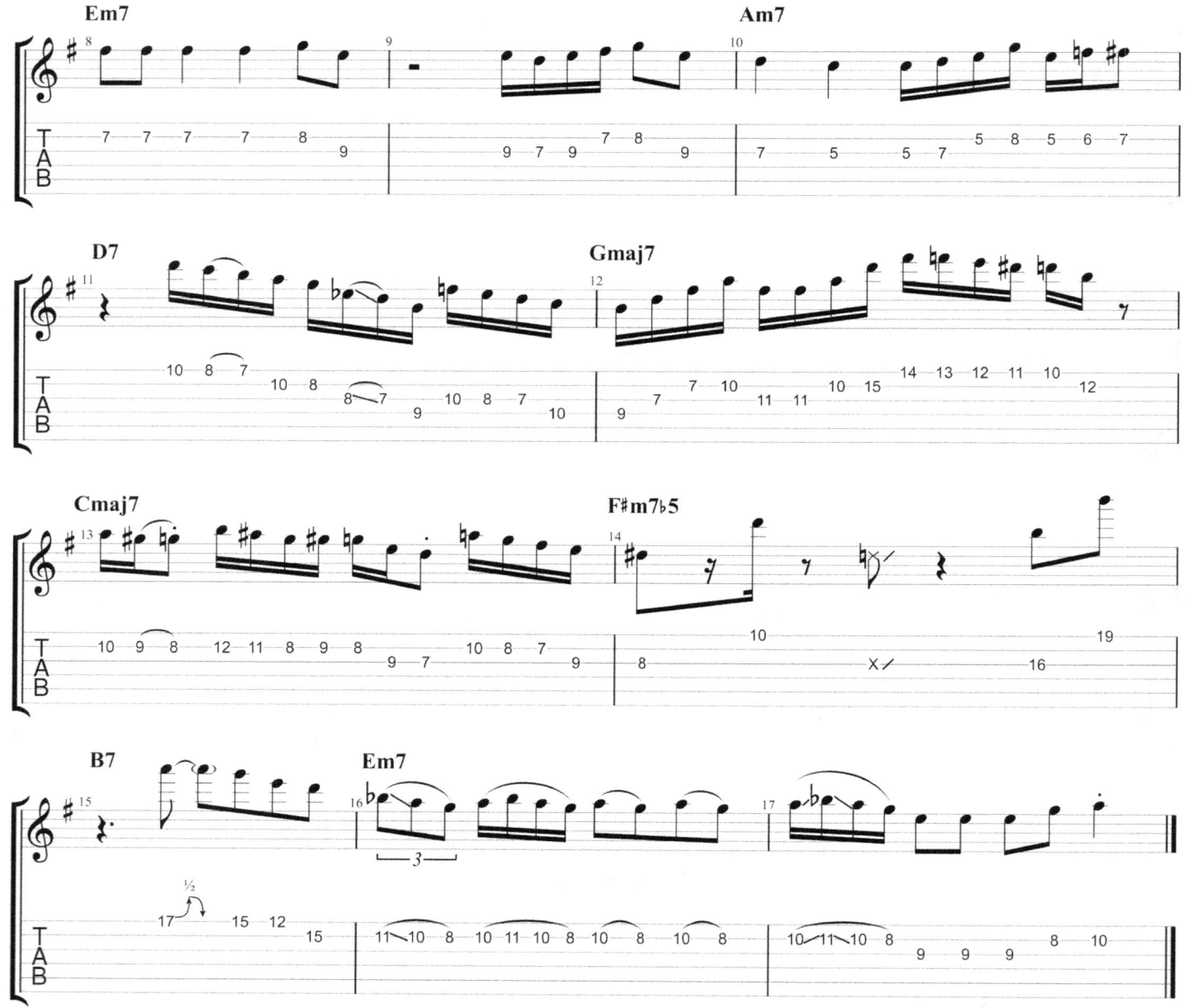

I begin the next section by combining different note durations, fast and slow, before I feel I need to balance the single note lines and introduce some octave textures.

Example 7f

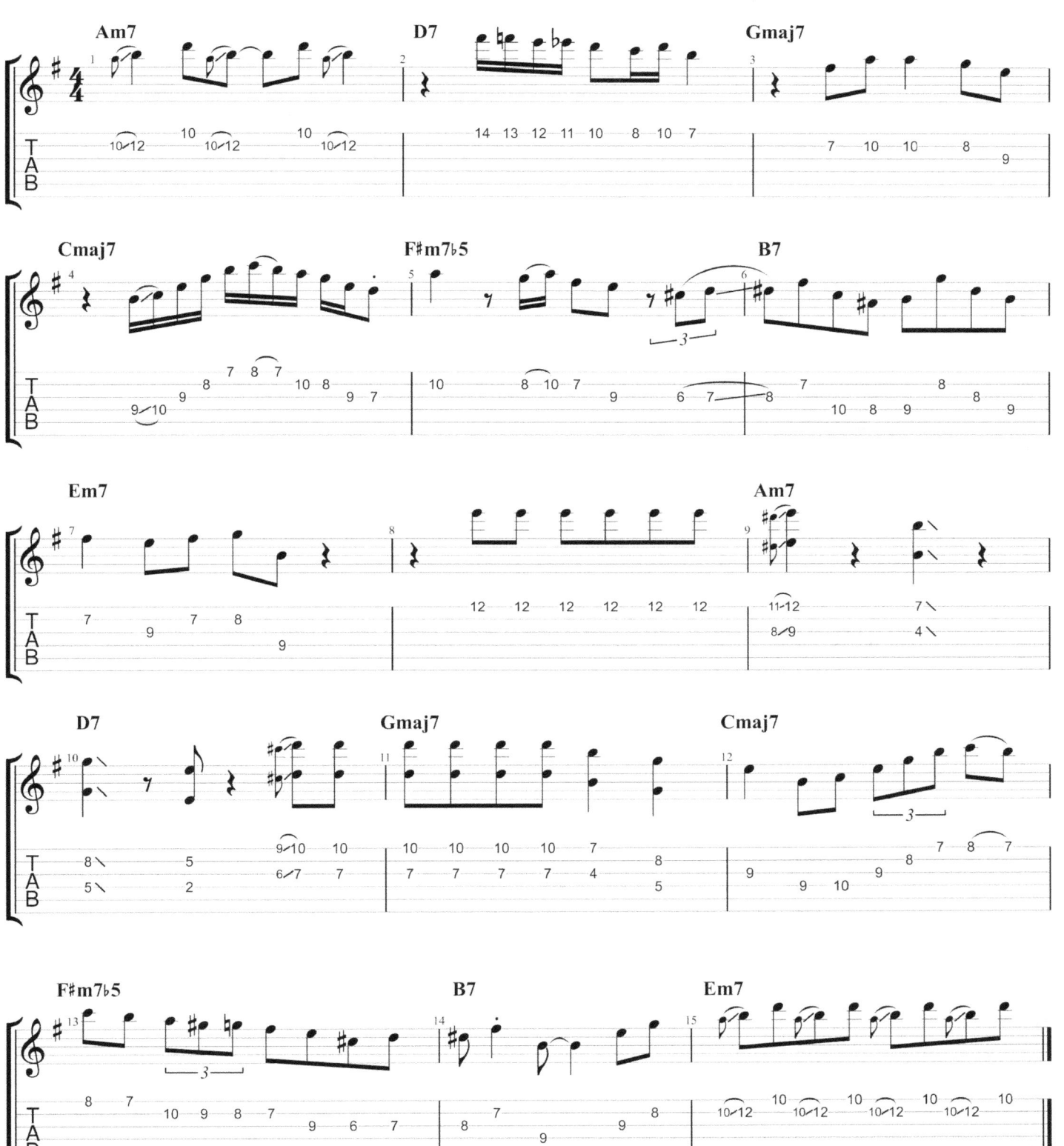

Now I raise the intensity again with some fast scale and chromatic based lines, which I again balance with some bouncy swing, and reintroduce the octaves. The solo finishes with me lowering the energy, almost bowing out to leave the room, so a following soloist could begin their solo. Notice how I play softer *and* play fewer notes.

Example 7g

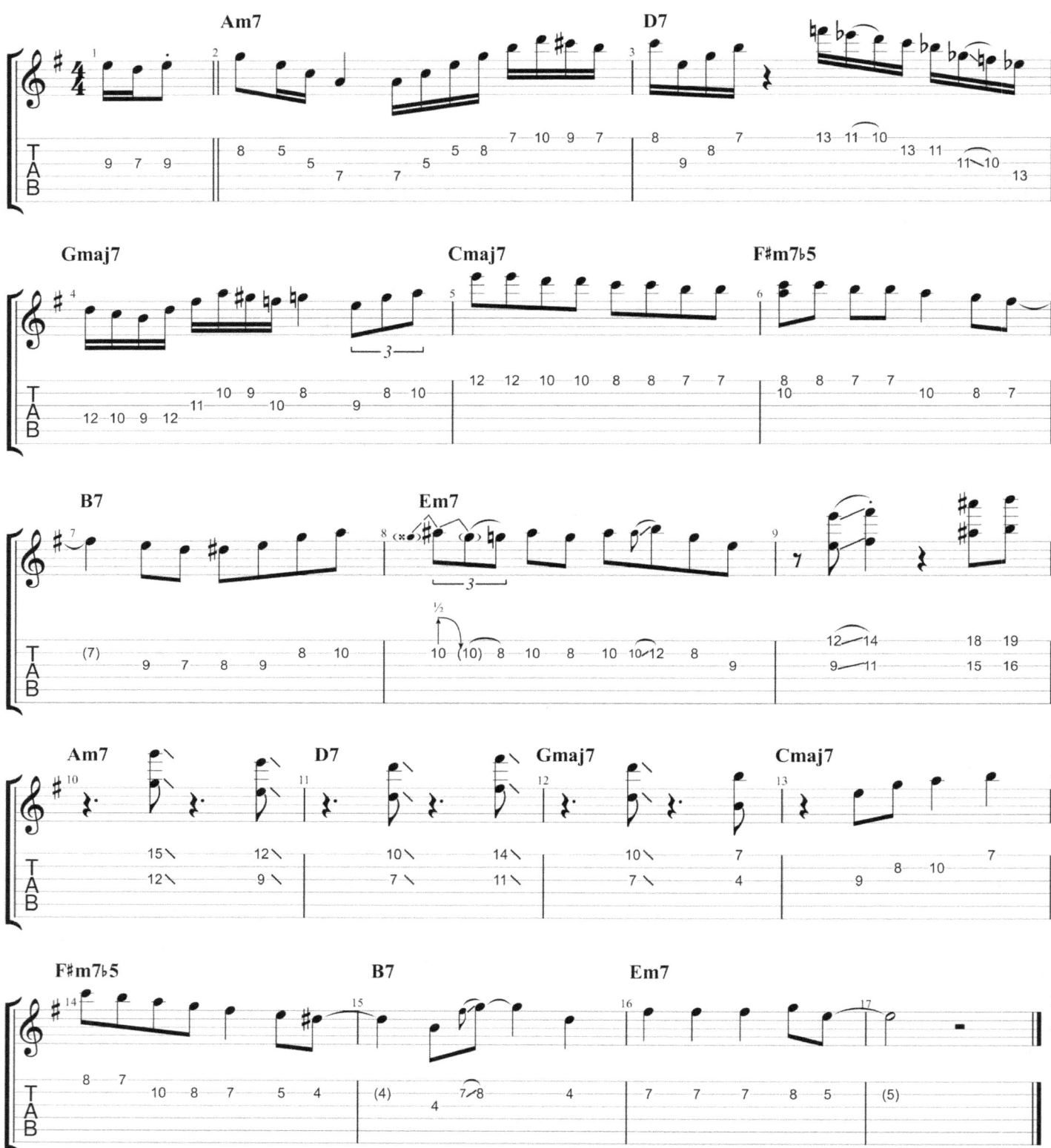

I'm sure you're wondering about some of those faster lines. These tend to be more scale based with chromatic notes filling in the gaps and targeting tones in the next chord. Really, I just double the amount I play on each chord. Here are a few ideas you can steal!

Example 7h

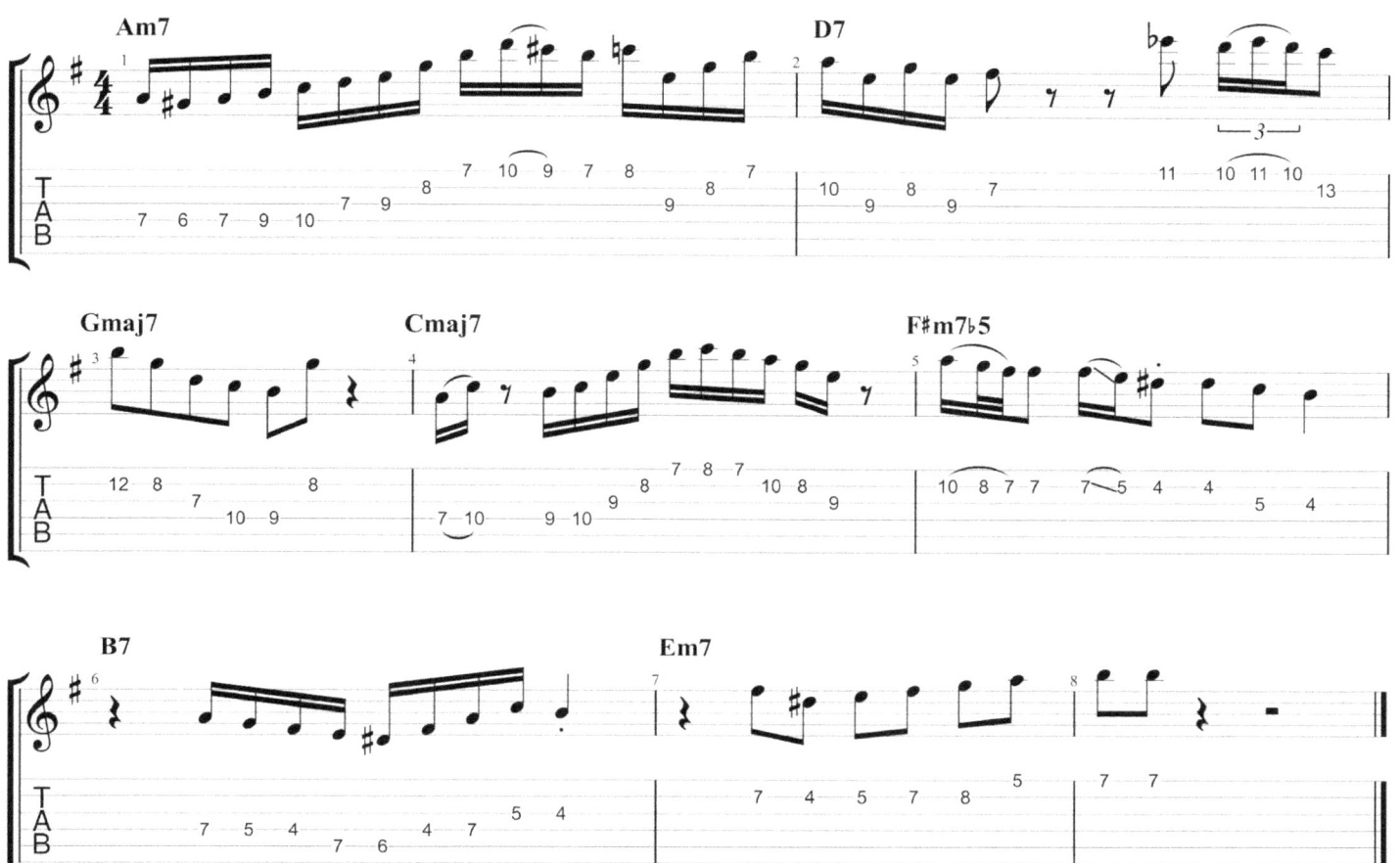

See how the fast phrases build tension while the slower phrases release it? This can work the other way around too, but fast then slow is a great starting point in your exploration of this idea.

Example 7i

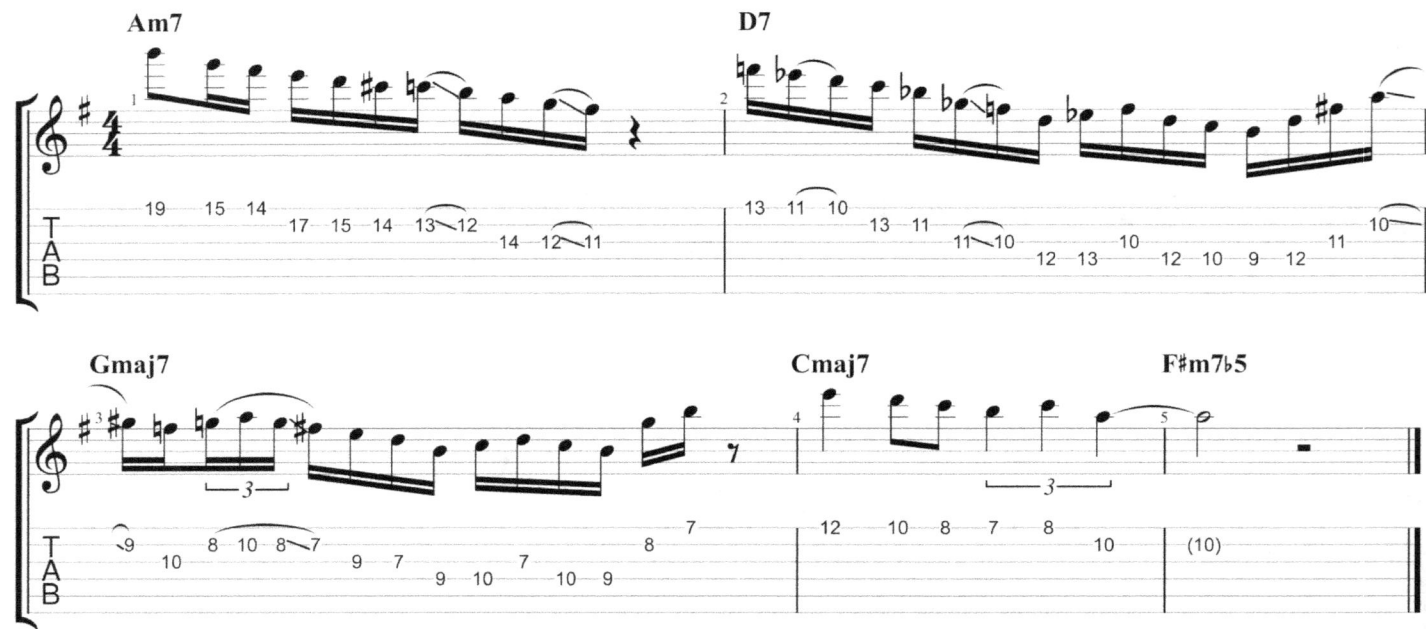

On the D7 chord, I often play the b9 (Eb) to create a slightly more tense sound. Here is some vocabulary that shows you how to do this.

Example 7j

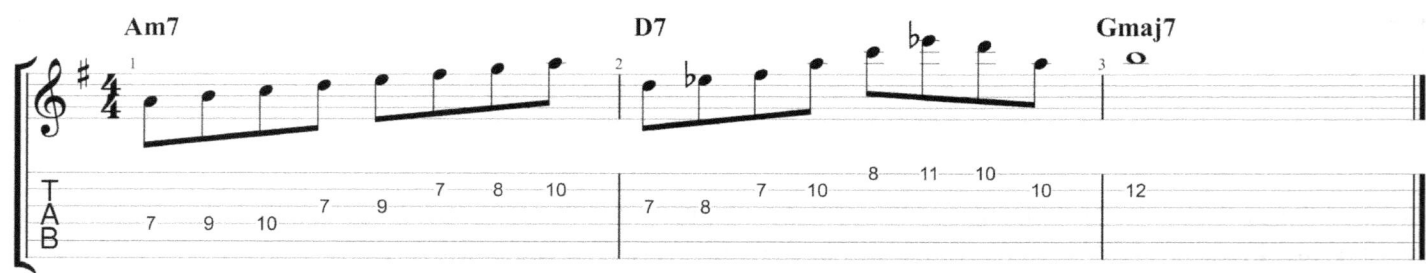

I hope this chapter has given you further insight and some tools to help you structure your solos and keep them interesting with pacing and dynamic hit points. Remember, it's not just what you play, it's a mindset. Plan ahead and have in mind the dynamics of your solo – the high points, the reflective points, the fast and slow, loud and soft. Embrace the notes you didn't mean to play and incorporate them into your variations because they'll take you in new creative directions you would never have imagined. Remember, when you play a note you didn't mean to, you're only ever one note away from a better one!

Chapter Eight – Piecing it all Together

We've covered a huge amount of ground in this book and many of the concepts will require months of work to perfect. I want to finish by applying all the concepts we've learnt into one complete solo. I'd like you to learn it, break down each idea and phrase to understand which notes I'm targeting, then compose your own variations on my lines. When I first learnt to play, I rarely memorised whole solos, I listened hard and figured out the lines I liked. I suggest you go through the solo and focus on learning the phrases that really leap out at you, then use them in your own playing as soon as possible.

In the following solo, you'll hear how I organically develop the initial melody using simple variations, then begin to stretch out a little as a soloist. Listen for my dynamics too and try to sketch out how the solo rises and falls in intensity. I begin with simple motifs.

Example 8a

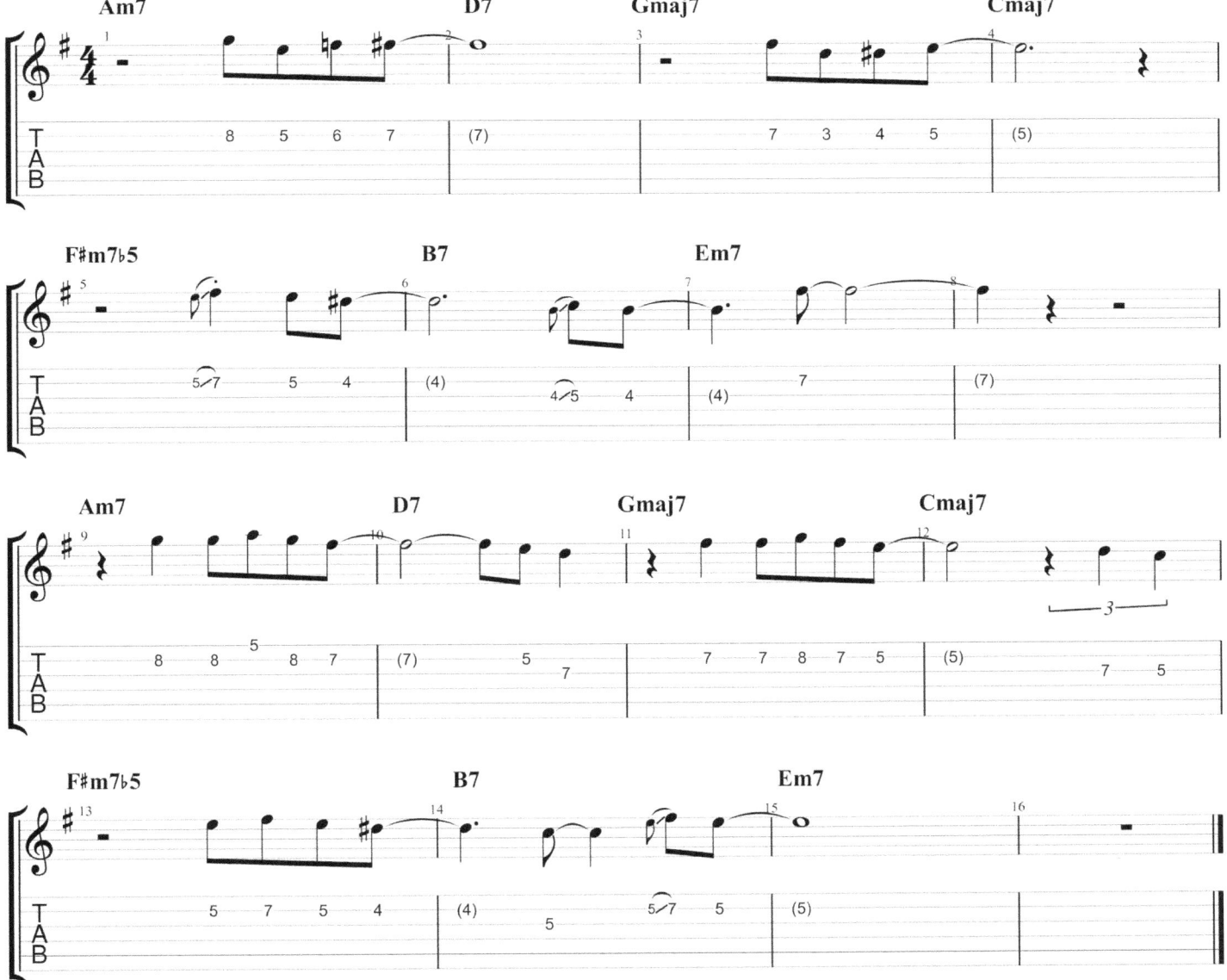

Then I begin to adapt a phrase I liked the sound of.

Example 8b

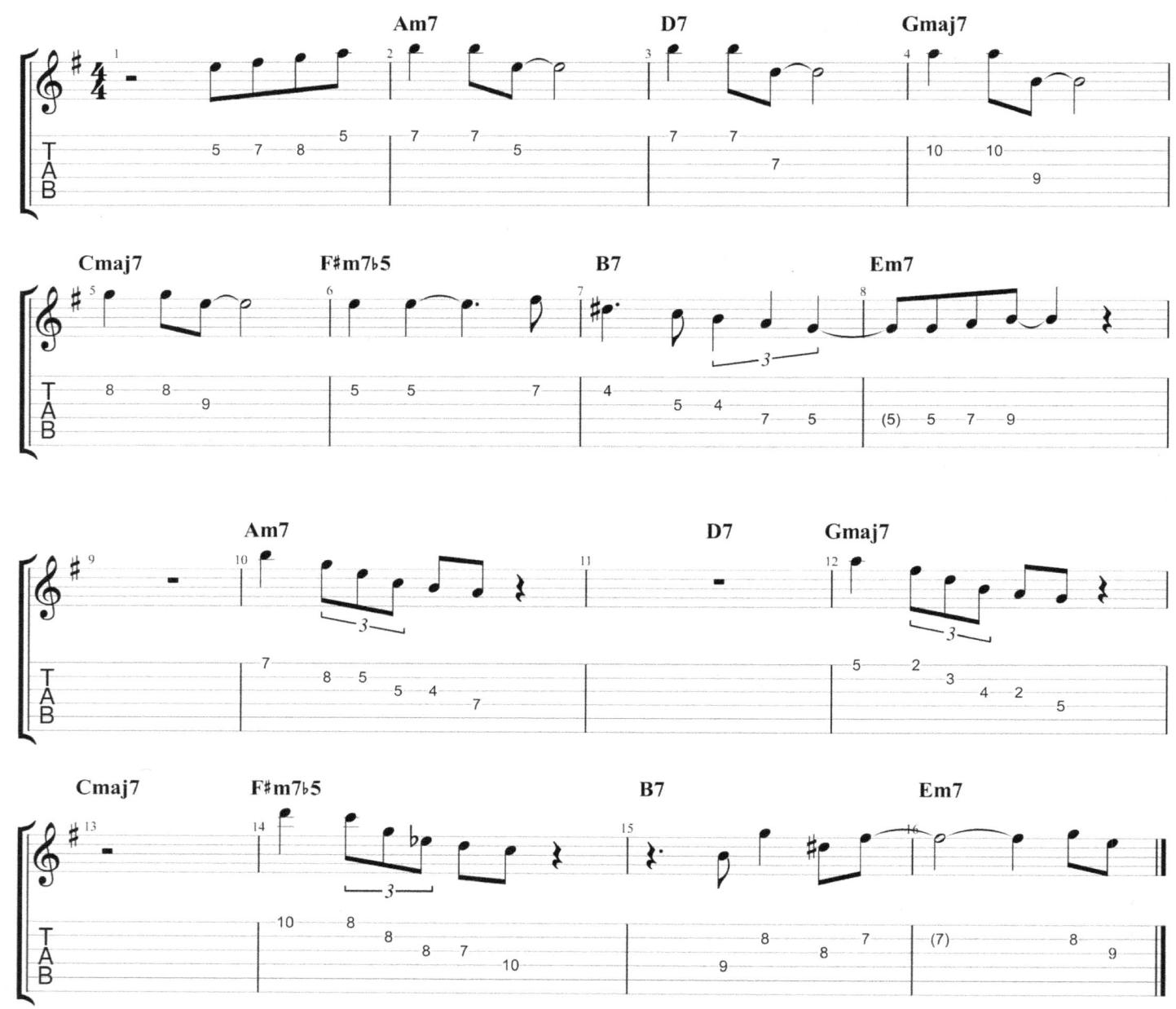

The next section uses a strong call and response idea.

Example 8c

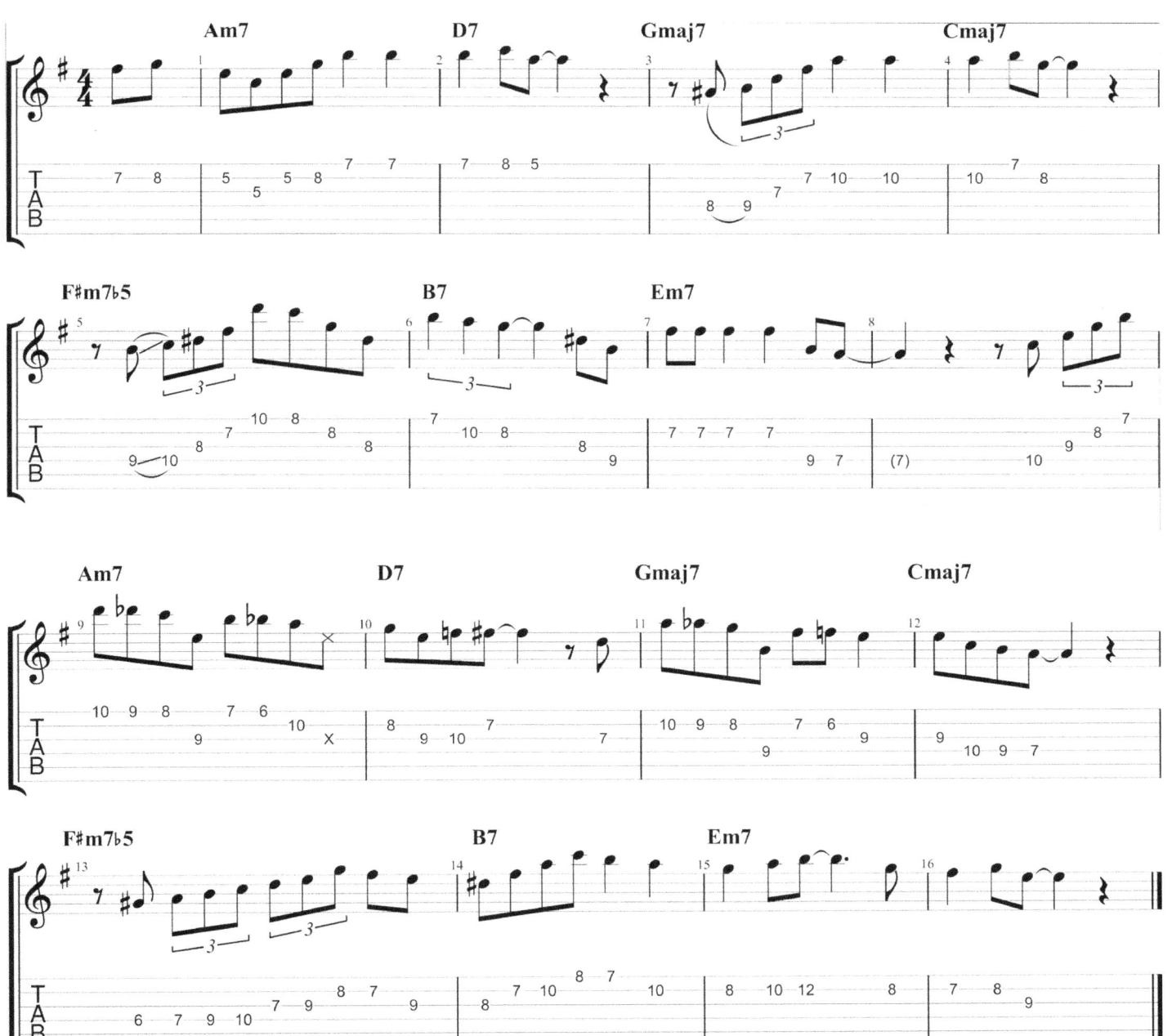

Hear how I develop some strong rhythmic patterns in the next few bars.

Example 8d

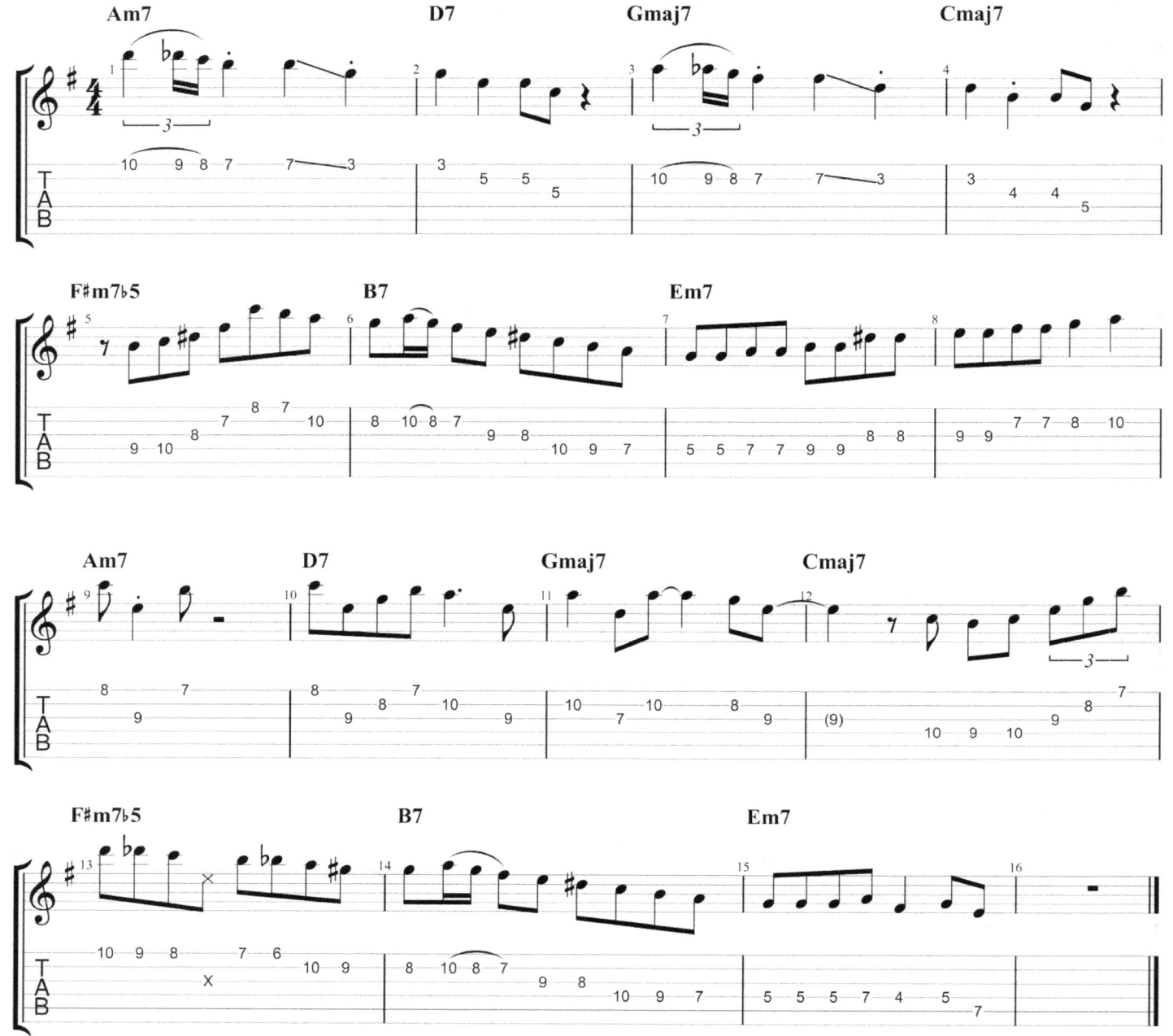

There are loads of repeating ideas in the next section that use different parts of the neck to demonstrate the use of range.

Example 8e

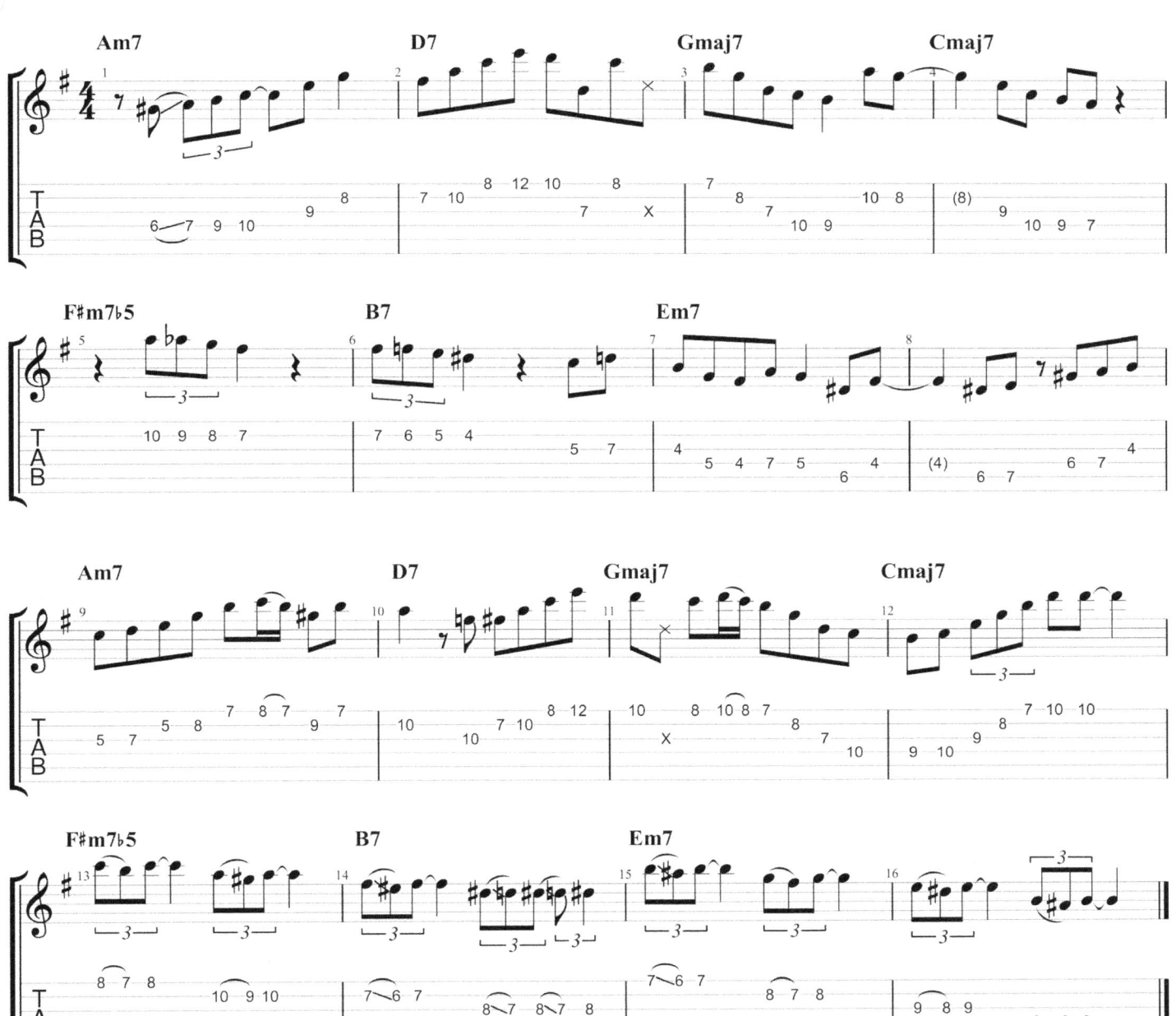

Now there is another mellow section before I play some flurries of chromatic notes to target chord tones.

Example 8f

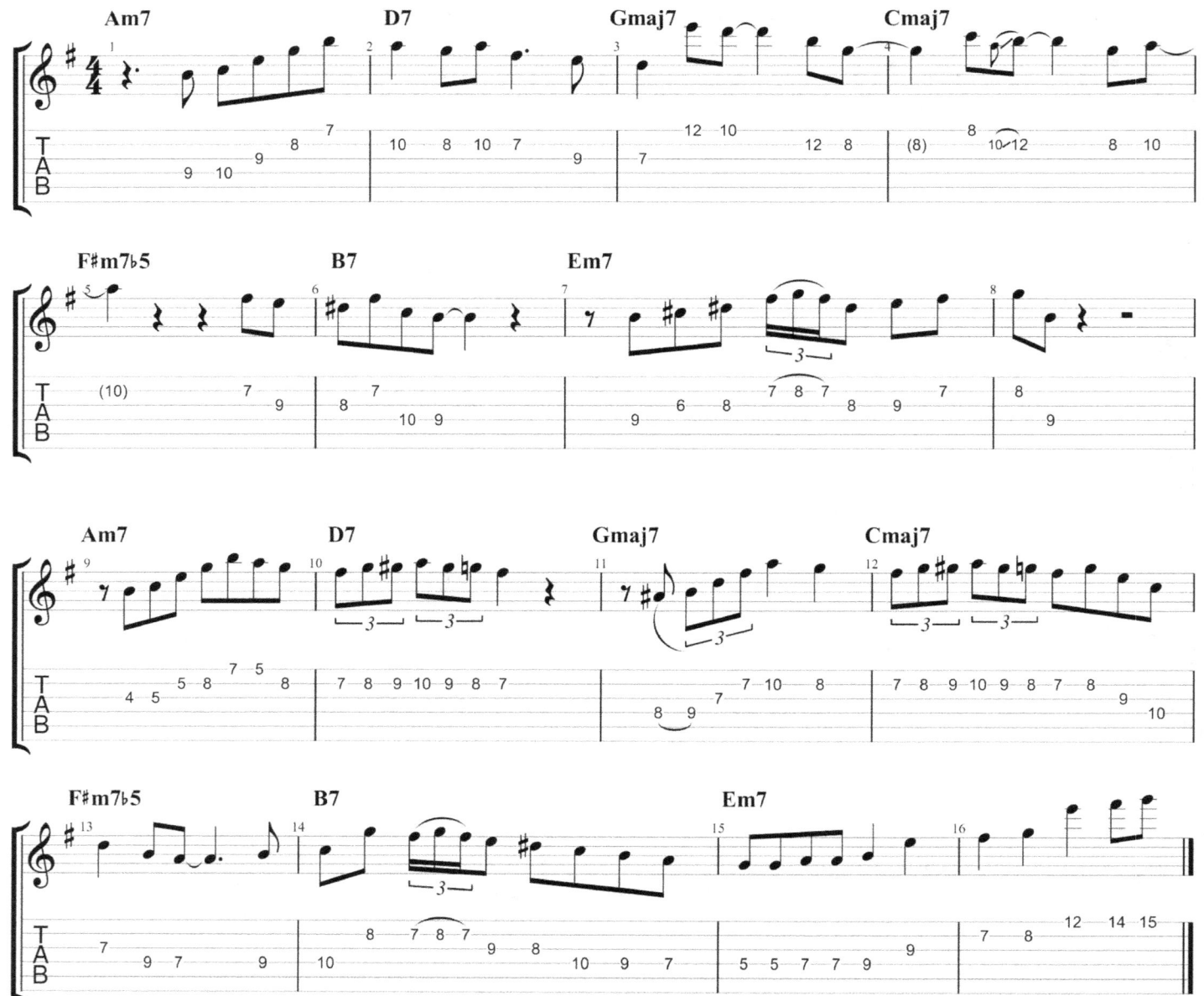

OK, now it's over to you to break down and learn my next three choruses. Listen out for strong motifs being moved around the changes, using range, note intensity, dynamics, legato and of course variation of melodies.

Example 8g

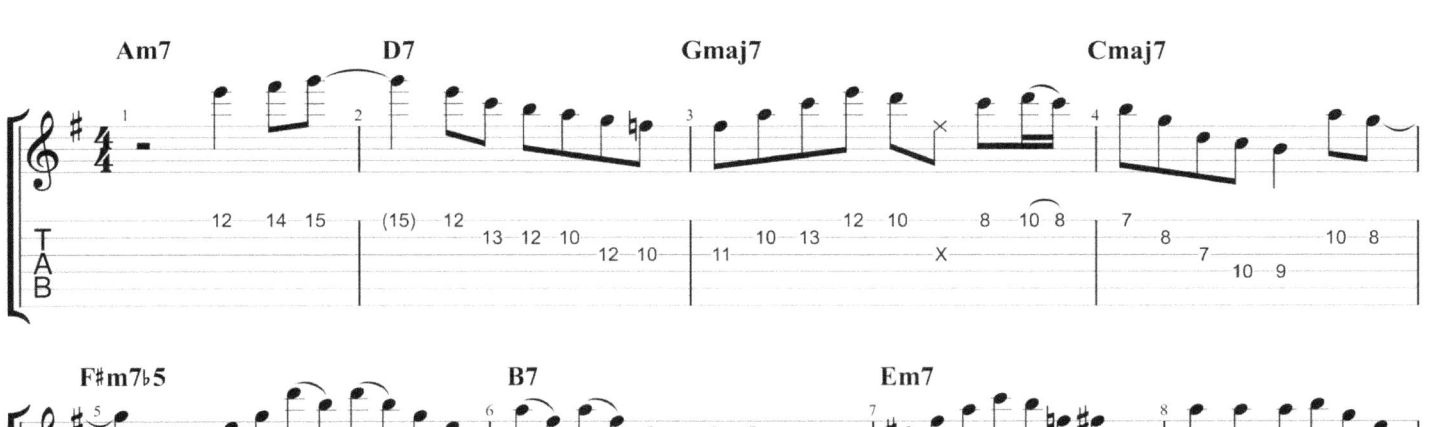
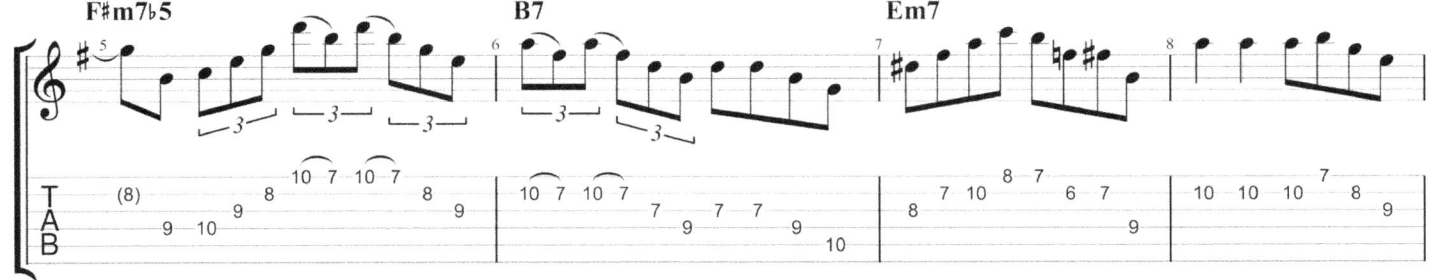
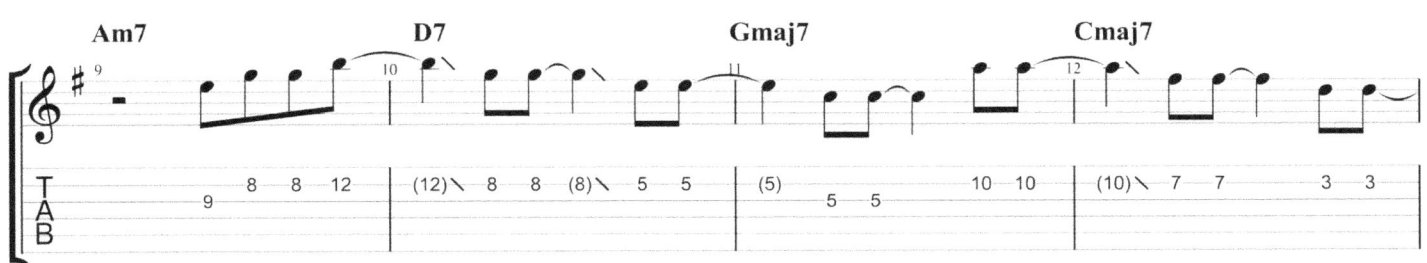
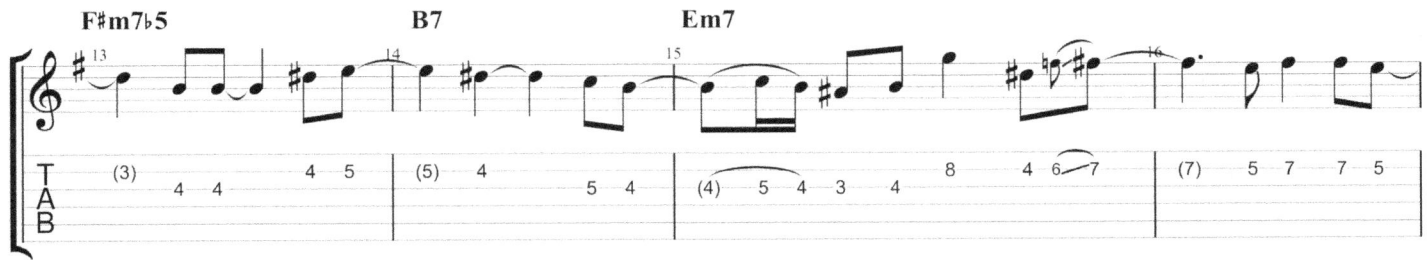

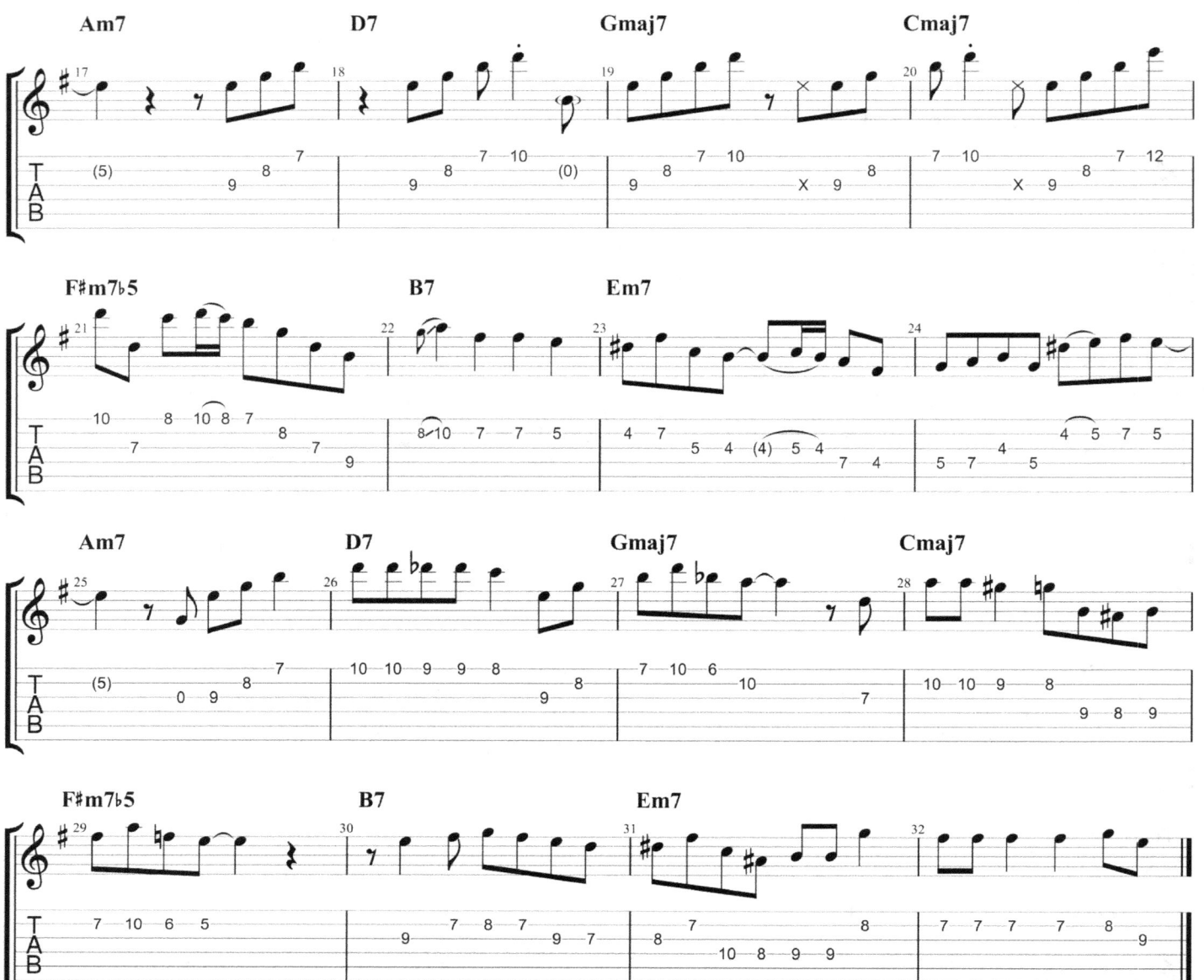

Example 8h

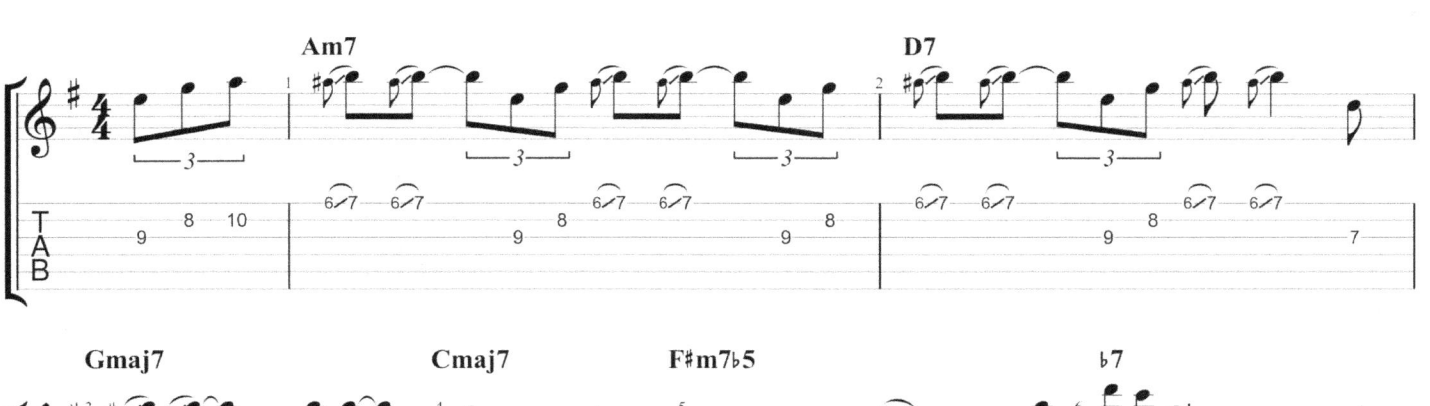

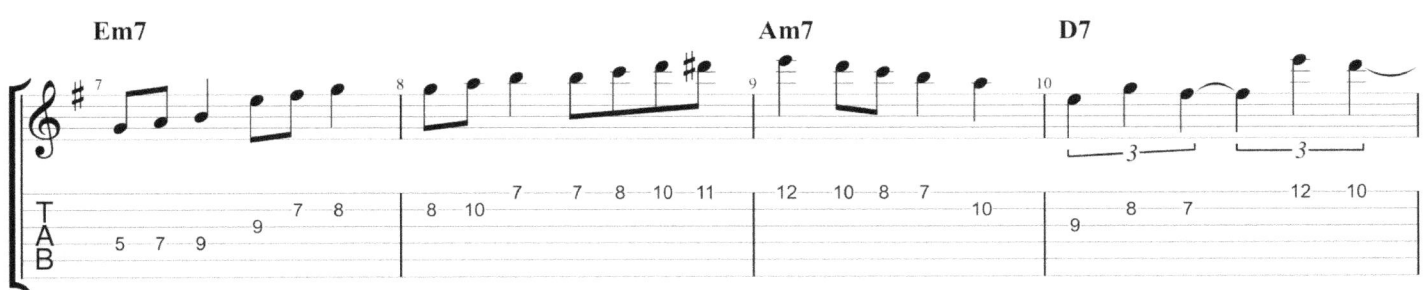

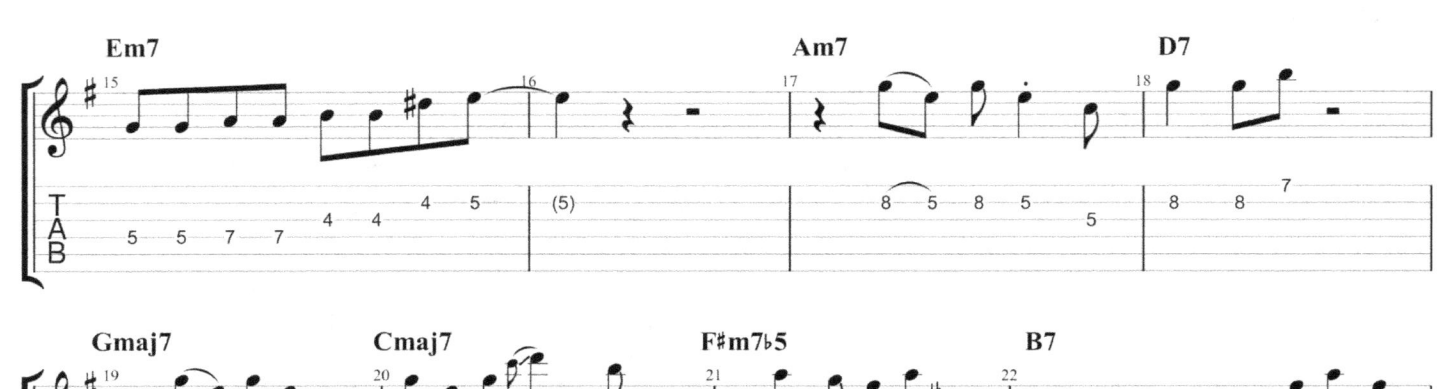

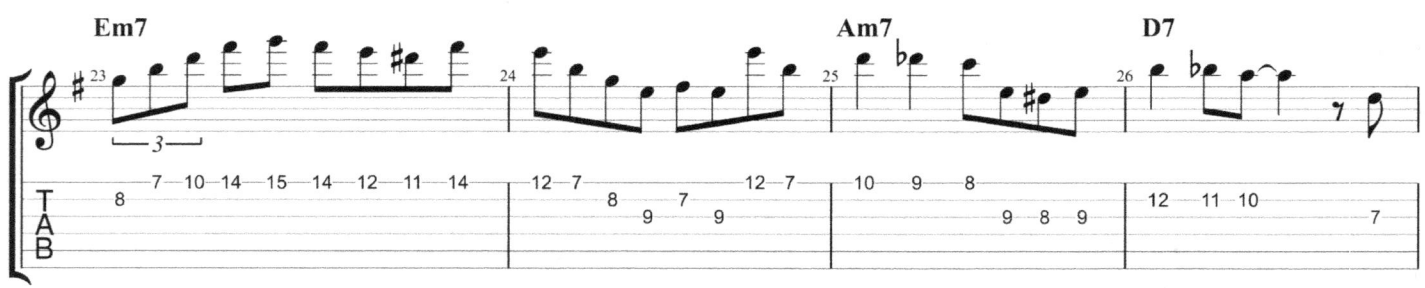
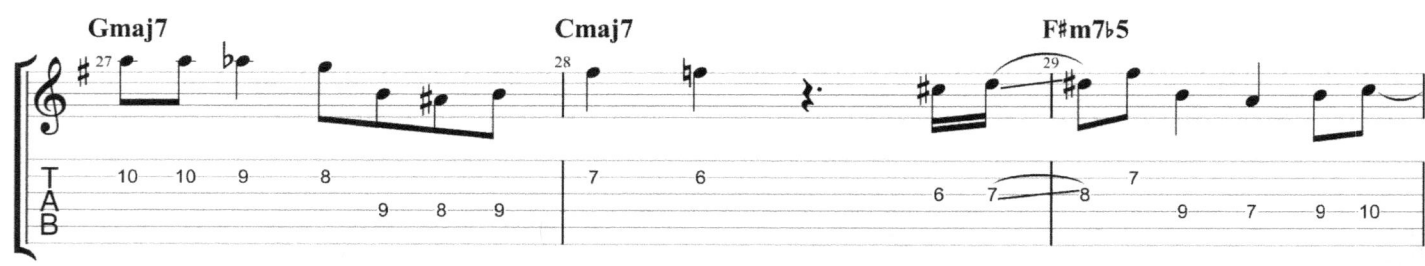
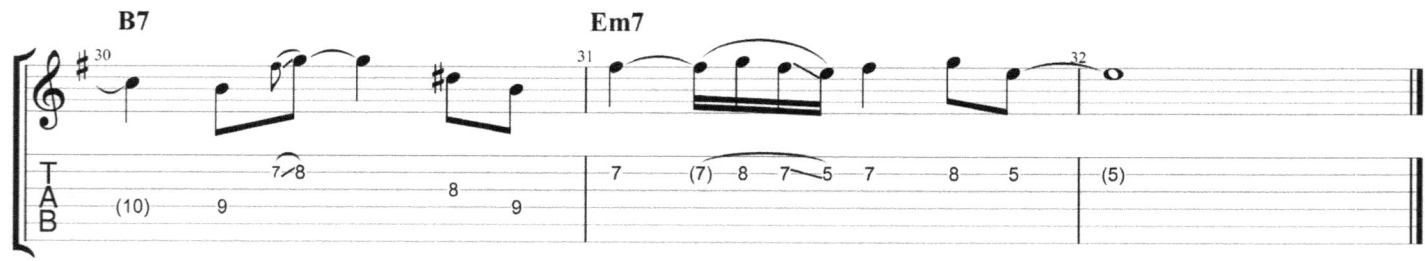

Example 8i

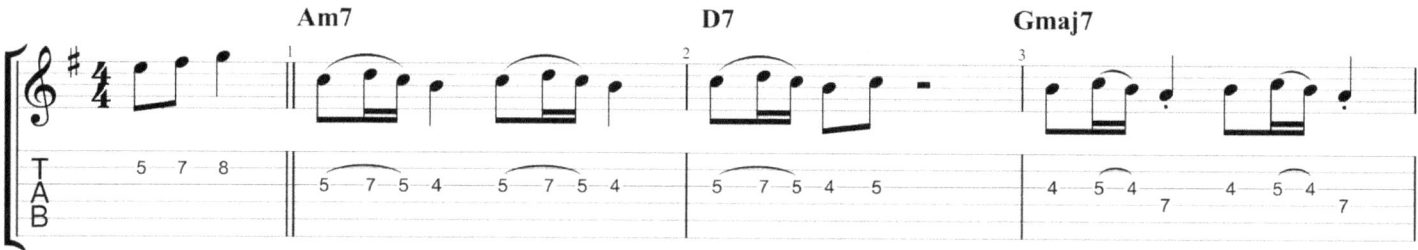
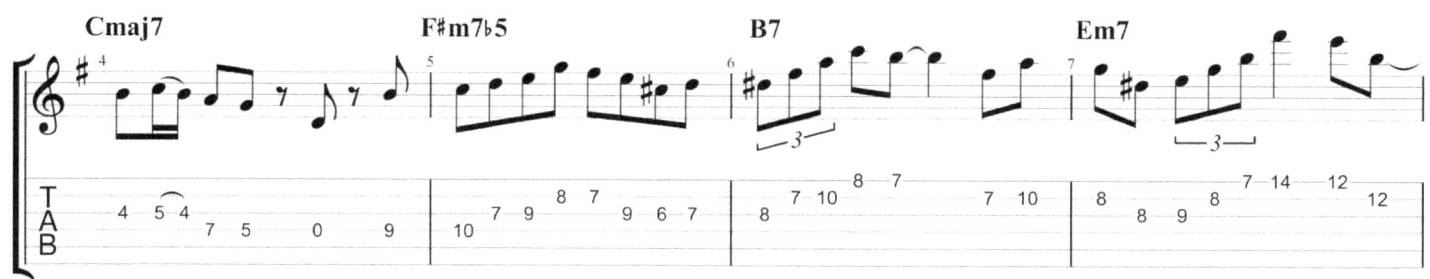
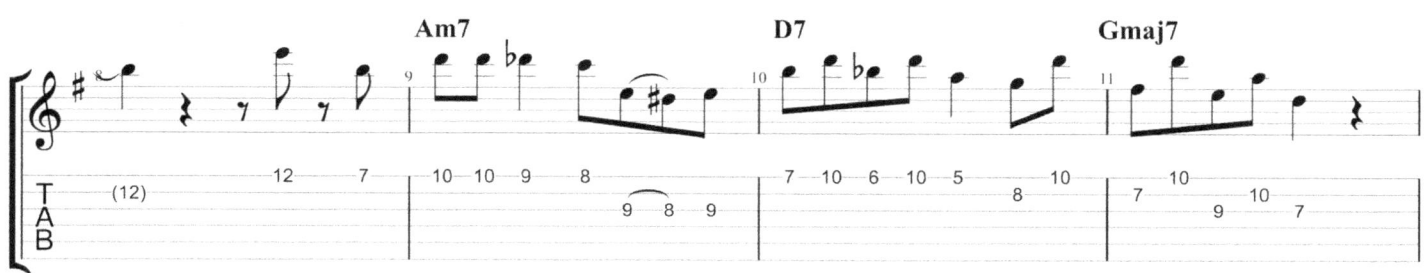
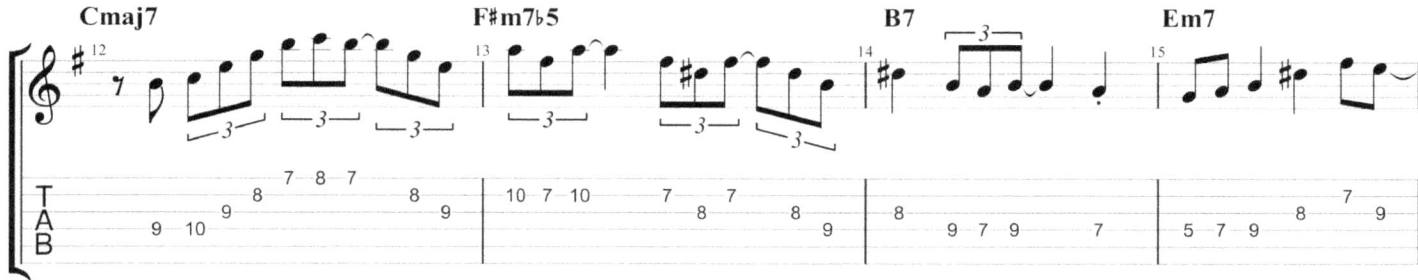

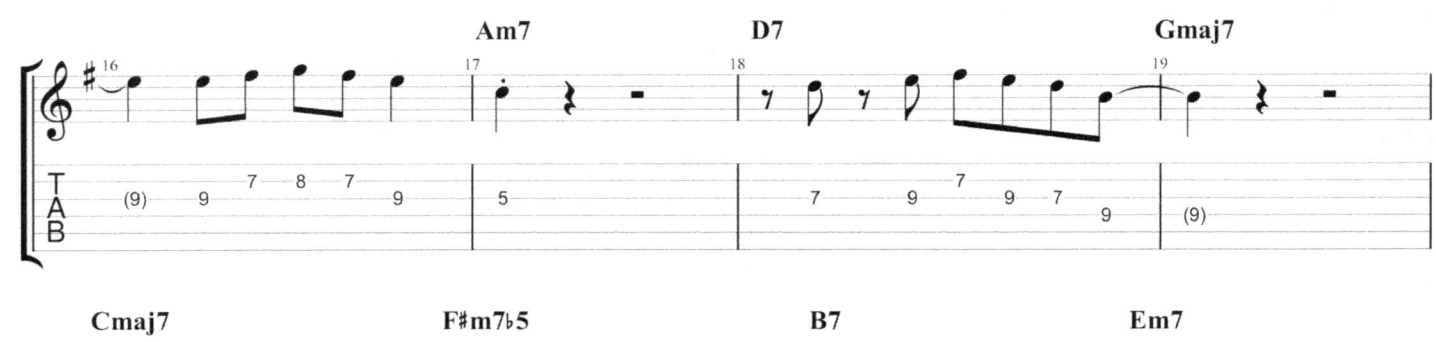
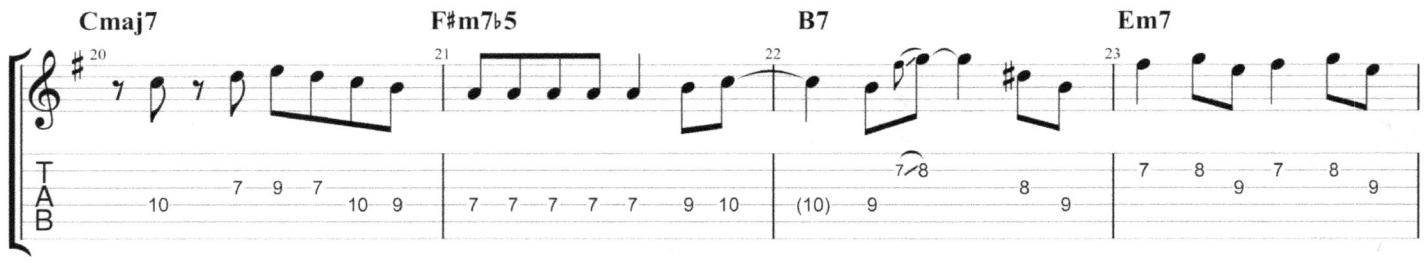
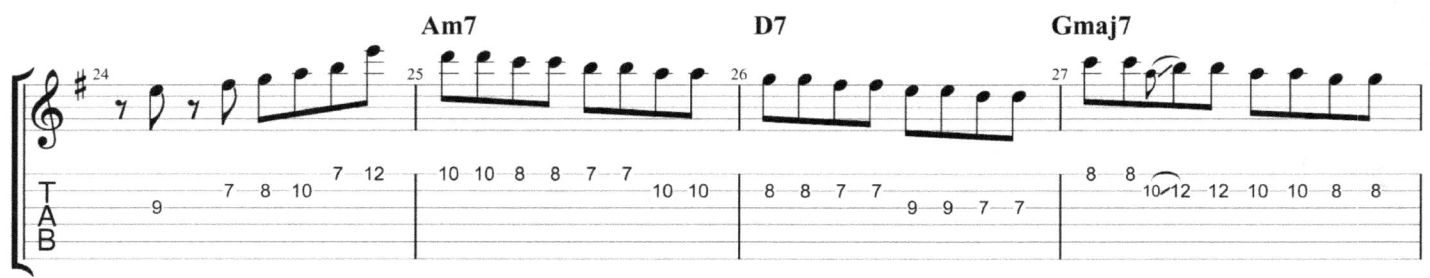
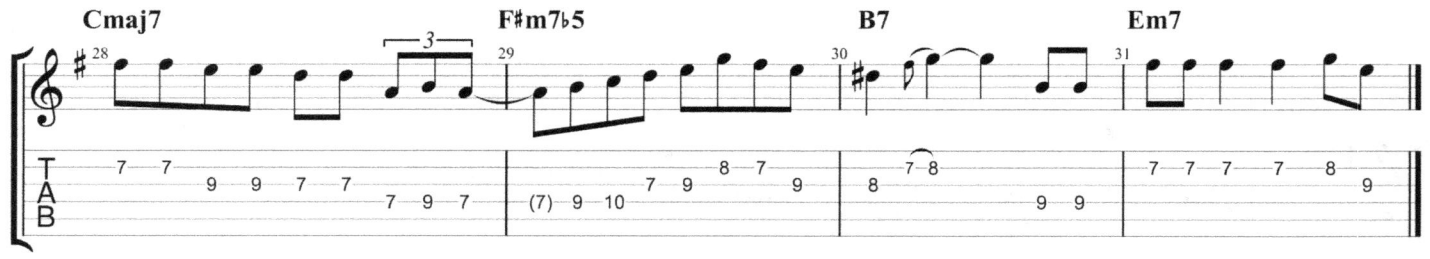

Conclusion and Further Reading

Congratulations, you made it!

I hope that what I've taught you in this book has given you a clear insight into the way I approach jazz guitar soloing. I've tried not to hold anything back and to explain my process as clearly as possible for you.

Remember, every solo begins by varying the melody of the tune and hearing those all-important hit points. When those are strong in your ears, you can target new intervals and take those variations further and further away from the original melody.

The golden rule to develop your jazz creativity and play whatever you hear in your head is to *think, sing then play*. If you practise this every day, your skills will quickly develop, and you will have much less reliance on "playing theory". Melody always comes first.

What I've taught you here will take you many years to perfect, but that's a good thing because the journey will be fun and you'll enjoy it. Don't be afraid to get out there and play as soon as possible. Find other musicians who are better than you and jam with them as much as possible – you'll get better much more quickly.

If you want more insight into my playing style, and want to learn how I play chords and basslines at the same time as soloing, I have two other books published through Fundamental Changes:

Beyond Chord Melody

and

Walking Basslines for Jazz Guitar

In them, I break down my approach to polyphonic playing and teach you the seven steps to chord melody mastery.

Also, look out for my new book of Christmas music arranged for chord melody guitar due to be released in November 2019. I think you'll get a lot out of it and it'll teach you my approach to arranging any song on guitar.

The most important rule in music is to always have fun and keep your mind open to new ideas and possibilities.

All the best,

Martin

Other Jazz Guitar Books From Fundamental Changes

100 Classic Jazz Licks For Guitar

Advanced Jazz Guitar Concepts

Fundamental Changes in Jazz Guitar

Jazz Bebop Blues Guitar

Jazz Blues Soloing For Guitar

Jazz Guitar Chord Mastery

Jazz Guitar Chord Tone Soloing

Martin Taylor – Beyond Chord Melody

Martin Taylor – Walking Bass for Jazz Guitar

Minor ii V Mastery For Guitar

Modern Jazz Guitar Concepts

Rhythm Changes For Jazz Guitar

The Jazz Guitar Soloing Compilation

The First 100 Jazz Chords For Guitar

The Jazz Guitar Chord Compilation

Voice Leading Jazz Guitar

Scan the QR code with your smartphone to discover more

www.ingramcontent.com/pod-product-compliance
Lightning Source LLC
Chambersburg PA
CBHW051148290426
44108CB00019B/2643